A Guide to

# DATA
# COMPRESSION
# METHODS

# Springer

*New York*
*Berlin*
*Heidelberg*
*Barcelona*
*Hong Kong*
*London*
*Milan*
*Paris*
*Singapore*
*Tokyo*

A Guide to

# DATA
# COMPRESSION
# METHODS

David Salomon

With 92 Illustrations

Includes a CD-ROM

Springer

David Salomon
Department of Computer Science
California State University, Northridge
Northridge, CA 91330-8281
USA
david.salomon@csun.edu

*Cover Illustration:* "Abstract: Yellow, Blue", 1993, Patricia S. Brown/Superstock.

Library of Congress Cataloging-in-Publication Data
Salomon, D. (David), 1938–
A guide to data compression methods/David Salomon.
     p.   cm.
   Includes bibliographical references and index.
   ISBN 0-387-95260-8 (pbk.: alk. paper)
   1. Data compression (Computer science).   I. Title.
QA76.9D33 S28   2001
005.74'6—dc21                               2001-032844

Printed on acid-free paper.

Production managed by Frank McGuckin; manufacturing supervised by Erica Bresler.
Camera-ready copy prepared from the author's TeX files.
Printed and bound by Hamilton Printing Co., Rensselaer, NY.
Printed in the United States of America.

9 8 7 6 5 4 3 2 1

ISBN 0-387-95260-8         SPIN  10796580

Springer-Verlag   New York  Berlin  Heidelberg
*A member of BertelsmannSpringer Science+Business Media GmbH*

*To the data compression community;*
*visionaries, researchers, and implementors.*

# Contents

# Contents

> Thus a rigidly chronological series of letters would
> present a patchwork of subjects, each of which would
> be difficult to follow. The Table of Contents will show
> in what way I have attempted to avoid this result.
>
> —Charles Darwin, *Life and Letters of Charles Darwin*

# Preface

In 1829, Louis Braille, a young organist in a Paris church, blind since age 3, invented the well-known code for the blind, still in common use today all over the world and named after him. Braille himself modified his code in 1834, and there have been several modifications since. However, the basic design of this code, where each character is represented by a group of $3 \times 2$ dots, has remained intact. The dots are embossed on thick paper and each can be raised or flat (i.e., present or absent). Each dot is therefore equivalent to one bit of information. As a result, the Braille code (Figure 1) is a 6-bit code and can therefore represent 64 symbols (the code of six flat dots indicates a blank space).

Braille's followers extended the capabilities of his code in several ways. One important extension is contractions. These are letters that, when they stand alone, mean words. For example, the letter "b" standing alone (or with punctuation) means the word "but," the letter "e" standing alone means "every," and "p" means "people." Another extension is short-form words. These are combinations of two or more codes that mean an entire word (short-form words may contain contractions). For example, "ab" means "about," "rcv" means "receive," and "(the)mvs" means "themselves." (The "the" in parentheses is a contraction, dots 2-3-4-6.) Figure 2 shows some examples of these special codes.

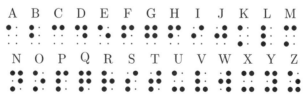

**Figure 1:** The 26 Braille letters

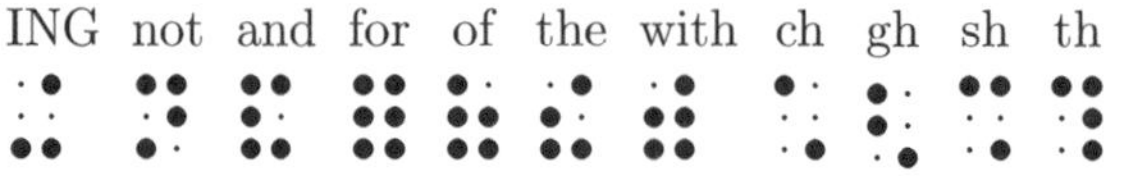

**Figure 2:** Some contractions and short words in Braille

The contractions, short words, and other extensions of the Braille code are examples of *intuitive data compression*. Those who developed the Braille code further and modified it for various languages realized that certain words and letter combinations are common and should be assigned special, short codes to facilitate rapid reading. The idea that common data items should be assigned short codes is one of the principles of the modern field of data compression.

---

### A Brief History of Braille

Louis Braille was born on 4 January, 1809, at Coupvray, near Paris. An accident at age 3 deprived him of his sight and he remained blind for the rest of his life. At age 10, he was sent to the Paris Blind School where he learned to read in a code of raised dots. This code was originally developed by M. Charles Barbier and later adopted by the military, which called it "night writing" and used it for soldiers to communicate after dark. Night writing was based on a twelve-dot cell, two dots wide by six dots high. Each dot or combination of dots within the cell stood for a letter or a phonetic sound. The problem with the military code was that the human fingertip could not feel all the dots with one touch.

Braille spent nine years developing and refining night writing, eventually ending up with the system of raised dots that today bears his name. His crucial improvement was to reduce the cell size from $6 \times 2$ to $3 \times 2$ dots. This meant that a fingertip could enclose the entire cell with one impression and advance fast from one cell to the next.

The Braille code was introduced to the United States in about 1860 and was taught with some success at the St. Louis School for the Blind. In 1868, the British and Foreign Blind Associations were founded. They introduced Braille into England and promoted it by printing and disseminating books in Braille.

In North America, the Braille organization is Braille Authority of North America (BANA), located at `http://www.brailleauthority.org/index.html`.

BANA's purpose is to promote and to facilitate the uses, teaching, and production of braille. It publishes rules and interprets and renders opinions pertaining to Braille in all existing and future codes.

---

The predecessor of this volume, *Data Compression: The Complete Reference*, was published in 1977, with a second edition published in late 2000. It was the immediate and enthusiastic readers' response that encouraged me to write this slim volume. Whereas the original book is large, attempting to cover both the principles of data compression and the details of many specific methods, this book is less ambitious. It aims to guide a lay reader through the field of compression by conveying the general flavor of this field. It does so by presenting the main approaches to compression and describing a few of the important algorithms. The book contains little mathematics, has no exercises, and includes simple examples.

The Introduction explains why data can be compressed, presents simple examples, and discusses the main technical terms of the field.

Chapter 1 discusses the statistical approach to data compression. This approach is based on estimating the probabilities of the elementary symbols in the data to be compressed and assigning them codes of varying sizes according to their probabilities.

The elementary symbols can be bits, ASCII codes, bytes, pixels, audio samples, or anything else. The main concept treated in this chapter is variable-size (prefix) codes. The methods described are Huffman coding, facsimile compression, and arithmetic coding.

The popular technique of dictionary compression is the topic of Chapter 2. A dictionary-based compression method saves bits and pieces of the file being compressed in a data structure called a dictionary. The dictionary is searched for each new fragment of data to be compressed. If that fragment is found, a pointer to the dictionary is written on the compressed file. The following compression methods are described in this chapter: LZ77, LZSS, LZ78, and LZW.

Images are common in computer applications, and image compression is especially important because an image can be large. Chapter 3 is devoted to image compression. Most of the chapter discusses various approaches to this problem, such as run-length encoding, context probability, pixel prediction, and image transforms. The only specific methods described are JPEG and JPEG-LS.

Chapter 4 is devoted to the wavelet transform. This technique is becoming more and more important in image, video, and audio compression. It is mathematically demanding, and a simple, nonmathematical presentation of its principles presents a challenge to both author and reader. The chapter starts with an intuitive technique based on the calculation of averages and differences. It then relates this technique to the Haar wavelet transform. The concept of filter banks is introduced next, followed by the discrete wavelet transform. The only wavelet-based specific compression method illustrated in this chapter is SPIHT.

A movie is, in some sense, a generalization of a single still picture. Movies are quickly becoming popular in computer multimedia applications, a trend that has created a demand for video compression. A movie file tends to be much bigger than a single image, so efficient video compression is a practical necessity. Another factor in video compression is the need for simple, fast decompression, so that a compressed video can be decompressed in real time. Chapter 5 covers the principles of video compression.

The last chapter, Chapter 6, examines the topic of audio compression. Sound is one of the "media" included in computer multimedia applications and is therefore very popular with computer users. Sound has to be digitized before it can be stored and used in a computer, and the resulting audio files tend to be large. The chapter presents the basic operation of the MP3 audio compression method (actually, this is the audio part of MPEG-1) and also includes a short introduction to sound, the properties of the human auditory system, and audio sampling.

The book is intended for those interested in a basic understanding of the important field of data compression but do not have the time or the technical background required to follow the details of the many different compression algorithms. It is my hope that the light use of mathematics will attract the lay reader and open up the "mysteries" of data compression to the nonexpert.

The CD-ROM included with the book is readable by PC and Macintosh computers. For each platform, the CD contains popular compression programs (freeware and shareware) and a catalog file listing the programs. In addition, there is one file with verbatim listings of the various code fragments (in Mathematica and Matlab) found in the book.

Domain name `BooksByDavidSalomon.com` has been registered and will always point to any future location of the book's Web site. The author's present email address is `david.salomon@csun.edu`, but some readers may find it easier to use the redirection address ⟨*anyname*⟩`@BooksByDavidSalomon.com`.

Readers willing to put up with eight seconds of advertisement can be redirected to the book's web site from `http://welcome.to/data.compression`. Email sent to `data.compression@welcome.to` will also be redirected.

Those interested in data compression in general should consult the short section titled "Joining the Data Compression Community" at the end of the book, as well as the useful URLs `http://www.internz.com/compression-pointers.html` and `http://www.hn.is.uec.ac.jp/~arimura/compression_links.html`.

Northridge, California                                        David Salomon

Math is hard.
—Barbie

Non mi legga chi non e matematico
(Let no one read me who is not a mathematician.)
—Leonardo da Vinci

# Introduction

Those who use compression software are familiar with terms such as "zip," "implode," "stuffit," "diet," and "squeeze." These are names of programs or methods for compressing data, names chosen to imply compression. However, such names do not reflect the true nature of data compression. Compressing data is not done by stuffing or squeezing it, but by removing any *redundancy* that's present in the data. The concept of redundancy is central to data compression. Data with redundancy can be compressed. Data without any redundancy cannot be compressed, period.

We all know what information is. We intuitively understand it but we consider it a qualitative concept. Information seems to be one of those entities that cannot be quantified and dealt with rigorously. There is, however, a mathematical field called *information theory*, where information is handled quantitatively. Among its other achievements, information theory shows how to precisely define redundancy. Here, we try to understand this concept intuitively by pointing out the redundancy in two common types of computer data and trying to understand why redundant data is used in the first place.

The first type of data is text. Text is an important example of computer data. Many computer applications, such as word processing and software compilation, are nonnumeric; they deal with data whose elementary components are characters of text. The computer can store and process only binary information (zeros and ones), so each character of text must be assigned a binary code. Present-day computers use the ASCII code (pronounced "ass-key," short for "American Standard Code for Information Interchange"), although more and more computers use the new Unicode. ASCII is a fixed-size code where each character is assigned an 8-bit code (the code itself occupies seven of the eight bits, and the eighth bit is parity, designed to increase the reliability of the code). A fixed-size code is a natural choice because it makes it easy for software applications to handle characters of text. On the other hand, a fixed-size code is inherently redundant.

In a file of random text, we expect each character to occur approximately the same number of times. However, files used in practice are rarely random. They contain meaningful text, and we know from experience that in typical English text certain letters, such as "E," "T," and "A" are common, whereas other letters, such as "Z" and

"Q," are rare. This explains why the ASCII code is redundant and also points the way to eliminating the redundancy. ASCII is redundant because it assigns to each character, common or rare, the same number (eight) of bits. Removing the redundancy can be done by assigning variable-size codes to the characters, with short codes assigned to the common characters and long codes assigned to the rare ones. This is precisely how Huffman coding (Section 1.4) works.

Imagine two text files $A$ and $B$ with the same text, where $A$ uses ASCII codes and $B$ has variable-size codes. We expect $B$ to be smaller than $A$ and we say that $A$ has been *compressed* to $B$. It is obvious that the amount of compression depends on the redundancy of the particular text and on the particular variable-size codes used in file $B$. Text where certain characters are very common while others are very rare has much redundancy and will compress well if the variable-size codes are properly assigned. In such a file, the codes of the common characters should be very short, while those of the rare characters can be long. The long codes would not degrade the compression because they would rarely appear in $B$. Most of $B$ would consist of the short codes. Random text, on the other hand, does not benefit from replacing ASCII with variable-size codes, because the compression achieved by the short codes is cancelled out by the long codes. This is a special case of a general rule that says that random data cannot be compressed because it has no redundancy.

The second type of common computer data is digital images. A digital image is a rectangular array of colored dots, called *pixels*. Each pixel is represented in the computer by its color code. (In the remainder of this section, the term "pixel" is used for the pixel's color code.) In order to simplify the software applications that handle images, the pixels are all the same size. The size of a pixel depends on the number of colors in the image, and this number is normally a power of 2. If there are $2^k$ colors in an image, then each pixel is a $k$-bit number.

There are two types of redundancy in a digital image. The first type is similar to redundancy in text. In any particular image, certain colors may dominate, while others may be infrequent. This redundancy can be removed by assigning variable-size codes to the pixels, as is done with text. The other type of redundancy is much more important and is the result of *pixel correlation*. As our eyes move along the image from pixel to pixel, we find that in most cases, adjacent pixels have similar colors. Imagine an image containing blue sky, white clouds, brown mountains, and green trees. As long as we look at a mountain, adjacent pixels tend to be similar; all or almost all of them are shades of brown. Similarly, adjacent pixels in the sky are shades of blue. It is only on the horizon, where mountain meets sky, that adjacent pixels may have very different colors. The individual pixels are therefore not completely independent, and we say that neighboring pixels in an image tend to be *correlated*. This type of redundancy can be exploited in many ways, as described in Chapter 3.

Regardless of the method used to compress an image, the effectiveness of the compression depends on the amount of redundancy in the image. One extreme case is a uniform image. Such an image has maximum redundancy because adjacent pixels are identical. Obviously, such an image is not interesting and is rarely, if ever, used in practice. However, it will compress very well under any image compression method. The other extreme example is an image with uncorrelated pixels. All adjacent pixels in such an image are very different, so the image redundancy is zero. Such an image will not compress, regardless of the compression method used. However, such an image tends to look like a random jumble of dots and is therefore uninteresting. We rarely need to keep and manipulate such an image, so we rarely need to compress it. Also, a truly random image features small or zero correlation between pixels.

---

What with all the ARC war flames going around, and arguments about which program is best, I decided to do something about it and write my OWN.

You've heard of crunching, jamming, squeezing, squashing, packing, crushing, imploding, etc....

Now there's TRASHING.

TRASH compresses a file to the smallest size possible: 0 bytes! NOTHING compresses a file better than TRASH! Date/time stamp are not affected, and since the file is zero bytes long, it doesn't even take up any space on your hard disk!

And TRASH is FAST! Files can be TRASHED in microseconds! In fact, it takes longer to go through the various parameter screens than it does to trash the file!

This prerelease version of TRASH is yours to keep and evaluate. I would recommend backing up any files you intend to TRASH first, though....

The next version of TRASH will have graphics and take wildcards:

TRASH C:\PAYROLL\*.*

...and will even work on entire drives:

TRASH D:

...or be first on your block to trash your system ON PURPOSE!

TRASH ALL

We're even hoping to come up with a way to RECOVER TRASHed files!

From *FIDO News*, 23 April 1990

---

The following simple argument illustrates the essence of the statement "Data compression is achieved by reducing or removing redundancy in the data." The argument shows that most data files cannot be compressed, no matter what compression method is used. This seems strange at first because we compress our data files all the time. The point is that most files cannot be compressed because they are random or close to random and therefore have no redundancy. The (relatively) few files that can be compressed are the ones that we *want* to compress; they are the files we use all the time. They have redundancy, are nonrandom and therefore useful and interesting.

Given two different files $A$ and $B$ that are compressed to files $C$ and $D$, respectively, it is clear that $C$ and $D$ must be different. If they were identical, there would be no way to decompress them and get back file $A$ or file $B$.

Suppose that a file of size $n$ bits is given and we want to compress it efficiently. Any compression method that can compress this file to, say, 10 bits would be welcome. Even compressing it to 11 bits or 12 bits would be great. We therefore (somewhat arbitrarily) assume that compressing such a file to half its size or better is considered good compression. There are $2^n$ $n$-bit files and they would have to be compressed into $2^n$ different files of sizes less than or equal $n/2$. However, the total number of these files is

$$N = 1 + 2 + 4 + \cdots + 2^{n/2} = 2^{1+n/2} - 1 \approx 2^{1+n/2},$$

so only $N$ of the $2^n$ original files have a chance of being compressed efficiently. The problem is that $N$ is much smaller than $2^n$. Here are two examples of the ratio between these two numbers.

For $n = 100$ (files with just 100 bits), the total number of files is $2^{100}$ and the number of files that can be compressed efficiently is $2^{51}$. The ratio of these numbers is the ridiculously small fraction $2^{-49} \approx 1.78 \cdot 10^{-15}$.

For $n = 1000$ (files with just 1000 bits, about 125 bytes), the total number of files is $2^{1000}$ and the number of files that can be compressed efficiently is $2^{501}$. The ratio of these numbers is the incredibly small fraction $2^{-499} \approx 9.82 \cdot 10^{-91}$.

Most files of interest are at least some thousands of bytes long. For such files, the percentage of files that can be efficiently compressed is so small that it cannot be computed with floating-point numbers even on a supercomputer (the result is zero).

It is therefore clear that no compression method can hope to compress all files or even a significant percentage of them. In order to compress a data file, the compression algorithm has to examine the data, find redundancies in it, and try to remove them. Since the redundancies in data depend on the type of data (text, images, sound, etc.), any compression method has to be developed for a specific type of data and works best on this type. There is no such thing as a universal, efficient data compression algorithm.

The rest of this introduction covers important technical terms used in the field of data compression.

■ The *compressor* or *encoder* is the program that compresses the raw data in the input file and creates an output file with compressed (low-redundancy) data. The *decompressor* or *decoder* converts in the opposite direction. Notice that the term *encoding* is very general and has wide meaning, but since we discuss only data compression, we use the name *encoder* to mean data compressor. The term *codec* is sometimes used to describe both the encoder and decoder. Similarly, the term *companding* is short for "compressing/expanding."

■ A *nonadaptive* compression method is rigid and does not modify its operations, its parameters, or its tables in response to the particular data being compressed. Such a method is best used to compress data that is all of a single type. Examples are the Group 3 and Group 4 methods for facsimile compression (Section 1.6). They are specifically designed for facsimile compression and would do a poor job compressing any other data. In contrast, an *adaptive* method examines the raw data and modifies its operations and/or its parameters accordingly. An example is the adaptive Huffman method of Section 1.5. Some compression methods use a two-pass algorithm, where the first pass reads the input file to collect statistics on the data to be compressed, and the second pass does the actual compressing using parameters or codes set by the first pass. Such a method may be called *semiadaptive*. A data compression method can also be *locally adaptive*, meaning it adapts itself to local conditions in the input file and varies this adaptation as it moves from area to area in the input. An example is the move-to-front method [Salomon 2000].

- *Lossy/lossless compression:* Certain compression methods are lossy. They achieve better compression by losing some information. When the compressed file is decompressed, the result is not identical to the original data. Such a method makes sense when compressing images, movies, or sounds. If the loss of data is small, we may not be able to tell the difference. In contrast, text files, especially files containing computer programs, may become worthless if even one bit gets modified. Such files should be compressed only by a lossless compression method. [Two points should be mentioned regarding text files: (1) If a text file contains the source code of a program, many blank spaces can normally be eliminated, since they are disregarded by the compiler anyway. (2) When the output of a word processor is saved in a text file, the file may contain information about the different fonts used in the text. Such information may be discarded if the user wants to save just the text.]

- *Symmetric compression* is the case where the compressor and decompressor use the same basic algorithm but work in "opposite" directions. Such a method makes sense for general work, where the same number of files are compressed as are decompressed. In an asymmetric compression method, either the compressor or the decompressor may have to work significantly harder. Such methods have their uses and are not necessarily bad. A compression method where the compressor executes a slow, complex algorithm and the decompressor is simple is a natural choice when files are compressed into an archive, where they will be decompressed and used very often, such as mp3 audio files on a CD. The opposite case is useful in environments where files are updated all the time and backups are made. There is only a small chance that a backup file will be used, so the decompressor isn't used very often.

- *Compression performance*: Several quantities are commonly used to express the performance of a compression method.

1. The *compression ratio* is defined as

$$\text{Compression ratio} = \frac{\text{size of the output file}}{\text{size of the input file}}.$$

A value of 0.6 means that the data occupies 60% of its original size after compression. Values greater than 1 indicate an output file bigger than the input file (negative compression). The compression ratio can also be called bpb (bit per bit), since it equals the number of bits in the compressed file needed, on average, to compress one bit in the input file. In image compression, the similar term bpp stands for "bits per pixel." In modern, efficient text compression methods, it makes sense to talk about bpc (bits per character), the number of bits it takes, on average, to compress one character in the input file.

Two more terms should be mentioned in connection with the compression ratio. The term *bitrate* (or "bit rate") is a general term for bpb and bpc. Thus, the main goal of data compression is to represent any given data at low bit rates. The term *bit budget* refers to the functions of the individual bits in the compressed file. Imagine a compressed file where 90% of the bits are variable-size codes of certain symbols and the remaining 10% are used to encode certain tables that are needed by the decompressor. The bit budget for the tables is 10% in this case.

2. The inverse of the compression ratio is the *compression factor*:

$$\text{Compression factor} = \frac{\text{size of the input file}}{\text{size of the output file}}.$$

In this case values greater than 1 indicate compression, and values less than 1 imply expansion. This measure seems natural to many people, since the bigger the factor, the better the compression. This measure is distantly related to the sparseness ratio, a performance measure discussed in Section 4.1.2.

3. The expression $100 \times (1 - \text{compression ratio})$ is also a reasonable measure of compression performance. A value of 60 means that the output file occupies 40% of its original size (or that the compression has resulted in savings of 60%).

4. In image compression, the quantity bpp (bits per pixel) is commonly used. It equals the number of bits needed, on average, to compress one pixel of the image. This quantity should always be compared with the bpp before compression.

■ The *probability model*. This concept is important in statistical data compression methods. Sometimes, a compression algorithm consists of two parts, a probability model and the compressor itself. Before the next data item (bit, byte, pixel, or anything else) can be compressed, the model is invoked and is asked to estimate the probability of the data item. The item and the probability are then sent to the compressor, which uses the estimated probability to compress the item. The better the probability, the better the item is compressed.

Here is an example of a simple model for a black and white image. Each pixel in such an image is a single bit. Assume that after reading 1000 pixels and compressing them, pixel 1001 is read. What is the probability that this pixel is black? The model can simply count the numbers of black and white pixels read so far. If 350 of the 1000 pixels were black, then the model can assign pixel 1001 a probability of $350/1000 = 0.35$ of being black. The probability and the pixel (which may, of course be either black or white) are then sent to the compressor. The point is that the decompressor can easily calculate the same probabilities before it decodes the 1001st pixel.

■ The term *alphabet* refers to the set of symbols in the data being compressed. An alphabet may consist of the two bits 0 and 1, of the 128 ASCII characters, of the 256 possible 8-bit bytes, or of any other symbols.

■ The performance of any compression method is limited. No method can compress all data files efficiently. Imagine applying a sophisticated compression algorithm $X$ to a data file $A$ and obtaining a compressed file of just 1 bit! Any method that can compress an entire file to a single bit is excellent. Even if the compressed file is 2 bits long, we still consider it to be highly compressed, and the same is true for compressed files of 3, 4, 5 and even more bits. It seems reasonable to define efficient compression as compressing a file to at most half its original size. Thus, we may be satisfied (even happy) if we discover a method $X$ that compresses any data file $A$ to a file $B$ of size less than or equal half the size of $A$.

The point is that different files $A$ should be compressed to different files $B$, since otherwise decompression is impossible. If method $X$ compresses two files $C$ and $D$ to the same file $E$, then the $X$ decompressor cannot decompress $E$. Once this is clear, it is easy to show that method $X$ cannot compress all files efficiently. If file $A$ is $n$ bits long, then there are $2^n$ different files $A$. At the same time, the total number of all files $B$ whose size is less than or equal half the size of $A$ is $2^{1+n/2} - 2$. For $n = 100$, the number of $A$ files is $N_A = 2^{100} \approx 1.27 \cdot 10^{30}$ but the number of $B$ files is only $N_B = 2^{1+50} - 2 \approx 2.25 \cdot 10^{15}$. The ratio $N_B/N_A$ is the incredibly small fraction $1.77 \cdot 10^{-15}$. For larger values of $n$ this ratio is much smaller.

The conclusion is that method $X$ can compress efficiently just a small fraction of all the files $A$. The great majority of files $A$ cannot be compressed efficiently since they are random or close to random.

This sad conclusion, however, should not cause any reader to close the book with a sigh and turn to more promising pursuits. The interesting fact is that out of the $2^n$ files $A$, the ones we actually *want* to compress are normally the ones that compress well. The ones that compress badly are normally random or close to random and are therefore uninteresting, unimportant, and not candidates for compression, transmission, or storage.

> The days just prior to marriage are like a
> snappy introduction to a tedious book.
> —Wilson Mizner

# 1
# Statistical Methods

Statistical data compression methods use the statistical properties of the data being compressed to assign variable-size codes to the individual symbols in the data. The term "statistical properties" normally means the probability (or equivalently, number of occurrences) of each symbol in the data, but this term may have other, more complex meanings. A *digram* is a pair of consecutive symbols, and long experience shows that in typical English text, certain digrams, such as "ta," "he," and "ca," are common while others, such as "xa," "hz," and "qe," are rare. A sophisticated statistical compression method may therefore assign variable-size codes to the many digrams (or even trigrams), rather than to the individual symbols in the data.

## 1.1 Entropy

Information theory is the creation, in 1948, of Claude Shannon of Bell Laboratories. This theory came upon the world as a surprise because we normally consider information a qualitative concept. The only information-theoretical concept needed to understand data compression is *entropy*. The entropy of a symbol $a$ with probability $P$ is interpreted as the amount of information included in $a$ and is defined as $-P \log_2 P$. For example, if the probability $P_a$ of symbol $a$ is 0.5, then its entropy is $-P_a \log_2 P_a = 0.5$.

Given an alphabet of symbols $a_1$ through $a_n$ with probabilities $P_1$ through $P_n$, respectively, the sum $\sum_n -P_i \log_2 P_i$ is the entropy of the entire alphabet. Given any string of symbols from the alphabet, its entropy is similarly calculated.

Based on the entropy, information theory shows how to calculate the probability of any string from the alphabet and predict its best compression, i.e., the minimum number of bits needed, on average, to represent the string. This is demonstrated by a simple example. Given the five symbols "ABCDE" with probabilities 0.5, 0.2, 0.1, 0.1, and 0.1, respectively, the probability of the string "AAAAABBCDE" is $P = 0.5^5 \times 0.2^2 \times 0.1^3 = 1.25 \times 10^{-6}$. The base-2 logarithm of this probability is $\log_2 P = -19.6096$. Thus, the minimum number of bits needed on average to encode the string is $-\lceil \log_2 P \rceil$ or 20.

An encoder that achieves this compression is called an *entropy encoder*.

**Example:** We analyze the entropy of an alphabet consisting of the two symbols $a_1$ and $a_2$, with probabilities $P_1$ and $P_2$, respectively. Since $P_1 + P_2 = 1$, the entropy of the alphabet is $-P_1 \log_2 P_1 - (1 - P_1) \log_2(1 - P_1)$. Table 1.1 shows the values of the expression $-\log_2 P_1 - \log_2(1 - P_1)$ for certain values of the probabilities. When $P_1 = P_2$, at least one bit is required to encode each symbol, reflecting the fact that the entropy is at its maximum, the redundancy is zero, and the data cannot be compressed. However, when the probabilities are very different, the minimum number of bits required per symbol drops significantly. We may not be able to devise a compression method using 0.08 bits per symbol, but we know that when $P_1 = 99\%$, such compression is theoretically possible.

| $P_1$ | $P_2$ | Entropy |
|-------|-------|---------|
| 99    | 1     | 0.08    |
| 90    | 10    | 0.47    |
| 80    | 20    | 0.72    |
| 70    | 30    | 0.88    |
| 60    | 40    | 0.97    |
| 50    | 50    | 1.00    |

**Table 1.1:** Probabilities and Entropies of Two Symbols.

## 1.2 Variable-Size Codes

The first rule of assigning variable-size codes is obvious. Short codes should be assigned to the common symbols and long codes should be assigned to the rare symbols. There is, however, another aspect to variable-size codes: they have to be assigned such that they can be decoded unambiguously. A simple example will serve to make this point clear.

Consider the four symbols $a_1$, $a_2$, $a_3$, and $a_4$. If they appear in our data strings with equal probabilities ($= 0.25$ each), then we can simply assign them the four 2-bit codes 00, 01, 10, and 11. The probabilities are equal, so variable-size codes will not compress the data. For each symbol with a short code there will be another symbol with a long code, and the average number of bits per symbol will be 2. The redundancy of a set of symbols with equal probabilities is zero and a string of such symbols cannot be compressed by the use of variable-size codes (or by anything else).

Next, consider the case where the four symbols occur with different probabilities as shown in Table 1.2, where $a_1$ appears in the data (on average) about half the time, $a_2$ and $a_3$ have equal probabilities, and $a_4$ is rare. In this case, the data has redundancy and variable-size codes can compress it to less than 2 bits per symbol. In fact, information theory tells us that the smallest number of bits needed, on average, to represent each symbol is 1.57 (the entropy of this set of symbols).

Code1 of Table 1.2 is designed such that the most common symbol, $a_1$, is assigned the shortest code. When long data strings are transmitted using Code1, the average number of bits per symbol is $1 \times 0.49 + 2 \times 0.25 + 3 \times 0.25 + 3 \times 0.01 = 1.77$, very close to

| Symbol | Prob. | Code1 | Code2 |
|--------|-------|-------|-------|
| $a_1$ | .49 | 1 | 1 |
| $a_2$ | .25 | 01 | 01 |
| $a_3$ | .25 | 010 | 000 |
| $a_4$ | .01 | 001 | 001 |

**Table 1.2:** Variable-size codes

the theoretical minimum. An illuminating example is the 20-symbol string

$$a_1a_3a_2a_1a_3a_3a_4a_2a_1a_1a_2a_2a_1a_1a_3a_1a_1a_2a_3a_1,$$

where the four symbols occur with (approximately) the right frequencies. Encoding this string with Code1 results in the 37 bits

$$1|010|01|1|010|010|001|01|1|1|01|01|1|1|010|1|1|01|010|1$$

(without the vertical bars). Using 37 bits to encode 20 symbols yields an average size of 1.85 bits/symbol, not far from the calculated average size. (The reader should bear in mind that our examples are short. To get results close to the best that's theoretically possible, an input file with at least thousands of symbols is needed.)

However, when we try to *decode* the binary string above, it becomes obvious that Code1 is bad. The first bit is 1, and since only $a_1$ is assigned this code, it ($a_1$) must be the first symbol. The next bit is 0, but the codes of $a_2$, $a_3$, and $a_4$ all start with a 0, so the decoder has to read the next bit. It is 1, but the codes of both $a_2$ and $a_3$ start with 01. The decoder does not know whether to decode the string as $1|010|01\ldots$, which is $a_1a_3a_2\ldots$, or as $1|01|001\ldots$, which is $a_1a_2a_4\ldots$. Code1 is thus *ambiguous*. In contrast, Code2, which has the same average size as Code1, can be decoded unambiguously.

The property of Code2 that makes it so much better than Code1 is called the *prefix property*. This property requires that once a certain bit pattern has been assigned as the code of a symbol, no other codes should start with that pattern (the pattern cannot be the *prefix* of any other code). Once the string "1" was assigned as the code of $a_1$, no other codes could start with 1 (i.e., they all had to start with 0). Once "01" was assigned as the code of $a_2$, no other codes could start with 01. This is why the codes of $a_3$ and $a_4$ had to start with 00. Naturally, they became 000 and 001.

Thus, designing a set of variable-size codes is done by observing two principles: (1) Assign short codes to the more frequent symbols and (2) obey the prefix property. Following these principles produces short, unambiguous codes but not necessarily the best (i.e., shortest) ones. In addition to these principles, an algorithm is needed that always produces a set of shortest codes (codes with minimum average size). The only input to such an algorithm is the frequencies (or the probabilities) of the symbols of the alphabet. Fortunately, there exists a simple algorithm, due to David Huffman and named after him, that does just that. It is the subject of Section 1.4.

(It should be noted that not all statistical compression methods assign variable-size codes to the individual symbols of the alphabet. A notable exception is arithmetic coding, Section 1.7.)

## 1.3 Decoding

Before we can describe any specific statistical compression methods, it is important to understand the way encoder and decoder (compressor and decompressor) communicate. Suppose that a data file (with text, images, or anything else) has been compressed by assigning variable-size (prefix) codes to the various symbols. In order to decompress the data, the decoder has to know the prefix code of every symbol. This problem can be approached in three ways:

1. A set of prefix codes is determined once and is used by all encoders and decoders. This approach is used in facsimile compression, Section 1.6. The designers of the fax compression standard have chosen a set of eight "representative" documents, analyzed their statistical properties, and used these as the basis for selecting the prefix codes shown in Table 1.20. In technical language we say that the documents were used to "train" the algorithm. Training an algorithm is a simple approach to statistical compression, but its performance depends on how much the file being compressed resembles the training documents.

2. The encoder performs a two-pass job. In the first pass, it reads the data file to be compressed and collects the necessary statistics. In the second pass, the file is actually compressed. In between the passes, the compressor uses the information from pass 1 to compute a set of best prefix codes for the particular file. This approach results in excellent compression but is normally too slow to be practical. It also has the added inconvenience that the prefix codes have to be included in the compressed file for the decoder's use. This degrades the overall performance but not by much. This approach to statistical compression is sometimes called semiadaptive compression.

3. Adaptive compression is used by both encoder and decoder. The encoder starts with no knowledge of the statistical properties of the data. The first part of the data is therefore poorly compressed, but while compressing it, the encoder collects more and more statistical information, improves the prefix codes that it uses, and thus improves its performance. The algorithm must be designed such that the decoder would be able to follow every step taken by the encoder, collect the same statistical information, and improve the prefix codes in the same way. An example of adaptive compression is shown in Section 1.5.

---

Buffy: It is a statistically impossible for a 16-year-old girl to unplug her phone.

—*Buffy the Vampire Slayer*

---

## 1.4 Huffman Coding

Huffman coding is a simple algorithm for generating a set of variable-size codes with the minimum average size. It is a well-known, popular algorithm, and it serves as the basis for several common software applications used on personal and other computers to compress text and images. Some of these applications use just the Huffman method, while others use it as one step in a multistep compression process. The Huffman method [Huffman 52] produces ideal compression (i.e., compression at the entropy of the data) when the probabilities of the symbols are negative powers of 2. The algorithm proceeds by constructing a code tree from the bottom up, then sliding down the tree to construct each individual code from right (least-significant bits) to left (most-significant bits). Since its development, in 1952, by D. Huffman, this method has been the subject of intensive research. (The last sentence of Section 3.8.1 shows that best variable-size codes can sometimes be obtained without this algorithm.)

The method starts by building a list of all the alphabet symbols in descending order of their probabilities. It then constructs a tree, with a symbol at every leaf, from the bottom up. This is done in steps, where at each step the two symbols with smallest probabilities are selected, added to the top of the partial tree, deleted from the list, and replaced with an auxiliary symbol representing both of them. When the list is reduced to just one auxiliary symbol (representing the entire alphabet), the tree is complete. The tree is then traversed to determine the codes of the symbols.

This is best illustrated by an example. Given five symbols with probabilities as shown in Figure 1.3a, they are paired in the following order:

1. $a_4$ is combined with $a_5$ and both are replaced by the combined symbol $a_{45}$, whose probability is 0.2.

2. There are now four symbols left, $a_1$, with probability 0.4, and $a_2$, $a_3$, and $a_{45}$, with probabilities 0.2 each. We arbitrarily select $a_3$ and $a_{45}$, combine them, and replace them with the auxiliary symbol $a_{345}$, whose probability is 0.4.

3. Three symbols are now left, $a_1$, $a_2$, and $a_{345}$, with probabilities 0.4, 0.2, and 0.4, respectively. We arbitrarily select $a_2$ and $a_{345}$, combine them, and replace them with the auxiliary symbol $a_{2345}$, whose probability is 0.6.

4. Finally, we combine the two remaining symbols, $a_1$ and $a_{2345}$, and replace them with $a_{12345}$ with probability 1.

The tree is now complete. It is shown in Figure 1.3a "lying on its side" with the root on the right and the five leaves on the left. To assign the codes, we arbitrarily assign a bit of 1 to the top edge and a bit of 0 to the bottom edge of every pair of edges. This results in the codes 0, 10, 111, 1101, and 1100. The assignments of bits to the edges is arbitrary.

The average size of this code is $0.4 \times 1 + 0.2 \times 2 + 0.2 \times 3 + 0.1 \times 4 + 0.1 \times 4 = 2.2$ bits/symbol, but even more important, the Huffman code is not unique. Some of the steps here were chosen arbitrarily, since there were more than two symbols with smallest probabilities. Figure 1.3b shows how the same five symbols can be combined differently to obtain a different Huffman code (11, 01, 00, 101, and 100). The average size of this code is $0.4 \times 2 + 0.2 \times 2 + 0.2 \times 2 + 0.1 \times 3 + 0.1 \times 3 = 2.2$ bits/symbol, the same as the previous code.

**Example:** Given the eight symbols A, B, C, D, E, F, G, and H with probabilities 1/30, 1/30, 1/30, 2/30, 3/30, 5/30, 5/30, and 12/30, we draw three different Huffman trees with heights 5 and 6 for these symbols (Figure 1.4a,b,c). The code sizes (in bits per symbol) for the trees are

$$(5 + 5 + 5 + 5 \cdot 2 + 3 \cdot 3 + 3 \cdot 5 + 3 \cdot 5 + 12)/30 = 76/30,$$
$$(5 + 5 + 4 + 4 \cdot 2 + 4 \cdot 3 + 3 \cdot 5 + 3 \cdot 5 + 12)/30 = 76/30,$$
$$(6 + 6 + 5 + 4 \cdot 2 + 3 \cdot 3 + 3 \cdot 5 + 3 \cdot 5 + 12)/30 = 76/30.$$

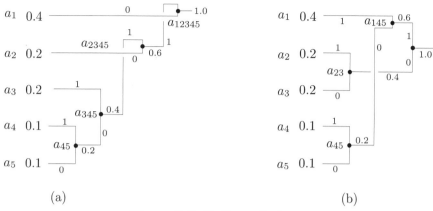

(a)                                              (b)

**Figure 1.3:** Huffman Codes.

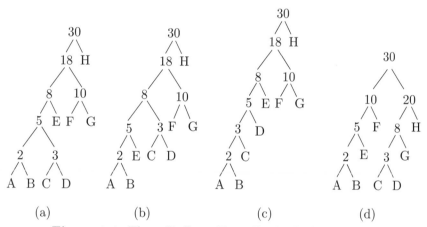

(a)             (b)             (c)             (d)

**Figure 1.4:** Three Huffman Trees For Eight Symbols.

**Example:** Figure 1.4d shows another Huffman tree, with height 4, for the eight symbols introduced in the previous example. As the following analysis shows, this tree is bad.

(Analysis.) After adding symbols A, B, C, D, E, F, and G to the tree we were left with the three symbols ABEF (with probability 10/30), CDG (with probability 8/30), and H (with probability 12/30). The two symbols with lowest probabilities were ABEF and CDG, so they had to be merged. Instead, symbols CDG and H were merged, creating a non-Huffman tree.

It turns out that the arbitrary decisions made in constructing the Huffman tree affect the individual codes but not the average size of the code. Still, we have to answer the obvious question, "Which of the different Huffman codes for a given set of symbols is best?" The answer, while not obvious, is simple: the code with the smallest variance.

The variance of a code measures how much the sizes of the individual codes deviate from the average size (the concept of variance is explained in any text on statistics). The variance of code 1.3a is

$$0.4(1 - 2.2)^2 + 0.2(2 - 2.2)^2 + 0.2(3 - 2.2)^2 + 0.1(4 - 2.2)^2 + 0.1(4 - 2.2)^2 = 1.36,$$

while that of code 1.3b is

$$0.4(2 - 2.2)^2 + 0.2(2 - 2.2)^2 + 0.2(2 - 2.2)^2 + 0.1(3 - 2.2)^2 + 0.1(3 - 2.2)^2 = 0.16.$$

Code 1.3b is thus preferable (see below). A careful look at the two trees shows how to select the one we want. In the tree of Figure 1.3a, symbol $a_{45}$ is combined with $a_3$, whereas in the tree of 1.3b it is combined with $a_1$. The rule is, when there are more than two smallest-probability nodes, select the ones that are lowest and highest in the tree and combine them. This will combine symbols of low probability with ones of high probability, thereby reducing the total variance of the code.

If the encoder simply writes the compressed file on a file, the variance of the code makes no difference. A small-variance Huffman code is preferable only in cases where the encoder *transmits* the compressed file, as it is being generated, over a communications line. In such a case, a code with large variance causes the encoder to generate bits at a rate that varies all the time. Since the bits have to be transmitted at a constant rate, the encoder has to use a buffer. Bits of the compressed file are entered into the buffer as they are being generated and are moved out of it at a constant rate to be transmitted. It is easy to see intuitively that a Huffman code with zero variance will enter bits into the buffer at a constant rate, so only a short buffer will be necessary. The larger the code variance, the more varied is the rate at which bits enter the buffer, requiring the encoder to use a larger buffer.

The following claim is sometimes found in the literature:

It can be shown that the size of the Huffman code of a symbol $a_i$ with probability $P_i$ is always less than or equal to $\lceil - \log_2 P_i \rceil$.

Even though it is correct in many cases, this claim is not true in general. I am indebted to Guy Blelloch for pointing this out and also for the example of Table 1.5. The second row of this table shows a symbol whose Huffman code is three bits long but for which $\lceil - \log_2 0.3 \rceil = \lceil 1.737 \rceil = 2$.

| $P_i$ | Code | $- \log_2 P_i$ | $\lceil - \log_2 P_i \rceil$ |
|---|---|---|---|
| .01 | 000 | 6.644 | 7 |
| *.30 | 001 | 1.737 | 2 |
| .34 | 01 | 1.556 | 2 |
| .35 | 1 | 1.515 | 2 |

**Table 1.5:** A Huffman Code Example.

The size of the Huffman code of symbol $a_i$ depends just on its probability $P_i$. However, the size also depends indirectly on the size of the alphabet. In a large alphabet, symbol probabilities tend to be small numbers, so Huffman codes are long. In a small alphabet, the situation is the opposite. This can also be understood intuitively. A small alphabet requires just a few codes, so they can all be short; a large alphabet requires many codes, so some must be long.

Figure 1.6 shows a Huffman code for the 26 letters.

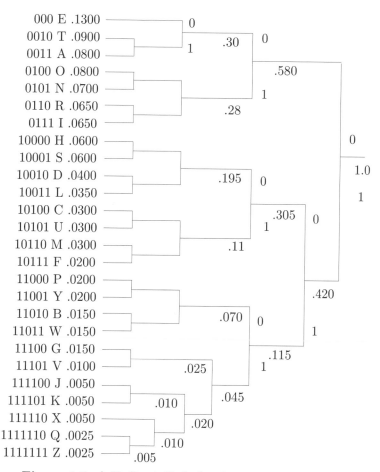

**Figure 1.6:** A Huffman Code for the 26-Letter Alphabet.

The case where all the alphabet symbols have equal probabilities is especially interesting. Figure 1.7 shows Huffman codes for 5, 6, 7, and 8 symbols with equal probabilities. In the case where $n$ is a power of 2, the codes are simply the fixed-size ones. In other cases the codes are very close to fixed-size. This shows that symbols with equal probabilities do not benefit from variable-size codes. Table 1.8 shows the codes and their average sizes and variances.

The fact that symbols with equal probabilities don't compress under the Huffman

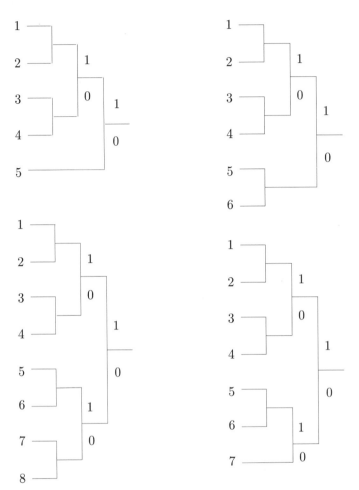

**Figure 1.7:** Huffman Codes for Equal Probabilities.

| $n$ | $p$ | $a_1$ | $a_2$ | $a_3$ | $a_4$ | $a_5$ | $a_6$ | $a_7$ | $a_8$ | Avg. size | Var. |
|---|---|---|---|---|---|---|---|---|---|---|---|
| 5 | 0.200 | 111 | 110 | 101 | 100 | 0 | | | | 2.6 | 0.64 |
| 6 | 0.167 | 111 | 110 | 101 | 100 | 01 | 00 | | | 2.672 | 0.2227 |
| 7 | 0.143 | 111 | 110 | 101 | 100 | 011 | 010 | 00 | | 2.86 | 0.1226 |
| 8 | 0.125 | 111 | 110 | 101 | 100 | 011 | 010 | 001 | 000 | 3 | 0 |

**Table 1.8:** Huffman Codes for 5–8 Symbols.

method suggests that strings of such symbols are normally random. There may be special cases where strings of symbols with equal probabilities are not random and can be compressed. A good example is the string $a_1a_1 \ldots a_1a_2a_2 \ldots a_2a_3a_3 \ldots$ in which each symbol appears in a long run. This string can be compressed with RLE but not with Huffman codes. (RLE stands for run-length encoding. This simple method is inefficient by itself but can be used as one step in a multistep compression method [Salomon 00].)

Notice that the Huffman method cannot be applied to a two-symbol alphabet. In such an alphabet, one symbol can be assigned the code 0 and the other code 1. The Huffman method cannot assign to any symbol a code shorter than one bit, so it cannot improve on this simple code. If the original data (the source) consists of individual bits, such as in the case of a bi-level (monochromatic) image, it is possible to combine several bits (perhaps 4 or 8) into a new symbol, and pretend that the alphabet consists of these (16 or 256) symbols. The problem with this approach is that the original binary data may have certain statistical correlations between the bits, and some of these correlations may be lost when the bits are combined into symbols. When a typical bi-level image (a painting or a diagram) is digitized by scan lines, a pixel is more likely to be followed by an identical pixel than by the opposite one. We thus have a file that can start with either a 0 or a 1 (each has 0.5 probability of being the first bit). A zero is more likely to be followed by another 0 and a 1 by another 1. Figure 1.9 is a finite-state machine illustrating this situation. If these bits are combined into, say, groups of eight, the bits inside a group will still be correlated, but the groups themselves will not be correlated by the original pixel probabilities. If the input file contains, e.g., the two adjacent groups 00011100 and 00001110, they will be encoded independently, ignoring the correlation between the last 0 of the first group and the first 0 of the next group. Selecting larger groups improves this situation but increases the number of groups, which implies more storage for the code table and also longer time to calculate the table. (Notice that when the group size increases from $s$ bits to $s + n$ bits, the number of groups increases exponentially from $2^s$ to $2^{s+n} = 2^s \times 2^n$.)

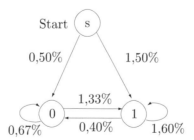

**Figure 1.9:** A Finite-State Machine.

A more complex approach to image compression by Huffman coding is to create several complete sets of Huffman codes. If the group size is, e.g., 8 bits, then several sets of 256 codes are generated. When a symbol S is to be encoded, one of the sets is selected, and S is encoded using its code in that set. The choice of set depends on the symbol preceding S.

**Example:** Imagine an image with 8-bit pixels where half the pixels have values 127 and the other half 128. We analyze the performance of RLE on the individual bitplanes of such an image and compare it to what can be achieved with Huffman coding.

(Analysis.) The binary value of 127 is 01111111 and that of 128 is 10000000. Half the pixels in each bitplane will therefore be 0 and the other half 1. In the worst case, each bitplane will be a checkerboard, i.e., will have many runs of size one. In such a case, each run requires a 1-bit code, leading to one codebit per pixel per bitplane, or eight codebits per pixel for the entire image, resulting in no compression at all. In comparison, a Huffman code for such an image requires just two codes (since there are just two pixel values) and they can be 1 bit each. This leads to one codebit per pixel, or a compression factor of eight.

---

### David Huffman (1925–1999)

David Huffman started his distinguished career as a brilliant student at MIT, where he developed his code in the early 1950s.

He joined the faculty at MIT in 1953. In 1967, he went to UC Santa Cruz as the founding faculty member of the Computer Science Department. He played a major role in the development of the department's academic programs and the hiring of its faculty and served as chair from 1970 to 1973. He retired in 1994 but remained active until 1999 as an emeritus professor, teaching information theory and signal analysis courses. He died in late 1999, at age 74.

Huffman made important contributions in many different areas, including information theory and coding, signal designs for radar and communications applications, and design procedures for asynchronous logical circuits. As an outgrowth of his work on the mathematical properties of "zero curvature" surfaces, Huffman developed his own techniques for folding paper into unusual sculptured shapes [Grafica 96].

---

### 1.4.1 Huffman Decoding

Before starting the compression of a data stream, the compressor (encoder) has to determine the codes. It does that based on the probabilities (or frequencies of occurrence) of the symbols. The probabilities or frequencies have to appear on the compressed file, so that any Huffman decompressor (decoder) will be able to decompress the file (but see Sections 1.3 and 1.5 for different approaches). This is easy, since the frequencies are integers and the probabilities can be written as scaled integers. It normally adds just a few hundred bytes to the compressed file. It is also possible to write the variable-size codes themselves on the file, but this may be awkward, since the codes have different sizes. It is also possible to write the Huffman tree on the file, but this may be longer than just the frequencies.

In any case, the decoder must know what's at the start of the file, read it, and construct the Huffman tree for the alphabet. Only then can it read and decode the rest of the file. The algorithm for decoding is simple. Start at the root and read the first bit off the compressed file. If it is zero, follow the bottom edge of the tree; if it is one, follow the top edge. Read the next bit and move another edge toward the leaves of the tree. When the decoder gets to a leaf, it finds the original uncompressed code of the symbol (normally, its ASCII code), and that code is emitted by the decoder. The process starts again at the root with the next input bit.

This process is illustrated for the five-symbol alphabet of Figure 1.10. The four-symbol input string "$a_4a_2a_5a_1$" is encoded into 1001100111. The decoder starts at the root, reads the first bit "1," and goes up. The second bit "0" sends it down, as does the third bit. This brings the decoder to leaf $a_4$, which it emits. It again returns to the root, reads 110, moves up, up, and down to reach leaf $a_2$, and so on.

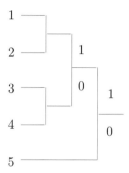

**Figure 1.10:** Huffman Codes for Equal Probabilities.

### 1.4.2 Average Code Size

Figure 1.13a shows a set of five symbols with their probabilities and a typical Huffman tree. Symbol A appears 55% of the time and is assigned a 1-bit code, so it contributes $0.55 \cdot 1$ bits to the average code size. Symbol E appears only 2% of the time and is assigned a 4-bit Huffman code, so it contributes $0.02 \cdot 4 = 0.08$ bits to the code size. The average code size is therefore calculated to be

$$0.55 \cdot 1 + 0.25 \cdot 2 + 0.15 \cdot 3 + 0.03 \cdot 4 + 0.02 \cdot 4 = 1.7 \text{ bits per symbol.}$$

Surprisingly, the same result is obtained by adding the values of the four internal nodes of the Huffman codetree $0.05 + 0.2 + 0.45 + 1 = 1.7$. This provides a way to calculate the average code size of a set of Huffman codes without any multiplications. Simply add the values of all the internal nodes of the tree. Table 1.11 illustrates why this works.

$$
\begin{aligned}
.05 &= & .02 + .03 \\
.20 &= .05 + .15 &= .02 + .03 + .15 \\
.45 &= .20 + .25 &= .02 + .03 + .15 + .25 \\
1.0 &= .45 + .55 &= .02 + .03 + .15 + .25 + .55
\end{aligned}
$$

**Table 1.11:** Composition of Nodes.

$$
\begin{aligned}
0.05 &= & = 0.02 + 0.03 + \cdots \\
a_1 &= 0.05 + \ldots &= 0.02 + 0.03 + \cdots \\
a_2 &= a_1 \ \ + \ldots &= 0.02 + 0.03 + \cdots \\
\vdots \ \ &= \\
a_{d-2} &= a_{d-3} + \ldots &= 0.02 + 0.03 + \cdots \\
1.0 &= a_{d-2} + \ldots &= 0.02 + 0.03 + \cdots
\end{aligned}
$$

**Table 1.12:** Composition of Nodes.

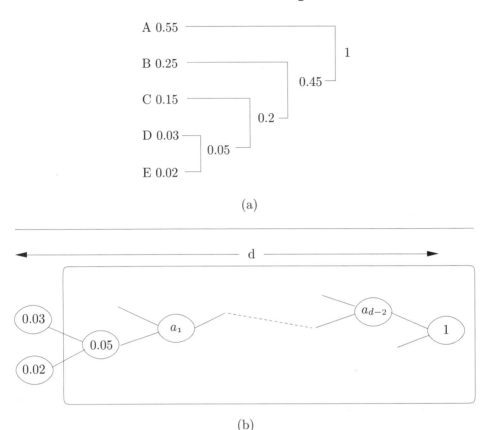

(a)

(b)

**Figure 1.13:** Huffman Code Trees.

(Internal nodes are shown in italics in this table.) The left column consists of the values of all the internal nodes. The right columns show how each internal node is the sum of some of the leaf nodes. Summing the values in the left column yields 1.7, and summing the other columns shows that this 1.7 is the sum of the four values 0.02, the four values 0.03, the three values 0.15, the two values 0.25, and the single value 0.55.

This argument can be extended to the general case. It is easy to show that, in a Huffman-like tree (a tree where each node is the sum of its children) the weighted sum of the leaves, where the weights are the distances of the leaves from the root, equals the sum of the internal nodes. (This property was communicated to me by John M. Motil.)

Figure 1.13b shows such a tree, where we assume that the two leaves 0.02 and 0.03 have $d$-bit Huffman codes. Inside the tree, these leaves become the children of internal node 0.05, which, in turn, is connected to the root by means of the $d-2$ internal nodes $a_1$ through $a_{d-2}$. Table 1.12 has $d$ rows and shows that the two values 0.02 and 0.03 are included in the various internal nodes exactly $d$ times. Adding the values of all the internal nodes produces a sum that includes the contributions $0.02 \cdot d + 0.03 \cdot d$ from the two leaves. Since these leaves are arbitrary, it is clear that this sum includes similar contributions from all the other leaves, so this sum is the average code size. Since this sum also equals the sum of the left column, which is the sum of the internal nodes, it is clear that the sum of the internal nodes equals the average code size.

Notice that this proof does not assume that the tree is binary. The property illustrated here exists for any tree where a node contains the sum of its children.

> Statistics are no substitute for judgment.
>                              —Henry Clay

## 1.5 Adaptive Huffman Coding

The Huffman method assumes that the frequencies of occurrence of all the symbols of the alphabet are known to the compressor. In practice, the frequencies are seldom, if ever, known in advance. One solution is for the compressor to read the original data twice. The first time it just calculates the frequencies. The second time it compresses the data. Between the two passes, the compressor constructs the Huffman tree. Such a method is called semiadaptive (Section 1.3) and is normally too slow to be practical. The method used in practice is called adaptive (or dynamic) Huffman coding. This method is the basis of the UNIX `compact` program.

For more information on the adaptive method described here and on other adaptive Huffman algorithms, see [Lelewer and Hirschberg 87], [Knuth 85], and [Vitter 87].

The main idea is for the compressor and the decompressor to start with an empty Huffman tree and to modify it as symbols are being read and processed (in the case of the compressor, the word "processed" means compressed; in the case of the decompressor, it means decompressed). The compressor and decompressor should modify the tree in the same way, so at any point in the process they should use the same codes, although those codes may change from step to step. We say that the compressor and decompressor are synchronized, or that they work in *lockstep* (although they don't necessarily work together; compression and decompression usually take place at different times). The term *mirroring* is perhaps a better choice. The decoder mirrors the operations of the encoder.

Initially, the compressor starts with an empty Huffman tree. No symbols have been assigned codes. The first symbol being input is simply written on the output file in its uncompressed form. The symbol is then added to the tree and a code is assigned to it. The next time this symbol is encountered, its current code is written on the file and its frequency is incremented by one. Since this modifies the tree, it (the tree) is examined to see whether it is still a Huffman tree (best codes). If not, it is rearranged, which entails changing the codes (Section 1.5.2).

The decompressor mirrors the same steps. When it reads the uncompressed form of a symbol, it adds it to the tree and assigns it a code. When it reads a compressed (variable-size) code, it uses the current tree to determine what symbol the code belongs to, and it updates the tree in the same way as the compressor.

The only subtle point is that the decompressor needs to know whether the item it has just input is an uncompressed symbol (normally, an 8-bit ASCII code, but see Section 1.5.1) or a variable-size code. To remove any ambiguity, each uncompressed symbol is preceded by a special, variable-size *escape code*. When the decompressor reads this code, it knows that the next 8 bits are the ASCII code of a symbol that appears in the compressed file for the first time.

The trouble is that the escape code should not be any of the variable-size codes used for the symbols. Since these codes are being modified every time the tree is rearranged, the escape code should also be modified. A natural way to do this is to add an empty leaf to the tree, a leaf with a zero frequency of occurrence, that's always assigned to the 0-branch of the tree. Since the leaf is in the tree, it is assigned a variable-size code. This code is the escape code preceding every uncompressed symbol. As the tree is being rearranged, the position of the empty leaf—and thus its code—change, but this escape code is always used to identify uncompressed symbols in the compressed file. Figure 1.14 shows how the escape code moves as the tree grows.

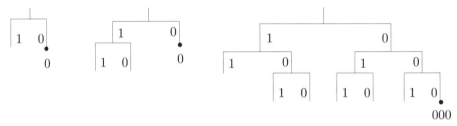

**Figure 1.14:** The Escape Code.

This method is used to compress/decompress data in the V.32 protocol for 14,400-baud modems.

### 1.5.1 Uncompressed Codes

If the symbols being compressed are ASCII characters, they may simply be assigned their ASCII codes as uncompressed codes. In the general case where there can be any symbols, uncompressed codes of two different sizes can be assigned by a simple method. Here is an example for the case $n = 24$. The first 16 symbols can be assigned the numbers 0 through 15 as their codes. These numbers require only 4 bits, but we encode them in 5 bits. Symbols 17 through 24 can be assigned the numbers $17 - 16 - 1 = 0$, $18 - 16 - 1 = 1$ through $24 - 16 - 1 = 7$ as 4-bit numbers. We end up with the sixteen 5-bit codes 00000, 00001,..., 01111, followed by the eight 4-bit codes 0000, 0001,..., 0111.

In general, we assume an alphabet that consists of the $n$ symbols $a_1, a_2, \ldots, a_n$. We select integers $m$ and $r$ such that $2^m \le n < 2^{m+1}$ and $r = n - 2^m$. The first $2^m$ symbols are encoded as the $(m + 1)$-bit numbers 0 through $2^m - 1$. The remaining symbols are encoded as $m$-bit numbers such that the code of $a_k$ is $k - 2^m - 1$. This code is also called a *phased-in binary code*.

> A single death is a tragedy, a million deaths is a statistic.
>
> —Joseph Stalin

### 1.5.2 Modifying the Tree

The main idea is to check the tree each time a symbol is input. If the tree is no longer a Huffman tree, it should be updated. A glance at Figure 1.15a shows what it means for a binary tree to be a Huffman tree. The tree in the figure contains five symbols: A, B, C, D, and E. It is shown with the symbols and their frequencies (in parentheses) after 16 symbols have been input and processed. The property that makes it a Huffman tree is that if we scan it level by level, scanning each level from left to right and going from the bottom (the leaves) to the top (the root), the frequencies will be in sorted, nondescending order. Thus the bottom left node (A) has the lowest frequency, and the top right one (the root) has the highest frequency. This is called the *sibling property*.

The reason a Huffman tree has this property is that a symbol with high frequency of occurrence should be assigned a shorter code and should therefore appear high in the tree. The requirement that at each level the frequencies be sorted from left to right is arbitrary. In principle it is not necessary, but it simplifies the process of updating the tree.

Here is a summary of the operations necessary to update the tree. The loop starts at the current node (the one corresponding to the symbol just input). This node is a leaf that we denote by $X$, with frequency of occurrence $F$. Each iteration of the loop involves three steps:

1. Compare $X$ to its successors in the tree (from left to right and bottom to top). If the immediate successor has frequency $F + 1$ or greater, the nodes are still in sorted order and there is no need to change anything. Otherwise, some successors of $X$ have identical frequencies of $F$ or smaller. In this case, $X$ should be swapped with the last node in this group (except that $X$ should not be swapped with its parent).
2. Increment the frequency of $X$ from $F$ to $F + 1$. Increment the frequencies of all its parents.
3. If $X$ is the root, the loop stops; otherwise, the loop repeats with the parent of node $X$.

Figure 1.15b shows the tree after the frequency of node A has been incremented from 1 to 2. It is easy to follow the three rules to see how incrementing the frequency of A results in incrementing the frequencies of all its parents. No swaps are needed in this simple case because the frequency of A hasn't exceeded the frequency of its immediate successor B. Figure 1.15c shows what happens when A's frequency has been incremented again, from 2 to 3. The three nodes following A, namely, B, C, and D, have frequencies of 2, so A is swapped with the last of them, D. The frequencies of the new parents of A are then incremented and each is compared to its successor, but no more swaps are needed.

Figure 1.15d shows the tree after the frequency of A has been incremented to 4. Once we decide that A is the current node, its frequency (which is still 3) is compared to that of its successor (4), and the decision is not to swap. A's frequency is incremented, followed by incrementing the frequencies of its parents.

In Figure 1.15e, A is again the current node. Its frequency (4) equals that of its successor, so they should be swapped. This is shown in Figure 1.15f, where A's frequency is 5. The next loop iteration examines the parent of A, with frequency 10.

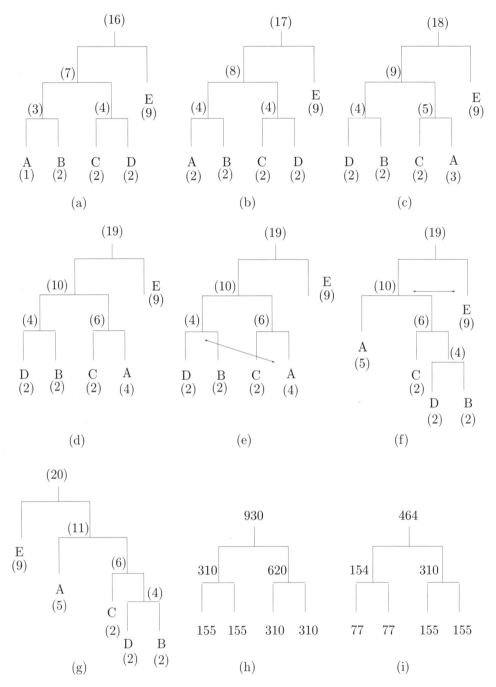

**Figure 1.15:** Updating the Huffman Tree.

It should be swapped with its successor E (with frequency 9), which leads to the final tree of Figure 1.15g.

> One that would have the fruit must climb the tree.
>
> —Thomas Fuller

### 1.5.3 Counter Overflow

The frequency counts are accumulated in the Huffman tree in fixed-size fields, and such fields may overflow. A 16-bit unsigned field can accommodate counts of up to $2^{16} - 1 = 65,535$. A simple solution is to watch the count field of the root each time it is incremented and, when it reaches its maximum value, to *rescale* all frequency counts by dividing them by 2 (integer division). In practice, this is done by dividing the count fields of the leaves, then updating the counts of the interior nodes. Each interior node gets the sum of the counts of its children. The problem is that the counts are integers, and integer division reduces precision. This may change a Huffman tree to one that does not satisfy the sibling property.

A simple example is shown in Figure 1.15h. After the counts of the leaves are halved, the three interior nodes are updated as shown in Figure 1.15i. The latter tree, however, is no longer a Huffman tree, since the counts are no longer in sorted order. The solution is to rebuild the tree each time the counts are rescaled, which does not happen very often. A Huffman data compression program intended for general use should thus have large count fields that would not overflow very often. A 4-byte count field overflows at $2^{32} - 1 \approx 4.3 \times 10^9$.

It should be noted that after rescaling the counts, the new symbols being read and compressed have more effect on the counts than the old symbols (those counted before the rescaling). This turns out to be fortuitous since it is known from experience that the probability of appearance of a symbol depends more on the symbols immediately preceding it than on symbols that appeared in the distant past.

### 1.5.4 Code Overflow

An even more serious problem is code overflow. This may happen when many symbols are added to the tree and it becomes tall. The codes themselves are not stored in the tree, since they change all the time, and the compressor has to figure out the code of a symbol $X$ each time $X$ is input. Here are the details:

1. The encoder has to locate symbol $X$ in the tree. The tree has to be implemented as an array of structures, each a node, and the array is searched linearly.

2. If $X$ is not found, the escape code is emitted, followed by the uncompressed code of $X$. $X$ is then added to the tree.

3. If $X$ is found, the compressor moves from node $X$ back to the root, building the code bit by bit as it goes along. Each time it goes from a left child to a parent, a "1" is appended to the code. Going from a right child to a parent appends a "0" bit to the code (or vice versa, but this should be consistent because it is mirrored by the decoder). Those bits have to be accumulated someplace, since they have to be emitted in the *reverse order* in which they are created. When the tree gets taller, the codes get longer.

If they are accumulated in a 16-bit integer, then codes longer than 16 bits would cause a malfunction.

One solution is to accumulate the bits of a code in a linked list, where new nodes can be created, limited in number only by the amount of available memory. This is general but slow. Another solution is to accumulate the codes in a large integer variable (perhaps 50 bits wide) and document a maximum code size of 50 bits as one of the limitations of the program.

Fortunately, this problem does not affect the decoding process. The decoder reads the compressed code bit by bit and uses each bit to go one step left or right down the tree until it reaches a leaf node. If the leaf is the escape code, the decoder reads the uncompressed code of the symbol off the compressed file (and adds the symbol to the tree). Otherwise, the uncompressed code is found in the leaf node.

**Example:** We apply the adaptive Huffman to the string "sir␣sid␣is". For each symbol input, we show the output, the tree after the symbol has been added to it, the tree after being rearranged (if necessary), and the list of nodes traversed left to right and bottom up.

Figure 1.16 shows the initial tree and how it is updated in the 11 steps (a) through (k). Notice how the *esc* symbol gets assigned different codes all the time, and how the different symbols move about in the tree and change their codes. Code 10, e.g., is the code of symbol "i" in steps (f) and (i), but is the code of "s" in steps (e) and (j). The code of a blank space is 011 in step (h), but 00 in step (k).

The final output is: "s0i00r100␣1010000d011101000". A total of $5 \times 8 + 22 = 62$ bits. The compression ratio is thus $62/88 \approx 0.7$.

### 1.5.5 A Variant

This variant of the adaptive Huffman method is simple but less efficient. The idea is to compute a set of $n$ variable-size codes based on equal probabilities, to assign those codes to the $n$ symbols at random, and to vary the assignments "on the fly," as symbols are being read and compressed. The method is inefficient because the codes are not based on the actual probabilities of the symbols in the input file. However, it is easier to implement and also faster than the adaptive method above, because it has to swap rows in a table, rather than update a tree, when updating the frequencies of the symbols.

The main data structure is an $n \times 3$ table where the three columns store the names of the $n$ symbols, their frequencies of occurrence so far, and their codes. The table is always kept sorted by the second column. When the frequency counts in the second column change, rows are swapped, but only columns 1 and 2 are moved. The codes in column 3 never change. Figure 1.17 shows an example of four symbols and the behavior of the method when the string "$a_2$, $a_4$, $a_4$" is compressed.

Figure 1.17a shows the initial state. After the first symbol $a_2$ is read, its count is incremented, and since it is now the largest count, rows 1 and 2 are swapped (Figure 1.17b). After the second symbol $a_4$ is read, its count is incremented and rows 2 and 4 are swapped (Figure 1.17c). Finally, after reading the last symbol $a_4$, its count is the largest, so rows 1 and 2 are swapped (Figure 1.17d).

The only point that can cause a problem with this method is overflow of the count fields. If such a field is $k$ bits wide, its maximum value is $2^k - 1$, so it will overflow

Initial tree

(a) Input: s. Output: 's'.
$esc\, s_1$

(b) Input: i. Output: 0'i'.
$esc\, i_1\, 1\, s_1$

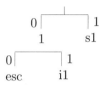

(c) Input: r. Output: 00'r'.
$esc\, r_1\, 1\, i_1\, 2\, s_1 \rightarrow$
$esc\, r_1\, 1\, i_1\, s_1\, 2$

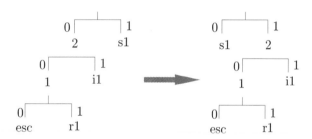

(d) Input: ␣. Output: 100'␣'.
$esc_{␣1}\, 1\, r_1\, 2\, i_1\, s_1\, 3 \rightarrow$
$esc_{␣1}\, 1\, r_1\, s_1\, i_1\, 2\, 2$

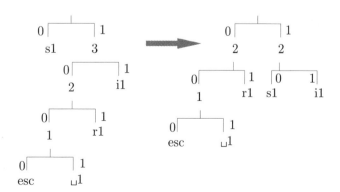

**Figure 1.16:** Adaptive Huffman Example: Part I.

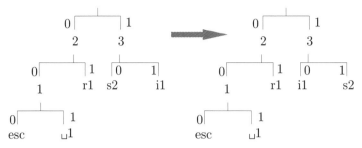

(e) Input: s. Output: 10.

$esc_{\sqcup 1}\, 1\, r_1\, s_2\, i_1\, 2\, 3 \rightarrow$

$esc_{\sqcup 1}\, 1\, r_1\, i_1\, s_2\, 2\, 3$

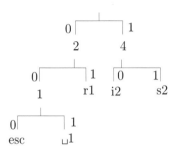

(f) Input: i. Output: 10.

$esc_{\sqcup 1}\, 1\, r_1\, i_2\, s_2\, 2\, 4$

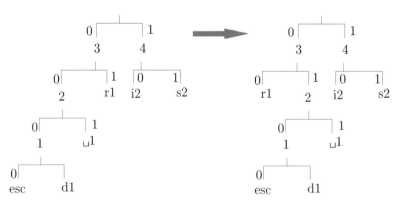

(g) Input: d. Output: 000'd'.

$esc\, d_1\, 1_{\sqcup 1}\, 2\, r_1\, i_2\, s_2\, 3\, 4 \rightarrow$

$esc\, d_1\, 1_{\sqcup 1}\, r_1\, 2\, i_2\, s_2\, 3\, 4$

**Figure 1.16:** Adaptive Huffman Example: Part II.

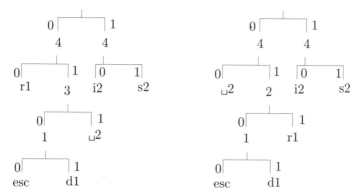

(h) Input: ⊔. Output: 011.
$esc\, d_1\, 1\, {}_{\sqcup 2}\, r_1\, 3\, i_2\, s_2\, 4\, 4 \rightarrow$
$esc\, d_1\, 1\, r_1\, {}_{\sqcup 2}\, 2\, i_2\, s_2\, 4\, 4$

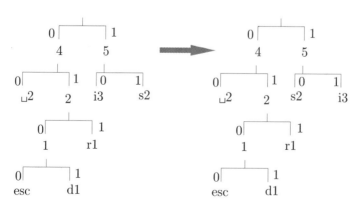

(i) Input: i. Output: 10.
$esc\, d_1\, 1\, r_1\, {}_{\sqcup 2}\, 2\, i_3\, s_2\, 4\, 5 \rightarrow$
$esc\, d_1\, 1\, r_1\, {}_{\sqcup 2}\, 2\, s_2\, i_3\, 4\, 5$

**Figure 1.16:** Adaptive Huffman Example: Part III.

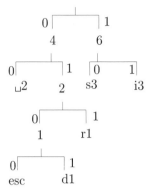

(j) Input: s. Output: 10.
$esc\, d_1\, 1\, r_1\, {}_{\sqcup 2}\, 2\, s_3\, i_3\, 4\, 6$

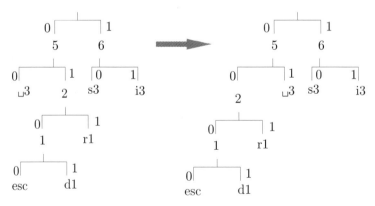

(k) Input: ⊔. Output: 00.
$esc\, d_1\, 1\, r_1\, {}_{\sqcup 3}\, 2\, s_3\, i_3\, 5\, 6 \rightarrow$
$esc\, d_1\, 1\, r_1\, 2\, {}_{\sqcup 3}\, s_3\, i_3\, 5\, 6$

**Figure 1.16:** Adaptive Huffman Example: Part IV.

| Name | Count | Code | Name | Count | Code | Name | Count | Code | Name | Count | Code |
|------|-------|------|------|-------|------|------|-------|------|------|-------|------|
| $a_1$ | 0 | 0 | $a_2$ | 1 | 0 | $a_2$ | 1 | 0 | $a_4$ | 2 | 0 |
| $a_2$ | 0 | 10 | $a_1$ | 0 | 10 | $a_4$ | 1 | 10 | $a_2$ | 1 | 10 |
| $a_3$ | 0 | 110 | $a_3$ | 0 | 110 | $a_3$ | 0 | 110 | $a_3$ | 0 | 110 |
| $a_4$ | 0 | 111 | $a_4$ | 0 | 111 | $a_1$ | 0 | 111 | $a_1$ | 0 | 111 |
| | (a) | | | (b) | | | (c) | | | (d) | |

**Figure 1.17:** Four Steps in a Huffman Variant.

when incremented for the $2^k$th time. This may happen if the size of the input file is not known in advance, which is very common. Fortunately, we do not really need to know the counts; we just need them in sorted order, making it easy to solve this problem.

One solution is to count the input symbols and, after $2^k - 1$ symbols are input and compressed, to (integer) divide all the count fields by 2 (or shift them one position to the right, if this is easier).

Another similar solution is to check each count field every time it is incremented and, if it has reached its maximum value (if it consists of all ones), to integer divide all the count fields by 2. This approach requires fewer divisions but more complex tests.

Whatever solution is adopted should be used by both the compressor and decompressor.

Get your facts first, and then you can distort them as much as you please. (Facts are stubborn, but statistics are more pliable.)

—Mark Twain

## 1.6 Facsimile Compression

Data compression is especially important when images are transmitted over a communications line, because the user is typically waiting at the receiver, eager to see something quickly. Documents transferred between fax machines are sent as bitmaps, so a standard data compression method was needed when those machines became popular. Several methods were developed and proposed by the ITU-T. [Anderson et al. 87], [Hunter and Robinson 80], [Marking 90], and [McConnell 92] are a few of the many references available for this popular standard. Formal descriptions can be found at [Ohio-state 01] and as files `7_3_01.ps.gz` and `7_3_02.ps.gz` in ftp site [ccitt 01].

The ITU-T is one of four permanent parts of the International Telecommunications Union (ITU), based in Geneva, Switzerland (`http://www.itu.ch/`). It issues recommendations for standards applying to modems, packet-switched interfaces, V.24 connectors, etc. Although it has no power of enforcement, the standards it recommends are generally accepted and adopted by industry. Until March 1993, the ITU-T was known as the Consultative Committee for International Telephone and Telegraph (Comité Consultatif International Télégraphique et Téléphonique, or CCITT).

The first data compression standards developed by the ITU-T were T2 (also known as Group 1) and T3 (Group 2). These are now obsolete and have been replaced by T4 (Group 3) and T6 (Group 4). Group 3 is currently used by all fax machines designed to operate with the Public Switched Telephone Network (PSTN). These are the machines we have at home, and at the time of writing, they operate at maximum speeds of 9,600 baud. Group 4 is used by fax machines designed to operate on a digital network, such as ISDN. They have typical speeds of 64K baud. Both methods can produce compression factors of 10:1 or better, reducing the transmission time of a typical page to about a minute with the former and a few seconds with the latter.

> The word facsimile comes from the Latin *facere* (make) and *similis* (like).)

### 1.6.1 One-Dimensional Coding

A fax machine scans a document line by line, converting each line to small black and white dots called *pels* (from Picture ELement). The horizontal resolution is always 8.05 pels per millimeter (about 205 pels per inch). An 8.5-inch-wide scan line is thus converted to 1728 pels. The T4 standard, though, recommends scanning only about 8.2 inches, thus producing 1664 pels per scan line (these numbers, as well as those in the next paragraph, are all to within $\pm 1\%$ accuracy).

The vertical resolution is either 3.85 scan lines per millimeter (standard mode) or 7.7 lines/mm (fine mode). Many fax machines have also a very-fine mode, where they scan 15.4 lines/mm. Table 1.18 assumes a 10-inch-high page (254 mm) and shows the total number of pels per page and typical transmission times for the three modes without compression. The times are long, which shows how important data compression is in fax transmissions.

| Scan lines | Pels per line | Pels per page | Time (sec) | Time (min) |
|---|---|---|---|---|
| 978 | 1664 | 1.670M | 170 | 2.82 |
| 1956 | 1664 | 3.255M | 339 | 5.65 |
| 3912 | 1664 | 6.510M | 678 | 11.3 |

Ten inches equal 254 mm. The number of pels is in the millions, and the transmission times, at 9600 baud without compression, are between 3 and 11 minutes, depending on the mode. However, if the page is shorter than 10 inches, or if most of it is white, the compression factor can be 10:1 or better, resulting in transmission times of between 17 and 68 seconds.

**Table 1.18:** Fax Transmission Times.

To derive the Group 3 code, the ITU-T counted all the run lengths of white and black pels in a set of eight "training" documents that they felt represent typical text and images sent by fax and applied the Huffman algorithm to assign a variable-size code to each run length. (The eight documents are described in Table 1.19. They are not shown, because they are copyrighted by the ITU-T, but they can be downloaded from [funet 01].) The most common run lengths were found to be 2, 3, and 4 black pixels, so they were assigned the shortest codes (Table 1.20). Next come run lengths of 2–7 white pixels, which were assigned slightly longer codes. Most run lengths were rare and were assigned long, 12-bit codes. Thus, the Group 3 standard uses a combination of RLE and Huffman coding.

It is interesting to notice that the run length of 1664 white pels was assigned the short code 011000. This is because a typical fax machine scans lines that are about 8.2 inches wide ($\approx$ 208 mm). A blank scan line produces 1,664 consecutive white pels, making this run length very common.

| Image | Description |
|:-----:|:------------|
| 1 | Typed business letter (English) |
| 2 | Circuit diagram (hand drawn) |
| 3 | Printed and typed invoice (French) |
| 4 | Densely typed report (French) |
| 5 | Printed technical article including figures and equations (French) |
| 6 | Graph with printed captions (French) |
| 7 | Dense document (Kanji) |
| 8 | Handwritten memo with very large white-on-black letters (English) |

**Table 1.19:** The Eight CCITT Training Documents.

Since run lengths can be long, the Huffman algorithm was modified. Codes were assigned to run lengths of 1 to 63 pels (they are the termination codes in Table 1.20a) and to run lengths that are multiples of 64 pels (the makeup codes in Table 1.20b). Group 3 is thus a *modified Huffman code* (also called MH). The code of a run length is either a single termination code (if the run length is short) or one or more makeup codes, followed by one termination code (if it is long). Here are some examples:

1. A run length of 12 white pels is coded as 001000.
2. A run length of 76 white pels (= 64 + 12) is coded as 11011|001000 (without the vertical bar).
3. A run length of 140 white pels (= 128 + 12) is coded as 10010|001000.
4. A run length of 64 black pels (= 64 + 0) is coded as 0000001111|0000110111.
5. A run length of 2561 black pels (2560 + 1) is coded as 000000011111|010.

The meticulous reader will notice that codes were assigned to runs of zero black and zero white pels, even though run lengths must have a positive value. These codes are needed for cases where the run length is 64, 128 or any length for which a makeup code has been assigned. There is also the question of the run length of 2561. An 8.5-inch-wide scan line results in only 1728 pels, so currently there is no need for codes for longer runs. However, there may be fax machines (now or in the future) built for wider paper, so the Group 3 code was designed to accommodate them.

Each scan line is coded separately, and its code is terminated by the special 12-bit EOL code 000000000001. Each line also gets one white pel appended to it on the left

| Run length | White code-word | Black code-word | Run length | White code-word | Black code-word |
|---|---|---|---|---|---|
| 0 | 00110101 | 0000110111 | 32 | 00011011 | 000001101010 |
| 1 | 000111 | 010 | 33 | 00010010 | 000001101011 |
| 2 | 0111 | 11 | 34 | 00010011 | 000011010010 |
| 3 | 1000 | 10 | 35 | 00010100 | 000011010011 |
| 4 | 1011 | 011 | 36 | 00010101 | 000011010100 |
| 5 | 1100 | 0011 | 37 | 00010110 | 000011010101 |
| 6 | 1110 | 0010 | 38 | 00010111 | 000011010110 |
| 7 | 1111 | 00011 | 39 | 00101000 | 000011010111 |
| 8 | 10011 | 000101 | 40 | 00101001 | 000001101100 |
| 9 | 10100 | 000100 | 41 | 00101010 | 000001101101 |
| 10 | 00111 | 0000100 | 42 | 00101011 | 000011011010 |
| 11 | 01000 | 0000101 | 43 | 00101100 | 000011011011 |
| 12 | 001000 | 0000111 | 44 | 00101101 | 000001010100 |
| 13 | 000011 | 00000100 | 45 | 00000100 | 000001010101 |
| 14 | 110100 | 00000111 | 46 | 00000101 | 000001010110 |
| 15 | 110101 | 000011000 | 47 | 00001010 | 000001010111 |
| 16 | 101010 | 0000010111 | 48 | 00001011 | 000001100100 |
| 17 | 101011 | 0000011000 | 49 | 01010010 | 000001100101 |
| 18 | 0100111 | 0000001000 | 50 | 01010011 | 000001010010 |
| 19 | 0001100 | 00001100111 | 51 | 01010100 | 000001010011 |
| 20 | 0001000 | 00001101000 | 52 | 01010101 | 000000100100 |
| 21 | 0010111 | 00001101100 | 53 | 00100100 | 000000110111 |
| 22 | 0000011 | 00000110111 | 54 | 00100101 | 000000111000 |
| 23 | 0000100 | 00000101000 | 55 | 01011000 | 000000100111 |
| 24 | 0101000 | 00000010111 | 56 | 01011001 | 000000101000 |
| 25 | 0101011 | 00000011000 | 57 | 01011010 | 000001011000 |
| 26 | 0010011 | 000011001010 | 58 | 01011011 | 000001011001 |
| 27 | 0100100 | 000011001011 | 59 | 01001010 | 000000101011 |
| 28 | 0011000 | 000011001100 | 60 | 01001011 | 000000101100 |
| 29 | 00000010 | 000011001101 | 61 | 00110010 | 000001011010 |
| 30 | 00000011 | 000001101000 | 62 | 00110011 | 000001100110 |
| 31 | 00011010 | 000001101001 | 63 | 00110100 | 000001100111 |

(a)

| Run length | White code-word | Black code-word | Run length | White code-word | Black code-word |
|---|---|---|---|---|---|
| 64 | 11011 | 0000001111 | 1344 | 011011010 | 0000001010011 |
| 128 | 10010 | 000011001000 | 1408 | 011011011 | 0000001010100 |
| 192 | 010111 | 000011001001 | 1472 | 010011000 | 0000001010101 |
| 256 | 0110111 | 000001011011 | 1536 | 010011001 | 0000001011010 |
| 320 | 00110110 | 000000110011 | 1600 | 010011010 | 0000001011011 |
| 384 | 00110111 | 000000110100 | 1664 | 011000 | 0000001100100 |
| 448 | 01100100 | 000000110101 | 1728 | 010011011 | 0000001100101 |
| 512 | 01100101 | 0000001101100 | 1792 | 00000001000 | same as |
| 576 | 01101000 | 0000001101101 | 1856 | 00000001100 | white |
| 640 | 01100111 | 0000001001010 | 1920 | 00000001101 | from this |
| 704 | 011001100 | 0000001001011 | 1984 | 000000010010 | point |
| 768 | 011001101 | 0000001001100 | 2048 | 000000010011 | |
| 832 | 011010010 | 0000001001101 | 2112 | 000000010100 | |
| 896 | 011010011 | 0000001110010 | 2176 | 000000010101 | |
| 960 | 011010100 | 0000001110011 | 2240 | 000000010110 | |
| 1024 | 011010101 | 0000001110100 | 2304 | 000000010111 | |
| 1088 | 011010110 | 0000001110101 | 2368 | 000000011100 | |
| 1152 | 011010111 | 0000001110110 | 2432 | 000000011101 | |
| 1216 | 011011000 | 0000001110111 | 2496 | 000000011110 | |
| 1280 | 011011001 | 0000001010010 | 2560 | 000000011111 | |

(b)

**Table 1.20:** Group 3 and 4 Fax Codes: (a) Termination Codes. (b) Makeup Codes.

when it is scanned. This is done to remove any ambiguity when the line is decoded on the receiving end. After reading the EOL for the previous line, the receiver assumes that the new line starts with a run of white pels, and it ignores the first of them. Examples:

1. The 14-pel line ▮▮▮ ▮ ▮▮          is coded as the run lengths 1w 3b 2w 2b 7w EOL, which become 000111|10|0111|11|1111|000000000001. The decoder ignores the single white pel at the start.

2. The line    ▮▮▮▮▮      ▮▮ is coded as the run lengths 3w 5b 5w 2b EOL, which becomes the binary string 1000|0011|1100|11|000000000001.

Notice that the codes of Table 1.20 have to satisfy the prefix property in each column but not between the columns. This is because each scan line starts with a white pel, so when the decoder inputs the next code it knows whether it is for a run of white or black pels. An example of where the prefix property is not preserved between columns is the code for a run length of five black pels (0011) that is also the prefix of the codes for run lengths of 61, 62, and 63 white pels.

The Group 3 code has no error correction, but many errors can be detected. Because of the nature of the Huffman code, even one bad bit in the transmission can cause the receiver to get out of synchronization and to produce a string of wrong pels. This is why each scan line is encoded separately. If the receiver detects an error, it skips bits, looking for an EOL. This way, one error can cause at most one scan line to be received incorrectly. If the receiver does not see an EOL after a certain number of lines, it assumes a high error rate, and it aborts the process, notifying the transmitter. Since the codes are between 2 and 12 bits long, the receiver detects an error if it cannot decode a valid code after reading 12 bits.

Each page of the coded document is preceded by one EOL and is followed by six EOL codes. Because each line is coded separately, this method is a *one-dimensional coding* scheme. The compression ratio depends on the image. Images with large contiguous black or white areas (text or black and white images) can be highly compressed. Images with many short runs can sometimes produce negative compression. This is especially true in the case of images with shades of gray (such as scanned photographs). Such shades are produced by halftoning, which covers areas with many alternating black and white pels (runs of length one).

Since the T4 standard is based on run lengths, it may result in poor compression or even in expansion when the document features only short lengths. An extreme (and unlikely) case is a hypothetical document where all the run lengths are of size 1. The code of a run length of one white pel is 000111, and that of one black pel is 010. Thus, two consecutive pels of different colors are coded into 9 bits. Since the uncoded data requires just two bits (01 or 10), the compression ratio is $9/2 = 4.5$ (the compressed file is 4.5 times longer than the uncompressed one, a large expansion).

The T4 standard also allows for fill bits to be inserted between the data bits and the EOL. This is done in cases where a pause is necessary or where the total number of bits transmitted for a scan line must be a multiple of 8. The fill bits are zeros.

**Example:** The binary string 000111|10|0111|11|1111|000000000001 becomes a bit longer 000111|10|0111|11|1111|00|0000000001 after two zeros are added as fill bits, bringing the total length of the string to 32 bits ($= 8 \times 4$). The decoder sees the two zeros of the fill, followed by the eleven zeros of the EOL, followed by the single 1, so it knows that it has encountered a fill followed by an EOL.

> 98% of all statistics are made up.
> —Unknown

### 1.6.2 Two-Dimensional Coding

Two-dimensional coding was developed because one-dimensional coding does not produce good results for images with gray areas. Two-dimensional coding is optional on fax machines that use Group 3 but is the only method used by machines intended to work on a digital network. When a fax machine using Group 3 supports two-dimensional coding as an option, each EOL is followed by one extra bit to indicate the compression method used for the next scan line. That bit is 1 if the next line is encoded with one-dimensional coding, 0 if it is encoded with two-dimensional coding.

The two-dimensional coding method is also called MMR, for *modified modified READ*, where READ stands for *relative element address designate*. The term "modified modified" is used because this is a modification of one-dimensional coding, which itself is a modification of the original Huffman method. The two-dimensional coding method works by comparing the current scan line (called the *coding line*) to its predecessor (which is called the *reference line*) and recording the differences between them, the assumption being that two consecutive lines in a document will normally differ by just a few pels. The method assumes that there is an all-white line above the page, which is used as the reference line for the first scan line of the page. After coding the first line, it becomes the reference line, and the second scan line is coded. As in one-dimensional coding, each line is assumed to start with a white pel, which is ignored by the receiver.

The two-dimensional coding method is less reliable than one-dimensional coding, since an error in decoding a line will cause errors in decoding all its successors and will propagate through the entire document. This is why the T.4 (Group 3) standard includes a requirement that after a line is encoded with the one-dimensional method, at most $K - 1$ lines will be encoded with the two-dimensional coding method. For standard resolution $K = 2$, and for fine resolution $K = 4$. The T.6 standard (Group 4) does not have this requirement and uses two-dimensional coding exclusively.

Scanning the coding line and comparing it to the reference line results in three cases, or modes. The mode is identified by comparing the next run length on the reference line [$(b_1 b_2)$ in Figure 1.21] with the current run length $(a_0 a_1)$ and the next one $(a_1 a_2)$ on the coding line. Each of these three runs can be black or white. The three modes are as follows:

1. **Pass mode.** This is the case where $(b_1 b_2)$ is to the left of $(a_1 a_2)$ and $b_2$ is to the left of $a_1$ (Figure 1.21a). This mode does not include the case where $b_2$ is above $a_1$. When this mode is identified, the length of run $(b_1 b_2)$ is coded using the codes of Table 1.22 and is transmitted. Pointer $a_0$ is moved below $b_2$, and the four values $b_1$, $b_2$, $a_1$, and $a_2$ are updated.

2. **Vertical mode.** $(b_1 b_2)$ overlaps $(a_1 a_2)$ by not more than three pels (Figure 1.21b1, b2). Assuming that consecutive lines do not differ by much, this is the most common case. When this mode is identified, one of seven codes is produced (Table 1.22) and is

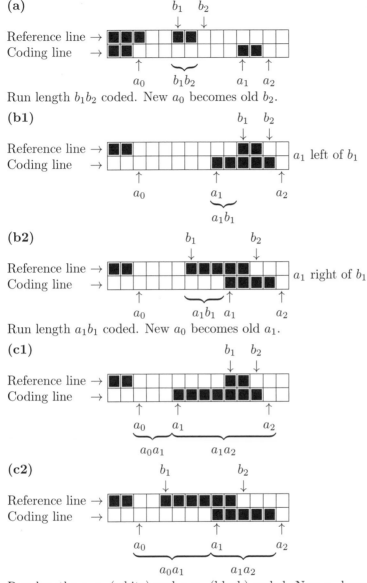

**Figure 1.21:** Five Run-Length Configurations: (a) Pass Mode. (b) Vertical Mode. (c) Horizontal Mode.

transmitted. Pointers are updated as in case 1. The performance of the two-dimensional coding method depends on this case being common.

3. **Horizontal mode.** $(b_1 b_2)$ overlaps $(a_1 a_2)$ by more than three pels (Figure 1.21c1, c2). When this mode is identified, the lengths of runs $(a_0 a_1)$ and $(a_1 a_2)$ are coded using the codes of Table 1.22 and are transmitted. Pointers are updated as in cases 1 and 2.

| Mode | Run length to be encoded | Abbreviation | Codeword |
|---|---|---|---|
| Pass | $b_1 b_2$ | P | 0001+coded length of $b_1 b_2$ |
| Horizontal | $a_0 a_1, a_1 a_2$ | H | 001+coded length of $a_0 a_1$ and $a_1 a_2$ |
| Vertical | $a_1 b_1 = 0$ | V(0) | 1 |
|  | $a_1 b_1 = -1$ | VR(1) | 011 |
|  | $a_1 b_1 = -2$ | VR(2) | 000011 |
|  | $a_1 b_1 = -3$ | VR(3) | 0000011 |
|  | $a_1 b_1 = +1$ | VL(1) | 010 |
|  | $a_1 b_1 = +2$ | VL(2) | 000010 |
|  | $a_1 b_1 = +3$ | VL(3) | 0000010 |
| Extension |  |  | 0000001000 |

**Table 1.22:** 2D Codes for the Group 4 Method.

When scanning starts, pointer $a_0$ is set to an imaginary white pel on the left of the coding line, and $a_1$ is set to point to the first black pel on the coding line. (Since $a_0$ corresponds to an imaginary pel, the first run length is $|a_0 a_1| - 1$.) Pointer $a_2$ is set to the first white pel following that. Pointers $b_1$, $b_2$ are set to point to the start of the first and second runs on the reference line, respectively.

After identifying the current mode and transmitting codes according to Table 1.22, $a_0$ is updated as shown in the flowchart, and the other four pointers are updated relative to the new $a_0$. The process continues until the end of the coding line is reached. The encoder assumes an extra pel on the right of the line, with a color opposite that of the last pel.

The extension code in Table 1.22 is used to abort the encoding process prematurely, before reaching the end of the page. This is necessary if the rest of the page is transmitted in a different code or even in uncompressed form.

**Example:** Figure 1.23 shows the modes and the actual code generated from two consecutive lines of pels.

The statistics on sanity are that one out of every four Americans is suffering from some form of mental illness. Think of your three best friends. If they're okay, then it's you.

—Rita Mae Brown

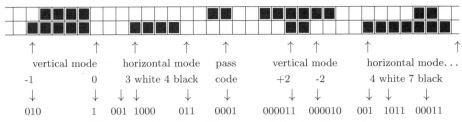

**Figure 1.23:** Two-Dimensional Coding Example.

## 1.7 Arithmetic Coding

The Huffman method is simple and efficient, but Section 1.4 shows that it produces the best variable-size codes (codes whose average size equals the entropy) only when the symbols have probabilities of occurrence that are negative powers of 2 (i.e., numbers such as 1/2, 1/4, or 1/8). This is because the Huffman method assigns a code with an integral number of bits to each symbol in the alphabet. Information theory shows that a symbol with probability 0.4 should ideally be assigned a 1.32-bit code, since $-\log_2 0.4 \approx 1.32$. The Huffman method, however, normally assigns such a symbol a code of 1 or 2 bits.

(Before we delve into the details of arithmetic coding, the two references [Moffat et al. 98] and [Witten et al. 87] should be mentioned. They discuss the principles and the details of practical arithmetic coding and show examples.)

Arithmetic coding overcomes this problem by assigning one (normally long) code to the entire input file, instead of assigning codes to the individual symbols. (The input file may be text, images, or any type of data.) The method reads the input file symbol by symbol and appends bits to the code each time a symbol is input and processed. To understand the method, it is useful to imagine the resulting code as a number in the range $[0, 1)$. [The notation $[a, b)$ means the range of real numbers from $a$ to $b$, not including $b$. The range is "closed" at $a$ and "open" at $b$.] Thus the code "9746509" should be interpreted as "0.9746509", although the "0." part will not be included in the output file.

The first step is to calculate, or at least to estimate, the frequencies of occurrence of each symbol. For best results, the exact frequencies are calculated by reading the entire input file in the first pass of a two-pass compression job. However, if the program can get good estimates of the frequencies from a different source, the first pass may be omitted.

The first example involves the three symbols $a_1$, $a_2$, and $a_3$, with probabilities $P_1 = 0.4$, $P_2 = 0.5$, and $P_3 = 0.1$, respectively. The interval $[0, 1)$ is divided among the three symbols by assigning each a subinterval proportional in size to its probability. The order of the subintervals is immaterial. In our example, the three symbols are assigned the subintervals $[0, 0.4)$, $[0.4, 0.9)$, and $[0.9, 1.0)$. To encode the string "$a_2 a_2 a_2 a_3$", we start with the interval $[0, 1)$. The first symbol $a_2$ reduces this interval to the subinterval from its 40% point to its 90% point. The result is $[0.4, 0.9)$. The second $a_2$ reduces $[0.4, 0.9)$ in the same way (see note below) to $[0.6, 0.85)$, the third $a_2$ reduces this to $[0.7, 0.825)$, and the $a_3$ reduces this to the stretch from the 90% point of $[0.7, 0.825)$ to its 100% point, producing $[0.8125, 0.8250)$. The final code our method produces can be any number in this final range. (Note: The subinterval $[0.6, 0.85)$ is obtained from the interval $[0.4, 0.9)$ by $0.4 + (0.9 - 0.4) \times 0.4 = 0.6$ and $0.4 + (0.9 - 0.4) \times 0.9 = 0.85$.)

With this example in mind, it should be easy to understand the following rules, which summarize the main steps of arithmetic coding:

1. Start by defining the "current interval" as $[0, 1)$.
2. Repeat the following two steps for each symbol $s$ in the input file:

    2.1. Divide the current interval into subintervals whose sizes are proportional to the symbols' probabilities.

    2.2. Select the subinterval for $s$ and make it the new current interval.

3. When the entire input file has been processed in this way, the output should be any number that uniquely identifies the current interval (i.e., any number inside the current interval).

For each symbol processed, the current interval gets smaller, so it takes more bits to express it, but the point is that the final output is a single number and does not consist of codes for the individual symbols. The average code size can be obtained by dividing the size of the output (in bits) by the size of the input (in symbols). Notice also that the probabilities used in step 2.1 may change all the time, since they may be supplied by an adaptive probability model (Section 1.8).

The next example is a little more involved. We show the compression steps for the short string "SWISS␣MISS". Table 1.24 shows the information prepared in the first step (the *statistical model* of the data). The five symbols appearing in the input may be arranged in any order. For each symbol, its frequency is counted first, followed by its probability of occurrence (the frequency divided by the string size, 10). The range $[0, 1)$ is then divided among the symbols, in any order, with each symbol getting a chunk, or a subrange, equal in size to its probability. Thus "S" gets the subrange $[0.5, 1.0)$ (of size 0.5), whereas the subrange of "I" is of size 0.2 $[0.2, 0.4)$. The cumulative frequencies column is used by the decoding algorithm on page 47.

| Char | Freq | Prob. | Range | CumFreq |
|------|------|-------|-------|---------|
| | | Total CumFreq= | | 10 |
| S | 5 | $5/10 = 0.5$ | $[0.5, 1.0)$ | 5 |
| W | 1 | $1/10 = 0.1$ | $[0.4, 0.5)$ | 4 |
| I | 2 | $2/10 = 0.2$ | $[0.2, 0.4)$ | 2 |
| M | 1 | $1/10 = 0.1$ | $[0.1, 0.2)$ | 1 |
| ␣ | 1 | $1/10 = 0.1$ | $[0.0, 0.1)$ | 0 |

**Table 1.24:** Frequencies and Probabilities of Five Symbols.

The symbols and frequencies in Table 1.24 are written on the output file before any of the bits of the compressed code. This table will be the first thing input by the decoder.

The encoding process starts by defining two variables, Low and High, and setting them to 0 and 1, respectively. They define an interval [Low, High). As symbols are being input and processed, the values of Low and High are moved closer together to narrow the interval.

After processing the first symbol "S", Low and High are updated to 0.5 and 1, respectively. The resulting code for the entire input file will be a number in this range $(0.5 \leq \text{Code} < 1.0)$. The rest of the input file will determine precisely where, in the interval $[0.5, 1)$, the final code will lie. A good way to understand the process is to imagine that the new interval $[0.5, 1)$ is divided among the five symbols of our alphabet using the same proportions as for the original interval $[0, 1)$. The result is the five subintervals $[0.5, 0.55)$, $[0.55, 0.60)$, $[0.60, 0.70)$, $[0.70, 0.75)$, and $[0.75, 1.0)$. When the next symbol W is input, the third of those subintervals is selected and is again divided into five subsubintervals.

As more symbols are being input and processed, Low and High are being updated according to

```
NewHigh:=OldLow+Range*HighRange(X);
NewLow:=OldLow+Range*LowRange(X);
```

where Range=OldHigh−OldLow and LowRange(X), HighRange(X) indicate the low and high limits of the range of symbol X, respectively. In the example, the second input symbol is W, so we update Low $:= 0.5 + (1.0 - 0.5) \times 0.4 = 0.70$, High $:= 0.5 + (1.0 - 0.5) \times 0.5 = 0.75$. The new interval $[0.70, 0.75)$ covers the stretch $[40\%, 50\%)$ of the subrange of S. Table 1.25 shows all the steps involved in coding the string "SWISS␣MISS". The final code is the final value of Low, 0.71753375, of which only the eight digits 71753375 need be written on the output file (a modification of this statement is discussed later).

The decoder works in the opposite way. It starts by inputting the symbols and their ranges and reconstructing Table 1.24. It then inputs the rest of the code. The first digit is "7", so the decoder immediately knows that the entire code is a number of the form $0.7\ldots.$ This number is inside the subrange $[0.5, 1)$ of S, so the first symbol is S. The decoder then eliminates the effect of symbol S from the code by subtracting the lower limit 0.5 of S and dividing by the width of the subrange of S (0.5). The result is 0.4350675, which tells the decoder that the next symbol is W (since the subrange of W is $[0.4, 0.5)$).

To eliminate the effect of symbol X from the code, the decoder performs the operation Code:=(Code−LowRange(X))/Range, where Range is the width of the subrange of X. Table 1.26 summarizes the steps for decoding our example string.

The next example is of three symbols with probabilities as shown in Table 1.27a. Notice that the probabilities are very different. One is large (97.5%) and the others are much smaller. This is a case of *skewed probabilities*.

Encoding the string $a_2a_2a_1a_3a_3$ produces the strange numbers (accurate to 16 digits) in Table 1.28, where the two rows for each symbol correspond to the Low and High values, respectively.

At first glance, it seems that the resulting code is longer than the original string, but Section 1.7.3 shows how to figure out the true compression achieved by arithmetic coding.

Decoding this string is shown in Table 1.29 and involves a special problem. After eliminating the effect of $a_1$, on line 3, the result is 0. Earlier, we implicitly assumed

| Char. | | The calculation of low and high |
|-------|---|----------------------------------|
| S | L | $0.0 + (1.0 - 0.0) \times 0.5 = 0.5$ |
|   | H | $0.0 + (1.0 - 0.0) \times 1.0 = 1.0$ |
| W | L | $0.5 + (1.0 - 0.5) \times 0.4 = 0.70$ |
|   | H | $0.5 + (1.0 - 0.5) \times 0.5 = 0.75$ |
| I | L | $0.7 + (0.75 - 0.70) \times 0.2 = 0.71$ |
|   | H | $0.7 + (0.75 - 0.70) \times 0.4 = 0.72$ |
| S | L | $0.71 + (0.72 - 0.71) \times 0.5 = 0.715$ |
|   | H | $0.71 + (0.72 - 0.71) \times 1.0 = 0.72$ |
| S | L | $0.715 + (0.72 - 0.715) \times 0.5 = 0.7175$ |
|   | H | $0.715 + (0.72 - 0.715) \times 1.0 = 0.72$ |
| ␣ | L | $0.7175 + (0.72 - 0.7175) \times 0.0 = 0.7175$ |
|   | H | $0.7175 + (0.72 - 0.7175) \times 0.1 = 0.71775$ |
| M | L | $0.7175 + (0.71775 - 0.7175) \times 0.1 = 0.717525$ |
|   | H | $0.7175 + (0.71775 - 0.7175) \times 0.2 = 0.717550$ |
| I | L | $0.717525 + (0.71755 - 0.717525) \times 0.2 = 0.717530$ |
|   | H | $0.717525 + (0.71755 - 0.717525) \times 0.4 = 0.717535$ |
| S | L | $0.717530 + (0.717535 - 0.717530) \times 0.5 = 0.7175325$ |
|   | H | $0.717530 + (0.717535 - 0.717530) \times 1.0 = 0.717535$ |
| S | L | $0.7175325 + (0.717535 - 0.7175325) \times 0.5 = 0.71753375$ |
|   | H | $0.7175325 + (0.717535 - 0.7175325) \times 1.0 = 0.717535$ |

**Table 1.25:** The Process of Arithmetic Encoding.

that this means the end of the decoding process, but now we know that there are two more occurrences of $a_3$ that should be decoded. These are shown on lines 4 and 5 of the table. This problem always occurs when the last symbol in the input file is the one whose subrange starts at zero.

In order to distinguish between such a symbol and the end of the input file, we need to define an additional symbol, the end-of-input (or end-of-file, eof). This symbol should be added, with a small probability, to the frequency table (see Table 1.27b), and it should be encoded at the end of the input file.

Tables 1.30 and 1.31 show how the string $a_3a_3a_3a_3a_3$eof is encoded into the very small fraction 0.000002878086184764172 and then decoded properly. Without the eof symbol, a string of all $a_3$s would have been encoded into a 0.

Notice how the low value is 0 until the eof is input and processed and how the high value quickly approaches 0. It has already been mentioned that the final code does not have to be the final low value but can be any number between the final low and high values. In the example of $a_3a_3a_3a_3a_3$eof, the final code can be the much shorter number 0.0000002878086 (or 0.0000002878087 or even 0.0000002878088).

(Figure 1.32 lists the *Mathematica* code that computed Table 1.28.)

| Char. | Code−low | Range |
|---|---|---|
| S | $0.71753375 - 0.5 = 0.21753375$ | $/0.5 = 0.4350675$ |
| W | $0.4350675 - 0.4 = 0.0350675$ | $/0.1 = 0.350675$ |
| I | $0.350675 - 0.2 = 0.150675$ | $/0.2 = 0.753375$ |
| S | $0.753375 - 0.5 = 0.253375$ | $/0.5 = 0.50675$ |
| S | $0.50675 - 0.5 = 0.00675$ | $/0.5 = 0.0135$ |
| ␣ | $0.0135 - 0 = 0.0135$ | $/0.1 = 0.135$ |
| M | $0.135 - 0.1 = 0.035$ | $/0.1 = 0.35$ |
| I | $0.35 - 0.2 = 0.15$ | $/0.2 = 0.75$ |
| S | $0.75 - 0.5 = 0.25$ | $/0.5 = 0.5$ |
| S | $0.5 - 0.5 = 0$ | $/0.5 = 0$ |

**Table 1.26:** The Process of Arithmetic Decoding.

| Char | Prob. | Range |
|---|---|---|
| $a_1$ | 0.001838 | $[0.998162, \quad 1.0)$ |
| $a_2$ | 0.975 | $[0.023162, 0.998162)$ |
| $a_3$ | 0.023162 | $[0.0, \quad 0.023162)$ |

(a)

| Char | Prob. | Range |
|---|---|---|
| eof | 0.000001 | $[0.999999, \quad 1.0)$ |
| $a_1$ | 0.001837 | $[0.998162, 0.999999)$ |
| $a_2$ | 0.975 | $[0.023162, 0.998162)$ |
| $a_3$ | 0.023162 | $[0.0, \quad 0.023162)$ |

(b)

**Table 1.27:** (Skewed) Probabilities of Three Symbols.

| | |
|---|---|
| $a_2$ | $0.0 + (1.0 - 0.0) \times 0.023162 = 0.023162$ |
| | $0.0 + (1.0 - 0.0) \times 0.998162 = 0.998162$ |
| $a_2$ | $0.023162 + .975 \times 0.023162 = 0.04574495$ |
| | $0.023162 + .975 \times 0.998162 = 0.99636995$ |
| $a_1$ | $0.04574495 + 0.950625 \times 0.998162 = 0.99462270125$ |
| | $0.04574495 + 0.950625 \times 1.0 = 0.99636995$ |
| $a_3$ | $0.99462270125 + 0.00174724875 \times 0.0 = 0.99462270125$ |
| | $0.99462270125 + 0.00174724875 \times 0.023162 = 0.994663171025547$ |
| $a_3$ | $0.99462270125 + 0.00004046977554749998 \times 0.0 = 0.99462270125$ |
| | $0.99462270125 + 0.00004046977554749998 \times 0.023162 = 0.994623638610941$ |

**Table 1.28:** Encoding the String $a_2a_2a_1a_3a_3$.

| Char. | Code−low | | Range | |
|---|---|---|---|---|
| $a_2$ | $0.99462270125 - 0.023162$ | $= 0.97146170125$ | $/0.975$ | $= 0.99636995$ |
| $a_2$ | $0.99636995 - 0.023162$ | $= 0.97320795$ | $/0.975$ | $= 0.998162$ |
| $a_1$ | $0.998162 - 0.998162$ | $= 0.0$ | $/0.00138$ | $= 0.0$ |
| $a_3$ | $0.0 - 0.0$ | $= 0.0$ | $/0.023162$ | $= 0.0$ |
| $a_3$ | $0.0 - 0.0$ | $= 0.0$ | $/0.023162$ | $= 0.0$ |

**Table 1.29:** Decoding the String $a_2a_2a_1a_3a_3$.

| | |
|---|---|
| $a_3$ | $0.0 + (1.0 - 0.0) \times 0.0 = 0.0$ |
| | $0.0 + (1.0 - 0.0) \times 0.023162 = 0.023162$ |
| $a_3$ | $0.0 + .023162 \times 0.0 = 0.0$ |
| | $0.0 + .023162 \times 0.023162 = 0.000536478244$ |
| $a_3$ | $0.0 + 0.000536478244 \times 0.0 = 0.0$ |
| | $0.0 + 0.000536478244 \times 0.023162 = 0.000012425909087528$ |
| $a_3$ | $0.0 + 0.000012425909087528 \times 0.0 = 0.0$ |
| | $0.0 + 0.000012425909087528 \times 0.023162 = 0.00000028780 89062853235$ |
| eof | $0.0 + 0.00000028780 89062853235 \times 0.999999 = 0.00000028780 86184764172$ |
| | $0.0 + 0.00000028780 89062853235 \times 1.0 = 0.00000028780 89062853235$ |

**Table 1.30:** Encoding the String $a_3a_3a_3a_3$eof.

| Char. | Code−low | | Range | |
|---|---|---|---|---|
| $a_3$ | $0.00000028780 86184764172\text{-}0$ | $=0.00000028780 86184764172$ | $/0.023162$ | $=0.0000124258 9666161891247$ |
| $a_3$ | $0.0000124258 9666161891247\text{-}0$ | $=0.0000124258 9666161891247$ | $/0.023162$ | $=0.000536477707521756$ |
| $a_3$ | $0.000536477707521756\text{-}0$ | $=0.000536477707521756$ | $/0.023162$ | $=0.023161976838$ |
| $a_3$ | $0.023161976838\text{-}0.0$ | $=0.023161976838$ | $/0.023162$ | $=0.999999$ |
| eof | $0.999999\text{-}0.999999$ | $=0.0$ | $/0.000001$ | $=0.0$ |

**Table 1.31:** Decoding the String $a_3a_3a_3a_3$eof.

**Example:** Table 1.33 shows the steps of encoding the string $a_2a_2a_2a_2$. Because of the high probability of $a_2$ the low and high variables start at very different values and approach each other slowly.

If the size of the input file is known, it is possible to do without an eof symbol. The encoder can start by writing this size (unencoded) on the output file. The decoder reads the size, starts decoding, and stops when the decoded file reaches this size. If the decoder reads the compressed file byte by byte, the encoder may have to add some zeros

```
lowRange={0.998162,0.023162,0.};
highRange={1.,0.998162,0.023162};
low=0.; high=1.;
enc[i_]:=Module[{nlow,nhigh,range},
range=high-low;
nhigh=low+range highRange[[i]];
nlow=low+range lowRange[[i]];
low=nlow; high=nhigh;
Print["r=",N[range,25]," l=",N[low,17]," h=",N[high,17]]]
enc[2]
enc[2]
enc[1]
enc[3]
enc[3]
```

**Figure 1.32:** *Mathematica* Code for Table 1.28.

| | |
|---|---|
| $a_2$ | $0.0 + (1.0 - 0.0) \times 0.023162 = 0.023162$ |
| | $0.0 + (1.0 - 0.0) \times 0.998162 = 0.998162$ |
| $a_2$ | $0.023162 + .975 \times 0.023162 = 0.04574495$ |
| | $0.023162 + .975 \times 0.998162 = 0.99636995$ |
| $a_2$ | $0.04574495 + 0.950625 \times 0.023162 = 0.06776322625$ |
| | $0.04574495 + 0.950625 \times 0.998162 = 0.99462270125$ |
| $a_2$ | $0.06776322625 + 0.926859375 \times 0.023162 = 0.08923124309375$ |
| | $0.06776322625 + 0.926859375 \times 0.998162 = 0.99291913371875$ |

**Table 1.33:** Encoding the String $a_2a_2a_2a_2$.

at the end to make sure the compressed file can be read in groups of 8 bits.

> Do not put faith in what statistics say until you have carefully considered what they do not say.
>
> —William W. Watt

### 1.7.1 Implementation Details

The encoding process described earlier is not practical, since it assumes that numbers of unlimited precision can be stored in Low and High. The decoding process described on page 42 ("The decoder then eliminates the effect of the S from the code by subtracting... and dividing ...") is simple in principle but also impractical. The code, which is a single number, is normally long and may be very long. A 1 MB file may be encoded into, say, a 500 KB one that consists of a single number. Dividing a 500 KB number is complex and slow.

Any practical implementation of arithmetic coding should use just integers (because floating-point arithmetic is slow and precision is lost), and they should not be very long (preferably just single precision). We describe such an implementation here, using two integer variables `Low` and `High`. In our example they are four decimal digits long, but in practice they might be 16 or 32 bits long. These variables hold the low and high limits of the current subinterval, but we don't let them grow too much. A glance at Table 1.25 shows that once the leftmost digits of `Low` and `High` become identical, they never change. We therefore shift such digits out of the two variables and write one digit on the output file. This way, the two variables have to hold not the entire code, but just the most recent part of it. As digits are shifted out of the two variables, a zero is shifted into the right end of `Low` and a 9 into the right end of `High`. A good way to understand this is to think of each of the two variables as the left end of an infinitely long number. `Low` contains $xxxx00\ldots$, and `High`$= yyyy99\ldots$.

One problem is that `High` should be initialized to 1, but the contents of `Low` and `High` should be interpreted as fractions less than 1. The solution is to initialize `High` to $9999\ldots$, since the infinite fraction $0.999\ldots$ equals 1.

(This is easy to prove. If $0.999\ldots < 1$, then their average $a = (1+0.999\ldots)/2$ would be a number between $0.999\ldots$ and 1, but there is no way to write $a$. It is impossible to give it more digits than to $0.999\ldots$, since the latter already has an infinite number of digits. It is impossible to make the digits any bigger, since they are already 9's. This is why the infinite fraction $0.999\ldots$ must equal 1. Similarly, there are two ways to write the number 0.5 in binary. It can be written either as $0.1000\ldots$ or $0.0111\ldots$.)

Table 1.34 describes the encoding process of the string "SWISS␣MISS". Column 1 shows the next input symbol. Column 2 shows the new values of `Low` and `High`. Column 3 shows these values as scaled integers, after `High` has been decremented by 1. Column 4 shows the next digit sent to the output file. Column 5 shows the new values of `Low` and `High` after being shifted to the left. Notice how the last step sends the four digits 3750 to the output file. The final output is 717533750.

Decoding is the opposite of encoding. We start with `Low=0000`, `High=9999`, and `Code=7175` (the first four digits of the compressed file). These are updated at each step of the decoding loop. `Low` and `High` approach each other (and both approach `Code`) until their most significant digits are the same. They are then shifted to the left, which separates them again, and `Code` is also shifted at that time. An index is calculated at each step and is used to search the cumulative frequencies column of Table 1.24 to figure out the current symbol.

Each iteration of the loop consists of the following steps:

1. Calculate `index:=((Code-Low+1)x10-1)/(High-Low+1)` and truncate it to the nearest integer. (The number 10 is the total cumulative frequency in our example.)
2. Use `index` to find the next symbol by comparing it to the cumulative frequencies column in Table 1.24. In the following example, the first value of `index` is 7.1759, truncated to 7. Seven is between the 5 and the 10 in the table, so it selects the "S".
3. Update `Low` and `High` according to

```
Low:=Low+(High-Low+1)LowCumFreq[X]/10;
High:=Low+(High-Low+1)HighCumFreq[X]/10-1;
```

where `LowCumFreq[X]` and `HighCumFreq[X]` are the cumulative frequencies of symbol `X` and of the symbol above it in Table 1.24.

| 1 | 2 | 3 | 4 | 5 |
|---|---|---|---|---|
| S | $L = 0+(1 - 0)\times0.5 = 0.5$ | 5000 | | 5000 |
|   | $H = 0+(1 - 0)\times1.0 = 1.0$ | 9999 | | 9999 |
| W | $L = 0.5+(1 - .5)\times0.4 = 0.7$ | 7000 | 7 | 0000 |
|   | $H = 0.5+(1 - .5)\times0.5 = 0.75$ | 7499 | 7 | 4999 |
| I | $L = 0 +(0.5 - 0)\times0.2 = 0.1$ | 1000 | 1 | 0000 |
|   | $H = 0 +(0.5 - 0)\times0.4 = 0.2$ | 1999 | 1 | 9999 |
| S | $L = 0+(1 - 0)\times0.5 = 0.5$ | 5000 | | 5000 |
|   | $H = 0+(1 - 0)\times1.0 = 1.0$ | 9999 | | 9999 |
| S | $L = 0.5+(1 - 0.5)\times0.5 = 0.75$ | 7500 | | 7500 |
|   | $H = 0.5+(1 - 0.5)\times1.0 = 1.0$ | 9999 | | 9999 |
| ␣ | $L = .75+(1 - .75)\times0.0 = 0.75$ | 7500 | 7 | 5000 |
|   | $H = .75+(1 - .75)\times0.1 = .775$ | 7749 | 7 | 7499 |
| M | $L = 0.5+(.75 - .5)\times0.1 = .525$ | 5250 | 5 | 2500 |
|   | $H = 0.5+(.75 - .5)\times0.2 = 0.55$ | 5499 | 5 | 4999 |
| I | $L = .25+(.5 - .25)\times0.2 = 0.3$ | 3000 | 3 | 0000 |
|   | $H = .25+(.5 - .25)\times0.4 = .35$ | 3499 | 3 | 4999 |
| S | $L = 0.0+(0.5 - 0)\times0.5 = .25$ | 2500 | | 2500 |
|   | $H = 0.0+(0.5 - 0)\times1.0 = 0.5$ | 4999 | | 4999 |
| S | $L = .25+(.5 - .25)\times0.5 = .375$ | 3750 | 3750 | |
|   | $H = .25+(.5 - .25)\times1.0 = 0.5$ | 4999 | | 4999 |

**Table 1.34:** Encoding "SWISS␣MISS" by Shifting.

4. If the leftmost digits of Low and High are identical, shift Low, High, and Code one position to the left. Low gets a 0 entered on the right, High gets a 9, and Code gets the next input digit from the compressed file.

Here are all the decoding steps for our example:

0. Initialize Low=0000, High=9999, and Code=7175.

1. index= $[(7175-0+1)\times10-1]/(9999-0+1) = 7.1759 \to 7$. Symbol "S" is selected. Low $= 0 + (9999 - 0 + 1) \times 5/10 = 5000$. High $= 0 + (9999 - 0 + 1) \times 10/10 - 1 = 9999$.

2. index= $[(7175-5000+1)\times10-1]/(9999-5000+1) = 4.3518 \to 4$. Symbol "W" is selected.
Low $= 5000+(9999-5000+1)\times4/10 = 7000$. High $= 5000+(9999-5000+1)\times5/10-1 = 7499$.
After the 7 is shifted out, we have Low=0000, High=4999, and Code=1753.

3. index= $[(1753-0+1)\times10-1]/(4999-0+1) = 3.5078 \to 3$. Symbol "I" is selected. Low $= 0 + (4999 - 0 + 1) \times 2/10 = 1000$. High $= 0 + (4999 - 0 + 1) \times 4/10 - 1 = 1999$.
After the 1 is shifted out, we have Low=0000, High=9999, and Code=7533.

4. index= $[(7533-0+1)\times10-1]/(9999-0+1) = 7.5339 \to 7$. Symbol "I" is selected. Low $= 0 + (9999 - 0 + 1) \times 5/10 = 5000$. High $= 0 + (9999 - 0 + 1) \times 10/10 - 1 = 9999$.

5. index= $[(7533 - 5000 + 1) \times 10 - 1]/(9999 - 5000 + 1) = 5.0678 \rightarrow 5$. Symbol "S" is selected.
Low $= 5000 + (9999 - 5000 + 1) \times 5/10 = 7500$. High $= 5000 + (9999 - 5000 + 1) \times 10/10 - 1 = 9999$.

6. index= $[(7533 - 7500 + 1) \times 10 - 1]/(9999 - 7500 + 1) = 0.1356 \rightarrow 0$. Symbol "␣" is selected.
Low $= 7500 + (9999 - 7500 + 1) \times 0/10 = 7500$. High $= 7500 + (9999 - 7500 + 1) \times 1/10 - 1 = 7749$.
After the 7 is shifted out, we have Low=5000, High=7499, and Code=5337.

7. index= $[(5337 - 5000 + 1) \times 10 - 1]/(7499 - 5000 + 1) = 1.3516 \rightarrow 1$. Symbol "M" is selected.
Low $= 5000 + (7499 - 5000 + 1) \times 1/10 = 5250$. High $= 5000 + (7499 - 5000 + 1) \times 2/10 - 1 = 5499$.
After the 5 is shifted out, we have Low=2500, High=4999, and Code=3375.

8. index= $[(3375 - 2500 + 1) \times 10 - 1]/(4999 - 2500 + 1) = 3.5036 \rightarrow 3$. Symbol "I" is selected.
Low $= 2500 + (4999 - 2500 + 1) \times 2/10 = 3000$. High $= 2500 + (4999 - 2500 + 1) \times 4/10 - 1 = 3499$.
After the 3 is shifted out, we have Low=0000, High=4999, and Code=3750.

9. index= $[(3750 - 0 + 1) \times 10 - 1]/(4999 - 0 + 1) = 7.5018 \rightarrow 7$. Symbol "S" is selected.
Low $= 0 + (4999 - 0 + 1) \times 5/10 = 2500$. High $= 0 + (4999 - 0 + 1) \times 10/10 - 1 = 4999$.

10. index= $[(3750 - 2500 + 1) \times 10 - 1]/(4999 - 2500 + 1) = 5.0036 \rightarrow 5$. Symbol "S" is selected.
Low $= 2500 + (4999 - 2500 + 1) \times 5/10 = 3750$. High $= 2500 + (4999 - 2500 + 1) \times 10/10 - 1 = 4999$.

It is now obvious that the eof symbol has to be included in the original table of frequencies and probabilities. This symbol is the last to be encoded and decoding it serves as a signal for the decoder to stop.

### 1.7.2 Underflow

Table 1.35 shows the steps in encoding the string $a_3a_3a_3a_3a_3$ by shifting. This table is similar to Table 1.34, and it illustrates the problem of underflow. Low and High approach each other, and since Low is always 0 in this example, High loses its significant digits as it approaches Low.

Underflow may happen not just in this case but in any case where Low and High need to converge very closely. Because of the finite size of the Low and High variables, they may reach values of, say, 499996 and 500003 and from there, instead of reaching values where their most significant digits are identical, they reach the values 499999 and 500000. Since the most significant digits are different, the algorithm will not output anything, there will not be any shifts, and the next iteration will add digits only beyond the first six. Those digits will be lost, and the first six digits will not change. The algorithm will iterate without generating any output until it reaches the eof.

The solution is to detect such a case early and *rescale* both variables. In the example above, rescaling should be done when the two variables reach values of 49xxxx

| 1 | 2 | 3 | 4 | 5 |
|---|---|---|---|---|
| 1 | L=0+(1    −    0)×0.0      = 0.0 | 000000 | 0 | 000000 |
|   | H=0+(1    −    0)×0.023162= 0.023162 | 023162 | 0 | 231629 |
| 2 | L=0+(0.231629 − 0)×0.0      = 0.0 | 000000 | 0 | 000000 |
|   | H=0+(0.231629 − 0)×0.023162= 0.00536478244 | 005364 | 0 | 053649 |
| 3 | L=0+(0.053649 − 0)×0.0      = 0.0 | 000000 | 0 | 000000 |
|   | H=0+(0.053649 − 0)×0.023162= 0.00124261813 | 001242 | 0 | 012429 |
| 4 | L=0+(0.012429 − 0)×0.0      = 0.0 | 000000 | 0 | 000000 |
|   | H=0+(0.012429 − 0)×0.023162= 0.00028788049 | 000287 | 0 | 002879 |
| 5 | L=0+(0.002879 − 0)×0.0      = 0.0 | 000000 | 0 | 000000 |
|   | H=0+(0.002879 − 0)×0.023162= 0.00006668339 | 000066 | 0 | 000669 |

**Table 1.35:** Encoding $a_3a_3a_3a_3a_3$ by Shifting.

and 50yyyy. Rescaling should squeeze out the second most significant digits, end up with 4xxxx0 and 5yyyy9, and increment a counter `cntr`. The algorithm may have to rescale several times before the most significant digits become equal. At that point, the most significant digit (which can be either 4 or 5) should be output, followed by `cntr` zeros (if the two variables converged to 4) or nines (if they converged to 5).

### 1.7.3 Final Remarks

All the examples so far have been in decimal, since the computations involved are easier to understand in this number base. It turns out that all the algorithms and rules described here apply to the binary case as well with only one change: Every occurrence of 9 (the largest decimal digit) should be replaced by 1 (the largest binary digit).

The examples above don't seem to show any compression at all. It seems that the three example strings "SWISS␣MISS", "$a_2a_2a_1a_3a_3$", and "$a_3a_3a_3a_3$eof" are encoded into very long numbers. In fact, it seems that the length of the final code depends on the probabilities involved. The long probabilities of Table 1.27a generate long numbers in the encoding process, whereas the shorter probabilities of Table 1.24 result in the more reasonable `Low` and `High` values of Table 1.25. This behavior demands an explanation.

To figure out the kind of compression achieved by arithmetic coding, we have to consider two facts: (1) In practice, all the operations are performed on binary numbers, so we have to translate the final results to binary before we can estimate the efficiency of the compression; (2) since the last symbol encoded is the eof, the final code does not have to be the final value of `Low`; it can be any value between `Low` and `High`. This makes it possible to select a shorter number as the final code that's being output.

Table 1.25 encodes the string "SWISS␣MISS" into Low and High values 0.71753375 and 0.717535 whose approximate binary values are 0.10110111101̇100000100101010111 and 0.1011011110110000010111111011. Thus, we can select "10110111101100000100" as our final, compressed output. The ten-symbol string has been encoded into a 20-bit number. Does this represent good compression?

The answer is yes. Using the probabilities of Table 1.24, it is easy to calculate the probability of the string "SWISS⎵MISS". It is $P = 0.5^5 \times 0.1 \times 0.2^2 \times 0.1 \times 0.1 = 1.25 \times 10^{-6}$. The entropy of this string is therefore $-\log_2 P = 19.6096$. Twenty bits is thus the minimum needed in practice to encode the string.

The symbols in Table 1.27a have probabilities 0.975, 0.001838, and 0.023162. These numbers require quite a few decimal digits, and as a result, the final Low and High values in Table 1.28 are the numbers 0.99462270125 and 0.994623638610941. Again it seems that there is no compression, but an analysis similar to the one above shows compression that's very close to the entropy.

The probability of the string "$a_2a_2a_1a_3a_3$" is $0.975^2 \times 0.001838 \times 0.023162^2 \approx 9.37361 \times 10^{-7}$, and $-\log_2 9.37361 \times 10^{-7} \approx 20.0249$.

The binary representations of the final values of Low and High in Table 1.28 are 0.11111110100111111100101111111001 and 0.11111110100111111010100111101. We can select any number between these two, so we select 1111111010011111100, a 19-bit number. (This should have been a 21-bit number, but the numbers in Table 1.28 have limited precision and are not exact.)

**Example:** Given the three symbols $a_1$, $a_2$, and eof, with probabilities $P_1 = 0.4$, $P_2 = 0.5$, and $P_{\text{eof}} = 0.1$, we encode the string "$a_2a_2a_2\text{eof}$" and show that the size of the final code equals the theoretical minimum.

The encoding steps are simple (see first example on page 40). We start with the interval $[0, 1)$. The first symbol $a_2$ reduces the interval to $[0.4, 0.9)$, the second one to $[0.6, 0.85)$, the third one to $[0.7, 0.825)$, and the eof symbol to $[0.8125, 0.8250)$. The approximate binary values of the last interval are 0.1101000000 and 0.1101001100, so we select the 7-bit number 1101000 as our code.

The probability of the string "$a_2a_2a_2\text{eof}$" is $(0.5)^3 \times 0.1 = 0.0125$, but since $-\log_2 0.125 \approx 6.322$, it follows that the theoretical minimum code size is 7 bits. (End of example.)

The following argument shows why arithmetic coding can, in principle, be a very efficient compression method. We denote by $s$ a sequence of symbols to be encoded and by $b$ the number of bits required to encode it. As $s$ gets longer, its probability $P(s)$ gets smaller and $b$ gets larger. Since the logarithm is the information function, it is easy to see that $b$ should grow at the same rate that $\log_2 P(s)$ shrinks. Their product should, therefore, be constant or close to a constant. Information theory shows that $b$ and $P(s)$ satisfy the double inequality

$$2 \leq 2^b P(s) < 4,$$

which implies

$$1 - \log_2 P(s) \leq b < 2 - \log_2 P(s). \tag{1.1}$$

As $s$ gets longer, its probability $P(s)$ shrinks, the quantity $-\log_2 P(s)$ becomes a large positive number, and the double inequality of Equation (1.1) shows that in the limit, $b$ approaches $-\log_2 P(s)$. This is why arithmetic coding can, in principle, compress a string of symbols to its theoretical limit.

## 1.8 Adaptive Arithmetic Coding

Two features of arithmetic coding make it easy to extend:

1. The main encoding step is

```
Low:=Low+(High-Low+1)LowCumFreq[X]/10;
High:=Low+(High-Low+1)HighCumFreq[X]/10-1;
```

This means that in order to encode symbol X, the encoder should be given the cumulative frequencies of the symbol and of the one above it (see Table 1.24 for an example of cumulative frequencies). This also implies that the frequency of X (or, equivalently, its probability) could be changed each time it is encoded, provided that the encoder and the decoder agree on how to do this.

2. The order of the symbols in Table 1.24 is unimportant. The symbols can even be swapped in the table during the encoding process as long as the encoder and decoder do it in the same way.

With this in mind, it is easy to understand how adaptive arithmetic coding works. The encoding algorithm has two parts: the probability model and the arithmetic encoder. The model reads the next symbol from the input file and invokes the encoder, sending to it the symbol and the two required cumulative frequencies. The model then increments the count of the symbol and updates the cumulative frequencies. The point is that the symbol's probability is determined by the model from its *old* count, and the count is incremented only after the symbol has been encoded. This makes it possible for the decoder to mirror the encoder's operations. The encoder knows what the symbol is even before it is encoded, but the decoder has to decode the symbol in order to find out what it is. The decoder can therefore use only the old counts when decoding a symbol. Once the symbol has been decoded, the decoder increments its count and updates the cumulative frequencies in exactly the same way as the encoder.

The model should keep the symbols, their counts (frequencies of occurrence), and their cumulative frequencies in an array. This array should be kept in sorted order of the counts. Each time a symbol is read and its count is incremented, the model updates the cumulative frequencies, then checks to see whether it is necessary to swap the symbol with another one to keep the counts in sorted order.

It turns out that there is a simple data structure that allows for both easy search and update. This structure is a balanced binary tree housed in an array. (A balanced binary tree is a complete binary tree in which some of the bottom-right nodes may be missing.) The tree should have a node for every symbol in the alphabet and, since it is balanced, its height is $\lceil \log_2 n \rceil$, where $n$ is the size of the alphabet. For $n = 256$ the height of the balanced binary tree is 8, so starting at the root and searching for a node takes at most eight steps. The tree is arranged such that the most probable symbols (the ones with high counts) are located near the root, which speeds up searches. Table 1.36a shows an example of a ten-symbol alphabet with counts. Table 1.36b shows the same symbols sorted by count.

The sorted array "houses" the balanced binary tree of Figure 1.38a. This is a simple, elegant way to build a tree. A balanced binary tree can be housed in an array without the use of pointers. The rule is that the first array location (with index 1)

| $a_1$ | $a_2$ | $a_3$ | $a_4$ | $a_5$ | $a_6$ | $a_7$ | $a_8$ | $a_9$ | $a_{10}$ |
|-------|-------|-------|-------|-------|-------|-------|-------|-------|----------|
| 11    | 12    | 12    | 2     | 5     | 1     | 2     | 19    | 12    | 8        |

(a)

| $a_8$ | $a_2$ | $a_3$ | $a_9$ | $a_1$ | $a_{10}$ | $a_5$ | $a_4$ | $a_7$ | $a_6$ |
|-------|-------|-------|-------|-------|----------|-------|-------|-------|-------|
| 19    | 12    | 12    | 12    | 11    | 8        | 5     | 2     | 2     | 1     |

(b)

**Table 1.36:** A Ten-Symbol Alphabet with Counts.

houses the root, the two children of the node at array location $i$ are housed at locations $2i$ and $2i+1$, and the parent of the node at array location $j$ is housed at location $\lfloor j/2 \rfloor$. It is easy to see how sorting the array has placed the symbols with largest counts at and near the root.

In addition to a symbol and its count, another value is now added to each tree node, the total counts of its left subtree. This will be used to compute cumulative frequencies. The corresponding array is shown in Table 1.37a.

Assume that the next symbol read from the input file is $a_9$. Its count is incremented from 12 to 13. The model keeps the array in sorted order by searching for the farthest array element to the left of $a_9$ that has a count smaller than that of $a_9$. This search can be a straight linear search if the array is short enough or a binary search if the array is long. In our case, symbols $a_9$ and $a_2$ should be swapped (Table 1.37b). Figure 1.38b shows the tree after the swap. Notice how the left subtree counts have been updated.

| $a_8$ | $a_2$ | $a_3$ | $a_9$ | $a_1$ | $a_{10}$ | $a_5$ | $a_4$ | $a_7$ | $a_6$ |
|-------|-------|-------|-------|-------|----------|-------|-------|-------|-------|
| 19    | 12    | 12    | 12    | 11    | 8        | 5     | 2     | 2     | 1     |
| 40    | 16    | 8     | 2     | 1     | 0        | 0     | 0     | 0     | 0     |

(a)

| $a_8$ | $a_9$ | $a_3$ | $a_2$ | $a_1$ | $a_{10}$ | $a_5$ | $a_4$ | $a_7$ | $a_6$ |
|-------|-------|-------|-------|-------|----------|-------|-------|-------|-------|
| 19    | 13    | 12    | 12    | 11    | 8        | 5     | 2     | 2     | 1     |
| 41    | 16    | 8     | 2     | 1     | 0        | 0     | 0     | 0     | 0     |

(b)

**Table 1.37:** A Ten-Symbol Alphabet with Counts.

Finally, here is how the cumulative frequencies are computed from this tree. When the cumulative frequency for a symbol X is needed, the model follows the tree branches from the root to the node containing X while adding numbers into an integer `af`. Each time a right branch is taken from an interior node N, `af` is incremented by the two numbers (the count and the left-subtree count) found in that node. When a left branch

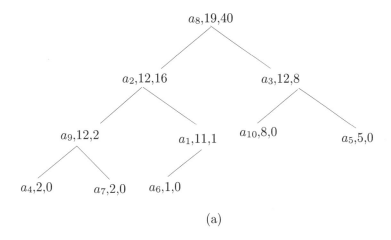

(a)

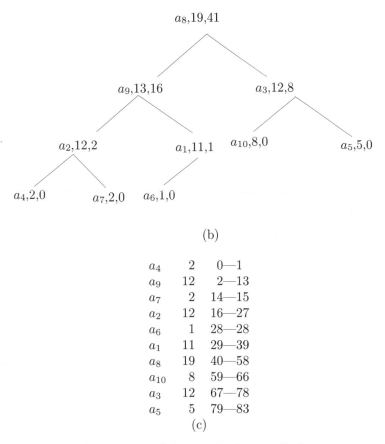

(b)

|       |    |       |
|-------|----|-------|
| $a_4$ | 2  | 0—1   |
| $a_9$ | 12 | 2—13  |
| $a_7$ | 2  | 14—15 |
| $a_2$ | 12 | 16—27 |
| $a_6$ | 1  | 28—28 |
| $a_1$ | 11 | 29—39 |
| $a_8$ | 19 | 40—58 |
| $a_{10}$ | 8 | 59—66 |
| $a_3$ | 12 | 67—78 |
| $a_5$ | 5  | 79—83 |

(c)

**Figure 1.38:** Adaptive Arithmetic Coding.

is taken, af is not modified. When the node containing X is reached, the left-subtree count of X is added to af, and af then contains the quantity LowCumFreq[X].

As an example, we trace the tree of Figure 1.38a from the root to symbol $a_6$, whose cumulative frequency is 28. A right branch is taken at node $a_2$, adding 12 and 16 to af. A left branch is taken at node $a_1$, adding nothing to af. When reaching $a_6$, its left-subtree count, 0, is added to af. The result in af is $12 + 16 = 28$, as can be verified from Figure 1.38c. The quantity HighCumFreq[X] is obtained by adding the count of $a_6$ (which is 1) to LowCumFreq[X].

To trace the tree and find the path from the root to $a_6$, the algorithm performs the following steps:

1. Find $a_6$ in the array housing the tree by means of a binary search. In our example the node with $a_6$ is found at array location 10.

2. Integer-divide 10 by 2. The remainder is 0, which means that $a_6$ is the left child of its parent. The quotient is 5, which is the array location of the parent.

3. Location 5 of the array contains $a_1$. Integer-divide 5 by 2. The remainder is 1, which means that $a_1$ is the right child of its parent. The quotient is 2, which is the array location of $a_1$'s parent.

4. Location 2 of the array contains $a_2$. Integer-divide 2 by 2. The remainder is 0, which means that $a_2$ is the left child of its parent. The quotient is 1, the array location of the root, so the process stops.

The PPM compression method [Cleary and Witten 84] and [Moffat 90], is a good example of a statistical model that invokes an arithmetic encoder as described here.

> Statistics are like bikinis. What they reveal
> is suggestive, but what they conceal is vital.
>
> Aaron Levenstein, *Why People Work*

# 2
# Dictionary Methods

Statistical compression methods use a statistical model of the data, so the quality of compression they achieve depends on how good that model is. Dictionary-based compression methods do not use a statistical model, nor do they use variable-size codes. Instead they select strings of symbols and encode each string as a *token* using a dictionary. The dictionary holds strings of symbols and it may be static or dynamic (adaptive). The former is permanent, sometimes allowing the addition of strings but no deletions, whereas the latter holds strings previously found in the input file, allowing for additions and deletions of strings as new input is read.

The simplest example of a static dictionary is a dictionary of the English language used to compress English text. Imagine a dictionary containing perhaps half a million words (without their definitions). A word (a string of symbols terminated by a space or a punctuation mark) is read from the input file and the dictionary is searched. If a match is found, an index to the dictionary is written into the output file. Otherwise, the uncompressed word itself is written. (This is an example of *logical compression*.)

As a result, the output file contains indexes and raw words, and we need to distinguish between them. One way to do this is to add an extra bit to every item written. In principle, a 19-bit index is sufficient to specify an item in a $2^{19} = 524,288$-word dictionary. Thus, when a match is found, we can write a 20-bit token consisting of a flag bit (perhaps a zero) followed by a 19-bit index. When no match is found, a flag of 1 is written, followed by the size of the unmatched word, followed by the word itself.

**Example:** Assuming that the word `bet` is found in dictionary entry 1025, it is encoded as the 20-bit number 0|0000000010000000001. Assuming that the word `xet` is not found, it is encoded as 1|0000011|01111000|01100101|01110100. This is a 4-byte number where the 7-bit field 0000011 indicates that three more bytes follow.

Assuming that the size is written as a 7-bit number and that an average word size is five characters, an uncompressed word occupies, on average, 6 bytes (= 48 bits) in the output file. Compressing 48 bits into 20 is excellent, provided that it happens often enough. Thus, we have to answer the question "How many matches are needed in order to have overall compression?" We denote the probability of a match (the case where the word is found in the dictionary) by $P$. After reading and compressing $N$ words, the size of the output file will be $N[20P + 48(1 - P)] = N[48 - 28P]$ bits. The size of the input file is (assuming five characters per word) $40N$ bits. Compression is achieved when $N[48 - 28P] < 40N$, which implies $P > 0.29$. We need a matching rate of 29% or better to achieve compression.

**Example:** If the probability of a match is large, say $P = 0.9$, the size of the output file is $N[48 - 28P] = N[48 - 25.2] = 22.8N$. The size of the input file is, as before, $40N$. The compression factor in such a case is $40/22.8 \approx 1.75$.

As long as the input file consists of English text, most words will be found in a 500,000-word dictionary. Other types of data, however, may not do that well. A file containing the source code of a computer program may contain "words" such as `cout`, `xor`, and `malloc` that may not be found in an English dictionary. A binary file normally contains gibberish when viewed in ASCII, so very few matches may be found, resulting in considerable expansion instead of compression.

This shows that a static dictionary is not a good choice for a general-purpose compressor. It may, however, be a good choice for a special-purpose one. Consider a chain of hardware stores, for example. Their files may contain words such as `nut`, `bolt`, and `paint` many times, but words such as `peanut`, `lightning`, and `painting` will be rare. Special-purpose compression software for such a company may benefit from a small, specialized dictionary containing, perhaps, just a few hundred words. The computers in each branch would each have a copy of the dictionary, making it easy to compress files and send them between stores and offices in the chain.

In general, an adaptive dictionary-based method is preferable. Such a method can start with an empty dictionary or with a small, default dictionary, add words to it as they are found in the input file, and delete old words, since a big dictionary results in slow search. Such a method consists of a loop where each iteration starts by reading the input file and breaking it up (parsing it) into words or phrases. It then should search the dictionary for each word and, if a match is found, write a token on the output file. Otherwise, the uncompressed word should be written and also added to the dictionary. The last step in each iteration checks to see whether an old word should be deleted from the dictionary. This may sound complicated but it has two advantages:

1. It involves string search and match operations, rather than numerical computations. Many programmers prefer that.

2. The decoder is simple (thus, this is an asymmetric compression method). In statistical compression methods, the decoder is normally the exact opposite of the encoder (resulting in symmetric compression). In an adaptive dictionary-based method, however, the decoder has to read its input file, determine whether the current item is a token or uncompressed data, use tokens to obtain data from the dictionary, and output the final, uncompressed data. It does not have to parse the input file in a complex way, and it does not have to search the dictionary to find matches. Many programmers like that, too.

Having one's name attached to a scientific discovery, technique, or phenomenon is considered a special honor in science. Having one's name associated with an entire field of science is even more so. This is what happened to Jacob Ziv and Abraham Lempel. In the 1970s these two researchers developed the first methods, LZ77 and LZ78, for dictionary-based compression. Their ideas have been a source of inspiration to many researchers, who generalized, improved, and combined them with RLE and statistical methods to form many commonly used lossless compression methods for text, images, and sound. The remainder of this chapter describes a few common LZ compression methods and shows how they were developed from the basic ideas of Ziv and Lempel.

## 2.1 LZ77 (Sliding Window)

The main idea of this method (sometimes referred to as LZ1) [Ziv 77] is to use part of the previously seen input file as the dictionary. The encoder maintains a window to the input file and shifts the input in that window from right to left as strings of symbols are being encoded. Thus, the method is based on a *sliding window*. The following window is divided into two parts. The part on the left is called the *search buffer*. This is the current dictionary, and it always includes symbols that have recently been input and encoded. The part on the right is the *look-ahead buffer*, containing text yet to be encoded. In practical implementations the search buffer is some thousands of bytes long, while the look-ahead buffer is only tens of bytes long. The vertical bar between the t and the e represents the current dividing line between the two buffers. We thus assume that the text "sir␣sid␣eastman␣easily␣t" has already been compressed, while the text "eases␣sea␣sick␣seals" still needs to be compressed.

← coded text... ⌐sir␣sid␣eastman␣easily␣t│eases␣sea␣sick␣seals⌐ ...← text to be read

The encoder scans the search buffer backward (from right to left) looking for a match to the first symbol e in the look-ahead buffer. It finds one at the e of the word easily. This e is at a distance (offset) of 8 from the end of the search buffer. The encoder then matches as many symbols following the two e's as possible. The three symbols eas match in this case, so the length of the match is 3. The encoder then continues the backward scan, trying to find longer matches. In our case, there is one more match, at the word eastman, with offset 16, and it has the same length. The encoder selects the longest match or, if they are all the same length, the last one found and prepares the token (16, 3, "e").

Selecting the last match rather than the first one simplifies the encoder, since it has to keep track of only the last match found. It is interesting to note that selecting the first match, while making the program somewhat more complex, also has an advantage. It selects the smallest offset. It would seem that this is not an advantage, since a token should have room for the largest possible offset. However, it is possible to follow LZ77 with Huffman or some other statistical coding of the tokens where small offsets are assigned shorter codes. This method, proposed by Bernd Herd, is called LZH. Having many small offsets implies better compression in LZH.

The following point is easy to grasp. The decoder doesn't know whether the encoder has selected the first match or the last match, but the point is that the decoder does not need to know! The decoder simply reads tokens and uses each offset to locate a

string of text in the search buffer without having to know whether the string was a first
or a last match.

In general, an LZ77 token has three parts: offset, length, and next symbol in the
look-ahead buffer (which, in our case, is the **second e** of the word `teases`). This token
is written on the output file, and the window is shifted to the right (or, alternatively,
the input file is moved to the left) four positions: three positions for the matched string
and one position for the next symbol.

$$\ldots \text{sir}_\sqcup \boxed{\text{sid}_\sqcup\text{eastman}_\sqcup\text{easily}_\sqcup\text{tease}\,|\,\text{s}_\sqcup\text{sea}_\sqcup\text{sick}_\sqcup\text{seals}\ldots}\ldots$$

If the backward search yields no match, an LZ77 token with zero offset and length
and with the unmatched symbol is written. This is also the reason a token has to have
a third component. Tokens with zero offset and length are common at the beginning of
any compression job, when the search buffer is empty or almost empty. The first seven
steps in encoding our example are the following:

| | |
|---|---|
| sir␣sid␣eastman␣ | ⇒ (0,0,"s") |
| s&#124;ir␣sid␣eastman␣e | ⇒ (0,0,"i") |
| si&#124;r␣sid␣eastman␣ea | ⇒ (0,0,"r") |
| sir&#124;␣sid␣eastman␣eas | ⇒ (0,0,"␣") |
| sir␣&#124;sid␣eastman␣easi | ⇒ (4,2,"d") |
| sir␣sid&#124;␣eastman␣easily␣ | ⇒ (4,1,"e") |
| sir␣sid␣e&#124;astman␣easily␣te | ⇒ (0,0,"a") |

Clearly, a token of the form $(0,0,\ldots)$, which encodes a single symbol, does not
provide good compression. It is easy to estimate its length. The size of the offset is
$\lceil \log_2 S \rceil$, where $S$ is the length of the search buffer. In practice, the search buffer may
be a few thousand bytes long, so the offset size is typically 10–12 bits. The size of the
"length" field is similarly $\lceil \log_2(L-1) \rceil$, where $L$ is the length of the look-ahead buffer
(see the next paragraph for the $-1$). In practice, the look-ahead buffer is only a few
tens of bytes long, so the size of the "length" field is just a few bits. The size of the
"symbol" field is typically 8 bits, but in general, it is $\lceil \log_2 A \rceil$, where $A$ is the alphabet
size. The total size of the 1-symbol token $(0,0,\ldots)$ may typically be $11+5+8=24$
bits, much longer than the raw 8-bit size of the (single) symbol it encodes.

Here is an example showing why the "length" field may be longer than the size of
the look-ahead buffer:

$$\ldots \text{Mr.}_\sqcup \boxed{\text{alf}_\sqcup\text{eastman}_\sqcup\text{easily}_\sqcup\text{grows}_\sqcup\text{alf}\,|\,\text{alfa}_\sqcup\text{in}_\sqcup\text{his}_\sqcup\text{garden}}\ldots$$

The first symbol `a` in the look-ahead buffer matches the 5 a's in the search buffer. It
seems that the two extreme a's match with a length of 3 and the encoder should select
the last (leftmost) of them and create the token (28,3,"a"). In fact, it creates the token
(3,4,"␣"). The four-symbol string `alfa` in the look-ahead buffer is matched to the last
three symbols `alf` in the search buffer *and* the first symbol `a` in the look-ahead buffer.
The reason for this is that the decoder can handle such a token naturally, without
any modifications. It starts at position 3 of its search buffer and copies the next four
symbols, one by one, extending its buffer to the right. The first three symbols are copies
of the old buffer contents, and the fourth one is a copy of the first of those three. The
next example is even more convincing (and only somewhat contrived):

$\cdots$ `alf␣eastman␣easily␣yells␣A` `AAAAAAAAAA` `AAAAAH`$\cdots$

The encoder creates the token (1,9,"`A`"), matching the first nine copies of `A` in the look-ahead buffer and including the tenth `A`. This is why, in principle, the length of a match can be up to the size of the look-ahead buffer minus 1.

The LZ77 decoder is much simpler than the encoder (thus, LZ77 is an asymmetric compression method). It has to maintain a buffer equal in size to the encoder's window. The decoder inputs a token, finds the match in its buffer, writes the match and the third token field on the output file, and shifts the matched string and the third field into the buffer. This implies that LZ77 or any of its variants is useful in cases where a file is compressed once (or just a few times) and is decompressed often. A heavily used archive of old compressed files is a good example.

At first it seems that this method does not make any assumptions about the input data. Specifically, it does not pay attention to symbol frequencies. A little thinking, however, shows that because of the nature of the sliding window, the LZ77 method always compares the look-ahead buffer to the recently input text in the search buffer, never to text that was input long ago (and has since been flushed out of the search buffer). The method therefore implicitly assumes that patterns in the input data occur close together. Data that satisfies this assumption will compress well.

The basic LZ77 method was improved in several ways by researchers and programmers during the 1980s and 1990s. One way to improve it is to use variable-size "offset" and "length" fields in the tokens. Another way is to increase the sizes of both buffers. Increasing the size of the search buffer makes it possible to find better matches, but the tradeoff is an increased search time. Obviously, a large search buffer requires a more sophisticated data structure that allows for fast search (Section 2.4.2). A third improvement has to do with sliding the window. The simplest approach is to move all the text in the window to the left after each match. A faster method is to replace the linear window with a *circular queue*, where sliding the window is done by resetting two pointers (Section 2.1.1). Yet another improvement is adding an extra bit (a flag) to each token, thereby eliminating the third field (Section 2.2).

### 2.1.1 A Circular Queue

The circular queue is a basic data structure. Physically, it is an array, but it is used differently. Figure 2.1 illustrates a simple example. It shows a 16-byte array with characters being appended at the "end" and others being deleted from the "start." Both the start and end positions move, and two pointers, `s` and `e`, point to them all the time. In (a) there are the 8 characters `sid␣east`, with the rest of the buffer empty. In (b) all 16 bytes are occupied, and `e` points to the end of the buffer. In (c), the first letter `s` has been deleted and the `l` of `easily` inserted. Notice how pointer `e` is now located *to the left* of `s`. In (d), the two letters `id` have been deleted just by moving the `s` pointer; the characters themselves are still present in the array but have been effectively deleted. In (e), the two characters `y␣` have been appended and the `e` pointer moved. In (f), the pointers show that the buffer ends at `teas` and starts at `tman`. Inserting new symbols into the circular queue and moving the pointers is thus equivalent to shifting the contents of the queue. No actual shifting or moving is necessary, though.

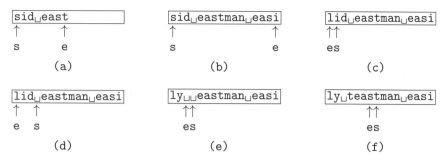

**Figure 2.1:** A Circular Queue.

## 2.2 LZSS

This version of LZ77 was developed by Storer and Szymanski in 1982 [Storer 82]. It improves LZ77 in three ways: (1) It holds the look-ahead buffer in a circular queue, (2) it holds the search buffer (the dictionary) in a binary search tree, and (3) it creates tokens with two fields instead of three.

A binary search tree is a binary tree where the left subtree of every node $A$ contains nodes smaller than $A$ and the right subtree contains nodes greater than $A$. Since the nodes of our binary search trees contain strings, we first need to know how to compare two strings and decide which one is "bigger." This is easily understood by imagining that the strings appear in a dictionary or a lexicon, where they are sorted alphabetically. Clearly, the string `rote` precedes the string `said` since r precedes s (even though o follows a), so we consider `rote` smaller than `said`. This is called *lexicographic order* (ordering strings lexicographically).

What about the string "␣abc"? Virtually all modern computers use ASCII codes to represent characters (although more and more use Unicode, discussed in the box on page 63, and some older IBM, Amdahl, Fujitsu, and Siemens mainframe computers use the old 8-bit EBCDIC code developed by IBM), and in ASCII the code of a blank space precedes those of the letters, so a string that starts with a space is considered smaller than any string that starts with a letter. In general, the *collating sequence* of the computer determines the sequence of characters arranged from small to big. Figure 2.2 shows two examples of binary search trees.

Notice the difference between the (almost) balanced tree in Figure 2.2a and the skewed one in Figure 2.2b. They contain the same 14 nodes, but they look and behave very differently. In the balanced tree any node can be found in at most four steps. In the skewed tree up to 14 steps may be needed. In either case, the maximum number of steps necessary to locate a node equals the height of the tree. For a skewed tree (which is really the same as a linked list), the height is the number of elements $n$; for a balanced tree, the height is $\lceil \log_2 n \rceil$, a much smaller number. More information on the properties of binary search trees may be found in any text on data structures.

**Example:** We show how a binary search tree can be used to speed up the search of the dictionary. The input file is "`sid␣eastman␣clumsily␣teases␣sea␣sick␣seals`". To keep the example simple, we assume a window of a 16-byte search buffer followed by

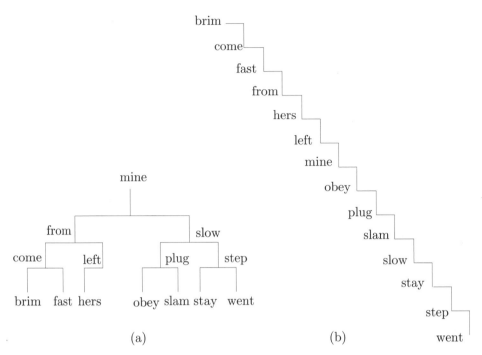

**Figure 2.2:** Two Binary Search Trees.

---

**Unicode**

A new international standard code, the Unicode, has been proposed and is being developed by an international Unicode organization (`www.unicode.org`). Unicode uses 16-bit codes for its characters, so it provides for $2^{16} = 64K = 65,536$ codes. (Doubling the size of a code thus more than doubles the number of possible codes.) Unicode includes all the ASCII codes plus codes for characters in foreign languages (including complete sets of Korean, Japanese, and Chinese characters) and many mathematical and other symbols. Currently, about 39,000 out of the 65,536 possible codes have been assigned, so there is room for adding more symbols in the future.

The Microsoft Windows NT operating system has adopted Unicode, as have also AT&T Plan 9 and Lucent Inferno.

---

The only place where success comes before work is in the dictionary.
—Vidal Sassoon

a 5-byte look-ahead buffer. After the first $16+5$ characters have been input, the sliding window is

| sid␣eastman␣clum | sily␣ | teases␣sea␣sick␣seals |

with the string "teases␣sea␣sick␣seals" still waiting to be input.

The encoder scans the search buffer, creating the twelve five-character strings of Table 2.3 (twelve since $16-5+1=12$), which are inserted into the binary search tree, each with its offset.

$$
\begin{array}{ll}
\text{sid␣e} & 16 \\
\text{id␣ea} & 15 \\
\text{d␣eas} & 14 \\
\text{␣east} & 13 \\
\text{eastm} & 12 \\
\text{astma} & 11 \\
\text{stman} & 10 \\
\text{tman␣} & 09 \\
\text{man␣c} & 08 \\
\text{an␣cl} & 07 \\
\text{n␣clu} & 06 \\
\text{␣clum} & 05 \\
\end{array}
$$

**Table 2.3:** Five-Character Strings.

The first symbol in the look-ahead buffer is s, so the encoder searches the tree for strings that start with an s. Two are found, at offsets 16 and 10, and the first of them, sid␣e (at offset 16), provides a longer match.

(We now have to sidetrack and discuss the case where a string in the tree completely matches that in the look-ahead buffer. In that case the encoder should go back to the search buffer to attempt to match longer strings. In principle, the maximum length of a match can be $L-1$.)

In our example, the match is of length 2, and the two-field token $(16, 2)$ is emitted. The encoder now has to slide the window two positions to the right and update the tree. The new window is

| si | d␣eastman␣clumsi | ly␣te | ases␣sea␣sick␣seals |

The tree should be updated by deleting strings sid␣e and id␣ea and inserting the new strings clums and lumsi. If a longer, $k$-letter string is matched, the window has to be shifted $k$ positions, and the tree should be updated by deleting $k$ strings and adding $k$ new strings—but which ones?

A little thinking shows that the $k$ strings to be deleted are the first ones in the search buffer before the shift, and the $k$ strings to be added are the last ones in it after the shift. A simple procedure for updating the tree is to prepare a string consisting of the first five letters in the search buffer, find it in the tree, and delete it. Then slide the buffer one position to the right (or shift the data to the left), prepare a string consisting of the last five letters in the search buffer, and append it to the tree. This should be repeated $k$ times. (End of example.)

Since each update deletes and adds the same number of strings, the tree size never changes. It always contains $T$ nodes, where $T$ is the length of the search buffer minus the length of the look-ahead buffer plus 1 ($T = S - L + 1$). The shape of the tree, however, may change significantly. As nodes are being added and deleted, the tree may change its shape between a completely skewed tree (the worst case for searching) and a balanced one, the ideal shape for searching.

The third improvement of LZSS over LZ77 is in the tokens created by the encoder. An LZSS token contains just an offset and a length. If no match was found, the encoder emits the uncompressed code of the next symbol instead of the wasteful three-field token $(0, 0, \ldots)$. To distinguish between tokens and uncompressed codes, each is preceded by a single bit (a flag).

In practice, the search buffer may be a few thousand bytes long, so the offset field would typically be 11–13 bits. The size of the look-ahead buffer should be selected such that the total size of a token would be 16 bits (2 bytes). For example, if the search buffer size is 2 KB ($= 2^{11}$), then the look-ahead buffer should be 32 bytes long ($= 2^5$). The offset field would be 11 bits long and the length field, 5 bits (the size of the look-ahead buffer). With this choice of buffer sizes the encoder will emit either 2-byte tokens or 1-byte uncompressed ASCII codes. But what about the flag bits? A good practical idea is to collect eight output items (tokens and ASCII codes) in a small buffer, then output one byte consisting of the eight flags, followed by the eight items (which are 1 or 2 bytes long each).

### 2.2.1 Deficiencies

Before we discuss LZ78, let's summarize the deficiencies of LZ77 and its variants. It has already been mentioned that LZ77 uses the built-in implicit assumption that patterns in the input data occur close together. Data files that don't satisfy this assumption compress poorly. A common example is text where a certain word, say "economy", occurs often but is uniformly distributed throughout the text. When this word is shifted into the look-ahead buffer, its previous occurrence may have already been shifted out of the search buffer. A better algorithm would save commonly occurring strings in the dictionary and not simply slide it all the time.

Another disadvantage of LZ77 is the limited size $L$ of the look-ahead buffer. The size of matched strings is limited to $L - 1$, but $L$ must be kept small, since the process of matching strings involves comparing individual symbols. If $L$ were doubled in size, compression would improve, since longer matches would be possible, but the encoder would be much slower when searching for long matches. The size $S$ of the search buffer is also limited. A large search buffer produces better compression but slows down the encoder, since searching takes longer (even with a binary search tree). Increasing the sizes of the two buffers also means creating longer tokens, thereby reducing the compression ratio. With 2-byte tokens, compressing a 2-character string into one token results in 2 bytes plus 1 flag. Writing the two characters as two raw ASCII codes results in 2 bytes plus 2 flags, a very small difference in size. The encoder should, in such a case, use the latter choice and write the two characters in uncompressed form, saving time and wasting just one bit. We say that the encoder has a 2-byte *breakeven* point. With longer tokens, the breakeven point increases to 3 bytes.

## 2.3 LZ78

The LZ78 method (sometimes referred to as LZ2) [Ziv 78] does not use any search buffer, look-ahead buffer, or sliding window. Instead, there is a dictionary of previously encountered strings. This dictionary starts empty (or almost empty), and its size is limited only by the amount of available memory. The encoder outputs two-field tokens. The first field is a pointer to the dictionary; the second is the code of a symbol. Tokens do not contain the length of a string, since this is implied in the dictionary. Each token corresponds to a string of input symbols, and that string is added to the dictionary after the token is written on the compressed file. Nothing is ever deleted from the dictionary, which is both an advantage over LZ77 (since future strings can match even strings seen in the distant past) and a liability (since the dictionary tends to grow fast).

The dictionary starts with the null string at position zero. As symbols are input and encoded, strings are added to the dictionary at positions 1, 2, and so on. When the next symbol x is read from the input file, the dictionary is searched for an entry with the one-symbol string x. If none are found, x is added to the next available position in the dictionary, and the token $(0, x)$ is output. This token indicates the string "null x" (a concatenation of the null string and x). If an entry with x is found (at, say, position 37), the next symbol y is read, and the dictionary is searched for an entry containing the two-symbol string xy. If none are found, then string xy is added to the next available position in the dictionary, and the token $(37, y)$ is output. This token indicates the string xy, since 37 is the dictionary position of string x. The process continues until the end of the input file is reached.

In general, the current symbol is read and becomes a one-symbol string. The encoder then tries to find it in the dictionary. If the symbol is found in the dictionary, the next symbol is read and concatenated with the first to form a two-symbol string that the encoder then tries to locate in the dictionary. As long as those strings are found in the dictionary, more symbols are read and concatenated to the string. At a certain point the string is not found in the dictionary, so the encoder adds it to the dictionary and outputs a token with the last dictionary match as its first field and the last symbol of the string (the one that caused the search to fail) as its second field. Table 2.4 shows the steps in encoding "sir␣sid␣eastman␣easily␣teases␣sea␣sick␣seals".

In each step, the string added to the dictionary is the one being encoded, minus its last symbol. In a typical compression run, the dictionary starts with short strings, but as more text is being input and processed, longer and longer strings are added to it. The size of the dictionary either can be fixed or may be determined by the size of the available memory each time the LZ78 compression program is executed. A large dictionary may contain more strings and so allow for longer matches, but the tradeoff is longer pointers (and thus bigger tokens) and slower dictionary search.

A good data structure for the dictionary is a tree, but not a binary one. The tree starts with the null string as the root. All the strings that start with the null string (strings for which the token pointer is zero) are added to the tree as children of the root. In the example those are s, i, r, ␣, d, a, m, y, e, c, and k. Each of them becomes the root of a subtree as shown in Figure 2.5. For example, all the strings that start with s (the four strings si, sil, st, and s(eof)) constitute the subtree of node s.

| Dictionary | | Token | Dictionary | | Token |
|---|---|---|---|---|---|
| 0 | null | | 14 | "y" | (0, "y") |
| 1 | "s" | (0, "s") | 15 | "␣t" | (4, "t") |
| 2 | "i" | (0, "i") | 16 | "e" | (0, "e") |
| 3 | "r" | (0, "r") | 17 | "as" | (8, "s") |
| 4 | "␣" | (0, "␣") | 18 | "es" | (16, "s") |
| 5 | "si" | (1, "i") | 19 | "␣s" | (4, "s") |
| 6 | "d" | (0, "d") | 20 | "ea" | (4, "a") |
| 7 | "␣e" | (4, "e") | 21 | "␣si" | (19, "i") |
| 8 | "a" | (0, "a") | 22 | "c" | (0, "c") |
| 9 | "st" | (1, "t") | 23 | "k" | (0, "k") |
| 10 | "m" | (0, "m") | 24 | "␣se" | (19, "e") |
| 11 | "an" | (8, "n") | 25 | "al" | (8, "l") |
| 12 | "␣ea" | (7, "a") | 26 | "s(eof)" | (1, "(eof)") |
| 13 | "sil" | (5, "l") | | | |

**Table 2.4:** Encoding Steps in LZ78.

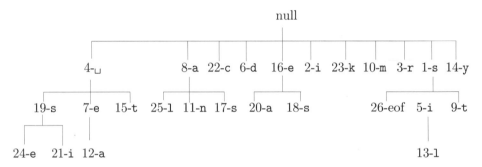

**Figure 2.5:** An LZ78 Dictionary Tree.

Given an alphabet with 8-bit symbols, there are 256 different symbols. In principle, each node in the tree could have up to 256 children. Adding a child to a tree node should therefore be a dynamic process. When the node is first created, it has no children and it should not reserve any memory space for them. As a child is added to the node, memory space should be claimed for it. Since no nodes are ever deleted, there is no need to reclaim memory space, which simplifies the memory management task somewhat.

Such a tree makes it easy to search for a string and to add strings. To search for `sil`, for example, the program looks for the child `s` of the root, then for the child `i` of `s`, and so on, going down the tree. Here are some examples:

1. When the `s` of `sid` is input in step 5, the encoder finds node "1-s" in the tree as a child of "null". It then inputs the next symbol `i`, but node `s` does not have a child `i` (in fact, it has no children at all at this point), so the encoder adds node "5-i" as a child of "1-s", which effectively adds the string `si` to the tree.

2. When the blank space between `eastman` and `easily` is input in step 12, a similar situation occurs. The encoder finds node "4-␣", inputs e, finds "7-e", inputs a, but "7-e" does not have "a" as a child, so the encoder adds node "12-a", which effectively adds the string "␣ea" to the tree.

A tree of the type described here is called a *trie*. In general, a trie is a tree in which the branching structure at any level is determined by just part of a data item, not the entire item. In the case of LZ78, each string added to the tree effectively adds just one symbol and does so by adding a branch.

Since the total size of the tree is limited, it may fill up during compression. This, in fact, happens all the time except when the input file is unusually small. The original LZ78 method does not specify what to do in such a case, so here are some possible solutions.

1. The simplest solution is to freeze the dictionary when it fills up. No new nodes should be added and the tree becomes a static dictionary, but it can still be used to encode strings.

2. Delete the entire tree once it fills up and start with a new, empty tree. This solution effectively breaks the input into blocks, each with its own dictionary. If the content of the input varies from block to block, this solution will produce good compression, since it will eliminate a dictionary with strings that are unlikely to be used in the future. We can say that this solution implicitly assumes that future symbols will benefit more from new data than from old (the same implicit assumption used by LZ77).

3. The UNIX `compress` utility uses a more complex solution. This utility (also called LZC) uses LZW (Section 2.4) with a growing dictionary. It starts with a small dictionary of just $2^9 = 512$ entries (with the first 256 of them already filled up). While this dictionary is being used, 9-bit pointers are written onto the output file. When the original dictionary fills up, its size is doubled to 1024 entries, and 10-bit pointers are used from then on. This process continues until the pointer size reaches a maximum set by the user (it can be set to between 9 and 16 bits, with 16 as the default value). When the largest allowed dictionary fills up, the program continues without changing the dictionary (which then becomes static) but with monitoring the compression ratio. If the ratio falls below a predefined threshold, the dictionary is deleted, and a new 512-entry dictionary is started. This way, the dictionary never gets too out of date.

4. When the dictionary is full, delete some of the least recently used entries to make room for new ones. Unfortunately there is no good algorithm to decide which entries to delete and how many.

The LZ78 decoder works by building and maintaining the dictionary in the same way as the encoder. It is therefore more complex than the LZ77 decoder.

> Words—so innocent and powerless as they are, as standing in a dictionary, how potent for good and evil they become in the hands of one who knows how to combine them.
>
> —Nathaniel Hawthorne

## 2.4 LZW

This is a popular variant of LZ78, developed by Terry Welch in 1984 ([Welch 84] and [Phillips 92]). Its main feature is eliminating the second field of a token. An LZW token consists of just a pointer to the dictionary. To best understand LZW, we should temporarily forget that the dictionary is a tree and should think of it as an array of variable-size strings. The LZW method starts by initializing the dictionary to all the symbols in the alphabet. In the common case of 8-bit symbols, the first 256 entries of the dictionary (entries 0 through 255) are occupied before any data is input. Because the dictionary is initialized, the next input symbol will always be found in the dictionary. This is why an LZW token can consist of just a pointer and does not have to contain a symbol code as in LZ77 and LZ78.

(LZW has been patented and its use requires a license. The issue of software patents is discussed in [Salomon 00].)

The principle of LZW is that the encoder inputs symbols one by one and accumulates them in a string I. After each symbol is input and is concatenated to I, the dictionary is searched for string I. As long as I is found in the dictionary, the process continues. At a certain point, adding the next symbol x causes the search to fail; string I is in the dictionary but string Ix (symbol x appended to I) is not. At this point the encoder (1) outputs the dictionary pointer that points to string I, (2) saves string Ix (which is now called a *phrase*) in the next available dictionary entry, and (3) initializes string I to symbol x. To illustrate this process, we again use the text string "sir␣sid␣eastman␣easily␣teases␣sea␣sick␣seals". The steps are as follows:

0. Initialize entries 0–255 of the dictionary to all 256 8-bit bytes.
1. The first symbol s is input and is found in the dictionary (in entry 115, since this is the ASCII code of s). The next symbol i is input, but si is not found in the dictionary. The encoder performs the following: (1) outputs 115, (2) saves string si in the next available dictionary entry (entry 256), and (3) initializes I to the symbol i.
2. The r of sir is input, but string ir is not in the dictionary. The encoder (1) outputs 105 (the ASCII code of i), (2) saves string ir in the next available dictionary entry (entry 257), and (3) initializes I to the symbol r.

Table 2.6 summarizes all the steps of this process. Table 2.7 shows some of the original 256 entries in the LZW dictionary plus the entries added during encoding of the string above. The complete output file is (only the numbers are output, not the strings in parentheses) as follows:

115 (s), 105 (i), 114 (r), 32 (␣), 256 (si), 100 (d), 32 (␣), 101 (e), 97 (a), 115 (s), 116 (t), 109 (m), 97 (a), 110 (n), 262 (␣e), 264 (as), 105 (i), 108 (l), 121 (y), 32 (␣), 116 (t), 263 (ea), 115 (s), 101 (e), 115 (s), 259 (␣s), 263 (ea), 259 (␣s), 105 (i), 99 (c), 107 (k), 280 (␣se), 97 (a), 108 (l), 115 (s), eof.

Figure 2.8 is a pseudo-code listing of the algorithm. We denote by λ the empty string and by <<a,b>> the concatenation of strings a and b.

The line "append <<di,ch>> to the dictionary" is of special interest. It is clear that in practice, the dictionary may fill up. This line should therefore include a test for a full dictionary and certain actions for the case where it is full.

| I | in dict? | new entry | output | I | in dict? | new entry | output |
|---|---|---|---|---|---|---|---|
| s | Y | | | y | Y | | |
| si | N | 256-si | 115 (s) | y⊔ | N | 274-y⊔ | 121 (y) |
| i | Y | | | ⊔ | Y | | |
| ir | N | 257-ir | 105 (i) | ⊔t | N | 275-⊔t | 32 (⊔) |
| r | Y | | | t | Y | | |
| r⊔ | N | 258-r⊔ | 114 (r) | te | N | 276-te | 116 (t) |
| ⊔ | Y | | | e | Y | | |
| ⊔s | N | 259-⊔s | 32 (⊔) | ea | Y | | |
| s | Y | | | eas | N | 277-eas | 263 (ea) |
| si | Y | | | s | Y | | |
| sid | N | 260-sid | 256 (si) | se | N | 278-se | 115 (s) |
| d | Y | | | e | Y | | |
| d⊔ | N | 261-d⊔ | 100 (d) | es | N | 279-es | 101 (e) |
| ⊔ | Y | | | s | Y | | |
| ⊔e | N | 262-⊔e | 32 (⊔) | s⊔ | N | 280-s⊔ | 115 (s) |
| e | Y | | | ⊔ | Y | | |
| ea | N | 263-ea | 101 (e) | ⊔s | Y | | |
| a | Y | | | ⊔se | N | 281-⊔se | 259 (⊔s) |
| as | N | 264-as | 97 (a) | e | Y | | |
| s | Y | | | ea | Y | | |
| st | N | 265-st | 115 (s) | ea⊔ | N | 282-ea⊔ | 263 (ea) |
| t | Y | | | ⊔ | Y | | |
| tm | N | 266-tm | 116 (t) | ⊔s | Y | | |
| m | Y | | | ⊔si | N | 283-⊔si | 259 (⊔s) |
| ma | N | 267-ma | 109 (m) | i | Y | | |
| a | Y | | | ic | N | 284-ic | 105 (i) |
| an | N | 268-an | 97 (a) | c | Y | | |
| n | Y | | | ck | N | 285-ck | 99 (c) |
| n⊔ | N | 269-n⊔ | 110 (n) | k | Y | | |
| ⊔ | Y | | | k⊔ | N | 286-k⊔ | 107 (k) |
| ⊔e | Y | | | ⊔ | Y | | |
| ⊔ea | N | 270-⊔ea | 262 (⊔e) | ⊔s | Y | | |
| a | Y | | | ⊔se | Y | | |
| as | Y | | | ⊔sea | N | 287-⊔sea | 281 (⊔se) |
| asi | N | 271-asi | 264 (as) | a | Y | | |
| i | Y | | | al | N | 288-al | 97 (a) |
| il | N | 272-il | 105 (i) | l | Y | | |
| l | Y | | | ls | N | 289-ls | 108 (l) |
| ly | N | 273-ly | 108 (l) | s | Y | | |
| | | | | s,eof | N | | 115 (s) |

**Table 2.6:** Encoding "sir⊔sid⊔eastman⊔easily⊔teases⊔sea⊔sick⊔seals".

| | | | | | | | |
|---|---|---|---|---|---|---|---|
| 0 | NULL | 110 | n | 262 | ␣e | 276 | te |
| 1 | SOH | ... | | 263 | ea | 277 | eas |
| ... | | 115 | s | 264 | as | 278 | se |
| 32 | SP | 116 | t | 265 | st | 279 | es |
| ... | | ... | | 266 | tm | 280 | s␣ |
| 97 | a | 121 | y | 267 | ma | 281 | ␣se |
| 98 | b | ... | | 268 | an | 282 | ea␣ |
| 99 | c | 255 | 255 | 269 | n␣ | 283 | ␣si |
| 100 | d | 256 | si | 270 | ␣ea | 284 | ic |
| 101 | e | 257 | ir | 271 | asi | 285 | ck |
| ... | | 258 | r␣ | 272 | il | 286 | k␣ |
| 107 | k | 259 | ␣s | 273 | ly | 287 | ␣sea |
| 108 | l | 260 | sid | 274 | y␣ | 288 | al |
| 109 | m | 261 | d␣ | 275 | ␣t | 289 | ls |

**Table 2.7:** An LZW Dictionary.

```
for i:=0 to 255 do
   append i as a 1-symbol string to the dictionary;
append λ to the dictionary;
di:=dictionary index of λ;
repeat
   read(ch);
   if <<di,ch>> is in the dictionary then
      di:=dictionary index of <<di,ch>>;
   else
      output(di);
      append <<di,ch>> to the dictionary;
      di:=dictionary index of ch;
   endif;
until end-of-input;
```

**Figure 2.8:** The LZW Algorithm.

Since the first 256 entries of the dictionary are occupied right from the start, pointers to the dictionary have to be longer than 8 bits. A simple implementation would typically use 16-bit pointers, which allow for a 64K-entry dictionary (where $64K = 2^{16} = 65,536$). Such a dictionary will, of course, fill up very quickly in all but the smallest compression jobs. The same problem exists with LZ78, and any solutions used with LZ78 can also be used with LZW. Another interesting fact about LZW is that strings in the dictionary become only one character longer at a time. It therefore takes a long time to get long strings in the dictionary and thus a chance to achieve really good compression. We can say that LZW adapts slowly to its input data.

**Example:** We apply LZW to encode the string "alf⎵eats⎵alfalfa". The encoder output and the new entries added by it to the dictionary are shown. Table 2.9 summarizes the steps. The output emitted by the encoder is

97 (a), 108 (l), 102 (f), 32 (⎵), 101 (e), 97 (a), 116 (t), 115 (s), 32 (⎵), 256 (al), 102 (f), 265 (alf), 97 (a),

and the following new entries are added to the dictionary:

(256: al), (257: lf), (258: f⎵), (259: ⎵e), (260: ea), (261: at), (262: ts), (263: s⎵), (264: ⎵a), (265: alf), (266: fa), (267: alfa).

| I | in dict? | new entry | output | I | in dict? | new entry | output |
|---|---|---|---|---|---|---|---|
| a | Y | | | s⎵ | N | 263-s⎵ | 115 (s) |
| al | N | 256-al | 97 (a) | ⎵ | Y | | |
| l | Y | | | ⎵a | N | 264-⎵a | 32 (⎵) |
| lf | N | 257-lf | 108 (l) | a | Y | | |
| f | Y | | | al | Y | | |
| f⎵ | N | 258-f⎵ | 102 (f) | alf | N | 265-alf | 256 (al) |
| ⎵ | Y | | | f | Y | | |
| ⎵e | N | 259-⎵e | 32 (w) | fa | N | 266-fa | 102 (f) |
| e | Y | | | a | Y | | |
| ea | N | 260-ea | 101 (e) | al | Y | | |
| a | Y | | | alf | Y | | |
| at | N | 261-at | 97 (a) | alfa | N | 267-alfa | 265 (alf) |
| t | Y | | | a | Y | | |
| ts | N | 262-ts | 116 (t) | a,eof | N | | 97 (a) |
| s | Y | | | | | | |

**Table 2.9:** LZW Encoding of "alf eats alfalfa".

**Example:** The LZW compression of the string "aaaa..." is analyzed. The encoder inputs the first a into I, searches and finds a in the dictionary. It inputs the next a but finds that Ix, which is now aa, is not in the dictionary. The encoder therefore adds string aa to the dictionary as entry 256 and outputs the token 97 (a). Variable I is initialized to the second a. The third a is input, so Ix is the string aa, which is now in the dictionary. I becomes this string, and the fourth a is input. Ix is now aaa, which is not in the dictionary. The encoder therefore adds string aaa to the dictionary as entry 257 and outputs 256 (aa). I is initialized to the fourth a. Continuing this process is straightforward.

The result is that strings aa, aaa, aaaa,... are added to the dictionary as entries 256, 257, 258,..., and the output is

$$97 \text{ (a)}, 256 \text{ (aa)}, 257 \text{ (aaa)}, 258 \text{ (aaaa)},....$$

The output consists of pointers pointing to longer and longer strings of as. Thus, the first $k$ pointers point at strings whose total length is $1 + 2 + \cdots + k = (k + k^2)/2$.

Assuming an input file that consists of 1 million as, we can find the size of the compressed output file by solving the quadratic equation $(k + k^2)/2 = 1000000$ for the unknown $k$. The solution is $k \approx 1414$. The original 8-million bit input is thus compressed into 1414 pointers, each at least 9 bits (and in practice, probably 16 bits) long. The compression factor is thus either $8M/(1414 \times 9) \approx 628.6$ or $8M/(1414 \times 16) \approx 353.6$.

This is an impressive result, but such input files are rare (notice that this particular input can best be compressed by generating an output file containing just "1000000 a" and without using LZW).

### 2.4.1 LZW Decoding

In order to understand how the LZW decoder works, we should first recall the three steps the encoder performs each time it writes something on the output file: (1) It outputs the dictionary pointer that points to string I, (2) it saves string Ix in the next available entry of the dictionary, and (3) it initializes string I to symbol x.

The decoder starts with the first entries of its dictionary initialized to all the symbols of the alphabet (normally 256 symbols). It then reads its input file (which consists of pointers to the dictionary) and uses each pointer to retrieve uncompressed symbols from its dictionary and write them on its output file. It also builds its dictionary in the same way as the encoder (this fact is usually expressed by saying that the encoder and decoder are *synchronized*, or that they work in *lockstep*).

In the first decoding step, the decoder inputs the first pointer and uses it to retrieve a dictionary item I. This is a string of symbols, and it is written on the decoder's output file. String Ix needs to be saved in the dictionary, but symbol x is still unknown; it will be the first symbol in the next string retrieved from the dictionary.

In each decoding step after the first, the decoder inputs the next pointer, retrieves the next string J from the dictionary, writes it on the output file, isolates its first symbol x, and saves string Ix in the next available dictionary entry (after checking to make sure string Ix is not already in the dictionary). The decoder then moves J to I and is ready for the next step.

In our "sir␣sid..." example, the first pointer that's input by the decoder is 115. This corresponds to the string s, which is retrieved from the dictionary, gets stored in I, and becomes the first item written on the decoder's output file. The next pointer is 105, so string i is retrieved into J and is also written on the output file. J's first symbol is concatenated with I to form string si, which does not exist in the dictionary, and is therefore added to it as entry 256. Variable J is moved to I, so I is now the string i.

The next pointer is 114, so string r is retrieved from the dictionary into J and is also written on the output file. J's first symbol is concatenated with I to form string ir, which does not exist in the dictionary, and is added to it as entry 257. Variable J is moved to I, so I is now the string r. The next step reads pointer 32, writes "␣" on the output file, and saves string "r␣".

**Example:** The string "alf␣eats␣alfalfa" is decoded by using the encoding results from the example on page 72. We simply follow the decoding steps described in the text.

1. Input 97. This is in the dictionary so set I="a" and output "a". String "ax" needs to be saved in the dictionary but x is still unknown..

2. Input 108. This is in the dictionary so set J="l" and output "l". Save "al" in entry 256. Set I="l".

3. Input 102. This is in the dictionary so set J="f" and output "f". Save "lf" in entry 257. Set I="f".

4. Input 32. This is in the dictionary so set J="␣" and output "␣". Save "f␣" in entry 258. Set I="␣".

5. Input 101. This is in the dictionary so set J="e" and output "e". Save "␣e" in entry 259. Set I="e".

6. Input 97. This is in the dictionary so set J="a" and output "a". Save "ea" in entry 260. Set I="a".

7. Input 116. This is in the dictionary so set J="t" and output "t". Save "at" in entry 261. Set I="t".

8. Input 115. This is in the dictionary so set J="s" and output "s". Save "ts" in entry 262. Set I="t".

9. Input 32. This is in the dictionary so set J="␣" and output "␣". Save "s␣" in entry 263. Set I="␣".

10. Input 256. This is in the dictionary so set J="al" and output "al". Save "␣a" in entry 264. Set I="al".

11. Input 102. This is in the dictionary so set J="f" and output "f". Save "alf" in entry 265. Set I="f".

12. Input 265. This has just been saved in the dictionary so set J="alf" and output "alf". Save "fa" in dictionary entry 266. Set I="alf".

13. Input 97. This is in the dictionary so set J="a" and output "a". Save "alfa" in entry 267 (even though it will never be used). Set I="a".

14. Read eof. Stop.

**Example:** Given a two-symbol alphabet with the symbols a and b, we show the first few steps for encoding and decoding the string "ababab...". We assume that the dictionary is initialized to just the two entries (1: a) and (2: b). The encoder outputs

$$1 \text{ (a)}, 2 \text{ (b)}, 3 \text{ (ab)}, 5(\text{aba}), 4(\text{ba}), 7 \text{ (bab)}, 6 \text{ (abab)}, 9 \text{ (ababa)}, 8 \text{ (baba)}, \ldots$$

and adds the new entries (3: ab), (4: ba), (5: aba), (6: abab), (7: bab), (8: baba), (9: ababa), (10: ababab), (11: babab),...to the dictionary. This behavior is regular, so it can easily be analyzed and the $k$th output pointer and dictionary entry predicted, but the results are not worth the effort required.

### 2.4.2 LZW Dictionary Structure

Until now, we have assumed that the LZW dictionary is an array of variable-size strings. To understand why a trie is a better data structure for the dictionary we need to recall how the encoder works. It inputs symbols and concatenates them into a variable I as long as the string in I is found in the dictionary. At a certain point the encoder inputs the first symbol x, which causes the search to fail (string Ix is not in the dictionary). It then adds Ix to the dictionary. This means that each string added to the dictionary effectively adds just one new symbol, x. (Phrased another way; for each dictionary string of more than one symbol, there exists a "parent" string in the dictionary that's one symbol shorter.)

A tree similar to the one used by LZ78 is therefore a good data structure, since adding string Ix to such a tree is done by adding one node with x. The main problem is that each node in the LZW tree may have many children (the tree is multiway, not binary). Imagine the node for the letter a in entry 97. Initially it has no children, but if the string ab is added to the tree, node 97 receives one child. Later, when, say, the string ae is added, node 97 receives a second child, and so on. The data structure for the tree should therefore be designed such that a node could have any number of children without having to reserve any memory for them in advance.

One way of designing such a data structure is to house the tree in an array of nodes, each a structure with two fields: a symbol and a pointer to the parent node. A node has no pointers to any child nodes. Moving down the tree from a node to one of its children is done by a *hashing process* in which the pointer to the node and the symbol of the child are hashed to create a new pointer.

Suppose that string abc has already been input, symbol by symbol, and has been stored in the tree in the three nodes at locations 97, 266, and 284. Following that, the encoder has just input the next symbol d. The encoder now searches for string abcd or, more specifically, for a node containing the symbol d whose parent is at location 284. The encoder hashes the 284 (the pointer to string abc) and the 100 (ASCII code of d) to create a pointer to some node, say, 299. The encoder then examines node 299. There are three cases:

1. The node is unused. This means that abcd is not yet in the dictionary and should be added to it. The encoder adds it to the tree by storing the parent pointer 284 and ASCII code 100 in the node. The result is the following:

| Node | | | | |
|---|---|---|---|---|
| Address   : | 97 | 266 | 284 | 299 |
| Contents  : | (-:"a") | (97:"b") | (266:"c") | (284:"d") |
| Represents: | "a" | "ab" | "abc" | "abcd" |

2. The node contains a parent pointer of 284 and the ASCII code of d. This means that string abcd is already in the tree. The encoder inputs the next symbol, say e, and searches the dictionary tree for string abcde.

3. The node contains something else. This means that another hashing of a pointer and an ASCII code has resulted in 299, and node 299 already contains information from another string. This is called a *collision*, and it can be dealt with in several ways. The

simplest way to deal with a collision is to increment pointer 299 and examine nodes 300, 301,... until an unused node is found or until a node with (284:"d") is found.

In practice, we build nodes that are structures with three fields, a pointer to the parent node, the pointer (or index) created by the hashing process, and the code (normally ASCII) of the symbol contained in the node. The second field is necessary because of collisions. A node can therefore be illustrated by the triplet

| parent |
|:---:|
| index |
| symbol |

**Example:** We illustrate this data structure using string "ababab..." (see example on page 74). The dictionary is an array dict where each entry is a structure with the three fields parent, index, and symbol. We refer to a field by, e.g., dict[pointer].parent, where pointer is an index to the array. The dictionary is initialized to the two entries a and b. (To keep the example simple we use no ASCII codes. We assume that a has code 1 and b, code 2.) The first few steps of the encoder are as follows:

*Step 0*: Mark all dictionary locations from 3 on as unused.

| / | / | / | / | / |
|:---:|:---:|:---:|:---:|:---:|
| 1 | 2 | - | - | - | ...
| a | b |   |   |   |

*Step 1*: The first symbol a is input into variable I. What is actually input is the code of "a", which in our example is 1, so I = 1. Since this is the first symbol, the encoder assumes that it is in the dictionary and so does not perform any search.

*Step 2*: The second symbol b is input into J, so J = 2. The encoder has to search for string ab in the dictionary. It executes pointer:=hash(I,J). Let's assume that the result is 5. Field dict[pointer].index contains "unused", since location 5 is still empty, so string ab is not in the dictionary. It is added by executing

```
dict[pointer].parent:=I;
dict[pointer].index:=pointer;
dict[pointer].symbol:=J;
```

with pointer=5. J is moved into I, so I = 2.

| / | / | / | / | 1 |
|:---:|:---:|:---:|:---:|:---:|
| 1 | 2 | - | - | 5 | ...
| a | b |   |   | b |

*Step 3*: The third symbol a is input into J, so J = 1. The encoder has to search for string ba in the dictionary. It executes pointer:=hash(I,J). Let's assume that the result is 8. Field dict[pointer].index contains "unused", so string ba is not in the dictionary. It is added as before by executing

```
dict[pointer].parent:=I;
dict[pointer].index:=pointer;
dict[pointer].symbol:=J;
```

with `pointer`=8. J is moved into I, so I = 1.

| / | / | / | / | 1 | / | / | 2 | / | |
|---|---|---|---|---|---|---|---|---|---|
| 1 | 2 | - | - | 5 | - | - | 8 | - | ... |
| a | b | | | b | | | a | | |

*Step 4*: The fourth symbol b is input into J, so J=2. The encoder has to search for string ab in the dictionary. It executes `pointer:=hash(I,J)`. We know from step 2 that the result is 5. Field `dict[pointer].index` contains "5", so string ab is in the dictionary. The value of `pointer` is moved into I, so I = 5.

*Step 5*: The fifth symbol a is input into J, so J = 1. The encoder has to search for string aba in the dictionary. It executes as usual `pointer:=hash(I,J)`. Let's assume that the result is 8 (a collision). Field `dict[pointer].index` contains 8, which looks good, but field `dict[pointer].parent` contains 2 instead of the expected 5, so the hash function knows that this is a collision and string aba is not in dictionary entry 8. It increments `pointer` as many times as necessary until it finds a dictionary entry with `index=8` and `parent=5` or until it finds an unused entry. In the former case, string aba is in the dictionary, and `pointer` is moved to I. In the latter case aba is not in the dictionary, and the encoder saves it in the entry pointed at by `pointer`, and moves J to I.

| / | / | / | / | 1 | / | / | 2 | 5 | / | |
|---|---|---|---|---|---|---|---|---|---|---|
| 1 | 2 | - | - | 5 | - | - | 8 | 8 | - | ... |
| a | b | | | b | | | a | a | | |

**Example:** The 15 hashing steps for encoding the string "alf␣eats␣alfalfa" are shown here. The encoding process itself was illustrated in detail in the example on page 72. The results of the hashing are arbitrary; they are not the results produced by a real hash function. The 12 trie nodes constructed for this string are shown in Figure 2.10.

1. Hash(l,97) → 278. Array location 278 is set to (97, 278, l).
2. Hash(f,108) → 266. Array location 266 is set to (108, 266, f).
3. Hash(␣,102) → 269. Array location 269 is set to (102, 269, ␣).
4. Hash(e,32) → 267. Array location 267 is set to (32, 267, e).
5. Hash(a,101) → 265. Array location 265 is set to (101, 265, a).
6. Hash(t,97) → 272. Array location 272 is set to (97, 272, t).
7. Hash(s,116) → 265. A collision! Skip to the next available location, 268, and set it to (116, 265, s). This is why the index needs to be stored.
8. Hash(␣,115) → 270. Array location 270 is set to (115, 270, ␣).
9. Hash(a,32) → 268. A collision! Skip to the next available location, 271, and set it to (32, 268, a).
10. Hash(l,97) → 278. Array location 278 already contains index 278 and symbol l from step 1, so there is no need to store anything else or to add a new trie entry.
11. Hash(f,278) → 276. Array location 276 is set to (278, 276, f).
12. Hash(a,102) → 274. Array location 274 is set to (102, 274, a).
13. Hash(l,97) → 278. Array location 278 already contains index 278 and symbol l from step 1, so there is no need to do anything.

| 265 | 266 | 267 | 268 | 269 | 270 | 271 | 272 | 273 | 274 | 275 | 276 | 277 | 278 |
|---|---|---|---|---|---|---|---|---|---|---|---|---|---|
| / | / | / | / | / | / | / | / | / | / | / | / | / | 97 |
| - | - | - | - | - | - | - | - | - | - | - | - | - | 278 |
|  |  |  |  |  |  |  |  |  |  |  |  |  | 1 |

| 265 | 266 | 267 | 268 | 269 | 270 | 271 | 272 | 273 | 274 | 275 | 276 | 277 | 278 |
|---|---|---|---|---|---|---|---|---|---|---|---|---|---|
| / | 108 | / | / | / | / | / | / | / | / | / | / | / | 97 |
| - | 266 | - | - | - | - | - | - | - | - | - | - | - | 278 |
|  | f |  |  |  |  |  |  |  |  |  |  |  | 1 |

| 265 | 266 | 267 | 268 | 269 | 270 | 271 | 272 | 273 | 274 | 275 | 276 | 277 | 278 |
|---|---|---|---|---|---|---|---|---|---|---|---|---|---|
| / | 108 | / | / | 102 | / | / | / | / | / | / | / | / | 97 |
| - | 266 | - | - | 269 | - | - | - | - | - | - | - | - | 278 |
|  | f |  |  | ␣ |  |  |  |  |  |  |  |  | 1 |

| 265 | 266 | 267 | 268 | 269 | 270 | 271 | 272 | 273 | 274 | 275 | 276 | 277 | 278 |
|---|---|---|---|---|---|---|---|---|---|---|---|---|---|
| / | 108 | 32 | / | 102 | / | / | / | / | / | / | / | / | 97 |
| - | 266 | 267 | - | 269 | - | - | - | - | - | - | - | - | 278 |
|  | f | e |  | ␣ |  |  |  |  |  |  |  |  | 1 |

| 265 | 266 | 267 | 268 | 269 | 270 | 271 | 272 | 273 | 274 | 275 | 276 | 277 | 278 |
|---|---|---|---|---|---|---|---|---|---|---|---|---|---|
| 101 | 108 | 32 | / | 102 | / | / | / | / | / | / | / | / | 97 |
| 265 | 266 | 267 | - | 269 | - | - | - | - | - | - | - | - | 278 |
| a | f | e |  | ␣ |  |  |  |  |  |  |  |  | 1 |

| 265 | 266 | 267 | 268 | 269 | 270 | 271 | 272 | 273 | 274 | 275 | 276 | 277 | 278 |
|---|---|---|---|---|---|---|---|---|---|---|---|---|---|
| 101 | 108 | 32 | / | 102 | / | / | 97 | / | / | / | / | / | 97 |
| 265 | 266 | 267 | - | 269 | - | - | 272 | - | - | - | - | - | 278 |
| a | f | e |  | ␣ |  |  | t |  |  |  |  |  | 1 |

| 265 | 266 | 267 | 268 | 269 | 270 | 271 | 272 | 273 | 274 | 275 | 276 | 277 | 278 |
|---|---|---|---|---|---|---|---|---|---|---|---|---|---|
| 101 | 108 | 32 | 116 | 102 | / | / | 97 | / | / | / | / | / | 97 |
| 265 | 266 | 267 | 265 | 269 | - | - | 272 | - | - | - | - | - | 278 |
| a | f | e | s | ␣ |  |  | t |  |  |  |  |  | 1 |

| 265 | 266 | 267 | 268 | 269 | 270 | 271 | 272 | 273 | 274 | 275 | 276 | 277 | 278 |
|---|---|---|---|---|---|---|---|---|---|---|---|---|---|
| 101 | 108 | 32 | 116 | 102 | 115 | / | 97 | / | / | / | / | / | 97 |
| 265 | 266 | 267 | 265 | 269 | 270 | - | 272 | - | - | - | - | - | 278 |
| a | f | e | s | ␣ | ␣ |  | t |  |  |  |  |  | 1 |

| 265 | 266 | 267 | 268 | 269 | 270 | 271 | 272 | 273 | 274 | 275 | 276 | 277 | 278 |
|---|---|---|---|---|---|---|---|---|---|---|---|---|---|
| 101 | 108 | 32 | 116 | 102 | 115 | 32 | 97 | / | / | / | / | / | 97 |
| 265 | 266 | 267 | 265 | 269 | 270 | 268 | 272 | - | - | - | - | - | 278 |
| a | f | e | s | ␣ | ␣ | a | t |  |  |  |  |  | 1 |

| 265 | 266 | 267 | 268 | 269 | 270 | 271 | 272 | 273 | 274 | 275 | 276 | 277 | 278 |
|---|---|---|---|---|---|---|---|---|---|---|---|---|---|
| 101 | 108 | 32 | 116 | 102 | 115 | 32 | 97 | / | / | / | 278 | / | 97 |
| 265 | 266 | 267 | 265 | 269 | 270 | 268 | 272 | - | - | - | 276 | - | 278 |
| a | f | e | s | ␣ | ␣ | a | t |  |  |  | f |  | 1 |

| 265 | 266 | 267 | 268 | 269 | 270 | 271 | 272 | 273 | 274 | 275 | 276 | 277 | 278 |
|---|---|---|---|---|---|---|---|---|---|---|---|---|---|
| 101 | 108 | 32 | 116 | 102 | 115 | 32 | 97 | / | 102 | / | 278 | / | 97 |
| 265 | 266 | 267 | 265 | 269 | 270 | 268 | 272 | - | 274 | - | 276 | - | 278 |
| a | f | e | s | ␣ | ␣ | a | t |  | a |  | f |  | 1 |

| 265 | 266 | 267 | 268 | 269 | 270 | 271 | 272 | 273 | 274 | 275 | 276 | 277 | 278 |
|---|---|---|---|---|---|---|---|---|---|---|---|---|---|
| 101 | 108 | 32 | 116 | 102 | 115 | 32 | 97 | / | 102 | 276 | 278 | / | 97 |
| 265 | 266 | 267 | 265 | 269 | 270 | 268 | 272 | - | 274 | 274 | 276 | - | 278 |
| a | f | e | s | ␣ | ␣ | a | t |  | a | a | f |  | 1 |

**Figure 2.10:** Growing an LZW Trie for "alf␣eats␣alfalfa".

14. Hash(f,278) → 276. Array location 276 already contains index 276 and symbol f from step 11, so there is no need to do anything.

15. Hash(a,276) → 274. A collision! Skip to the next available location, 275, and set it to (276, 274, a).

Readers who have carefully followed the discussion up to this point will be happy to learn that the LZW decoder's use of the dictionary tree array is simple and no hashing is needed. The decoder starts, like the encoder, by initializing the first 256 array locations. It then reads pointers from its input file and uses each pointer to locate a symbol in the dictionary.

In the first decoding step, the decoder inputs the first pointer and uses it to retrieve a dictionary item I. This is a symbol that is now written by the decoder on its output file. String Ix needs to be saved in the dictionary, but symbol x is still unknown; it will be the first symbol in the next string retrieved from the dictionary.

In each decoding step after the first, the decoder inputs the next pointer and uses it to retrieve the next string J from the dictionary and write it on the output file. If the pointer is, say, 8, the decoder examines field dict[8].index. If this field equals 8, then this is the right node. Otherwise, the decoder examines consecutive array locations until it finds the right one.

Once the right tree node is found, the parent field is used to go back up the tree and retrieve the individual symbols of the string *in reverse order*. The symbols are then placed in J in the right order (see point 2 of the string reversal discussion after the example) and the decoder isolates the first symbol x of J, and saves string Ix in the next available array location. (String I was found in the previous step, so only one node, with symbol x, needs be added.) The decoder then moves J to I and is ready for the next step.

Retrieving a complete string from the LZW tree therefore involves following the pointers in the parent fields. This is equivalent to moving *up* the tree, which is why the hash function is no longer needed.

**Example:** The previous example describes the 15 hashing steps in the encoding of string "alf␣eats␣alfalfa". The last step sets array location 275 to (276,274,a) and writes 275 (a pointer to location 275) on the compressed file. When this file is read by the decoder, pointer 275 is the last item input and processed by the decoder. The decoder finds symbol a in the symbol field of location 275 (indicating that the string stored at 275 ends with an a) and a pointer to location 276 in the parent field. The decoder then examines location 276 where it finds symbol f and parent pointer 278. In location 278 the decoder finds symbol l and a pointer to 97. Finally, in location 97 the decoder finds symbol a and a null pointer. The (reversed) string is thus afla. There is no need for the decoder to do any hashing or to use the index fields.

The last point to discuss is string reversal. Two commonly used approaches are outlined here:

1. Use a stack. A stack is a common data structure in modern computers. It is an array in memory that is accessed at one end only. At any time, the item that was last pushed into the stack will be the first one to be popped out (last-in-first-out, or LIFO). Symbols retrieved from the dictionary are pushed into the stack. When the last one

has been retrieved and pushed, the stack is popped, symbol by symbol, into variable J. When the stack is empty, the entire string has been reversed. This is a common way to reverse a string.

2. Retrieve symbols from the dictionary and concatenate them into J *from right to left*. When done, the string will be stored in J in the right order. Variable J must be long enough to accommodate the longest possible string, but then it has to be long enough even when a stack is used.

### 2.4.3 LZW in Practice

The 1984 publication of the LZW algorithm has strongly affected the data compression community and has influenced many to come up with implementations and variants of this method. Some of the most important LZW spin-offs are described in [Salomon 00].

> [Ramsay] MacDonald has the gift of compressing the largest amount of words into the smallest amount of thoughts.
>
> —Winston Churchill

## 2.5 Summary

The dictionary-based methods presented here are different but are based on the same principle. They read the input file symbol by symbol and add phrases to the dictionary. The phrases are symbols or strings of symbols from the input. The main difference between the methods is in deciding what phrases to add to the dictionary. When a string in the input file matches a dictionary phrase, the encoder outputs the position of the match in the dictionary. If that position requires fewer bits than the matched string, compression results.

In general, dictionary-based methods, when carefully implemented, give better compression than statistical methods. This is why many popular compression programs are dictionary based or involve a dictionary as one of several compression steps. More dictionary-based methods can be found in [Salomon 00].

> Luckily, he went on, you have come to exactly the right place with your interesting problem, for there is no such word as "impossible" in my dictionary. In fact, he added, brandishing the abused book, everything between "herring" and "marmalade" appears to be missing.
>
> Douglas Adams, *Dirk Gently's Holistic Detective Agency*

# 3
# Image Compression

The modern field of data compression is vast, encompassing many methods and approaches for the compression of different types of data, such as text, images, video, and audio. Of these types, image compression is special because (1) it was the first field where users routinely had large files that needed efficient compression and (2) it was the first field that allowed the development of *lossy* compression methods.

In ASCII, each character occupies one byte. A typical book of a quarter of a million words may consist of about a million characters and therefore occupies about 1 MB. However, if one image is added to the book, its size may double, since the image file may easily be 1 MM or even bigger.

Image files tend to be large because an image is two-dimensional and because present-day displays can handle many colors, requiring each dot (pixel) in the image to be represented by many (typically 24) bits.

Text compression is always lossless. There may be documents where some of the text is unimportant and may be omitted during compression, but no algorithms exist that allow a computer to independently decide what text can be dropped. In contrast, there are many efficient lossy algorithms for image compression. Such an algorithm may delete much image information when the image is compressed, thereby resulting in excellent compression. The test for the performance of such an algorithm is for a person to visually compare the original image to its decompressed (lossy) version. If the person cannot tell which is which, the lossy compression is acceptable. Sometimes a person can tell the difference but may still judge the decompressed image acceptable.

The discussion of image compression in this chapter is mostly general. Most of the chapter describes approaches to image compression. Of the few specific methods that are included, the most important one is JPEG (Section 3.7).

## 3.1 Introduction

Modern computers employ graphics extensively. Window-based operating systems display the disk's file directory graphically. The progress of many system operations, such as downloading a file, may also be displayed graphically. Many applications provide a graphical user interface (GUI), which makes it easier to use the program and to interpret displayed results. Computer graphics is used in many areas in everyday life to convert many types of complex information to images. Images are therefore important, but they tend to be big! Since modern hardware can display many colors, it is common to have a pixel represented internally as a 24-bit number, where the percentages of red, green, and blue occupy 8 bits each. Such a 24-bit pixel can specify one of $2^{24} \approx 16.78$ million colors. Thus, an image at a resolution of $512 \times 512$ that consists of such pixels occupies 786,432 bytes. At a resolution of $1024 \times 1024$ it becomes four times as big, requiring 3,145,728 bytes. Movies are also commonly used in computers, making for even bigger images. This is why image compression is so important. An important feature of image compression is that it can be lossy. An image, after all, exists for people to look at, so, when it is compressed, it is acceptable to lose image features to which the human eye is not sensitive. This is one of the main ideas behind the many lossy image compression methods developed in the past three decades.

In general, information can be compressed if it is redundant. It has been mentioned several times that data compression amounts to reducing or removing redundancy in the data. With lossy compression, however, we have a new concept, namely, compressing by removing *irrelevancy*. An image can be lossy-compressed by removing irrelevant information even if the original image does not have any redundancy.

Notice that an image with no redundancy is not necessarily random. Page 2 discusses two types of image redundancy, the more important of which is pixel correlation. In rare cases, an image may have little or no correlation between its pixels and yet be nonrandom and even interesting.

The idea of losing image information becomes more palatable when we consider how digital images are created. Here are three examples: (1) A real-life image may be scanned from a photograph or a painting and digitized (converted to pixels); (2) an image may be recorded by a video camera that creates pixels and stores them directly in memory; (3) an image may be painted on the screen by means of a paint program. In all these cases, some information is lost when the image is digitized. The fact that the viewer is willing to accept this loss suggests that further loss of information might be tolerable if done properly.

(Digitizing an image involves two steps, sampling and quantization. Sampling is dividing the two-dimensional original image into small regions: pixels. Quantization is the process of assigning an integer value to each pixel. Notice that digitizing sound involves the same two steps, with the difference that sound is one-dimensional.)

Here is a simple process to determine qualitatively the amount of data loss in a compressed image. Given an image $A$, (1) compress it to $B$, (2) decompress $B$ to $C$, and (3) subtract $D = C - A$. If $A$ was compressed without any loss and decompressed properly, then $C$ should be identical to $A$ and image $D$ should be uniformly white. The more data was lost in the compression, the further will $D$ be from uniformly white.

How should an image be compressed? The main approaches to compression discussed so far are RLE, statistical methods, and dictionary-based methods. We have implicitly assumed that these approaches can be applied to the compression of any type of data, but we know from experience that they do a better job when applied to text. This is why new methods have to be developed that take into account the three main differences between text and images:

1. Text is one-dimensional while an image is two-dimensional. An entire text file may be considered one long row of symbols. Each character of text has two neighbors, on its left and right, and there is very little correlation between the neighbors. In this paragraph, for example, the letter "i" is preceded by "d," "s," "h," "t," "f," and others, and it is followed by "m," "o," "l," "r," "d," and others. In other paragraphs, the same "i" may have different neighbors. In an image, a pixel has four immediate neighbors and eight near neighbors (except the pixels on the edges of the image; see Figure 3.1, where the near neighbors of pixel "*" are shown in black) and there is strong correlation between them.

2. Text consists of a relatively small number of symbols. These are normally the 128 ASCII characters or the 256 8-bit bytes. In contrast, each pixel in an image may be represented by 24 bits, so there can be up to $2^{24} \approx 16.78$ different pixels. The number of elementary "symbols" in an image may therefore be very large.

3. There is no known algorithm to determine what parts of any given text are unimportant or irrelevant and can be deleted, but there are ways to automatically delete unimportant image information and thereby achieve high compression factors.

**Figure 3.1:** Four Immediate and Eight Near Neighbors of a Pixel.

Text compression methods are therefore unsatisfactory for image compression, which is why this chapter discusses novel approaches. These approaches are all different, but they remove redundancy from an image by using the following principle:

**The Principle of Image Compression**. If we select a pixel in the image at random, there is a good chance that its near neighbors will have the same color or very similar colors.

Image compression is therefore based on the fact that neighboring pixels are *highly correlated*. This correlation is also called *spatial redundancy*.

Here is a simple example that illustrates what can be done with correlated pixels. The following sequence of values gives the intensities of 24 adjacent pixels in a row of a continuous-tone image:

12, 17, 14, 19, 21, 26, 23, 29, 41, 38, 31, 44, 46, 57, 53, 50, 60, 58, 55, 54, 52, 51, 56, 60.

Only two of the 24 pixels are identical. Their average value is 40.3. Subtracting pairs of adjacent pixels results in the sequence

12, 5, −3, 5, 2, 4, −3, 6, 11, −3, −7, 13, 4, 11, −4, −3, 10, −2, −3, 1, −2, −1, 5, 4.

The two sequences are illustrated graphically in Figure 3.2.

**Figure 3.2:** Values and Differences of 24 Adjacent Pixels.

The sequence of difference values has three properties that illustrate its compression potential: (1) The difference values are smaller than the original pixel values. Their average is 2.58. (2) They repeat. There are just 15 distinct difference values, so in principle they can be coded by 4 bits each. (3) They are *decorrelated*: adjacent difference values tend to be different. This can be seen by subtracting them, which results in the sequence of 24 second differences

12, −7, −8, 8, −3, 2, −7, 9, 5, −14, −4, 20, −11, 7, −15, 1, 13, −12, −1, 4, −3, 1, 6, 1.

They are larger than the differences themselves.

Figure 3.3 provides another illustration of the meaning of the words "correlated quantities." A $32 \times 32$ matrix $A$ is constructed of random numbers, and its elements are displayed in part (a) as shaded squares. The random nature of the elements is obvious. The matrix is then inverted and stored in $B$, which is shown in part (b). This time, there seems to be more structure to the $32 \times 32$ squares. A direct calculation using the Pearson correlation coefficient of Equation (3.1) shows that the cross-correlation between the top two rows of $A$ is the small value 0.0412, whereas the cross-correlation between the top two rows of $B$ is the large value $-0.9831$. The elements of $B$ are correlated since each depends on *all* the elements of $A$

$$R = \frac{n \sum x_i y_i - \sum x_i \sum y_i}{\sqrt{[n \sum x_i^2 - (\sum x_i)^2][n \sum y_i^2 - (\sum y_i)^2]}}. \qquad (3.1)$$

**Example:** Mathematical software is used in this example to illustrate the covariance matrices of (1) a matrix with correlated values and (2) a matrix with decorrelated values. Figure 3.4 shows two 32×32 matrices. The first one, $a$, has random (and therefore decorrelated) values and the second one, $b$, is its inverse (and therefore with correlated values). Their covariance matrices are also shown, and it is obvious that matrix cov($a$)

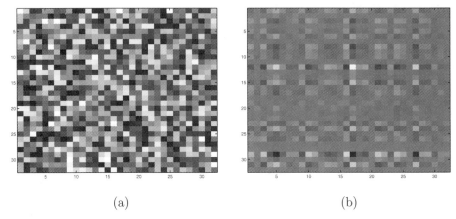

(a)                                                              (b)

**Figure 3.3:** Maps of (a) a Random Matrix and (b) Its Inverse.

```
n=32; a=rand(n); imagesc(a); colormap(gray)
b=inv(a); imagesc(b)
```

Matlab Code for Figure 3.3.

is close to diagonal (the off-diagonal elements are zero or close to zero), whereas matrix cov($b$) is far from diagonal. The Matlab code for this figure is also given.

Once the concept of correlated quantities is clear, it is easy to answer the question "How can we test the values of pixels after they have been transformed to find out whether they are really decorrelated?" The answer is that if a matrix $M$ contains decorrelated values, the covariance of any of its rows with any of its columns is zero. As a result, the covariance matrix of $M$ is diagonal. The statistical concepts of variance, covariance, and correlation are discussed in any text (elementary or advanced) on statistics.

The principle of image compression has another aspect. We know from experience that the *brightness* of neighboring pixels is also correlated. Two adjacent pixels may have different colors. One may be mostly red and the other mostly green. Yet if the red component of the first is bright, the green component of its neighbor will, in most cases, also be bright. This property can be exploited by converting pixel representations from RGB to three other components, one of which is the brightness, the other two of which (the chromatic components) represent color. One such format (or *color space*) is YCbCr, where Y (the "luminance" component) represents the brightness of a pixel and Cb and Cr define its color. This format is discussed in Section 3.7.1, but its advantage is easy to understand. The eye is sensitive to small changes in brightness but not to small changes in color. Thus, losing information in the Cb and Cr components compresses the image while introducing distortions to which the eye is not sensitive. Losing information in the Y component, on the other hand, is very noticeable to the eye.

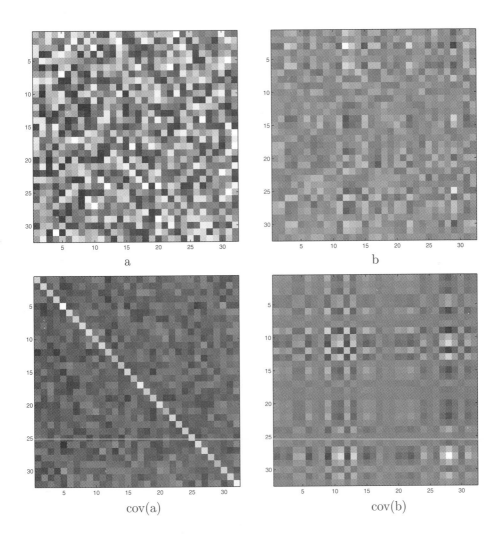

a

b

cov(a)

cov(b)

```
a=rand(32); b=inv(a);
figure(1), imagesc(a), colormap(gray); axis square
figure(2), imagesc(b), colormap(gray); axis square
figure(3), imagesc(cov(a)), colormap(gray); axis square
figure(4), imagesc(cov(b)), colormap(gray); axis square
```

**Figure 3.4:** Covariance Matrices of Correlated and Decorrelated Values.

## 3.2 Image Types

A digital image is a rectangular array of dots, or picture elements, arranged in $m$ rows and $n$ columns. The expression $m \times n$ is called the *resolution* of the image (although sometimes the term *resolution* refers to the number of pixels per unit length of the image), and the dots are called *pixels* (except in the cases of fax images and video compression, where they are referred to as *pels*). For the purpose of image compression it is useful to distinguish the following types of images:

1. *Bi-level* (or monochromatic) image. This is an image where the pixels can have one of two values, normally referred to as black (binary 1, or foreground) and white (binary 0, or background). Each pixel in such an image is represented by 1 bit, so this is the simplest type of image.

2. *Grayscale* image. A pixel in such an image can have one of the $n$ values 0 through $n - 1$, indicating one of $2^n$ shades of gray (or shades of some other color). The value of $n$ is normally compatible with a byte size, i.e., it is 4, 8, 12, 16, 24, or some other convenient multiple of 4 or of 8. The set of the most significant bits of all the pixels is the most significant bitplane. Thus, a grayscale image with $2^n$ shades of gray has $n$ bitplanes.

3. *Color* image. There are various methods for defining colors, but each requires the use of three parameters. Therefore, a color image requires three-part pixels. Currently, it is common to have color images where each pixel consists of three bytes specifying the three parameters of the pixel's color. Typical color models are RGB, HLS, and CMYK. A detailed description of color models is outside the scope of this book, but there is a basic discussion of luminance and chrominance in Section 3.7.1.

4. *Continuous-tone* image. This type of image can have many similar colors (or grayscales). When adjacent pixels differ by just one unit, it is hard or even impossible for the eye to distinguish their colors. As a result, such an image may contain areas with colors that seem to vary continuously as the eye moves along the area. A pixel in such an image is represented by either a single large number (in the case of many grayscales) or by three components (in the case of a color image). A continuous-tone image is normally a natural image (natural as opposed to artificial) and is obtained by taking a photograph with a digital camera or by scanning a photograph or a painting.

5. *Discrete-tone* image (also called a graphical image or a synthetic image). This is normally an artificial image. It may have few colors or many colors, but it does not have the noise and blurring of a natural image. Examples of this type of image are a photograph of an artificial object or machine, a page of text, a chart, a cartoon, and the contents of a computer screen. (Not every artificial image is discrete-tone. A computer-generated image that's meant to look natural is a continuous-tone image in spite of being artificially generated.) Artificial objects, text, and line drawings have sharp, well-defined edges and are therefore highly contrasted from the rest of the image (the background). Adjacent pixels in a discrete-tone image often are either identical or vary significantly in value. Such an image does not compress well with lossy methods, since the loss of just a few pixels may render a letter illegible or change a familiar pattern to an unrecognizable one. Compression methods for continuous-tone images often do not handle the sharp edges of a discrete-tone image very well, so special methods are

needed for efficient compression of these images. Notice that a discrete-tone image may be highly redundant, since the same character or pattern may appear many times in the image.

6. *Cartoon-like* image. This is a color image that consists of uniform areas. Each area has a uniform color but adjacent areas may have very different colors. This feature may be exploited to obtain better compression.

It is intuitively clear that each type of image may feature redundancy, but they are redundant in different ways. This is why any given compression method may not perform well for all images and why different methods are needed to compress the different image types. There are compression methods for bi-level images, for continuous-tone images, and for discrete-tone images. There are also methods that try to break an image up into continuous-tone and discrete-tone parts and compress each separately.

> It's the weird color-scheme that freaks me. Every time you try to operate one of these weird black controls, which are labeled in black on a black background, a small black light lights up black to let you know you've done it!
>
> —Mark Wing-Davey (as Zaphod Beeblebrox) in *The Hitchhiker's Guide to the Galaxy* (1981).

## 3.3 Approaches to Image Compression

An image compression method is normally designed for a specific type of image, and this section lists various approaches to compressing images of different types. Only the general principles are discussed here; specific methods are described later in this chapter and in [Salomon 00].

**Approach 1**: For compressing a bi-level image. A pixel in such an image is represented by one bit. Applying the principle of image compression to a bi-level image therefore means that the immediate neighbors of a pixel $P$ tend to be *identical* to $P$. Thus, it makes sense to use run length encoding (RLE) to compress such an image. A compression method for such an image may scan it in raster order (row by row) and compute the lengths of runs of black and white pixels. The lengths are encoded by variable-size (prefix) codes and are written on the compressed file. An example of such a method is facsimile compression (Section 1.6).

It should be stressed that this is just an approach to bi-level image compression. The details of specific methods vary. For instance, a method may scan the image column by column or in zigzag (Figure 3.5a), it may convert the image to a quadtree, or it may scan it region by region using a space-filling curve (see [Salomon 00] for these techniques).

**Approach 2**: Also for bi-level images. The principle of image compression tells us that the near neighbors of a pixel tend to resemble it. We can extend this principle and conclude that if the current pixel has color $c$ (where $c$ is either black or white), then pixels of the same color seen in the past (and also those that will be found in the future) tend to have the same immediate neighbors.

This approach looks at $n$ of the near neighbors of the current pixel and considers them an $n$-bit number. This number is the *context* of the pixel. In principle there can

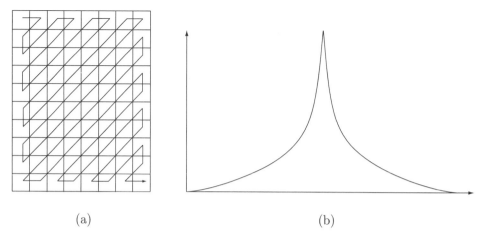

(a) (b)

**Figure 3.5:** (a) Zigzag Scan of an Image. (b) Laplace Distribution.

be $2^n$ contexts, but because of image redundancy we expect them to be distributed in a nonuniform way. Some contexts should be common while the rest will be rare.

The encoder counts how many times each context has already been found for a pixel of color $c$ and assigns probabilities to the contexts accordingly. If the current pixel has color $c$ and its context has probability $p$, the encoder can use adaptive arithmetic coding to encode the pixel with that probability. This approach is used by JBIG [Salomon 00].

Next, we turn to grayscale images. A pixel in such an image is represented by $n$ bits and can have one of $2^n$ values. Applying the principle of image compression to a grayscale image implies that the immediate neighbors of a pixel $P$ tend to be similar to $P$ but are not necessarily identical. Thus, RLE should not be used to compress such an image. Instead, two approaches are discussed.

**Approach 3**: Separate the grayscale image into $n$ bi-level images and compress each with RLE and prefix codes. The principle of image compression seems to imply intuitively that two adjacent pixels that are similar in the grayscale image will be identical in most of the $n$ bi-level images. This, however, is not true, as the following example makes clear. Imagine a grayscale image with $n = 4$ (i.e., 4-bit pixels, or 16 shades of gray). The image can be separated into four bi-level images. If two adjacent pixels in the original grayscale image have values 0000 and 0001, then they are similar. They are also identical in three of the four bi-level images. However, two adjacent pixels with values 0111 and 1000 are also similar in the grayscale image (their values are 7 and 8, respectively) but differ in all four bi-level images.

This problem occurs because the binary codes of adjacent integers may differ by several bits. The binary codes of 0 and 1 differ by one bit, those of 1 and 2 differ by two bits, and those of 7 and 8 differ by four bits. The solution is to design special binary codes where the codes of any consecutive integers $i$ and $i + 1$ will differ by one bit only. An example of such a code is the *reflected Gray codes* of Section 3.3.1.

**Approach 4**: Use the *context* of a pixel to *predict* its value. The context of a pixel consists of the values of some of its neighbors. We can examine some neighbors of a pixel $P$, compute an average $A$ of their values, and predict that $P$ will have the value $A$. The principle of image compression tells us that our prediction will be correct in most cases, almost correct in many cases, and completely wrong in a few cases. We can say that the predicted value of pixel $P$ represents the redundant information in $P$. We now calculate the difference

$$\Delta \overset{\text{def}}{=} P - A$$

and assign variable-size (prefix) codes to the different values of $\Delta$ such that small values (which we expect to be common) are assigned short codes and large values (which are expected to be rare) are assigned long codes. If $P$ can have the values 0 through $m-1$, then values of $\Delta$ are in the range $[-(m-1), +(m-1)]$, and the number of codes needed is $2(m-1)+1$ or $2m-1$.

Experiments with a large number of images suggest that the values of $\Delta$ tend to be distributed according to the Laplace distribution (Figure 3.5b), a well-known statistical distribution. A compression method can, therefore, use this distribution to assign a probability to each value of $\Delta$ and use arithmetic coding to encode the $\Delta$ values very efficiently. This is the principle of the MLP image compression method [Salomon 00].

The context of a pixel may consist of just one or two of its immediate neighbors. However, better results may be obtained when several neighbor pixels are included in the context. The average $A$ in such a case should be weighted, with near neighbors assigned higher weights. Another important consideration is the decoder. In order for it to decode the image, it should be able to calculate the context of every pixel before it decodes that pixel. This means that the context should contain only pixels that have already been encoded. If the image is scanned in raster order (i.e., row by row from top to bottom and each row from left to right), the context should include only pixels located above the current pixel or on the same row and to its left.

**Approach 5**: Transform the values of the pixels, and encode the transformed values. The concept of a transform, as well as the most important transforms used in image compression, are discussed in Section 3.5. Chapter 4 is devoted to the wavelet transform. Recall that compression is achieved by reducing or removing redundancy. The redundancy of an image is caused by the correlation between pixels, so transforming the pixels to a representation where they are *decorrelated* eliminates the redundancy. Quantizing the transformed values can produce efficient lossy image compression. We want the transformed values to be independent because coding independent values makes it simpler to construct a statistical model.

> The best way to predict the future is to create it.
> —Peter Drucker, *Reader's Digest*, August 1997

We now turn to color images. A pixel in such an image consists of three color components, such as red, green, and blue. Most color images are either continuous-tone or discrete-tone.

**Approach 6**: The principle of this approach is to separate a continuous-tone color image into three grayscale images and compress each of the three separately, using approach 2, 3, or 4.

For a continuous-tone image, the principle of image compression implies that adjacent pixels have similar although perhaps not identical colors. However, similar colors do not mean similar pixel values. Consider, for example, 12-bit pixel values where each color component is expressed in 4 bits. Thus, the 12 bits 1000|0100|0000 represent a pixel whose color is a mixture of eight units of red (about 50%, since the maximum is 15 units), four units of green (about 25%), and no blue. Now imagine two adjacent pixels with values 0011|0101|0011 and 0010|0101|0011. They have similar colors, since only their red components differ and only by one unit. However, when considered as 12-bit numbers, the two numbers 001101010011 = 851 and 001001010011 = 595 are very different, since they differ in one of their most significant bits.

An important feature of this approach is to use a luminance chrominance color representation instead of the more common RGB. The concepts of luminance and chrominance are discussed in Section 3.7.1 and in [Salomon 99]. The advantage of the luminance chrominance color representation is that the eye is sensitive to small changes in luminance but not in chrominance. This allows the loss of considerable data in the chrominance components, while making it possible to decode the image without a significant visible loss of quality.

**Approach 7**: A different approach is needed for discrete-tone images. Recall that such an image contains uniform regions, and a region may appear several times in the image. A good example is a screen dump. Such an image consists of text and icons. Each character of text and each icon is a region, and any region may appear several times in the image. A possible way to compress such an image is to scan it, identify regions, and find repeating regions. If a region $B$ is identical to an already found region $A$, then $B$ can be compressed by writing a pointer to $A$ on the compressed file. The block decomposition method (FABD, [Salomon 00]) is an example of how this approach can be implemented.

**Approach 8**: Partition the image into parts (overlapping or not) and compress it by processing the parts one by one. Suppose that the next unprocessed image part is part number 15. Try to match it with parts 1–14 that have already been processed. If part 15 can be expressed, for example, as a combination of parts 5 (scaled) and 11 (rotated), then only the few numbers that specify the combination need be saved, and part 15 can be discarded. If part 15 cannot be expressed as a combination of already processed parts, it is declared processed and is saved in raw format.

This approach is the basis of the various *fractal* methods for image compression. It applies the principle of image compression to image parts instead of to individual pixels. Applied this way, the principle tells us that "interesting" images (i.e., those that are being compressed in practice) have a certain amount of *self-similarity*. Parts of the image are identical or similar to the entire image or to other parts.

Image compression methods are not limited to these basic approaches. [Salomon 00] discusses methods that use the concepts of context trees, Markov models, and wavelets, among others. In addition, the concept of *progressive image compression* (Section 3.6) should be mentioned, since it adds another dimension to the compression of images.

> Art is a technique of communication. The image is the most complete technique of all communication.
>
> —Claes Thure Oldenburg

### 3.3.1 Gray Codes

An image compression method that has been developed specifically for a certain image type can sometimes be used for other types. Any method for compressing bi-level images, for example, can be used to compress grayscale images by separating the bitplanes and compressing each individually, as if it were a bi-level image. Imagine, for example, an image with 16 grayscale values. Each pixel is defined by 4 bits, so the image can be separated into four bi-level images. The trouble with this approach is that it violates the general principle of image compression. Imagine two adjacent 4-bit pixels with values $7 = 0111_2$ and $8 = 1000_2$. These pixels have close values, but when separated into four bitplanes, the resulting 1-bit pixels are different in every bitplane! This is because the binary representations of the consecutive integers 7 and 8 differ in all four bit positions. In order to apply any bi-level compression method to grayscale images, a binary representation of the integers is needed where consecutive integers have codes differing by 1 bit only. Such a representation exists and is called *reflected Gray code* (RGC). This code is easy to generate with the following recursive construction.

Start with the two 1-bit codes $(0, 1)$. Construct two sets of 2-bit codes by duplicating $(0, 1)$ and appending, either on the left or on the right, first a zero, then a one, to the original set. The result is $(00, 01)$ and $(10, 11)$. We now reverse (reflect) the second set and concatenate the two. The result is the 2-bit RGC $(00, 01, 11, 10)$, a binary code of the integers 0 through 3 where consecutive codes differ by exactly one bit. Applying the rule again produces the two sets $(000, 001, 011, 010)$ and $(110, 111, 101, 100)$, which are concatenated to form the 3-bit RGC. Note that the first and last codes of any RGC also differ by one bit. Here are the first three steps for computing the 4-bit RGC:

$$\text{Add a zero } (0000, 0001, 0011, 0010, 0110, 0111, 0101, 0100),$$
$$\text{Add a one } (1000, 1001, 1011, 1010, 1110, 1111, 1101, 1100),$$
$$\text{reflect } (1100, 1101, 1111, 1110, 1010, 1011, 1001, 1000).$$

Table 3.6 shows how individual bits change when moving through the binary codes of the first 32 integers. The 5-bit binary codes of these integers are listed in the odd-numbered columns of the table, with the bits of integer $i$ that differ from those of $i - 1$ shown in boldface. It is easy to see that the least-significant bit (bit $b_0$) changes all the time, bit $b_1$ changes every other number, and, in general, bit $b_k$ changes every $k$ integers. The even-numbered columns list one of the several possible reflected Gray codes for these integers. The table also lists a recursive Matlab function to compute RGC.

It is also possible to generate the reflected Gray code of an integer $n$ with the following nonrecursive rule: Exclusive-OR $n$ with a copy of itself that's logically shifted one position to the right. In the C programming language this is denoted by n^(n>>1). Table 3.7 (similar to Table 3.6) was generated by this expression.

The conclusion is that the most significant bitplanes of an image obey the principle of image compression more than the least significant ones. When adjacent pixels have values that differ by one unit (such as $p$ and $p+1$), chances are that the least significant bits are different and the most significant ones are identical. Any image compression

| 43210 | Gray | 43210 | Gray | 43210 | Gray | 43210 | Gray |
|-------|------|-------|------|-------|------|-------|------|
| 00000 | 00000 | 01000 | 10010 | 10000 | 00011 | 11000 | 10001 |
| 00001 | 00100 | 01001 | 10110 | 10001 | 00111 | 11001 | 10101 |
| 00010 | 01100 | 01010 | 11110 | 10010 | 01111 | 11010 | 11101 |
| 00011 | 01000 | 01011 | 11010 | 10011 | 01011 | 11011 | 11001 |
| 00100 | 11000 | 01100 | 01010 | 10100 | 11011 | 11100 | 01001 |
| 00101 | 11100 | 01101 | 01110 | 10101 | 11111 | 11101 | 01101 |
| 00110 | 10100 | 01110 | 00110 | 10110 | 10111 | 11110 | 00101 |
| 00111 | 10000 | 01111 | 00010 | 10111 | 10011 | 11111 | 00001 |

```
function b=rgc(a,i)
[r,c]=size(a);
b=[zeros(r,1),a; ones(r,1),flipud(a)];
if i>1, b=rgc(b,i-1); end;
```

**Table 3.6:** First 32 Binary and Reflected Gray Codes.

| 43210 | Gray | 43210 | Gray | 43210 | Gray | 43210 | Gray |
|-------|------|-------|------|-------|------|-------|------|
| 00000 | 00000 | 01000 | 01100 | 10000 | 11000 | 11000 | 10100 |
| 00001 | 00001 | 01001 | 01101 | 10001 | 11001 | 11001 | 10101 |
| 00010 | 00011 | 01010 | 01111 | 10010 | 11011 | 11010 | 10111 |
| 00011 | 00010 | 01011 | 01110 | 10011 | 11010 | 11011 | 10110 |
| 00100 | 00110 | 01100 | 01010 | 10100 | 11110 | 11100 | 10010 |
| 00101 | 00111 | 01101 | 01011 | 10101 | 11111 | 11101 | 10011 |
| 00110 | 00101 | 01110 | 01001 | 10110 | 11101 | 11110 | 10001 |
| 00111 | 00100 | 01111 | 01000 | 10111 | 11100 | 11111 | 10000 |

```
a=linspace(0,31,32); b=bitshift(a,-1);
b=bitxor(a,b); dec2bin(b)
```

**Table 3.7:** First 32 Binary and Gray Codes.

method that compresses bitplanes individually should therefore treat the least significant bitplanes differently from the most significant ones, or should use RGC instead of the binary code to represent pixels. Figures 3.10, 3.11, and 3.12 (prepared by the Matlab code of Figure 3.8) show the eight bitplanes of the well-known "parrots" image in both the binary code (the left column) and in RGC (the right column). The bitplanes are numbered 8 (the leftmost or most significant bits) through 1 (the rightmost or least significant bits). It is obvious that the least significant bitplane doesn't show any correlations between the pixels; it is random or very close to random in both binary and RGC. Bitplanes 2 through 5, however, exhibit better pixel correlation in the Gray code. Bitplanes 6 through 8 look different in Gray code and binary but seem to be highly correlated in either representation.

```
clear;                                clear;
filename='parrots128'; dim=128;       filename='parrots128'; dim=128;
fid=fopen(filename,'r');              fid=fopen(filename,'r');
img=fread(fid,[dim,dim])';            img=fread(fid,[dim,dim])';
mask=1; % between 1 and 8             mask=1 % between 1 and 8
                                      a=bitshift(img,-1);
                                      b=bitxor(img,a);
nimg=bitget(img,mask);               nimg=bitget(b,mask);
imagesc(nimg), colormap(gray)        imagesc(nimg), colormap(gray)
```

           Binary code                            Gray Code

**Figure 3.8:** Matlab Code to Separate Image Bitplanes.

Figure 3.13 is a graphic representation of two versions of the first 32 reflected
Gray codes. Part (b) shows the codes of Table 3.6, and part (c) shows the codes of
Table 3.9. Even though both are Gray codes, they differ in the way the bits in each
bitplane alternate between 0 and 1. In part (b), the bits of the most significant bitplane
alternate four times between 0 and 1. Those of the second most significant bitplane
alternate eight times between 0 and 1, and the bits of the remaining three bitplanes
alternate 16, 2, and 1 times between 0 and 1. When the bitplanes are separated, the
middle bitplane features the smallest correlation between the pixels, since the Gray
codes of adjacent integers tend to have different bits in this bitplane. The Gray codes
shown in Figure 3.13c, on the other hand, alternate more and more between 0 and 1
as we move from the most significant bitplanes to the least significant ones. The least
significant bitplanes of this version feature less and less correlation between the pixels
and therefore tend to be random. For comparison, Figure 3.13a shows the binary code.
It is obvious that bits in this code alternate more often between 0 and 1.

| 43210 | Gray | 43210 | Gray | 43210 | Gray | 43210 | Gray |
|-------|-------|-------|-------|-------|-------|-------|-------|
| 00000 | 00000 | 01000 | 01100 | 10000 | 11000 | 11000 | 10100 |
| 00001 | 00001 | 01001 | 01101 | 10001 | 11001 | 11001 | 10101 |
| 00010 | 00011 | 01010 | 01111 | 10010 | 11011 | 11010 | 10111 |
| 00011 | 00010 | 01011 | 01110 | 10011 | 11010 | 11011 | 10110 |
| 00100 | 00110 | 01100 | 01010 | 10100 | 11110 | 11100 | 10010 |
| 00101 | 00111 | 01101 | 01011 | 10101 | 11111 | 11101 | 10011 |
| 00110 | 00101 | 01110 | 01001 | 10110 | 11101 | 11110 | 10001 |
| 00111 | 00100 | 01111 | 01000 | 10111 | 11100 | 11111 | 10000 |

```
a=linspace(0,31,32); b=bitshift(a,-1);
b=bitxor(a,b); dec2bin(b)
```

**Table 3.9:** First 32 Binary and Gray Codes.

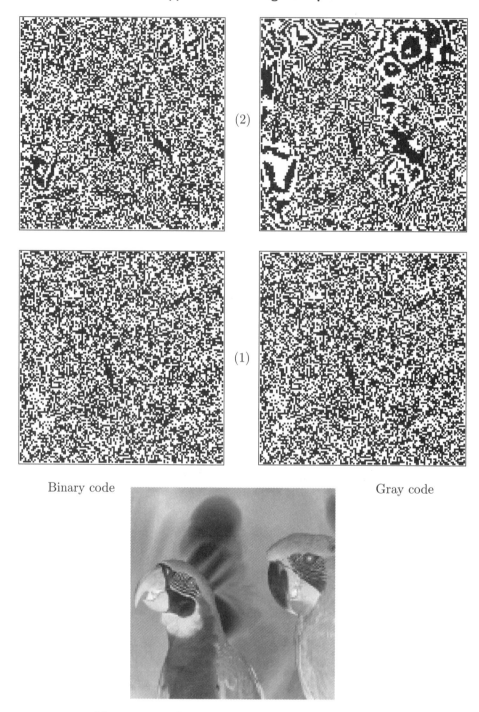

**Figure 3.10:** Bitplanes 1 and 2 of the Parrots Image.

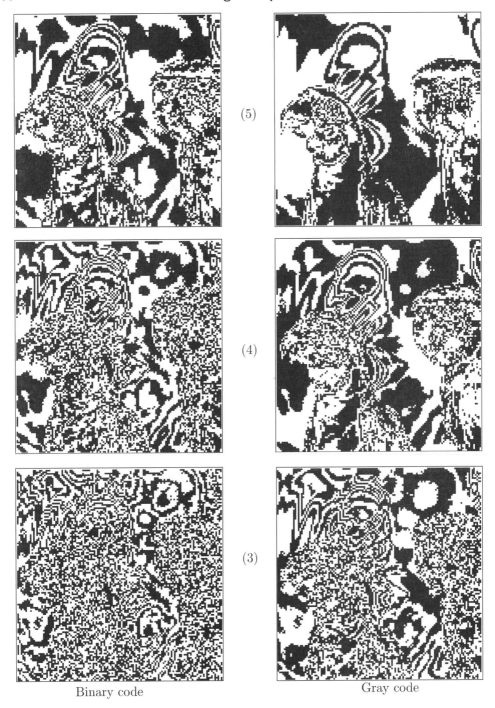

Binary code                                        Gray code

**Figure 3.11:** Bitplanes 3, 4, and 5 of the Parrots Image.

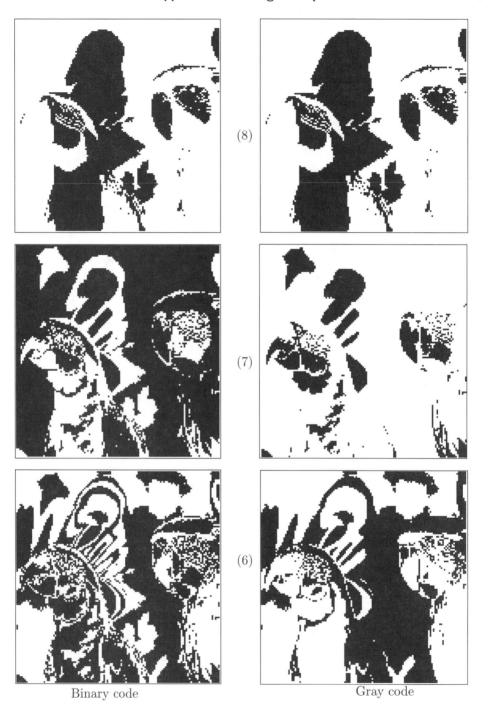

(8)

(7)

(6)

Binary code　　　　　　　　　　Gray code

**Figure 3.12:** Bitplanes 6, 7, and 8 of the Parrots Image.

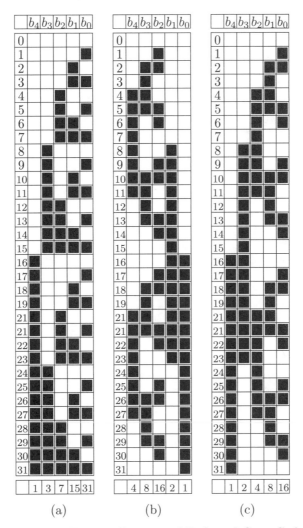

**Table 3.13:** First 32 Binary and Reflected Gray Codes.

> The binary Gray code is fun,
> For in it strange things can be done.
> Fifteen, as you know,
> Is one, oh, oh, oh,
> And ten is one, one, one, one.
>                                    —Anonymous

Even a cursory look at the Gray codes of Figure 3.13c shows that they exhibit some regularity. A careful examination of these codes identifies two features that may be used to calculate the codes. One feature is the regular way in which each of the five code bits alternates periodically between 0 and 1. It is easy to write a program that will set all five bits to 0, will flip the rightmost bit after two codes have been calculated, and will flip any of the other four code bits in the middle of the period of its immediate neighbor on the right. The other feature is the fact that the second half of the table is a mirror image of the first half, but with the most significant bit set to one. After the first half of the table has been computed, using any method, this symmetry can be used to quickly calculate the second half.

Figure 3.14 is an *angular code wheel* representation of the 4 and 6-bit RGC codes (part a) and the 4- and 6-bit binary codes (part b). The individual bitplanes are shown as rings, with the most significant bits as the innermost ring. It is easy to see that the maximum angular frequency of the RGC is half that of the binary code. Such a circular representation of the RGC is possible because the first and last codes of any RCG code sequence also differ by one bit only.

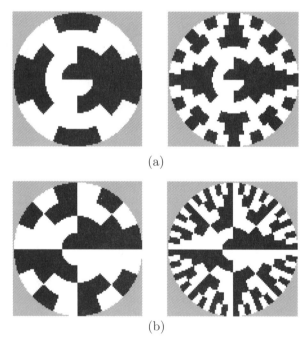

(a)

(b)

**Figure 3.14:** Angular Code Wheels of RGC and Binary Codes.

Color images provide another example of using the same compression method across image types. Any compression method for grayscale images can be used to compress color images. In a color image, each pixel is represented by three color components (such as RGB). Imagine a color image where each color component is represented by one byte. A pixel is represented by three bytes, or 24 bits, but these bits should not be considered a single number. The two pixels 118|206|12 and 117|206|12 differ by just one unit in the first component, so they have very similar colors. Considered as 24-bit numbers, however, these pixels are very different, since they differ in one of their most-significant bits. Any compression method that treats these pixels as 24-bit numbers would consider these pixels very different, and its performance would suffer as a result. A compression method for grayscale images can be applied to compressing color images, but the color image should first be separated into three color components and each component compressed individually as a grayscale image.

The context-tree weighting method for images ([Salomon 00] and [Ekstrand 96]) is an example of the use of RGC for image compression.

---

### History of Gray Codes

Gray codes are named after Frank Gray, who patented their use for shaft encoders in 1953 [Gray 53]. However, the work was performed much earlier; the patent was applied for in 1947. Gray was a researcher at Bell Telephone Laboratories. During the 1930s and 1940s he was awarded numerous patents for work related to television. According to [Heath 72] the code was, in fact, first used by J. M. E. Baudot for telegraphy in the 1870s, although it is only since the advent of computers that the code has become widely known.

The Baudot code uses five bits per symbol. It can represent $32 \times 2 - 2 = 62$ characters (each code can have two meanings, the meaning being indicated by the LS and FS codes). It became popular and, by 1950, was designated the International Telegraph Code No. 1. It was used by many first- and second-generation computers.

The August 1972 issue of *Scientific American* contains two articles of interest, one on the origin of binary codes [Heath 72] and another [Gardner 72] on some entertaining aspects of the Gray codes.

---

### 3.3.2 Error Metrics

Developers and implementers of lossy image compression methods need a standard metric to measure the quality of reconstructed images compared with the original ones. The better a reconstructed image resembles the original one, the bigger should be the value produced by this metric (which suggests that "similarity metric" may be a more appropriate name). Such a metric should also produce a dimensionless number, and that number should not be very sensitive to small variations in the reconstructed image. A common measure used for this purpose is the *peak signal to noise ratio* (PSNR). It is familiar to workers in the field, it is also simple to calculate, but it has only a limited, approximate relationship with the perceived errors noticed by the human visual system. This is why higher PSNR values imply closer resemblance between the reconstructed and the original images, but they do not provide a guarantee that viewers will like the reconstructed image.

Denoting the pixels of the original image by $P_i$ and the pixels of the reconstructed image by $Q_i$ (where $1 \le i \le n$), we first define the *mean square error* (MSE) between the two images as

$$\text{MSE} = \frac{1}{n} \sum_{i=1}^{n} (P_i - Q_i)^2. \tag{3.2}$$

It is the average of the square of the errors (pixel differences) of the two images. The *root mean square error* (RMSE) is defined as the square root of the MSE, and the PSNR is defined as

$$\text{PSNR} = 20 \log_{10} \frac{\max_i |P_i|}{\text{RMSE}}.$$

The absolute value is normally not needed, since pixel values are rarely negative. For a bi-level image, the numerator is 1. For a grayscale image with 8 bits per pixel, the numerator is 255. For color images, only the luminance component is used.

Greater resemblance between the images implies smaller RMSE and, as a result, larger PSNR. The PNSR is dimensionless, since the units of both numerator and denominator are pixel values. However, because of the use of the logarithm, we say that the PSNR is expressed in *decibels* (dB, Section 6.1). The use of the logarithm also implies less sensitivity to changes in the RMSE. For example, dividing the RMSE by 10 multiplies the PSNR by 2. Notice that the PSNR has no absolute meaning. It is meaningless to say that a PSNR of, say, 25 is good. PSNR values are used only to compare the performance of different lossy compression methods or the effects of different parametric values on the performance of an algorithm. The MPEG committee, for example, uses an informal threshold of PSNR $= 0.5$ dB to decide whether to incorporate a coding optimization, since they believe that an improvement of that magnitude would be visible to the eye.

Typical PSNR values range between 20 and 40. Assuming pixel values in the range $[0, 255]$, an RMSE of 25.5 results in a PSNR of 20, and an RMSE of 2.55 results in a PSNR of 40. An RMSE of zero (i.e., identical images) results in an infinite (or, more precisely, undefined) PSNR. An RMSE of 255 results in a PSNR of zero, and RMSE values greater than 255 yield negative PSNRs.

The reader may find it useful to answer the following: If the maximum pixel value is 255, can RMSE values be greater than 255? The answer is no. If pixel values are in the range $[0, 255]$, a difference $(P_i - Q_i)$ can be at most 255. The worst case is where all the differences are 255. It is easy to see that such a case yields an RMSE of 255.

Some authors define the PSNR as

$$\text{PSNR} = 10 \log_{10} \frac{\max_i |P_i|^2}{\text{MSE}}.$$

In order for the two formulations to produce the same result, the logarithm is multiplied in this case by 10 instead of by 20, since $\log_{10} A^2 = 2 \log_{10} A$. Either definition is useful, because only relative PSNR values are used in practice.

A related measure is *signal to noise ratio* (SNR). This is defined as (the numerator is the root mean square of the original image)

$$\text{SNR} = 20 \log_{10} \frac{\sqrt{\frac{1}{n} \sum_{i=1}^{n} P_i^2}}{\text{RMSE}}.$$

Figure 3.15 is a Matlab function to compute the PSNR of two images. A typical call is PSNR(A,B), where A and B are image files. They must have the same resolution and have pixel values in the range $[0, 1]$.

```
function PSNR(A,B)
if A==B
 error('Images are identical; PSNR is undefined')
end
max2_A=max(max(A)); max2_B=max(max(B));
min2_A=min(min(A)); min2_B=min(min(B));
if max2_A>1 | max2_B>1 | min2_A<0 | min2_B<0
   error('pixels must be in [0,1]')
end
differ=A-B;
decib=20*log10(1/(sqrt(mean(mean(differ.^2)))));
disp(sprintf('PSNR = +%5.2f dB',decib))
```

**Figure 3.15:** A Matlab Function to Compute PSNR.

Another cousin of the PSNR is the *signal to quantization noise ratio* (SQNR). This is a measure of the effect of quantization on signal quality. It is defined as

$$SQNR = 10 \log_{10} \frac{\text{signal power}}{\text{quantization error}},$$

where the quantization error is the difference between the quantized signal and the original signal.

Another approach to the comparison of an original and a reconstructed image is to generate the difference image and judge it visually. Intuitively, the difference image is $D_i = P_i - Q_i$, but such an image is hard to judge visually because its pixel values $D_i$ tend to be small numbers. If a pixel value of zero represents white, such a difference image would be almost invisible. In the opposite case, where pixel values of zero represent black, such a difference would be too dark to judge. Better results are obtained by calculating

$$D_i = a(P_i - Q_i) + b,$$

where $a$ is a magnification parameter (typically a small number such as 2) and $b$ is half the maximum value of a pixel (typically 128). Parameter $a$ serves to magnify small differences, while $b$ shifts the difference image from extreme white (or extreme black) to a more comfortable gray.

## 3.4 Intuitive Methods

It is easy to come up with simple, intuitive methods for compressing images. They are included here for the purpose of illustration, since much more sophisticated (and efficient) methods are used in practice.

### 3.4.1 Subsampling

Subsampling is perhaps the simplest way to compress an image. One approach to subsampling is simply to ignore some of the pixels. The encoder may, for example, ignore every other row and every other column of the image and write the remaining pixels (which constitute 25% of the image) on the compressed file. The decoder inputs the compressed data and uses each pixel to generate four identical pixels of the reconstructed image. This, of course, involves the loss of much image detail and is rarely acceptable. Notice that the compression ratio is known in advance.

A slight improvement is achieved when the encoder calculates the average of each block of four pixels and writes this average on the compressed file. No pixel is totally ignored, but the method is still primitive, since a good lossy image compression method should lose data to which the eye is not sensitive.

Better results (but worse compression) are obtained when the color representation of the image is transformed from the original (normally RGB) to luminance and chrominance. The encoder subsamples the two chrominance components of a pixel but not its luminance component. Assuming that each component uses the same number of bits, the two chrominance components make up 2/3 of the image size. Subsampling them reduces this to 25% of 2/3, or 1/6. The size of the compressed image is thus 1/3 (for the uncompressed luminance component) plus 1/6 (for the two chrominance components) or 1/2 of the original size.

### 3.4.2 Quantization

The term "quantization" as used in data compression means to truncate a real value to an integer or to transform an integer to a smaller integer. There are two types of quantization, scalar and vector. The former is an intuitive, lossy method where the information that's lost is not necessarily the least important. The latter can obtain better results, and an intuitive version of it is described here.

The image is partitioned into equal-size blocks (called *vectors*) of pixels, and the encoder has a list (called a *codebook*) of blocks of the same size. Each image block $B$ is compared to all the blocks of the codebook and is matched with the "closest" one. If $B$ is matched with codebook block $C$, then the encoder writes a pointer to $C$ on the compressed file. If the pointer is smaller than the block size, compression is achieved. Figure 3.16 shows an example.

The details of selecting and maintaining the codebook and of matching blocks are discussed in [Salomon 00], with an algorithm described in [Linde et al. 80]. Notice that vector quantization is a method where the compression ratio is known in advance.

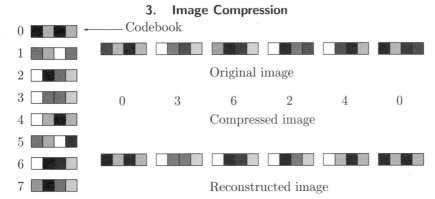

**Figure 3.16:** Intuitive Vector Quantization.

## 3.5 Image Transforms

The concept of a transform is familiar to mathematicians. It is a standard mathematical tool used to solve problems in many areas. The idea is to change a mathematical quantity (a number, a vector, a function, or anything else) to another form, where it may look unfamiliar but may exhibit useful features. The transformed quantity is used to solve a problem or to perform a calculation, and the result is then transformed back to the original form.

A simple, illustrative example of how a transform can be useful is arithmetic operations on Roman numerals. The ancient Romans presumably knew how to operate on such numbers, but when we have to, say, multiply two Roman numerals, we may find it more convenient to transform them into modern (Arabic) notation, multiply, then transform the result back into a Roman numeral. Here is a simple example:

$$\text{XCVI} \times \text{XII} \to 96 \times 12 = 1152 \to \text{MCLII}.$$

An image can be compressed by transforming its pixels (which are correlated) to a representation where they are *decorrelated*. Compression is achieved if the new values are smaller, on average, than the original ones. Lossy compression can be achieved by quantizing the transformed values. The decoder inputs the transformed values from the compressed file and reconstructs the (precise or approximate) original data by applying the opposite transform. The transforms discussed in this section are *orthogonal*. Section 4.3 discusses *subband transforms*.

The term *decorrelated* means that the transformed values are independent of one another. As a result, they can be encoded independently, which makes it simpler to construct a statistical model. An image can be compressed if its representation has redundancy. The redundancy in images stems from pixel correlation. If we transform the image to a representation where the pixels are decorrelated, we have eliminated the redundancy and the image has been fully compressed.

We start with a simple example, where we scan an image in raster order and group pairs of adjacent pixels. Because the pixels are correlated, the two pixels $(x, y)$ of a pair normally have similar values. We now consider the pairs of pixels as points in two-dimensional space and plot them. We know that all the points of the form $(x, x)$ are located on the 45° line $y = x$, so we expect our points to be concentrated around this line. Figure 3.17a shows the results of plotting the pixels of a typical image—where a pixel has values in the interval $[0, 255]$—in such a way. Most points form a cloud around this line, and only a few points are located away from it. We now transform the image by rotating all the points $45°$ clockwise about the origin such that the $45°$ line now coincides with the $x$ axis (Figure 3.17b). This is done by the simple transformation

$$(x^*, y^*) = (x, y) \begin{pmatrix} \cos 45° & -\sin 45° \\ \sin 45° & \cos 45° \end{pmatrix} = (x, y) \frac{1}{\sqrt{2}} \begin{pmatrix} 1 & -1 \\ 1 & 1 \end{pmatrix} = (x, y)\mathbf{R}, \qquad (3.3)$$

where the rotation matrix $\mathbf{R}$ is orthonormal (i.e., the dot product of a row with itself is 1, the dot product of different rows is 0, and the same is true for columns). The inverse transformation is

$$(x, y) = (x^*, y^*)\mathbf{R}^{-1} = (x^*, y^*)\mathbf{R}^T = (x^*, y^*) \frac{1}{\sqrt{2}} \begin{pmatrix} 1 & 1 \\ -1 & 1 \end{pmatrix}. \qquad (3.4)$$

(The inverse of an orthonormal matrix is its transpose.)

It is obvious that most points end up having $y$ coordinates that are zero or close to zero, while the $x$ coordinates don't change much. Figure 3.18a,b shows the distributions of the $x$ and $y$ coordinates (i.e., the odd-numbered and even-numbered pixels) of the $128 \times 128 \times 8$ grayscale Lena image before the rotation. It is clear that the two distributions don't differ by much. Figure 3.18c,d shows that the distribution of the $x$ coordinates stays about the same (with greater variance) but the $y$ coordinates are concentrated around zero. The Matlab code that generated these results is also shown. (Figure 3.18d shows that the $y$ coordinates are concentrated around 100, but this is because a few were as small as $-101$, so they had to be scaled by 101 to fit in a Matlab array, which always starts at index 1.)

Once the coordinates of points are known before and after the rotation, it is easy to measure the reduction in correlation. A simple measure is the sum $\sum_i x_i y_i$, also called the *cross-correlation* of points $(x_i, y_i)$.

Here is an example that illustrates the meaning of this term. Given the five points $(5, 5)$, $(6, 7)$, $(12.1, 13.2)$, $(23, 25)$, and $(32, 29)$, we rotate them $45°$ clockwise and calculate their cross-correlations before and after the rotation. The code of Figure 3.19 yields the coordinates of the rotated points

$$(7.071, 0), (9.19, 0.7071), (17.9, 0.78), (33.9, 1.41), (43.13, -2.12)$$

(notice how all the $y$ coordinates are small numbers) and shows that the cross-correlation drops from 1729.72 before the rotation to $-23.0846$ after it. A significant reduction!

We can now compress the image by simply writing the transformed pixels on the compressed file. If lossy compression is acceptable, then all the pixels can be quantized, resulting in even smaller numbers. We can also write all the odd-numbered pixels (those that make up the $x$ coordinates of the pairs) on the compressed file, followed by all the even-numbered pixels. These two sequences are called the *coefficient vectors* of the transform. The latter sequence consists of small numbers and may, after quantization, have runs of zeros, resulting in even better compression.

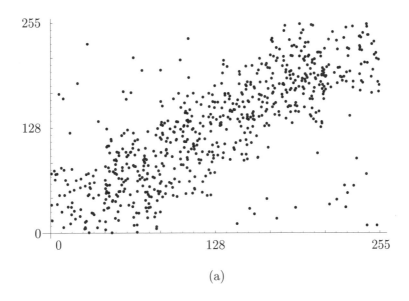

(a)

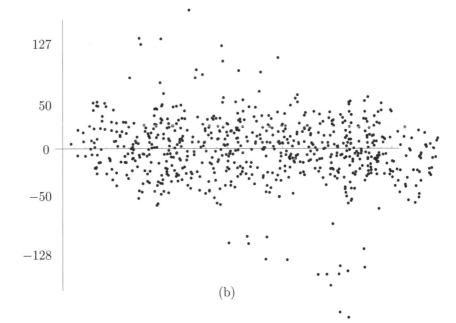

(b)

**Figure 3.17:** Rotating a Cloud of Points.

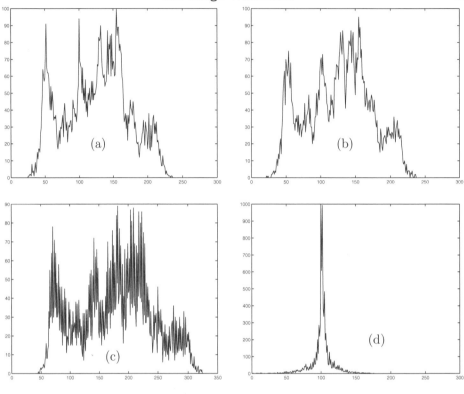

```
filename='lena128'; dim=128;
xdist=zeros(256,1); ydist=zeros(256,1);
fid=fopen(filename,'r');
img=fread(fid,[dim,dim])';
for col=1:2:dim-1
 for row=1:dim
  x=img(row,col)+1; y=img(row,col+1)+1;
  xdist(x)=xdist(x)+1; ydist(y)=ydist(y)+1;
 end
end
figure(1), plot(xdist), colormap(gray) %dist of x&y values
figure(2), plot(ydist), colormap(gray) %before rotation
xdist=zeros(325,1); % clear arrays
ydist=zeros(256,1);
for col=1:2:dim-1
 for row=1:dim
  x=round((img(row,col)+img(row,col+1))*0.7071);
  y=round((-img(row,col)+img(row,col+1))*0.7071)+101;
  xdist(x)=xdist(x)+1; ydist(y)=ydist(y)+1;
 end
end
figure(3), plot(xdist), colormap(gray) %dist of x&y values
figure(4), plot(ydist), colormap(gray) %after rotation
```

**Figure 3.18:** Distribution of Image Pixels before and after Rotation.

```
p={{5,5},{6, 7},{12.1,13.2},{23,25},{32,29}};
rot={{0.7071,-0.7071},{0.7071,0.7071}};
Sum[p[[i,1]]p[[i,2]], {i,5}]
q=p.rot
Sum[q[[i,1]]q[[i,2]], {i,5}]
```

**Figure 3.19:** Code for Rotating Five Points.

It can be shown that the total variance of the pixels (defined as the sum $\sum_i x_i^2 + y_i^2$) does not change by the rotation, because a rotation matrix is orthonormal. However, since the variance of the new $y$ coordinates is small, most of the variance is now concentrated in the $x$ coordinates. The variance is sometimes called the *energy* of the distribution of pixels, so we can say that the rotation has concentrated (or compacted) the energy in the $x$ coordinate and has created compression this way.

Concentrating the energy in one coordinate has another advantage. It makes it possible to quantize that coordinate more finely than the other coordinates. This type of quantization results in better (lossy) compression.

The following simple example illustrates the power of this basic transform. We start with the point $(4, 5)$, whose two coordinates are similar. Using Equation (3.3) the point is transformed to $(4, 5)\mathbf{R} = (9, 1)/\sqrt{2} \approx (6.36396, 0.7071)$. The energies of the point and its transform are $4^2 + 5^2 = 41 = (9^2 + 1^2)/2$. If we delete the smaller coordinate (4) of the point, we end up with an error of $4^2/41 = 0.39$. If, on the other hand, we delete the smaller of the two transform coefficients (0.7071), the resulting error is just $0.7071^2/41 = 0.012$. Another way to obtain the same error is to consider the reconstructed point. Passing $(9, 1)/\sqrt{2}$ through the inverse transform [Equation (3.4)] results in the original point $(4, 5)$. Doing the same with $(9, 0)/\sqrt{2}$ results in the approximate reconstructed point $(4.5, 4.5)$. The energy difference between the original and reconstructed points is the same small quantity

$$\frac{\left[(4^2 + 5^2) - (4.5^2 + 4.5^2)\right]}{4^2 + 5^2} = \frac{41 - 40.5}{41} = 0.012.$$

This simple transform can easily be extended to any number of dimensions. Instead of selecting pairs of adjacent pixels, we can select triplets. Each triplet becomes a point in three-dimensional space, and these points form a cloud concentrated around the line that forms 45° angles with the three coordinate axes. When this line is rotated such that it coincides with the $x$ axis, the $y$ and $z$ coordinates of the transformed points become small numbers. The transformation is done by multiplying each point by a $3 \times 3$ rotation matrix, and such a matrix is, of course, orthonormal. The transformed points are then separated into three coefficient vectors, of which the last two consist of small numbers. For maximum compression each coefficient vector should be quantized separately.

This can be extended to more than three dimensions, with the only difference being that we cannot visualize spaces of dimensions higher than three. However, the mathematics can easily be extended. An important point is that the number of dimensions should not be too large because the performance of the rotation depends on the correlation between adjacent pixels. If we collect, say, 24 adjacent pixels and consider them a point in 24-dimensional space, that point would generally not be near the "45° line" because there is no correlation between a pixel and its far neighbors. When the point is rotated, its last 23 dimensions will not end up near their corresponding axes, so the last 23 numbers will generally not be small. Experience shows that a pixel is generally correlated with neighbors up to a distance of eight, but rarely further away.

The JPEG method of Section 3.7 divides an image into blocks of $8 \times 8$ pixels each and rotates each block twice by means of Equation (3.9), as shown in Section 3.5.3. This double rotation produces a set of 64 transformed values of which the first—termed the "DC coefficient"—is large and the other 63 (called the "AC coefficients") are normally small. Thus, this transform concentrates the energy in the first of 64 dimensions. The set of DC coefficients and each of the sets of 63 AC coefficients should, in principle, be quantized separately (JPEG does this a little differently, though; see Section 3.7.4).

### 3.5.1 Orthogonal Transforms

Image transforms that are used in practice should be fast and preferably also simple to implement. This suggests the use of *linear transforms*. In such a transform, each transformed value $c_i$ is a weighted sum of the data items (the pixels) $d_j$, where each item is multiplied by a weight (or a transform coefficient) $w_{ij}$. Thus, $c_i = \sum_j d_j w_{ij}$, for $i, j = 1, 2, \ldots, n$. For the case $n = 4$, this is expressed in matrix notation:

$$\begin{pmatrix} c_1 \\ c_2 \\ c_3 \\ c_4 \end{pmatrix} = \begin{pmatrix} w_{11} & w_{12} & w_{13} & w_{14} \\ w_{21} & w_{22} & w_{23} & w_{24} \\ w_{31} & w_{32} & w_{33} & w_{34} \\ w_{41} & w_{42} & w_{43} & w_{44} \end{pmatrix} \begin{pmatrix} d_1 \\ d_2 \\ d_3 \\ d_4 \end{pmatrix}.$$

For the general case, we can write $\mathbf{C} = \mathbf{W} \cdot \mathbf{D}$. Each row of $\mathbf{W}$ is called a "basis vector."

The important issue is the determination of the values of the weights $w_{ij}$. The guiding principle is that we want the first transformed value $c_1$ to be large and the remaining values $c_2$, $c_3, \ldots$ to be small. The basic relation $c_i = \sum_j d_j w_{ij}$ suggests that $c_i$ will be large when each weight $w_{ij}$ reinforces the corresponding data item $d_j$. This happens, for example, when the vectors $w_{ij}$ and $d_j$ have similar values and signs. Conversely, $c_i$ will be small if all the weights $w_{ij}$ are small and half of them have the opposite sign of $d_j$. Thus, when we get a large $c_i$ we know that the basis vector $w_{ij}$ resembles the data vector $d_j$. A small $c_i$, on the other hand, means that $w_{ij}$ and $d_j$ have different shapes. We can therefore interpret the basis vectors $w_{ij}$ as tools to extract features from the data vector.

In practice, the weights should be independent of the data items. Otherwise, the weights would have to be included in the compressed file, for the use of the decoder. This, combined with the fact that our data items are pixel values, which are normally nonnegative, suggests a way to choose the basis vectors. The first vector, the one that produces $c_1$, should consist of positive, perhaps even identical, values. This will reinforce the nonnegative values of the pixels. Each of the other vectors should have half its elements positive, and the other half negative. When multiplied by nonnegative data items, such a vector tends to produce a small value. (This is especially true when the data items are similar, and we know that adjacent pixels tend to be similar.) Recall that we can interpret the basis vectors as tools for extracting features from the data vector. A good choice would therefore be a set of basis vectors that are very different from each other and so can extract different features. This leads to the idea of basis vectors that are *mutually orthogonal*. If the transform matrix $\mathbf{W}$ is orthogonal, the transform itself is called orthogonal. Another observation that helps to select the basis vectors is that they should feature higher and higher frequencies, thereby extracting higher-frequency features from the data as we go along, computing more transformed values.

These considerations are satisfied by the orthogonal matrix

$$\mathbf{W} = \begin{pmatrix} 1 & 1 & 1 & 1 \\ 1 & 1 & -1 & -1 \\ 1 & -1 & -1 & 1 \\ 1 & -1 & 1 & -1 \end{pmatrix}. \tag{3.5}$$

The first basis vector (the top row of $\mathbf{W}$) consists of all 1's, so its frequency is zero. Each of the subsequent vectors has two $+1$'s and two $-1$'s, so they produce small transformed values, and their frequencies (measured as the number of sign changes along the basis vector) get higher. This matrix is similar to the Walsh-Hadamard transform [Equation (3.11)]. As an example, we transform the data vector $(4, 6, 5, 2)$:

$$\begin{pmatrix} 1 & 1 & 1 & 1 \\ 1 & 1 & -1 & -1 \\ 1 & -1 & -1 & 1 \\ 1 & -1 & 1 & -1 \end{pmatrix} \begin{pmatrix} 4 \\ 6 \\ 5 \\ 2 \end{pmatrix} = \begin{pmatrix} 17 \\ 3 \\ -5 \\ 1 \end{pmatrix}.$$

The results are encouraging, since $c_1$ is large (compared to the original data items), and two of the remaining $c_i$'s are small. However, the energy of the original data items is $4^2 + 6^2 + 5^2 + 2^2 = 81$, whereas the energy of the transformed values is $17^2 + 3^2 + (-5)^2 + 1^2 = 324$, four times as much. It is possible to conserve the energy by multiplying the transformation matrix $\mathbf{W}$ by the scale factor $1/2$. The new product $\mathbf{W} \cdot (4, 6, 5, 2)^T$ now produces $(17/2, 3/2, -5/2, 1/2)$. The energy is conserved, but it is concentrated in the first component, which contains $8.5^2/81 = 89\%$ of the total energy, compared to the original data, where the first component contained $4^2/81 \approx 20\%$ of the energy.

Another advantage of $\mathbf{W}$ is that it also performs the inverse transform. The product $\mathbf{W} \cdot (17/2, 3/2, -5/2, 1/2)^T$ reconstructs the original data $(4, 6, 5, 2)$.

We are now in a position to appreciate the power of a transform. We quantize the transformed vector $(8.5, 1.5, -2.5, 0.5)$ to the integers $(9, 1, -3, 0)$ and perform the inverse transform to get back $(3.5, 6.5, 5.5, 2.5)$. In a similar experiment, we completely delete the two smallest elements and inverse-transform the coarsely quantized vector $(8.5, 0, -2.5, 0)$. This produces the reconstructed data $(3, 5.5, 5.5, 3)$, still very close to the original values. The conclusion is that even this simple, intuitive transform is a powerful tool for "squeezing out" the redundancy in data. More sophisticated transforms produce results that can be quantized coarsely and still be used to reconstruct the original data to a high degree.

> Some painters transform the sun into a yellow spot; others transform a yellow spot into the sun.
>
> —Pablo Picasso

### 3.5.2 Two-Dimensional Transforms

Given two-dimensional data such as the $4 \times 4$ matrix

$$\mathbf{D} = \begin{pmatrix} 4 & 7 & 6 & 9 \\ 6 & 8 & 3 & 6 \\ 5 & 4 & 7 & 6 \\ 2 & 4 & 5 & 9 \end{pmatrix}$$

(where the first column is identical to the previous example), we can apply our simple one-dimensional transform to the columns of $\mathbf{D}$. The result is

$$\mathbf{C}' = \mathbf{W} \cdot \mathbf{D} = \frac{1}{2} \begin{pmatrix} 1 & 1 & 1 & 1 \\ 1 & 1 & -1 & -1 \\ 1 & -1 & -1 & 1 \\ 1 & -1 & 1 & -1 \end{pmatrix} = \begin{pmatrix} 8.5 & 11.5 & 10.5 & 15 \\ 1.5 & 3.5 & -1.5 & 0 \\ -2.5 & -0.5 & 0.5 & 3 \\ 0.5 & -0.5 & 2.5 & 0 \end{pmatrix}.$$

Each column of $\mathbf{C}'$ is the transform of a column of $\mathbf{D}$. Notice that the top element of each column of $\mathbf{C}'$ is dominant. Also, all the columns have the same energy. We can consider $\mathbf{C}'$ the first stage in a two-stage process that produces the two-dimensional transform of matrix $\mathbf{D}$. The second stage should transform each *row* of $\mathbf{C}'$, and this is done by multiplying $\mathbf{C}'$ by the transpose $\mathbf{W}^T$. Our particular $\mathbf{W}$, however, is symmetric, so we end up with $\mathbf{C} = \mathbf{C}' \cdot \mathbf{W}^T = \mathbf{W} \cdot \mathbf{D} \cdot \mathbf{W}^T = \mathbf{W} \cdot \mathbf{D} \cdot \mathbf{W}$ or

$$\mathbf{C} = \begin{pmatrix} 8.5 & 11.5 & 10.5 & 15 \\ 1.5 & 3.5 & -1.5 & 0 \\ -2.5 & -0.5 & 0.5 & 3 \\ 0.5 & -0.5 & 2.5 & 0 \end{pmatrix} \frac{1}{2} \begin{pmatrix} 1 & 1 & 1 & 1 \\ 1 & 1 & -1 & -1 \\ 1 & -1 & -1 & 1 \\ 1 & -1 & 1 & -1 \end{pmatrix}$$

$$= \begin{pmatrix} 22.75 & -2.75 & 0.75 & -3.75 \\ 1.75 & 3.25 & -0.25 & -1.75 \\ 0.25 & -3.25 & 0.25 & -2.25 \\ 1.25 & -1.25 & -0.75 & 1.75 \end{pmatrix}.$$

The top left element is dominant. It contains 89% of the total energy of 579 in the original $\mathbf{D}$. The double-stage, two-dimensional transformation has reduced the correlation in both the horizontal and vertical dimensions.

The rest of this section discusses the following popular transforms:

1. The discrete cosine transform (DCT, Sections 3.5.3 and 3.7.2) is a well-known, efficient transform used by popular compression mathods such as JPEG and MPEG

audio. Several fast algorithms for DCT calculation are known, making the use of this method even more attractive.

2. The Karhunen-Loève transform (KLT, Section 3.5.8) is the best one, theoretically, in the sense of energy compaction (or, equivalently, pixel decorrelation). However, its coefficients are not fixed; they depend on the data to be compressed. Calculating these coefficients (the basis of the transform) is slow, as is the calculation of the transformed values themselves. Since the coefficients are data dependent, they have to be included in the compressed file. For these reasons, and because the DCT performs almost as well, the KLT is not generally used in practice.

3. The Walsh-Hadamard transform (WHT, Section 3.5.6) is fast to calculate (it requires only additions and subtractions), but its performance, in terms of energy compaction, is lower than that of the DCT.

4. The Haar transform [Stollnitz 96] is a simple, fast transform. It is the simplest wavelet transform and is discussed in Section 3.5.7 and in Chapter 4.

### 3.5.3 Discrete Cosine Transform

We first look at the one-dimensional DCT (in practice, the *two-dimensional* DCT is used to compress images, but the one-dimensional DCT is easier to understand, and it is based on the same principles). Figure 3.20 shows eight cosine waves, $w(f) = \cos(f\theta)$, for $0 \le \theta \le \pi$, with frequencies $f = 0, 1, \ldots, 7$. Each wave $w(f)$ is sampled at the eight points

$$\theta = \frac{\pi}{16}, \quad \frac{3\pi}{16}, \quad \frac{5\pi}{16}, \quad \frac{7\pi}{16}, \quad \frac{9\pi}{16}, \quad \frac{11\pi}{16}, \quad \frac{13\pi}{16}, \quad \frac{15\pi}{16} \tag{3.6}$$

to form one basis vector $\mathbf{v}_f$, and the resulting eight vectors $\mathbf{v}_f$, $f = 0, 1, \ldots, 7$ (a total of 64 numbers) are shown in Table 3.21. They serve as the basis of the one-dimensional DCT. Notice the similarity between this table and matrix $\mathbf{W}$ of Equation (3.5). In both cases the rows have increasing frequencies.

```
dct[pw_]:=Plot[Cos[pw t], {t,0,Pi}, DisplayFunction->Identity,
  AspectRatio->Automatic];
dcdot[pw_]:=ListPlot[Table[{t,Cos[pw t]},{t,Pi/16,15Pi/16,Pi/8}],
  DisplayFunction->Identity]
Show[dct[0],dcdot[0], Prolog->AbsolutePointSize[4],
  DisplayFunction->$DisplayFunction]
...
Show[dct[7],dcdot[7], Prolog->AbsolutePointSize[4],
  DisplayFunction->$DisplayFunction]
```

Code for Figure 3.20.

It can be shown that these $\mathbf{v}_i$ vectors are orthonormal (because of the particular choice of the eight sample points), and it is also easy, with appropriate mathematical software, to check this by direct calculations. This set of eight orthonormal vectors can therefore be considered an $8 \times 8$ transformation matrix. Since this matrix is orthonormal,

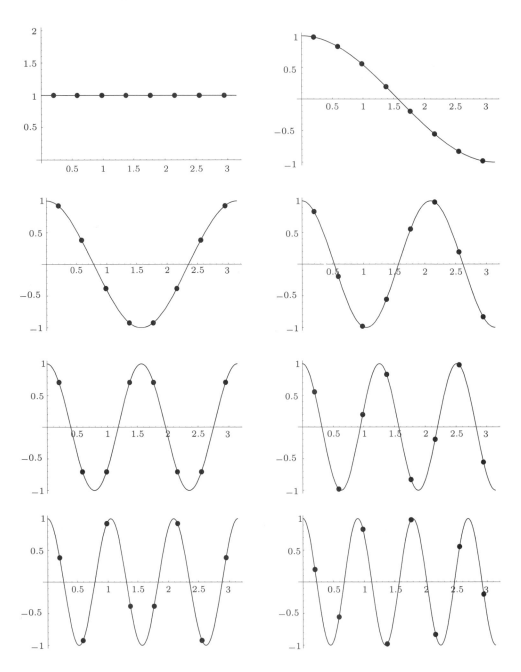

**Figure 3.20:** Calculating a One-Dimensional DCT.

| $\theta$ | 0.196 | 0.589 | 0.982 | 1.374 | 1.767 | 2.160 | 2.553 | 2.945 |
|---|---|---|---|---|---|---|---|---|
| $\cos 0\theta$ | 1. | 1. | 1. | 1. | 1. | 1. | 1. | 1. |
| $\cos 1\theta$ | 0.981 | 0.831 | 0.556 | 0.195 | $-0.195$ | $-0.556$ | $-0.831$ | $-0.981$ |
| $\cos 2\theta$ | 0.924 | 0.383 | $-0.383$ | $-0.924$ | $-0.924$ | $-0.383$ | 0.383 | 0.924 |
| $\cos 3\theta$ | 0.831 | $-0.195$ | $-0.981$ | $-0.556$ | 0.556 | 0.981 | 0.195 | $-0.831$ |
| $\cos 4\theta$ | 0.707 | $-0.707$ | $-0.707$ | 0.707 | 0.707 | $-0.707$ | $-0.707$ | 0.707 |
| $\cos 5\theta$ | 0.556 | $-0.981$ | 0.195 | 0.831 | $-0.831$ | $-0.195$ | 0.981 | $-0.556$ |
| $\cos 6\theta$ | 0.383 | $-0.924$ | 0.924 | $-0.383$ | $-0.383$ | 0.924 | $-0.924$ | 0.383 |
| $\cos 7\theta$ | 0.195 | $-0.556$ | 0.831 | $-0.981$ | 0.981 | $-0.831$ | 0.556 | $-0.195$ |

```
Table[N[t],{t,Pi/16,15Pi/16,Pi/8}]
dctp[pw_]:=Table[N[Cos[pw t]],{t,Pi/16,15Pi/16,Pi/8}]
dctp[0]
dctp[1]
...
dctp[7]
```

**Table 3.21:** Calculating a One-Dimensional DCT.

it is a rotation matrix. Thus, we can interpret the one-dimensional DCT as a rotation. The two-dimensional DCT can also be interpreted as a (double) rotation, and this is discussed on page 118.

The one-dimensional DCT has another interpretation. We can consider the eight orthonormal vectors $\mathbf{v}_i$ the basis of a vector space and express any other vector $\mathbf{p}$ in this space as a linear combination of the $\mathbf{v}_i$'s. As an example, we select the eight (correlated) numbers $\mathbf{p} = (.6, .5, .4, .5, .6, .5, .4, .55)$ as our test data. We express vector $\mathbf{p}$ as a linear combination $\mathbf{p} = \sum w_i \mathbf{v}_i$ of the eight basis vectors $\mathbf{v}_i$. Solving this system of eight equations yields the eight weights

$$w_0 = 0.506, \quad w_1 = 0.0143, \quad w_2 = 0.0115, \quad w_3 = 0.0439,$$
$$w_4 = 0.0795, \quad w_5 = -0.0432, \quad w_6 = 0.00478, \quad w_7 = -0.0077.$$

Weight $w_0$ is not much different from the elements of $\mathbf{p}$, but the other seven weights are much smaller. This is how the DCT (or any other orthogonal transform) produces compression. We can simply write the eight weights on the compressed file, where they will occupy less space than the eight components of $\mathbf{p}$. Quantizing the eight weights may increase compression considerably while resulting in just a small loss of data.

Figure 3.22 illustrates this linear combination graphically. Each of the eight $\mathbf{v}_i$'s is shown as a row of eight small, gray rectangles where a value of $+1$ is painted white and $-1$ is black. Each of the eight elements of vector $\mathbf{p}$ is expressed as the weighted sum of eight grayscales.

The simplest way to calculate the one-dimensional DCT in practice is by

$$G_f = \frac{1}{2} C_f \sum_{t=0}^{7} p_t \cos\left(\frac{(2t+1)f\pi}{16}\right), \tag{3.7}$$

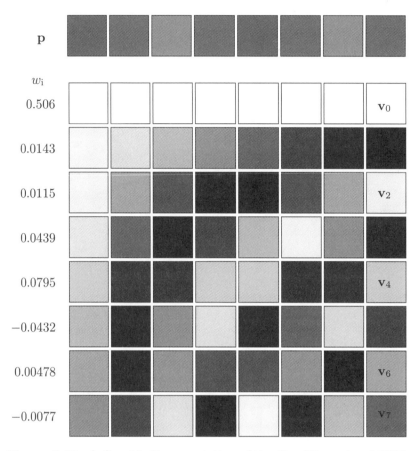

**Figure 3.22:** A Graphic Representation of the One-Dimensional DCT.

$$\text{where } C_f = \begin{cases} \frac{1}{\sqrt{2}}, & f = 0, \\ 1, & f > 0, \end{cases} \quad \text{for } f = 0, 1, \ldots, 7.$$

This starts with a set of eight data values $p_t$ (pixels, sound samples, or other data) and produces a set of eight DCT coefficients $G_f$. It is straightforward but slow (Section 3.7.3 discusses faster versions). The decoder inputs the DCT coefficients in sets of eight and uses the *inverse* DCT (IDCT) to reconstruct the original data values (also in groups of eight). The simplest way to calculate the IDCT is by

$$p_t = \frac{1}{2} \sum_{j=0}^{7} C_j G_j \cos\left(\frac{(2t+1)j\pi}{16}\right), \quad \text{for } t = 0, 1, \ldots, 7. \tag{3.8}$$

The following experiment illustrates the power of the DCT. We start with the set of eight data items $\mathbf{p} = (12, 10, 8, 10, 12, 10, 8, 11)$, apply the one-dimensional DCT to them, and end up with the eight coefficients

28.6375, 0.571202, 0.46194, 1.757, 3.18198, −1.72956, 0.191342, −0.308709.

These can be used to precisely reconstruct the original data (except for small errors caused by limited machine precision). Our goal, however, is to improve compression by quantizing the coefficients. We quantize them to $28.6, 0.6, 0.5, 1.8, 3.2, −1.8, 0.2, −0.3$, and apply the IDCT to get back

12.0254, 10.0233, 7.96054, 9.93097, 12.0164, 9.99321, 7.94354, 10.9989.

We then quantize the coefficients even more, to $28, 1, 1, 2, 3, −2, 0, 0$, and apply the IDCT to get back

12.1883, 10.2315, 7.74931, 9.20863, 11.7876, 9.54549, 7.82865, 10.6557.

Finally, we quantize the coefficients to $28, 0, 0, 2, 3, −2, 0, 0$ and still get back from the IDCT the sequence

11.236, 9.62443, 7.66286, 9.57302, 12.3471, 10.0146, 8.05304, 10.6842,

where the largest difference between an original value (12) and a reconstructed one (11.236) is 0.764 (or 6.4% of 12). The code that does all that is listed in Figure 3.23.

```
p={12.,10.,8.,10.,12.,10.,8.,11.};
c={.7071,1,1,1,1,1,1,1};
dct[i_]:=(c[[i+1]]/2)Sum[p[[t+1]]Cos[(2t+1)i Pi/16],{t,0,7}];
q=Table[dct[i],{i,0,7}] (* use precise DCT coefficients *)
q={28,0,0,2,3,-2,0,0}; (* or use quantized DCT coefficients *)
idct[t_]:=(1/2)Sum[c[[j+1]]q[[j+1]]Cos[(2t+1)j Pi/16],{j,0,7}];
ip=Table[idct[t],{t,0,7}]
```

**Figure 3.23:** Experiments with the One-Dimensional DCT.

These simple experiments illustrate the power of the DCT. The set of coarsely quantized DCT coefficients $28, 0, 0, 2, 3, −2, 0, 0$ has four properties that make it ideal for compression, yet it also produces excellent lossy decompression. The four properties are (1) it consists of integers only, (2) only four of the eight coefficients are nonzero, (3) the zero coefficients are concentrated in runs, and (4) of the nonzero coefficients, only the first is large; the rest are smaller than the original data items. These properties can be exploited by applying RLE, Huffman codes, and other techniques (Sections 3.7.4 and 3.7.5) to further compress this set.

**Example:** The one-dimensional DCT [Equation (3.7)] of the eight correlated values $11, 22, 33, 44, 55, 66, 77$, and $88$ produces the 8 coefficients $140, −71, 0, −7, 0, −2, 0, 0$.

```
Clear[Pixl, G, Gq, RecP];
Cr[i_]:=If[i==0, Sqrt[2]/2, 1];
DCT[i_]:={(1/2)Cr[i]Sum[Pixl[[x+1]]Cos[(2x+1)i Pi/16], {x,0,7,1}]};
IDCT[x_]:={(1/2)Sum[Cr[i]Gq[[i+1]]Cos[(2x+1)i Pi/16], {i,0,7,1}]};
Pixl={11,22,33,44,55,66,77,88};
G=Table[SetAccuracy[N[DCT[m]],0], {m,0,7}]
Gq={140.,-71,.0,0,0,0,0,0};
RecP=Table[SetAccuracy[N[IDCT[m]],0], {m,0,7}]
```

**Figure 3.24:** *Mathematica* Code for One-Dimensional DCT Example.

They are quantized to $140, -71, 0, 0, 0, 0, 0, 0$ and the IDCT applied. The result is $15, 20, 30, 43, 56, 69, 79$, and $84$. These are very close to the original values, with a maximum difference of only 4. Figure 3.24 lists *Mathematica* code for this example.

When reaching this point in the text, some readers tend to claim: "Amazing; reconstructing eight data items from just two numbers is magic." Those who understand the concept of a transform, however, know the simple explanation. The reconstruction is done not just by the two numbers 140 and $-71$ but also by their positions in the sequence of eight coefficients. Also, the original data has been reconstructed to a high degree because it has redundancy.

An extreme case of redundant data is a sequence of identical data items. They are, of course, perfectly correlated, and we feel intuitively that only one number is needed to perfectly reconstruct them. Reconstructing a highly correlated sequence such as $20, 31, 42, 53, \dots$ requires just two numbers. They can be the initial value (10) and the step size (11), but they can also be other values. In general, the less correlated a sequence is, the more numbers are required to reconstruct it.

**Two-Dimensional DCT**: We know from experience that the pixels of an image are correlated in two dimensions, not in just one dimension (a pixel is correlated with its neighbors on the left and right as well as above and below). This is why image compression methods use the two-dimensional DCT, given by

$$G_{ij} = \frac{1}{\sqrt{2n}} C_i C_j \sum_{x=0}^{n-1} \sum_{y=0}^{n-1} p_{xy} \cos\left(\frac{(2y+1)j\pi}{2n}\right) \cos\left(\frac{(2x+1)i\pi}{2n}\right) \tag{3.9}$$

for $0 \le i, j \le n - 1$. The image is broken up into blocks of $n \times n$ pixels $p_{xy}$ (we use $n = 8$ as an example), and Equation (3.9) is used to produce a block of $8 \times 8$ DCT coefficients $G_{ij}$ for each block of pixels. If lossy compression is required, the coefficients are quantized. The decoder reconstructs a block of (approximate or precise) data values by computing the inverse DCT (IDCT):

$$p_{xy} = \frac{1}{4} \sum_{i=0}^{7} \sum_{j=0}^{7} C_i C_j G_{ij} \cos\left(\frac{(2x+1)i\pi}{16}\right) \cos\left(\frac{(2y+1)j\pi}{16}\right),$$

$$\text{where } C_f = \begin{cases} \frac{1}{\sqrt{2}}, & f = 0, \\ 1, & f > 0. \end{cases} \tag{3.10}$$

The two-dimensional DCT can be interpreted in two different ways, as a rotation (actually, two separate rotations) and as a basis of an $n$-dimensional vector space. The first interpretation starts with a block of $n \times n$ pixels (Figure 3.25a, where the elements are labeled "L"). It first considers each row of this block a point $(p_{x,0}, p_{x,1}, \ldots, p_{x,n-1})$ in $n$-dimensional space, and it rotates the point by means of the innermost sum

$$G1_{x,j} = C_j \sum_{y=0}^{n-1} p_{xy} \cos\left(\frac{(2y+1)j\pi}{2n}\right)$$

of Equation (3.9). This results in a block $G1_{x,j}$ of $n \times n$ coefficients where the first element of each row is dominant (labeled "L" in Figure 3.25b) and the remaining elements are small (labeled "S" in that figure). The outermost sum of Equation (3.9) is

$$G_{ij} = \frac{1}{\sqrt{2n}} C_i \sum_{x=0}^{n-1} G1_{x,j} \cos\left(\frac{(2x+1)i\pi}{2n}\right).$$

Here, the *columns* of $G1_{x,j}$ are considered points in $n$-dimensional space and are rotated. The result is one large coefficient at the top left corner of the block ("L" in Figure 3.25c) and $n^2 - 1$ small coefficients elsewhere ("S" and "s" in that figure). This interpretation looks at the two-dimensional DCT as two separate rotations in $n$ dimensions. It is interesting to note that two rotations in $n$ dimensions are faster than one rotation in $n^2$ dimensions, since the latter requires an $n^2 \times n^2$ rotation matrix.

```
L L L L L L L L        L S S S S S S S        L S S S S S S S
L L L L L L L L        L S S S S S S S        S s s s s s s s
L L L L L L L L        L S S S S S S S        S s s s s s s s
L L L L L L L L        L S S S S S S S        S s s s s s s s
L L L L L L L L        L S S S S S S S        S s s s s s s s
L L L L L L L L        L S S S S S S S        S s s s s s s s
L L L L L L L L        L S S S S S S S        S s s s s s s s
L L L L L L L L        L S S S S S S S        S s s s s s s s
        (a)                    (b)                    (c)
```

**Figure 3.25:** The Two-Dimensional DCT as a Double Rotation.

The second interpretation (assuming $n = 8$) applies Equation (3.9) to create 64 blocks of $8 \times 8$ values each. The 64 blocks are then used as a basis of a 64-dimensional vector space (they are basis images). Any block $B$ of $8 \times 8$ pixels can be expressed as a linear combination of the basis images, and the 64 weights of this linear combination are the DCT coefficients of $B$.

Figure 3.26 shows the graphic representation of the 64 basis images of the two-dimensional DCT for $n = 8$. A general element $(i, j)$ in this figure is the $8 \times 8$ block obtained by calculating the product $\cos(i \cdot s) \cos(j \cdot t)$ where $s$ and $t$ are varied independently over the values listed in Equation (3.6). This figure can easily be generated by

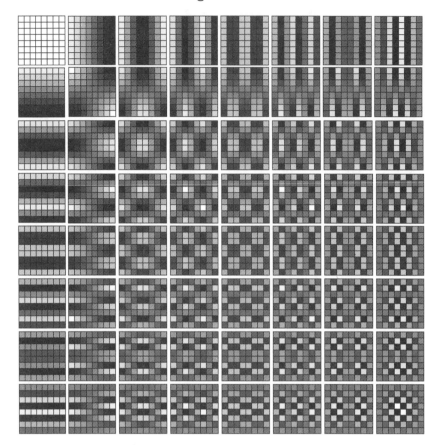

**Figure 3.26:** The 64 Basis Images of the Two-Dimensional DCT.

```
dctp[fs_,ft_]:=Table[SetAccuracy[N[(1.-Cos[fs s]Cos[ft t])/2],3],
 {s,Pi/16,15Pi/16,Pi/8},{t,Pi/16,15Pi/16,Pi/8}]//TableForm
dctp[0,0]
dctp[0,1]
...
dctp[7,7]
```

Code for Figure 3.26

```
Needs["GraphicsImage'"] (* Draws 2D DCT Coefficients *)
DCTMatrix=Table[If[k==0,Sqrt[1/8],Sqrt[1/4]Cos[Pi(2j+1)k/16]],
 {k,0,7}, {j,0,7}] //N;
DCTTensor=Array[Outer[Times, DCTMatrix[[#1]],DCTMatrix[[#2]]]&,
 {8,8}];
Show[GraphicsArray[Map[GraphicsImage[#, {-.25,.25}]&,
 DCTTensor,{2}]]]
```

Alternative Code for Figure 3.26

the *Mathematica* code shown with it. The alternative code shown is a modification of code in [Watson 94], and it requires the `GraphicsImage.m` package, which is not widely available.

Using appropriate software, it is easy to perform DCT calculations and display the results graphically. Figure 3.29a shows a random $8 \times 8$ data unit made up of zeros and ones. The same unit is shown in Figure 3.29b graphically, with 1 as white and 0 as black. Figure 3.29c shows the weights by which each of the 64 DCT coefficients has to be multiplied in order to reproduce the original data unit. In this figure, zero is shown in neutral gray, positive numbers are bright (notice how bright the DC coefficient is), and negative numbers are shown as dark. Figure 3.29d shows the weights numerically. The *Mathematica* code that does all that is also listed. Figure 3.30 is similar, but it is for a very regular data unit.

Next, we illustrate the performance of the two-dimensional DCT by applying it to two blocks of $8 \times 8$ values. The first block (Table 3.27) has highly correlated integer values in the range $[8, 12]$ and the second one has random values in the same range. The first block results in a large DC coefficient, followed by small (including 20 zeros) AC coefficients. In contrast, the coefficients for the second block (Table 3.28) include just one zero.

(It is easy to see why the values of Table 3.27 are correlated. The eight values in the top row of the table are close (the distances between them are either 2 or 3). Each of the other rows is obtained as a right circular shift of the preceding row.)

```
12 10  8 10 12 10  8 11     81    0     0     0      0     0      0      0
11 12 10  8 10 12 10  8      0  1.57  0.61  1.90   0.38 -1.81   0.20  -0.32
 8 11 12 10  8 10 12 10      0 -0.61  0.71  0.35      0  0.07      0   0.02
10  8 11 12 10  8 10 12      0  1.90 -0.35  4.76   0.77 -3.39   0.25  -0.54
12 10  8 11 12 10  8 10      0 -0.38     0 -0.77   8.00  0.51      0   0.07
10 12 10  8 11 12 10  8      0 -1.81 -0.07 -3.39  -0.51  1.57   0.56   0.25
 8 10 12 10  8 11 12 10      0 -0.20     0 -0.25      0 -0.56  -0.71   0.29
10  8 10 12 10  8 11 12      0 -0.32 -0.02 -0.54  -0.07  0.25  -0.29  -0.90
```

**Table 3.27:** Two-Dimensional DCT of a Block of Correlated Values.

```
 8 10  9 11 11  9  9 12     79.12  0.98  0.64 -1.51 -0.62 -0.86  1.22  0.32
11  8 12  8 11 10 11 10      0.15 -1.64 -0.09  1.23  0.10  3.29  1.08 -2.97
 9 11  9 10 12  9  9  8     -1.26 -0.29 -3.27  1.69 -0.51  1.13  1.52  1.33
 9 12 10  8  8  9  8  9     -1.27 -0.25 -0.67 -0.15  1.63 -1.94  0.47 -1.30
12  8  9  9 12 10  8 11     -2.12 -0.67 -0.07 -0.79  0.13 -1.40  0.16 -0.15
 8 11 10 12  9 12 12 10     -2.68  1.08 -1.99 -1.93 -1.77 -0.35     0 -0.80
10 10 12 10 12 10 10 12      1.20  2.10 -0.98  0.87 -1.55 -0.59 -0.98  2.76
12  9 11 11  9  8  8 12     -2.24  0.55  0.29  0.75 -2.40 -0.05  0.06  1.14
```

**Table 3.28:** Two-Dimensional DCT of a Block of Random Values.

> The teeth and hair, the colour of the skin and of the hair, are more or less correlated.                                    —Charles Darwin, *The Ascent of Man*

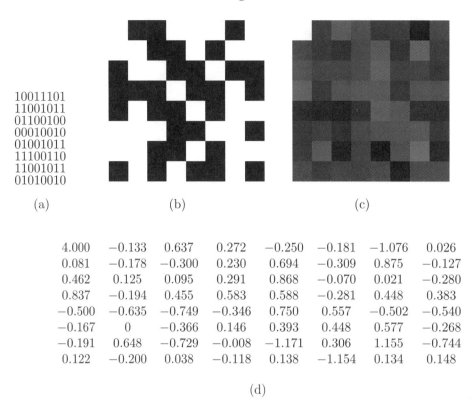

10011101
11001011
01100100
00010000
01001011
11100110
11001011
01010010

(a)       (b)       (c)

| 4.000 | −0.133 | 0.637 | 0.272 | −0.250 | −0.181 | −1.076 | 0.026 |
|---|---|---|---|---|---|---|---|
| 0.081 | −0.178 | −0.300 | 0.230 | 0.694 | −0.309 | 0.875 | −0.127 |
| 0.462 | 0.125 | 0.095 | 0.291 | 0.868 | −0.070 | 0.021 | −0.280 |
| 0.837 | −0.194 | 0.455 | 0.583 | 0.588 | −0.281 | 0.448 | 0.383 |
| −0.500 | −0.635 | −0.749 | −0.346 | 0.750 | 0.557 | −0.502 | −0.540 |
| −0.167 | 0 | −0.366 | 0.146 | 0.393 | 0.448 | 0.577 | −0.268 |
| −0.191 | 0.648 | −0.729 | −0.008 | −1.171 | 0.306 | 1.155 | −0.744 |
| 0.122 | −0.200 | 0.038 | −0.118 | 0.138 | −1.154 | 0.134 | 0.148 |

(d)

```
DCTMatrix=Table[If[k==0,Sqrt[1/8],Sqrt[1/4]Cos[Pi(2j+1)k/16]],
 {k,0,7}, {j,0,7}] //N;
DCTTensor=Array[Outer[Times, DCTMatrix[[#1]],DCTMatrix[[#2]]]&,
 {8,8}];
img={{1,0,0,1,1,1,0,1},{1,1,0,0,1,0,1,1},
{0,1,1,0,0,1,0,0},{0,0,0,1,0,0,1,0},
{0,1,0,0,1,0,1,1},{1,1,1,0,0,1,1,0},
{1,1,0,0,1,0,1,1},{0,1,0,1,0,0,1,0}};
ShowImage[Reverse[img]]
dctcoeff=Array[(Plus @@ Flatten[DCTTensor[[#1,#2]] img])&,{8,8}];
dctcoeff=SetAccuracy[dctcoeff,4];
dctcoeff=Chop[dctcoeff,.001];
MatrixForm[dctcoeff]
ShowImage[Reverse[dctcoeff]]
```

**Figure 3.29:** A Two-Dimensional DCT Example.

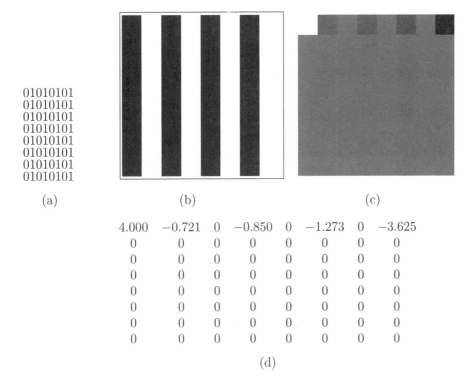

01010101
01010101
01010101
01010101
01010101
01010101
01010101
01010101

(a)                    (b)                              (c)

| 4.000 | −0.721 | 0 | −0.850 | 0 | −1.273 | 0 | −3.625 |
|---|---|---|---|---|---|---|---|
| 0 | 0 | 0 | 0 | 0 | 0 | 0 | 0 |
| 0 | 0 | 0 | 0 | 0 | 0 | 0 | 0 |
| 0 | 0 | 0 | 0 | 0 | 0 | 0 | 0 |
| 0 | 0 | 0 | 0 | 0 | 0 | 0 | 0 |
| 0 | 0 | 0 | 0 | 0 | 0 | 0 | 0 |
| 0 | 0 | 0 | 0 | 0 | 0 | 0 | 0 |
| 0 | 0 | 0 | 0 | 0 | 0 | 0 | 0 |

(d)

```
DCTMatrix=Table[If[k==0,Sqrt[1/8],Sqrt[1/4]Cos[Pi(2j+1)k/16]],
 {k,0,7}, {j,0,7}] //N;
DCTTensor=Array[Outer[Times, DCTMatrix[[#1]],DCTMatrix[[#2]]]&,
 {8,8}];
img={{0,1,0,1,0,1,0,1},{0,1,0,1,0,1,0,1},
 {0,1,0,1,0,1,0,1},{0,1,0,1,0,1,0,1},{0,1,0,1,0,1,0,1},
 {0,1,0,1,0,1,0,1},{0,1,0,1,0,1,0,1},{0,1,0,1,0,1,0,1}};
ShowImage[Reverse[img]]
dctcoeff=Array[(Plus @@ Flatten[DCTTensor[[#1,#2]] img])&,{8,8}];
dctcoeff=SetAccuracy[dctcoeff,4];
dctcoeff=Chop[dctcoeff,.001];
MatrixForm[dctcoeff]
ShowImage[Reverse[dctcoeff]]
```

**Figure 3.30:** A Two-Dimensional DCT Example.

Compressing an image with DCT can now be done as follows:

1. Divide it into $k$ blocks of $n \times n$ (typically $8 \times 8$) pixels each.

2. Apply the two-dimensional DCT to each block $B_i$. This expresses the block as a linear combination of the 64 basis images of Figure 3.26. The result is a block (we'll call it a vector) $W^{(i)}$ of 64 weights $w_j^{(i)}$ (where $j = 0, 1, \ldots, 63$).

3. The $k$ vectors $W^{(i)}$ $(i = 1, 2, \ldots, k)$ are separated into 64 coefficient vectors $C^{(j)}$, where the $k$ elements of $C^{(j)}$ are $\left(w_j^{(1)}, w_j^{(2)}, \ldots, w_j^{(k)}\right)$. The first coefficient vector $C^{(0)}$ consists of the $k$ DC coefficients.

4. Each coefficient vector $C^{(j)}$ is quantized separately to produce a quantized vector $Q^{(j)}$ that is written (after being further encoded by RLE, Huffman, and perhaps other methods) on the compressed file.

The decoder reads the 64 quantized coefficient vectors $Q^{(j)}$, uses them to construct $k$ weight vectors $W^{(i)}$, and applies the IDCT to each weight vector to reconstruct (approximately) the 64 pixels of block $B_i$. Notice that JPEG works differently.

### 3.5.4 Example

This example illustrates the difference in performance of the DCT when applied to a continuous-tone image and to a discrete-tone image. We start with the very correlated pattern of Table 3.31. This is an idealized example of a continuous-tone image, since adjacent pixels differ by a constant amount. The 64 DCT coefficients of this pattern are listed in Table 3.32. It is clear that there are just a few dominant coefficients. Table 3.33 lists the coefficients after they have been coarsely quantized. In fact, just four coefficients are nonzero. The results of performing the IDCT on these quantized coefficients are shown in Table 3.34. It is obvious that the four nonzero coefficients have reconstructed the original pattern to a high degree.

Tables 3.35 through 3.38 show the same process applied to a Y-shaped pattern, typical of a discrete-tone image. The quantization, shown in Table 3.37, is light. The coefficients have simply been truncated to the nearest integer. It is easy to see that the reconstruction, shown in Table 3.38, isn't as good as before. Quantities that should have been 10 are between 8.96 and 10.11. Quantities that should have been zero are as big as 0.86.

### 3.5.5 Discrete Sine Transform

Readers who have made it to this point ask why the cosine function, and not the sine, is used in the transform. Is it possible to use the sine function in a similar way to the DCT to create a discrete sine transform? Is there a DST, and if not, why? This short section discusses the differences between the sine and cosine functions and shows why these differences lead to a very ineffective sine transform.

A function $f(x)$ that satisfies $f(x) = -f(-x)$ is called *odd*. Similarly, a function for which $f(x) = f(-x)$ is called *even*. For an odd function, it is always true that $f(0) = -f(-0) = -f(0)$, so $f(0)$ must be 0. Most functions are neither odd nor even, but the trigonometric functions sine and cosine are important examples of odd and even functions, respectively. Figure 3.39 shows that even though the only difference between them is phase (i.e., the cosine is a shifted version of the sine), this difference is enough to

| 00 | 10 | 20 | 30 | 30 | 20 | 10 | 00 |
|----|----|----|----|----|----|----|----|
| 10 | 20 | 30 | 40 | 40 | 30 | 20 | 10 |
| 20 | 30 | 40 | 50 | 50 | 40 | 30 | 20 |
| 30 | 40 | 50 | 60 | 60 | 50 | 40 | 30 |
| 30 | 40 | 50 | 60 | 60 | 50 | 40 | 30 |
| 20 | 30 | 40 | 50 | 50 | 40 | 30 | 20 |
| 10 | 20 | 30 | 40 | 40 | 30 | 12 | 10 |
| 00 | 10 | 20 | 30 | 30 | 20 | 10 | 00 |

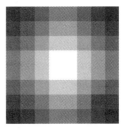

Table 3.31: A Highly Correlated Pattern.

| 239 | 1.19 | −89.76 | −0.28 | 1.00 | −1.39 | −5.03 | −0.79 |
|-----|------|--------|-------|------|-------|-------|-------|
| 1.18 | −1.39 | 0.64 | 0.32 | −1.18 | 1.63 | −1.54 | 0.92 |
| −89.76 | 0.64 | −0.29 | −0.15 | 0.54 | −0.75 | 0.71 | −0.43 |
| −0.28 | 0.32 | −0.15 | −0.08 | 0.28 | −0.38 | 0.36 | −0.22 |
| 1.00 | −1.18 | 0.54 | 0.28 | −1.00 | 1.39 | −1.31 | 0.79 |
| −1.39 | 1.63 | −0.75 | −0.38 | 1.39 | −1.92 | 1.81 | −1.09 |
| −5.03 | −1.54 | 0.71 | 0.36 | −1.31 | 1.81 | −1.71 | 1.03 |
| −0.79 | 0.92 | −0.43 | −0.22 | 0.79 | −1.09 | 1.03 | −0.62 |

Table 3.32: Its DCT Coefficients.

| 239 | 1 | -90 | 0 | 0 | 0 | 0 | 0 |
|-----|---|-----|---|---|---|---|---|
| 0 | 0 | 0 | 0 | 0 | 0 | 0 | 0 |
| -90 | 0 | 0 | 0 | 0 | 0 | 0 | 0 |
| 0 | 0 | 0 | 0 | 0 | 0 | 0 | 0 |
| 0 | 0 | 0 | 0 | 0 | 0 | 0 | 0 |
| 0 | 0 | 0 | 0 | 0 | 0 | 0 | 0 |
| 0 | 0 | 0 | 0 | 0 | 0 | 0 | 0 |
| 0 | 0 | 0 | 0 | 0 | 0 | 0 | 0 |

Table 3.33: Quantized Heavily to Just Four Nonzero Coefficients.

| 0.65 | 9.23 | 21.36 | 29.91 | 29.84 | 21.17 | 8.94 | 0.30 |
|------|------|-------|-------|-------|-------|------|------|
| 9.26 | 17.85 | 29.97 | 38.52 | 38.45 | 29.78 | 17.55 | 8.91 |
| 21.44 | 30.02 | 42.15 | 50.70 | 50.63 | 41.95 | 29.73 | 21.09 |
| 30.05 | 38.63 | 50.76 | 59.31 | 59.24 | 50.56 | 38.34 | 29.70 |
| 30.05 | 38.63 | 50.76 | 59.31 | 59.24 | 50.56 | 38.34 | 29.70 |
| 21.44 | 30.02 | 42.15 | 50.70 | 50.63 | 41.95 | 29.73 | 21.09 |
| 9.26 | 17.85 | 29.97 | 38.52 | 38.45 | 29.78 | 17.55 | 8.91 |
| 0.65 | 9.23 | 21.36 | 29.91 | 29.84 | 21.17 | 8.94 | 0.30 |

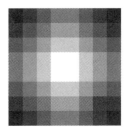

Table 3.34: Results of IDCT.

| 00 | 10 | 00 | 00 | 00 | 00 | 00 | 10 |
|----|----|----|----|----|----|----|----|
| 00 | 00 | 10 | 00 | 00 | 00 | 10 | 00 |
| 00 | 00 | 00 | 10 | 00 | 10 | 00 | 00 |
| 00 | 00 | 00 | 00 | 10 | 00 | 00 | 00 |
| 00 | 00 | 00 | 00 | 10 | 00 | 00 | 00 |
| 00 | 00 | 00 | 00 | 10 | 00 | 00 | 00 |
| 00 | 00 | 00 | 00 | 10 | 00 | 00 | 00 |
| 00 | 00 | 00 | 00 | 10 | 00 | 00 | 00 |

**Table 3.35:** A Pattern of Y.

| 13.75 | −3.11 | −8.17 | 2.46  | 3.75  | −6.86 | −3.38 | 6.59  |
|-------|-------|-------|-------|-------|-------|-------|-------|
| 4.19  | −0.29 | 6.86  | −6.85 | −7.13 | 4.48  | 1.69  | −7.28 |
| 1.63  | 0.19  | 6.40  | −4.81 | −2.99 | −1.11 | −0.88 | −0.94 |
| −0.61 | 0.54  | 5.12  | −2.31 | 1.30  | −6.04 | −2.78 | 3.05  |
| −1.25 | 0.52  | 2.99  | −0.20 | 3.75  | −7.39 | −2.59 | 1.16  |
| −0.41 | 0.18  | 0.65  | 1.03  | 3.87  | −5.19 | −0.71 | −4.76 |
| 0.68  | −0.15 | −0.88 | 1.28  | 2.59  | −1.92 | 1.10  | −9.05 |
| 0.83  | −0.21 | −0.99 | 0.82  | 1.13  | −0.08 | 1.31  | −7.21 |

**Table 3.36:** Its DCT Coefficients.

| 13.75 | −3 | −8 | 2  | 3  | −6 | −3 | 6  |
|-------|----|----|----|----|----|----|----|
| 4     | −0 | 6  | −6 | −7 | 4  | 1  | −7 |
| 1     | 0  | 6  | −4 | −2 | −1 | −0 | −0 |
| −0    | 0  | 5  | −2 | 1  | −6 | −2 | 3  |
| −1    | 0  | 2  | −0 | 3  | −7 | −2 | 1  |
| −0    | 0  | 0  | 1  | 3  | −5 | −0 | −4 |
| 0     | −0 | −0 | 1  | 2  | −1 | 1  | −9 |
| 0     | −0 | −0 | 0  | 1  | −0 | 1  | −7 |

**Table 3.37:** Quantized Lightly by Truncating to Integer.

| -0.13 | 8.96  | 0.55  | -0.27 | 0.27  | 0.86  | 0.15  | 9.22  |
|-------|-------|-------|-------|-------|-------|-------|-------|
| 0.32  | 0.22  | 9.10  | 0.40  | 0.84  | -0.11 | 9.36  | -0.14 |
| 0.00  | 0.62  | -0.20 | 9.71  | -1.30 | 8.57  | 0.28  | -0.33 |
| -0.58 | 0.44  | 0.78  | 0.71  | 10.11 | 1.14  | 0.44  | -0.49 |
| -0.39 | 0.67  | 0.07  | 0.38  | 8.82  | 0.09  | 0.28  | 0.41  |
| 0.34  | 0.11  | 0.26  | 0.18  | 8.93  | 0.41  | 0.47  | 0.37  |
| 0.09  | -0.32 | 0.78  | -0.20 | 9.78  | 0.05  | -0.09 | 0.49  |
| 0.16  | -0.83 | 0.09  | 0.12  | 9.15  | -0.11 | -0.08 | 0.01  |

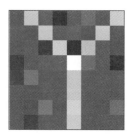

**Table 3.38:** The IDCT. Bad Results.

reverse their parity. When the (odd) sine curve is shifted, it becomes the (even) cosine
curve, which has the same shape.

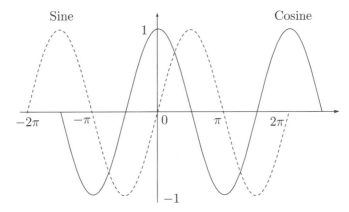

**Figure 3.39:** The Sine and Cosine as Odd and Even Functions, Respectively.

To understand the difference between the DCT and the DST we examine the one-
dimensional case. The one-dimensional DCT, Equation (3.7), employs the function
$\cos((2t + 1)f\pi/16)$ for $f = 0, 1, \ldots, 7$. For the first term, where $f = 0$, this function
becomes $\cos(0)$, which is 1. This term is the familiar and important DC coefficient,
which produces the average of the eight data values being transformed. The DST is
similarly based on the function $\sin((2t + 1)f\pi/16)$, resulting in a zero first term [since
$\sin(0) = 0$]. The first term contributes nothing to the transform, so the DST does not
have a DC coefficient.

The disadvantage can be seen when we consider the example of eight identical
data values to be transformed. Such values are, of course, perfectly correlated. When
plotted, they become a horizontal line. Applying the DCT to these values produces just
a DC coefficient: All the AC coefficients are zero. The DCT compacts all the energy of
the data into the single DC coefficient whose value is identical to the values of the data
items. The IDCT can reconstruct the eight values perfectly (except for minor changes
due to limited machine precision). Applying the DST to the same eight values, on the
other hand, results in seven AC coefficients whose sum is a wave function that passes
through the eight data points but oscillates between the points. This behavior, which is
illustrated in Figure 3.40, has three disadvantages, (1) The energy of the original data
values is not compacted, (2) the seven coefficients are not decorrelated (since the data
points are perfectly correlated), and (3) quantizing the seven coefficients may greatly
reduce the quality of the reconstruction done by the inverse DST.

**Example:** Applying the DST to the eight identical values 100 results in the eight
coefficients $(0, 256.3, 0, 90, 0, 60.1, 0, 51)$. Using these coefficients, the IDST can reconstruct the original values, but it is easy to see that the AC coefficients do not behave
like those of the DCT. They are not getting smaller and smaller, and there are no
runs of zeros between them. Applying the DST to the eight highly correlated values

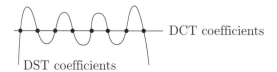

**Figure 3.40:** The DCT and DST of Eight Identical Data Values.

$11, 22, 33, 44, 55, 66, 77, 88$ results in the even worse set of coefficients

$$0, 126.9, -57.5, 44.5, -31.1, 29.8, -23.8, 25.2.$$

There is no energy compaction at all.

These arguments and examples, together with the fact (discussed in [Ahmed et al. 74]) that the DCT produces highly decorrelated coefficients, argue strongly for the use of the DCT as opposed to the DST in data compression.

Figure 3.41 shows the 64 basis images of the DST for $n = 8$ (and the Matlab code that generated them). The result resembles Figure 3.26.

### 3.5.6 Walsh-Hadamard Transform

As mentioned earlier (page 112), this transform has low compression efficiency, so it is not used much in practice. It is, however, fast, since it can be computed with just additions, subtractions, and an occasional right shift (to efficiently divide by a power of 2).

Given an $N \times N$ block of pixels $P_{xy}$ (where $N$ must be a power of 2, $N = 2^n$), its two-dimensional WHT and inverse WHT are defined by Equations (3.11) and (3.12):

$$H(u, v) = \sum_{x=0}^{N-1} \sum_{y=0}^{N-1} p_{xy} g(x, y, u, v)$$

$$= \frac{1}{N} \sum_{x=0}^{N-1} \sum_{y=0}^{N-1} p_{xy} (-1)^{\sum_{i=0}^{n-1} [b_i(x)p_i(u) + b_i(y)p_i(v)]}, \quad (3.11)$$

$$P_{xy} = \sum_{u=0}^{N-1} \sum_{v=0}^{N-1} H(u, v) h(x, y, u, v)$$

$$= \frac{1}{N} \sum_{u=0}^{N-1} \sum_{v=0}^{N-1} H(u, v) (-1)^{\sum_{i=0}^{n-1} [b_i(x)p_i(u) + b_i(y)p_i(v)]}, \quad (3.12)$$

where $H(u, v)$ are the results of the transform (i.e., the WHT coefficients), the quantity $b_i(u)$ is bit $i$ of the binary representation of the integer $u$, and $p_i(u)$ is defined in terms

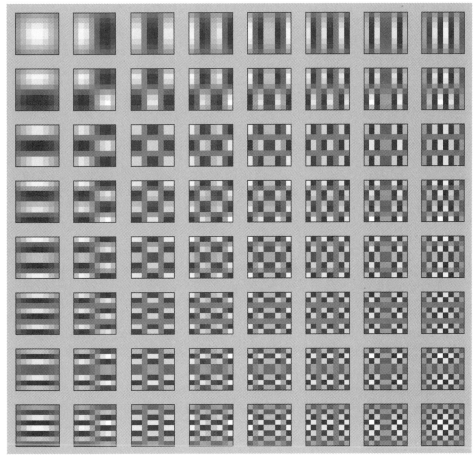

```
N=8;
m=[1:N]'*ones(1,N); n=m';
% can also use cos instead of sin
%A=sqrt(2/N)*cos(pi*(2*(n-1)+1).*(m-1)/(2*N));
A=sqrt(2/N)*sin(pi*(2*(n-1)+1).*(m-1)/(2*N));
A(1,:)=sqrt(1/N);
C=A';
for row=1:N
  for col=1:N
    B=C(:,row)*C(:,col).'; %tensor product
    subplot(N,N,(row-1)*N+col)
    imagesc(B)
    drawnow
  end
end
```

**Figure 3.41:** The 64 Basis Images of the Two-Dimensional DST.

of the $b_j(u)$ by Equation (3.13):

$$p_0(u) = b_{n-1}(u),$$
$$p_1(u) = b_{n-1}(u) + b_{n-2}(u),$$
$$p_2(u) = b_{n-2}(u) + b_{n-3}(u), \tag{3.13}$$
$$\cdots$$
$$p_{n-1}(u) = b_1(u) + b_0(u).$$

(Recall that $n$ is defined above by $N = 2^n$.) As an example consider $u = 6 = 110_2$. Bits zero, one, and two of 6 are 0, 1, and 1, respectively, so $b_0(6) = 0$, $b_1(6) = 1$, and $b_2(6) = 1$.

The quantities $g(x, y, u, v)$ and $h(x, y, u, v)$ are called the *kernels* (or *basis images*) of the WHT. These matrices are identical. Their elements are just $+1$ and $-1$, and they are multiplied by the factor $\frac{1}{N}$. As a result, the WHT transform consists in multiplying each image pixel by $+1$ or $-1$, summing, and dividing the sum by $N$. Since $N = 2^n$ is a power of 2, dividing by it can be done by shifting $n$ positions to the right.

The WHT kernels are shown, in graphical form, for $N = 4$, in Figure 3.42, where white denotes $+1$ and black denotes $-1$ (the factor $\frac{1}{N}$ is ignored). The rows and columns of blocks in this figure correspond to values of $u$ and $v$ from 0 to 3, respectively. The rows and columns inside each block correspond to values of $x$ and $y$ from 0 to 3, respectively. The number of sign changes across a row or a column of a matrix is called the *sequency* of the row or column. The rows and columns in the figure are ordered in increased sequency. Some authors show similar but unordered figures, because this transform was defined by Walsh and by Hadamard in slightly different ways (see [Gonzalez 92] for more information).

Compressing an image with the WHT is done similarly to the DCT, except that Equations (3.11) and (3.12) are used, instead of Equations (3.9) and (3.10).

**Example:** Figure 3.43 shows the 64 basis images and the Matlab code to calculate and display the basis images of the WHT for $N = 8$. Each basis image is an $8 \times 8$ matrix.

### 3.5.7 Haar Transform

The Haar transform [Stollnitz 92] is used in practice as a subband transform and is discussed as such in Chapter 4. However, since it is such a simple transform, it can also be understood in terms of basis images, which is why it is also discussed in this section. The Haar transform is based on the Haar functions $h_k(x)$, which are defined for $x \in [0, 1]$ and for $k = 0, 1, \ldots, N - 1$, where $N = 2^n$.

Before we discuss the actual transform, we have to mention that any integer $k$ can be expressed as the sum $k = 2^p + q - 1$, where $0 \le p \le n - 1$, $q = 0$ or 1 for $p = 0$, and $1 \le q \le 2^p$ for $p \ne 0$. For $N = 4 = 2^2$, for example, we get $0 = 2^0 + 0 - 1$, $1 = 2^0 + 1 - 1$, $2 = 2^1 + 1 - 1$, and $3 = 2^1 + 2 - 1$.

The Haar basis functions are now defined as

$$h_0(x) \overset{\text{def}}{=} h_{00}(x) = \frac{1}{\sqrt{N}} \quad \text{for } 0 \le x \le 1 \tag{3.14}$$

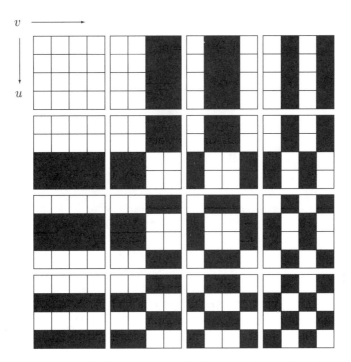

**Figure 3.42:** The Ordered WHT Kernel For $N = 4$.

and

$$h_k(x) \overset{\text{def}}{=} h_{pq}(x) = \frac{1}{\sqrt{N}} \begin{cases} 2^{p/2}, & \frac{q-1}{2^p} \le x < \frac{q-1/2}{2^p}, \\ -2^{p/2}, & \frac{q-1/2}{2^p} \le x < \frac{q}{2^p}, \\ 0, & \text{otherwise for } x \in [0,1]. \end{cases} \tag{3.15}$$

The Haar transform matrix $\mathbf{A}_N$ of order $N \times N$ can now be constructed. A general element $i, j$ of this matrix is the basis function $h_i(j)$, where $i = 0, 1, \ldots, N - 1$ and $j = 0/N, 1/N, \ldots, (N-1)/N$. For example,

$$\mathbf{A}_2 = \begin{pmatrix} h_0(0/2) & h_0(1/2) \\ h_1(0/2) & h_1(1/2) \end{pmatrix} = \frac{1}{\sqrt{2}} \begin{pmatrix} 1 & 1 \\ 1 & -1 \end{pmatrix} \tag{3.16}$$

(recall that $i = 1$ implies $p = 0$ and $q = 1$). Figure 3.44 shows code to calculate this matrix for any $N$, and also the Haar basis images for $N = 8$. As an example, the Haar coefficient matrices $\mathbf{A}_4$ and $\mathbf{A}_8$ are shown here. $\mathbf{A}_4$ is the $4 \times 4$ matrix

$$\mathbf{A}_4 = \begin{pmatrix} h_0(0/4) & h_0(1/4) & h_0(2/4) & h_0(3/4) \\ h_1(0/4) & h_1(1/4) & h_1(2/4) & h_1(3/4) \\ h_2(0/4) & h_2(1/4) & h_2(2/4) & h_2(3/4) \\ h_3(0/4) & h_3(1/4) & h_3(2/4) & h_3(3/4) \end{pmatrix} = \frac{1}{\sqrt{4}} \begin{pmatrix} 1 & 1 & 1 & 1 \\ 1 & 1 & -1 & -1 \\ \sqrt{2} & -\sqrt{2} & 0 & 0 \\ 0 & 0 & \sqrt{2} & -\sqrt{2} \end{pmatrix},$$

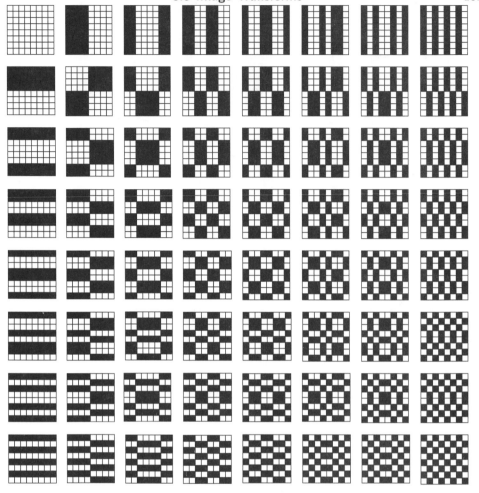

```
M=3; N=2^M; H=[1 1; 1 -1]/sqrt(2);
for m=1:(M-1) % recursion
  H=[H H; H -H]/sqrt(2);
end
A=H';
map=[1 5 7 3 4 8 6 2]; % 1:N
for n=1:N, B(:,n)=A(:,map(n)); end;
A=B;
sc=1/(max(abs(A(:))).^2); % scale factor
for row=1:N
  for col=1:N
    BI=A(:,row)*A(:,col).'; % tensor product
    subplot(N,N,(row-1)*N+col)
    oe=round(BI*sc); % results in -1, +1
    imagesc(oe), colormap([1 1 1; .5 .5 .5; 0 0 0])
    drawnow
  end
end
```

**Figure 3.43:** The $8 \times 8$ WHT Basis Images and Matlab Code.

and $\mathbf{A}_8$ is

$$
\mathbf{A}_8 = \frac{1}{\sqrt{8}} \begin{pmatrix}
1 & 1 & 1 & 1 & 1 & 1 & 1 & 1 \\
1 & 1 & 1 & 1 & -1 & -1 & -1 & -1 \\
\sqrt{2} & \sqrt{2} & -\sqrt{2} & -\sqrt{2} & 0 & 0 & 0 & 0 \\
0 & 0 & 0 & 0 & \sqrt{2} & \sqrt{2} & -\sqrt{2} & -\sqrt{2} \\
2 & -2 & 0 & 0 & 0 & 0 & 0 & 0 \\
0 & 0 & 2 & -2 & 0 & 0 & 0 & 0 \\
0 & 0 & 0 & 0 & 2 & -2 & 0 & 0 \\
0 & 0 & 0 & 0 & 0 & 0 & 2 & -2
\end{pmatrix}
$$

Given an image block $\mathbf{P}$ of order $N \times N$ where $N = 2^n$, its Haar transform is the matrix product $\mathbf{A}_N \mathbf{P} \mathbf{A}_N$ (Section 4.2.1).

### 3.5.8 Karhunen-Loève Transform

The Karhunen-Loève transform (also called the Hotelling transform) has the best efficiency in the sense of energy compaction, but for of the reasons mentioned earlier, it has more theoretical than practical value. Given an image, we break it up into $k$ blocks of $n$ pixels each, where $n$ is typically 64 but can have other values and $k$ depends on the image size. We consider the blocks vectors and denote them by $\mathbf{b}^{(i)}$ for $i = 1, 2, \ldots, k$. The average vector is $\overline{\mathbf{b}} = (\sum_i \mathbf{b}^{(i)})/k$. A new set of vectors $\mathbf{v}^{(i)} = \mathbf{b}^{(i)} - \overline{\mathbf{b}}$ is defined, causing the average $(\sum \mathbf{v}^{(i)})/k$ to be zero. We denote the $n \times n$ KLT transform matrix that we are seeking by $\mathbf{A}$. The result of transforming a vector $\mathbf{v}^{(i)}$ is the weight vector $\mathbf{w}^{(i)} = \mathbf{A}\mathbf{v}^{(i)}$. The average of the $\mathbf{w}^{(i)}$ is also zero. We now construct a matrix $\mathbf{V}$ whose columns are the $\mathbf{v}^{(i)}$ vectors and another matrix $\mathbf{W}$ whose columns are the weight vectors $\mathbf{w}^{(i)}$:

$$
\mathbf{V} = \left( \mathbf{v}^{(1)}, \mathbf{v}^{(2)}, \ldots, \mathbf{v}^{(k)} \right), \quad \mathbf{W} = \left( \mathbf{w}^{(1)}, \mathbf{w}^{(2)}, \ldots, \mathbf{w}^{(k)} \right).
$$

Matrices $\mathbf{V}$ and $\mathbf{W}$ have $n$ rows and $k$ columns each. From the definition of $\mathbf{w}^{(i)}$ we get $\mathbf{W} = \mathbf{A} \cdot \mathbf{V}$.

The $n$ coefficient vectors $\mathbf{c}^{(j)}$ of the Karhunen-Loève transform are given by

$$
\mathbf{c}^{(j)} = \left( w_j^{(1)}, w_j^{(2)}, \ldots, w_j^{(k)} \right), \quad j = 1, 2, \ldots, n.
$$

Thus, vector $\mathbf{c}^{(j)}$ consists of the $j$th elements of all the weight vectors $\mathbf{w}^{(i)}$, for $i = 1, 2, \ldots, k$ ($\mathbf{c}^{(j)}$ is the $j$th coordinate of the $\mathbf{w}^{(i)}$ vectors).

We now examine the elements of the matrix product $\mathbf{W} \cdot \mathbf{W}^T$ (this is an $n \times n$ matrix). A general element in row $a$ and column $b$ of this matrix is the sum of products

$$
\left( \mathbf{W} \cdot \mathbf{W}^T \right)_{ab} = \sum_{i=1}^k w_a^{(i)} w_b^{(i)} = \sum_{i=1}^k c_i^{(a)} c_i^{(b)} = \mathbf{c}^{(a)} \bullet \mathbf{c}^{(b)}, \quad \text{for } a, b \in [1, n]. \qquad (3.17)
$$

The fact that the average of each $\mathbf{w}^{(i)}$ is zero implies that a general diagonal element $(\mathbf{W} \cdot \mathbf{W}^T)_{jj}$ of the product matrix is the variance (up to a factor $k$) of the $j$th element (or

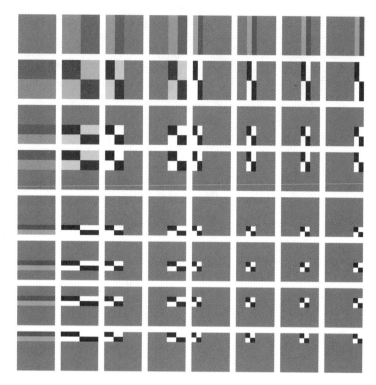

```
Needs["GraphicsImage'"] (* Draws 2D Haar Coefficients *)
n=8;
h[k_,x_]:=Module[{p,q}, If[k==0, 1/Sqrt[n],            (* h_0(x) *)
 p=0; While[2^p<=k ,p++]; p--; q=k-2^p+1; (* if k>0, calc. p, q *)
 If[(q-1)/(2^p)<=x && x<(q-.5)/(2^p),2^(p/2),
  If[(q-.5)/(2^p)<=x && x<q/(2^p),-2^(p/2),0]]]];
HaarMatrix=Table[h[k,x], {k,0,7}, {x,0,7/n,1/n}] //N;
HaarTensor=Array[Outer[Times, HaarMatrix[[#1]],HaarMatrix[[#2]]]&,
 {n,n}];
Show[GraphicsArray[Map[GraphicsImage[#, {-2,2}]&, HaarTensor,{2}]]]
```

**Figure 3.44:** The Basis Images of the Haar Transform for $n = 8$.

$j$th coordinate) of the $\mathbf{w}^{(i)}$ vectors. This diagonal element turns out to be the variance of coefficient vector $\mathbf{c}^{(j)}$ because the average of vector $\mathbf{w}^{(i)}$ is zero, so Equation (3.17) yields

$$\left(\mathbf{W}\cdot\mathbf{W}^T\right)_{jj} = \sum_{i=1}^{k} w_j^{(i)} w_j^{(i)} = \sum_{i=1}^{k} \left(w_j^{(i)} - 0\right)^2 = \sum_{i=1}^{k} \left(c_i^{(j)} - 0\right)^2 = k \, \text{variance}(\mathbf{c}^{(j)}).$$

The off-diagonal elements of $\left(\mathbf{W}\cdot\mathbf{W}^T\right)$ are the covariances of the $\mathbf{w}^{(i)}$ vectors such that element $\left(\mathbf{W}\cdot\mathbf{W}^T\right)_{ab}$ is the covariance of the $a$th and $b$th coordinates of the $\mathbf{w}^{(i)}$s.

Equation (3.17) shows that this is also the dot product $\mathbf{c}^{(a)} \cdot \mathbf{c}^{(b)}$. One of the main aims of image transform is to decorrelate the coordinates of the vectors, and probability theory tells us that two coordinates are decorrelated if their covariance is zero (the other aim is energy compaction, but the two goals go hand in hand). Thus, our aim is to find a transformation matrix $\mathbf{A}$ such that the product $\mathbf{W} \cdot \mathbf{W}^T$ will be diagonal.

From the definition of matrix $\mathbf{W}$ we get

$$\mathbf{W} \cdot \mathbf{W}^T = (\mathbf{A}\mathbf{V}) \cdot (\mathbf{A}\mathbf{V})^T = \mathbf{A}(\mathbf{V} \cdot \mathbf{V}^T)\mathbf{A}^T.$$

Matrix $\mathbf{V} \cdot \mathbf{V}^T$ is symmetric, and its elements are the covariances of the coordinates of vectors $\mathbf{v}^{(i)}$, i.e.,

$$\left(\mathbf{V} \cdot \mathbf{V}^T\right)_{ab} = \sum_{i=1}^{k} v_a^{(i)} v_b^{(i)}, \quad \text{for } a, b \in [1, n].$$

Since $\mathbf{V} \cdot \mathbf{V}^T$ is symmetric, its eigenvectors are orthogonal. We therefore normalize these vectors (i.e., make them orthonormal) and choose them as the rows of matrix $\mathbf{A}$. This produces the result

$$\mathbf{W} \cdot \mathbf{W}^T = \mathbf{A}(\mathbf{V} \cdot \mathbf{V}^T)\mathbf{A}^T = \begin{pmatrix} \lambda_1 & 0 & 0 & \cdots & 0 \\ 0 & \lambda_2 & 0 & \cdots & 0 \\ 0 & 0 & \lambda_3 & \cdots & 0 \\ \vdots & \vdots & & \vdots & \vdots \\ 0 & 0 & \cdots & 0 & \lambda_n \end{pmatrix}.$$

This choice of $\mathbf{A}$ results in a diagonal matrix $\mathbf{W} \cdot \mathbf{W}^T$ whose diagonal elements are the eigenvalues of $\mathbf{V} \cdot \mathbf{V}^T$. Matrix $\mathbf{A}$ is the Karhunen-Loève transformation matrix; its rows are the basis vectors of the KLT, and the energies (variances) of the transformed vectors are the eigenvalues $\lambda_1, \lambda_2, \ldots, \lambda_n$ of $\mathbf{V} \cdot \mathbf{V}^T$.

The basis vectors of the KLT are calculated from the original image pixels, and are therefore data dependent. In a practical compression method, these vectors have to be included in the compressed file for the decoder's use, and this, combined with the fact that no fast method has been discovered for the calculation of the KLT, makes this transform less than ideal for practical applications.

> Honesty is the best image.
> —Ziggy (Tom Wilson)

## 3.6 Progressive Image Compression

Most modern image compression methods are either progressive or optionally so. Progressive compression is an attractive choice when compressed images are transmitted over a communications line and are decompressed and viewed in real time (as is done, for example, in a Web browser). When such an image is received and decompressed, the decoder can very quickly display the entire image in a low-quality format and improve the display quality as more and more of the image is being received and decompressed. A user watching the image develop on the screen can normally recognize most of the image features after only 5–10% of it has been decompressed.

This should be compared to raster-scan image compression. When an image is raster scanned and compressed, a user normally cannot tell much about the image when only 5–10% of it has been decompressed and displayed. Since images are supposed to be viewed by humans, progressive compression makes sense even in cases where it is slower or less efficient than nonprogressive.

Perhaps a good way to think of progressive image compression is to imagine that the encoder compresses the most important image information first, then compresses less important information and appends it to the compressed file, and so on. This explains why all progressive image compression methods have a natural lossy option; simply stop compressing at a certain point. The user can control the amount of loss by means of a parameter that tells the encoder how soon to stop the progressive encoding process. The sooner encoding is stopped, the better the compression ratio and the bigger the data loss.

Another advantage of progressive compression becomes apparent when the compressed file has to be decompressed several times and displayed with different resolutions. The decoder can, in each case, stop the decompression when the image has reached the resolution of the particular output device used.

Progressive image compression has already been mentioned in connection with JPEG (page 142). JPEG uses the DCT to break the image up into its spatial frequency components, and it compresses the low-frequency components first. The decoder can therefore display these parts quickly, and it is these low-frequency parts that contain the general image information. The high-frequency parts contain image details. Thus, JPEG encodes spatial frequency data progressively.

> Education is a progressive discovery of our own ignorance.
>
> —Will Durant

It is useful to think of progressive decoding as the process of improving image features over time, and this can be done in three ways:

1. Encode spatial frequency data progressively. An observer watching such an image being decoded sees the image changing from blurred to sharp. Methods that work this way typically feature medium-speed encoding and slow decoding. This type of progressive compression is sometimes called *SNR progressive* or *quality progressive*.

2. Start with a gray image and add colors or shades of gray to it. An observer watching such an image being decoded will see all the image details from the start and will see them improve as more color is continuously added to them. Vector quantization

methods use this kind of progressive compression. Such a method normally features slow encoding and fast decoding.

3. Encode the image in layers, where early layers consist of a few large low-resolution pixels, followed by later layers with smaller higher-resolution pixels. A person watching such an image being decoded will see more detail added to the image over time. Such a method therefore adds detail (or resolution) to the image as it is being decompressed. This way of progressively encoding an image is called *pyramid coding* or *hierarchical coding*. Most progressive compression methods use this principle, so this section discusses general ideas for implementing pyramid coding. Figure 3.46 illustrates the three principles of progressive compression mentioned here. It should be contrasted with Figure 3.45, which illustrates sequential decoding.

**Figure 3.45:** Sequential Decoding.

Assuming that the image size is $2^n \times 2^n = 4^n$ pixels, the simplest method that comes to mind in trying to do progressive compression is to calculate each pixel of layer $i-1$ as the average of a group of $2 \times 2$ pixels of layer $i$. Thus, layer $n$ is the entire image ($4^n$ pixels), layer $n-1$ contains $2^{n-1} \times 2^{n-1} = 4^{n-1}$ large pixels of size $2 \times 2$, and so on, down to layer 1, with $4^{n-n} = 1$ large pixel representing the entire image. If the image isn't too large, all the layers can be saved in memory. The pixels are then written on the compressed file in reverse order, starting with layer 1. The single pixel of layer 1 is the "parent" of the four pixels of layer 2, each of which is the parent of four pixels in layer 3, and so on. This process creates a progressive image file but no compression, since the total number of pixels in the pyramid is

$$4^0 + 4^1 + \cdots + 4^{n-1} + 4^n = (4^{n+1} - 1)/3 \approx 4^n(4/3) \approx 1.33 \times 4^n = 1.33(2^n \times 2^n),$$

which is 33% more than the original number!

**Figure 3.46:** Progressive Decoding.

A simple way to bring the total number of pixels in the pyramid down to $4^n$ is to include only three of the four pixels of a group in layer $i$ and to compute the value of the fourth pixel using the parent of the group (from the preceding layer, $i-1$) and its three siblings.

**Example:** Figure 3.47c shows a $4 \times 4$ image that becomes the third layer in its progressive compression. Layer two is shown in Figure 3.47b, where, for example, pixel 81.25 is the average of the four pixels 90, 72, 140, and 23 of layer three. The single pixel of layer one is shown in Figure 3.47a.

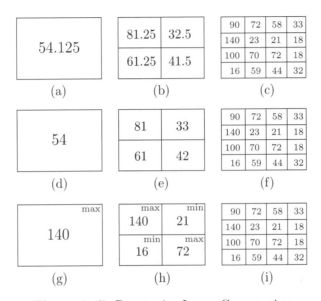

**Figure 3.47:** Progressive Image Compression.

The compressed file should contain just the numbers

$$54.125, \ 32.5, 41.5, 61.25, \ 72, 23, 140, \ 33, 18, 21, \ 18, 32, 44, \ 70, 59, 16$$

(properly encoded, of course) from which all the missing pixel values can easily be calculated. The missing pixel 81.25, for example, can be calculated from the equation $(x + 32.5 + 41.5 + 61.25)/4 = 54.125$.

A small complication with this method is that averages of integers may be nonintegers. If we want our pixel values to remain integers, we either have to lose precision or to keep using longer and longer integers. Assuming that pixels are represented by 8 bits, adding four 8-bit integers produces a 10-bit integer. Dividing it by 4, to create the average, reduces the sum back to an 8-bit integer, but some precision may be lost. If we don't want to lose precision, we should represent our second-layer pixels as 10-bit numbers and our first-layer (single) pixel as a 12-bit number. Figure 3.47d,e,f shows the results of rounding off our pixel values and thus losing some image information. The contents of the compressed file in this case should be

$$54, \ 33, 42, 61, \ 72, 23, 140, \ 33, 18, 21, \ 18, 32, 44, \ 70, 59, 16.$$

The first missing pixel, 81, of layer three can be calculated from the equation $(x + 33 + 42 + 61)/4 = 54$, which yields the (slightly wrong) value 80.

A better method is to let the parent of a group help in calculating the values of its four children. This can be done by calculating the differences between the parent and its children and writing the differences (suitably coded) in layer $i$ of the compressed file. The decoder decodes the differences, then uses the parent from layer $i-1$ to compute the values of the four pixels. Either Huffman or arithmetic coding can be used to encode the differences. If all the layers are calculated and saved in memory, then the distribution of difference values can be found and used to achieve the best statistical compression.

If there is no room in memory for all the layers, a simple adaptive model can be implemented. It starts by assigning a count of 1 to every difference value (to avoid the zero-probability problem, [Salomon 00]). When a particular difference is calculated, it is assigned a probability and is encoded according to its count, and its count is then updated. It is a good idea to update the counts by incrementing them by a value greater than 1, since this way the original counts of 1 become insignificant very quickly.

Some improvement can be achieved if the parent is used to help calculate the values of three child pixels, and then these three plus the parent are used to calculate the value of the fourth pixel of the group. If the four pixels of a group are $a$, $b$, $c$, and $d$, then their average is $v = (a + b + c + d)/4$. The average becomes part of layer $i - 1$, and layer $i$ need contain only the three differences $k = a - b$, $l = b - c$, and $m = c - d$. Once the decoder has read and decoded the three differences, it can use their values, together with the value of $v$ from the previous layer, to compute the values of the four pixels of the group. Calculating $v$ by a division by 4 still causes the loss of two bits, but this 2-bit quantity can be isolated before the division, and retained by encoding it separately, following the three differences.

The parent pixel of a group does not have to be its average. One alternative is to select the maximum (or the minimum) pixel of a group as the parent. This has the advantage that the parent is identical to one of the pixels in the group. The encoder has to encode just three pixels in each group, and the decoder decodes three pixels (or differences) and uses the parent as the fourth pixel to complete the group. When encoding consecutive groups in a layer, the encoder should alternate between selecting the maximum and the minimum as parents, since always selecting the same creates progressive layers that are either too dark or too bright. Figure 3.47g,h,i shows the three layers in this case.

The compressed file should contain the numbers

$$140, \ (0), 21, 72, 16, \ (3), 90, 72, 23, \ (3), 58, 33, 18, \ (0), 18, 32, 44, \ (3), 100, 70, 59,$$

where the numbers in parentheses are two bits each. They tell where (in what quadrant) the parent from the previous layer should go. Notice that quadrant numbering is $\left(\begin{smallmatrix} 0 & 1 \\ 3 & 2 \end{smallmatrix}\right)$.

Selecting the median of a group is a little slower than selecting the maximum or the minimum, but it improves the appearance of the layers during progressive decompression. In general, the median of a sequence $(a_1, a_2, \ldots, a_n)$ is an element $a_i$ such that half the elements (or very close to half) are smaller than $a_i$ and the other half are bigger. If the four pixels of a group satisfy $a < b < c < d$, then either $b$ or $c$ can serve as the median pixel of the group. The main advantage of selecting the median as the group's parent is that it tends to smooth large differences in pixel values that may occur because of one extreme pixel. In the group 1, 2, 3, 100, for example, selecting 2 or 3 as the parent is much more representative than selecting the average. Finding the median of four pixels requires a few comparisons, but calculating the average requires a division by 4 (or, alternatively, a right shift).

Once the median has been selected and encoded as part of layer $i-1$, the remaining three pixels can be encoded in layer $i$ by encoding their (three) differences, preceded by a 2-bit code telling which of the four is the parent. Another small advantage of using the median is that once the decoder reads this 2-bit code, it knows how many of the three pixels are smaller and how many are bigger than the median. If the code says, for example, that one pixel is smaller and the other two are bigger than the median, and the decoder reads a pixel that's smaller than the median, it knows that the next two pixels decoded will be bigger than the median. This knowledge changes the distribution of the differences, and it can be taken advantage of by using three count tables to estimate probabilities when the differences are encoded. One table is used when a pixel is encoded that the decoder will know is bigger than the median. Another table is used to encode pixels that the decoder will know are smaller than the median, and the third table is used for pixels where the decoder will not know in advance their relations to the median. This improves compression by a few percent and is an example of how adding more features to a compression method brings diminishing returns.

Some of the important progressive image compression methods used in practice, such as SPIHT and EZW, are described in [Salomon 00].

## 3.7 JPEG

JPEG is a sophisticated lossy/lossless compression method for color or grayscale still images (not movies). It does not handle bi-level (black and white) images very well. It also works best on continuous-tone images, where adjacent pixels tend to have similar colors. One advantage of JPEG is the existence of many parameters that allow the user to adjust the amount of the data lost (and thereby also the compression ratio) over a very wide range. Often, the eye cannot see any image degradation even at compression factors of 10 or 20. There are two main modes: lossy (also called baseline) and lossless (which isn't very efficient and typically produces compression factors of around 2). Most implementations support just the lossy mode. This mode includes progressive and hierarchical coding.

JPEG is a compression method, not a complete standard for image representation. This is why it does not specify image features such as pixel aspect ratio, color space, or interleaving of bitmap rows.

JPEG has been developed as a compression method for continuous-tone images. The main goals of JPEG compression are the following:

1. High compression ratios, especially in cases where image quality is judged as very good to excellent.

2. The use of many parameters, allowing sophisticated users to experiment and achieve the desired compression/quality tradeoff.

3. Obtaining good results with any kind of continuous-tone image, regardless of image dimensions, color space, pixel aspect ratio, or other features.

4. A sophisticated but not too complex compression method, allowing software and hardware implementations on many platforms.

5. Several modes of operation: (a) Sequential mode: each color component is compressed in a single left-to-right, top-to-bottom scan; (b) Progressive mode: the image is compressed in multiple blocks (known as "scans") to be decompressed and viewed from coarse to fine detail; (c) Lossless mode: important for cases where the user decides that no pixels should be lost (the tradeoff is low compression ratio compared to the lossy modes); and (d) Hierarchical mode: the image is compressed at multiple resolutions allowing lower-resolution blocks to be viewed without first having to decompress the following higher-resolution blocks.

The term JPEG is an acronym that stands for Joint Photographic Experts Group. The JPEG project was a joint effort by the CCITT and the ISO (the International Standards Organization) that started in June 1987 and produced the first JPEG draft proposal in 1991. The JPEG standard has proved successful and has become widely used for image compression, especially in Web pages.

The main JPEG compression steps are outlined below, and each step is then described in detail later.

1. Color images are transformed from RGB into a luminance/chrominance color space (Section 3.7.1; this step is skipped for grayscale images). The eye is sensitive to small changes in luminance but not in chrominance, so the chrominance parts can later lose much data and thus be highly compressed without visually impairing the overall image quality much. This step is optional but important since the remainder of the algorithm works on each color component separately. Without transforming the color space, none of the three color components will tolerate much loss, leading to worse compression.

2. Color images are downsampled by creating low-resolution pixels from the original ones (this step is used only when hierarchical compression is needed; it is always skipped for grayscale images). The downsampling is not done for the luminance component. Downsampling (Figure 3.48) is done either at a ratio of 2:1 both horizontally and vertically (the so-called 2h2v or "4:1:1" sampling) or at ratios of 2:1 horizontally and 1:1 vertically (2h1v or "4:2:2" sampling). Since this is done on two of the three color components, 2h2v reduces the image to $1/3 + (2/3) \times (1/4) = 1/2$ its original size, while 2h1v reduces it to $1/3 + (2/3) \times (1/2) = 2/3$ its original size. Since the luminance component is not touched, there is no noticeable loss of image quality. Grayscale images don't go through this step.

3. The pixels of each color component are organized in groups of $8 \times 8$ pixels called *data units*. If the number of image rows or columns is not a multiple of 8, the bottom row and the rightmost column are duplicated as many times as necessary. In the noninterleaved mode, the encoder handles all the data units of the first image component, then the

**Figure 3.48:** 2h2v and 2h1v Sampling.

data units of the second component, and finally those of the third component. In the interleaved mode, the encoder processes the three top left (#1) data units of the three image components, then the three data units (#2) to their right, and so on.

4. The *discrete cosine transform* (DCT, Section 3.5.3) is then applied to each data unit to create an $8 \times 8$ data unit (or block) of frequency components (Section 3.7.2). They represent the average pixel value and successive higher-frequency changes within the group. This prepares the image data for the crucial step of losing information. Since DCT involves the transcendental function cosine, it must involve some loss of information due to the limited precision of computer arithmetic. This means that even without the main lossy step (step 5 below), there will be some loss of image quality, but this is normally very small.

5. Each of the 64 frequency components in a data unit is divided by a separate number called its *quantization coefficient* (QC) and then rounded to an integer (Section 3.7.4). This is where information is irretrievably lost. Large QCs cause more loss, so the high-frequency components typically have larger QCs. Each of the 64 QCs is a JPEG parameter and can, in principle, be specified by the user. In practice, most JPEG implementations use the QC tables recommended by the JPEG standard for the luminance and chrominance image components (Table 3.50).

6. The 64 quantized frequency coefficients (which are now integers) of each data unit are encoded using a combination of RLE and Huffman coding (Section 3.7.5). An arithmetic coding variant known as the QM coder [Salomon 00] can be used instead of Huffman coding.

7. The last step adds headers and the values of all the JPEG parameters used and outputs the result. The compressed file may be in one of three formats: (1) the *interchange* format, in which the file contains the compressed image and all the tables needed by the decoder (mostly quantization tables and tables of Huffman codes), (2) the *abbreviated* format for compressed image data, where the file contains the compressed image and may contain no tables (or just a few tables), and (3) the *abbreviated* format for table-specification data, where the file contains just tables, and no compressed image. The second format makes sense in cases where the same encoder/decoder pair is used, and they have the same tables built in. The third format is used in cases where many images have been compressed by the same encoder, using the same tables. When those images need to be decompressed, they are sent to a decoder preceded by one file with table-specification data.

The JPEG decoder performs the reverse steps. (Thus, JPEG is a symmetric compression method).

The progressive mode is a JPEG option. In this mode, higher-frequency DCT coefficients are written on the compressed file in blocks called "scans." Each scan read and processed by the decoder results in a sharper image. The idea is to use the first few scans to quickly create a low-quality, blurred preview of the image, then either input the remaining scans or stop the process and reject the image. The tradeoff is that the encoder has to save all the coefficients of all the data units in a memory buffer before they are sent in scans (this is because they are sent in scans in the reverse order in which they are generated; see page 136) and also go through all the steps for each scan, slowing down the progressive mode.

Figure 3.49a shows an example of an image with resolution $1024 \times 512$. The image is divided into $128 \times 64 = 8192$ data units, and each is DCT transformed, becoming a set of 64 8-bit numbers. Figure 3.49b is a block whose depth corresponds to the 8,192 data units, whose height corresponds to the 64 DCT coefficients (the DC coefficient is the top one, numbered 0), and whose width corresponds to the 8 bits of each coefficient.

After preparing all the data units in a memory buffer, the encoder writes them on the compressed file in one of two methods, *spectral selection* or *successive approximation* (Figure 3.49c,d). The first scan in either method is the set of DC coefficients. If spectral selection is used, each successive scan consists of several consecutive (a *band* of) AC coefficients. If successive approximation is used, the second scan consists of the four most significant bits of all AC coefficients, and each of the following four scans, numbers 3 through 6, adds one more significant bit (bits 3 through 0, respectively).

In the hierarchical mode, the encoder stores the image several times in the output file at several resolutions. However, each high-resolution part uses information from the low-resolution parts of the output file, so the total amount of information is less than that required to store the different resolutions separately. Each hierarchical part may use the progressive mode.

The hierarchical mode is useful in cases where a high-resolution image needs to be output in low resolution. Older dot-matrix printers may be a good example of a low-resolution output device still in use.

The lossless mode of JPEG (Section 3.7.6) calculates a "predicted" value for each pixel, generates the difference between the pixel and its predicted value for relative encoding, and encodes the difference using the same method (i.e., Huffman or arithmetic coding) as in step 5 above. The predicted value is calculated using values of pixels above and to the left of the current pixel (pixels that have already been input and encoded). The following sections discuss these steps in more detail.

> When in doubt, predict that the present trend will continue.
>
> —Merkin's Maxim

### 3.7.1 Luminance

The main international organization devoted to light and color is the International Committee on Illumination (Commission Internationale de l'Éclairage), abbreviated CIE. It is responsible for developing standards and definitions in this area. One of the early achievements of the CIE was its *chromaticity diagram* [Salomon 99], developed in 1931. It shows that no fewer than three parameters are required to define color. Expressing a certain color by the triplet $(x, y, z)$ is similar to denoting a point in three-

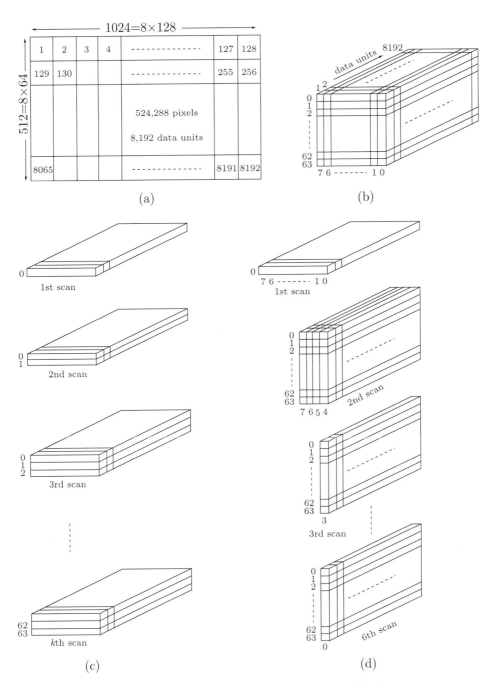

**Figure 3.49:** Scans in the JPEG Progressive Mode.

dimensional space, hence the term *color space*. The most common color space is RGB, where the three parameters are the intensities of red, green, and blue in a color. When used in computers, these parameters are normally in the range 0–255 (8 bits) each.

The CIE defines color as the perceptual result of light in the visible region of the spectrum, having wavelengths in the region of 400 nm to 700 nm incident on the retina (a nanometer, nm, equals $10^{-9}$ meter). Physical power (or radiance) is expressed in a spectral power distribution (SPD), often in 31 components each representing a 10 nm band.

The CIE defines brightness as the attribute of a visual sensation according to which an area appears to emit more or less light. The brain's perception of brightness is impossible to define, so the CIE defines a more practical quantity called *luminance*. It is defined as radiant power weighted by a spectral sensitivity function that is characteristic of vision. The luminous efficiency of the standard observer is defined by the CIE as a positive function of the wavelength, which has a maximum at about 555 nm. When a spectral power distribution is integrated using this function as a weighting function, the result is CIE luminance, which is denoted by Y. Luminance is an important quantity in the fields of digital image processing and compression.

Luminance is proportional to the power of the light source. It is similar to intensity, but the spectral composition of luminance is related to the brightness sensitivity of human vision. Based on the results of many experiments, luminance is defined as a weighted sum of red, green, and blue, with weights 77/256, 150/256, and 29/256, respectively.

The eye is very sensitive to small changes in luminance, which is why it is useful to have color spaces that use Y as one of their three parameters. A simple way to do this is to subtract Y from the blue and red components of RGB and use the three components Y, $Cb = B - Y$, and $Cr = R - Y$ as a new color space. The last two components are called chroma. They represent color in terms of the presence or absence of blue (Cb) and red (Cr) for a given luminance intensity.

Various number ranges are used in $B - Y$ and $R - Y$ for different applications. The YPbPr ranges are optimized for component analog video. The YCbCr ranges are appropriate for component digital video such as studio video, JPEG, JPEG 2000, and MPEG-1.

The YCbCr color space was developed as part of Recommendation ITU-R BT.601 (formerly CCIR 601) during the development of a worldwide digital component video standard. Y is defined to have a range of 16 to 235; Cb and Cr are defined to have a range of 16 to 240, with 128 equal to zero. There are several YCbCr sampling formats, such as 4:4:4, 4:2:2, 4:1:1, and 4:2:0, which are also described in the recommendation.

Conversions between RGB with a 16–235 range and YCbCr are linear and therefore simple. Transforming RGB to YCbCr is done by (notice the small weight assigned to blue)

$$Y = (77/256)R + (150/256)G + (29/256)B,$$
$$Cb = -(44/256)R - (87/256)G + (131/256)B + 128,$$
$$Cr = (131/256)R - (110/256)G - (21/256)B + 128,$$

while the opposite transformation is

$$R = Y + 1.371(Cr - 128),$$
$$G = Y - 0.698(Cr - 128) - 0.336(Cb - 128),$$
$$B = Y + 1.732(Cb - 128).$$

When performing YCbCr to RGB conversion, the resulting RGB values have a nominal range of 16–235, with possible occasional values in 0–15 and 236–255.

## 3.7.2 DCT

The discrete cosine transform (DCT) is discussed in Section 3.5.3. The JPEG committee elected to use the DCT because of its good performance, because it does not assume anything about the structure of the data being compressed, and because there are ways to speed up the DCT (Section 3.7.3).

The JPEG standard does not apply the DCT to the entire image but to data units (blocks) of $8 \times 8$ pixels each: (1) Applying the DCT to the entire image involves many arithmetic operations and is therefore slow. Applying the DCT to individual data units is faster. (2) Experience shows that, in a continuous-tone image, correlations between pixels are short range. A pixel in such an image has a value (color component or shade of gray) that's close to those of its near neighbors, but has nothing to do with the values of far neighbors. Applying the DCT to the entire image may therefore not result in better compression.

It should be noted that the principle of transforming individual data units has its downside. Applying the DCT to the entire image produces a better-looking image after lossy compression and decompression. Applying the DCT to data units is faster, but when an image is compressed and then decompressed, it may feature blocky artifacts due to the way the various blocks respond to the quantization step that follows the DCT.

The JPEG DCT is computed by Equation (3.9), duplicated here:

$$G_{ij} = \frac{1}{4} C_i C_j \sum_{x=0}^{7} \sum_{y=0}^{7} p_{xy} \cos\left(\frac{(2x+1)i\pi}{16}\right) \cos\left(\frac{(2y+1)j\pi}{16}\right), \tag{3.9}$$
$$\text{where } C_f = \begin{cases} \frac{1}{\sqrt{2}}, & f = 0, \\ 1, & f > 0, \end{cases} \quad \text{and } 0 \leq i, j \leq 7.$$

The DCT is JPEG's key to lossy compression. JPEG "loses" unimportant image information by dividing each of the 64 DCT coefficients (especially the ones located toward the right bottom part of the data unit) by a quantization coefficient (QC). In general, each of the 64 DCT coefficients is divided by a different quantization coefficient, and all 64 QCs are parameters that can, in principle, be controlled by the user (Section 3.7.4).

The JPEG decoder works by computing the inverse DCT (IDCT), Equation (3.10), duplicated here:

$$p_{xy} = \frac{1}{4} \sum_{i=0}^{7} \sum_{j=0}^{7} C_i C_j G_{ij} \cos\left(\frac{(2x+1)i\pi}{16}\right) \cos\left(\frac{(2y+1)j\pi}{16}\right),$$

$$\text{where } C_f = \begin{cases} \frac{1}{\sqrt{2}}, & f = 0; \\ 1, & f > 0. \end{cases}$$

(3.10)

It takes the 64 quantized DCT results and calculates 64 pixels $p_{xy}$. Mathematically, the DCT is a one-to-one mapping of 64-point vectors from the image domain to the frequency domain. The IDCT is the reverse mapping. If the DCT and IDCT could be calculated with infinite precision and if the DCT coefficients were not quantized, the original 64 pixels could be exactly reconstructed. In practice, quantization is often used, but if done carefully, the new 64 pixels will be very similar to the original ones.

### 3.7.3 Practical DCT

Equation (3.9) can be coded directly in any higher-level language. However, several improvements are possible, which speed it up considerably. Since this equation is the "heart" of JPEG, its fast calculation is essential. Here are some ideas.

1. Regardless of the image size, only 32 cosine functions are involved (see the next paragraph). They can be precomputed once and used repeatedly to calculate all the $8 \times 8$ data units. Calculating the expression

$$p_{xy} \cos\left(\frac{(2x+1)i\pi}{16}\right) \cos\left(\frac{(2y+1)j\pi}{16}\right)$$

now amounts to performing two multiplications. The double sum of (3.9) thus requires $64 \times 2 = 128$ multiplications and 63 additions.

(The arguments of the cosine functions used by the DCT are of the form $(2x+1)i\pi/16$, where $i$ and $x$ are integers in the range $[0, 7]$. Such an argument can be written in the form $n\pi/16$, where $n$ is an integer in the range $[0, 15 \times 7]$. Since the cosine function is periodic, it satisfies $\cos(32\pi/16) = \cos(0\pi/16)$, $\cos(33\pi/16) = \cos(\pi/16)$, and so on. As a result, only the 32 values $\cos(n\pi/16)$ for $n = 0, 1, 2, \ldots, 31$ are needed. I am indebted to V. Saravanan for pointing out this feature of the DCT.)

2. A little algebraic tinkering shows that the double sum of (3.9) can be written as the matrix product $\mathbf{C}\mathbf{P}\mathbf{C}^T$, where $\mathbf{P}$ is the $8 \times 8$ matrix of the pixels, $\mathbf{C}$ is the matrix defined by

$$C_{ij} = \begin{cases} \frac{1}{\sqrt{8}}, & i = 0, \\ \frac{1}{2} \cos\left(\frac{(2j+1)i\pi}{16}\right), & i > 0, \end{cases}$$

and $\mathbf{C}^T$ is the transpose of $\mathbf{C}$.

Calculating one matrix element of the product $\mathbf{C}\mathbf{P}$ thus requires eight multiplications and seven (but for simplicity let's say eight) additions. Multiplying the two $8 \times 8$ matrices $\mathbf{C}$ and $\mathbf{P}$ requires $64 \times 8 = 8^3$ multiplications and the same number of additions. Multiplying the product $\mathbf{C}\mathbf{P}$ by $\mathbf{C}^T$ requires the same number of operations, so the DCT of one $8\times8$ data unit requires $2\times8^3$ multiplications (and the same number of additions). Assuming that the entire image consists of $n\times n$ pixels, and that $n = 8q$, there are $q\times q$ data units, so the DCT of all the data units requires $2q^2 8^3$ multiplications (and the same number of additions). In comparison, performing one DCT for the entire image would require $2n^3 = 2q^3 8^3 = (2q^2 8^3)q$ operations. By dividing the image into data units we reduce the number of multiplications (and also of additions) by a factor of $q$. Unfortunately, $q$ cannot be too large, since that would mean very small data units.

We should remember that a color image consists of three components (normally RGB, but usually converted to YCbCr or YPbPr). Each is DCT-transformed separately, bringing the total number of arithmetic operations to $3\cdot2q^2 8^3 = 3,072q^2$. For a $512\times512$-pixel image, this means $3,072\times64^2 = 12,582,912$ multiplications (and the same number of additions).

3. Another way to speed up the DCT is to perform all the arithmetic operations on fixed-point (scaled integer) rather than floating-point numbers. On many computers, operations on fixed-point numbers require (somewhat) sophisticated programming techniques but are considerably faster than floating-point operations (some high-performance computers—such as the CDC 6400, the CDC 7600, and the various Cray systems—are notable exceptions).

Arguably, the best DCT algorithm is described in [Feig and Linzer 90]. It uses 54 multiplications and 468 additions and shifts. Today, there are also various VLSI chips that perform this calculation efficiently. The interested reader should also check [Loeffler et al. 89] for a fast one-dimensional DCT algorithm that uses 11 multiplications and 29 additions.

### 3.7.4 Quantization

After each $8\times8$ matrix of DCT coefficients $G_{ij}$ is calculated, it is quantized. This is the step where the information loss (except for some unavoidable loss because of finite precision calculations in other steps) occurs. Each number in the DCT coefficients matrix is divided by the corresponding number from the particular "quantization table" used, and the result is rounded to the nearest integer. As has already been mentioned, three such tables are needed for the three color components. The JPEG standard allows for up to four tables, and the user can select any of the four for quantizing each color component. The 64 numbers constituting each quantization table are all JPEG parameters. In principle, they can all be specified and fine-tuned by the user for maximum compression. In practice, few users have the time or expertise to experiment with so many parameters, so JPEG software normally uses two approaches:

1. Default quantization tables. Two such tables, one for the luminance (grayscale) and one for the chrominance components, are the result of many experiments performed by the JPEG committee. They are included in the JPEG standard and are reproduced here as Table 3.50. It is easy to see how the QCs in the table generally grow as we move from the upper left corner to the bottom right one. This is how JPEG reduces the DCT coefficients with high spatial frequencies.

2. A simple quantization table $Q$ is computed, based on one parameter $R$ supplied by the user. A simple expression such as $Q_{ij} = 1 + (i + j) \times R$ guarantees that QCs start small at the upper left corner and get bigger toward the bottom right corner.

| 16 | 11 | 10 | 16 | 24 | 40 | 51 | 61 |
|----|----|----|----|----|----|----|----|
| 12 | 12 | 14 | 19 | 26 | 58 | 60 | 55 |
| 14 | 13 | 16 | 24 | 40 | 57 | 69 | 56 |
| 14 | 17 | 22 | 29 | 51 | 87 | 80 | 62 |
| 18 | 22 | 37 | 56 | 68 | 109 | 103 | 77 |
| 24 | 35 | 55 | 64 | 81 | 104 | 113 | 92 |
| 49 | 64 | 78 | 87 | 103 | 121 | 120 | 101 |
| 72 | 92 | 95 | 98 | 112 | 100 | 103 | 99 |

| 17 | 18 | 24 | 47 | 99 | 99 | 99 | 99 |
|----|----|----|----|----|----|----|----|
| 18 | 21 | 26 | 66 | 99 | 99 | 99 | 99 |
| 24 | 26 | 56 | 99 | 99 | 99 | 99 | 99 |
| 47 | 66 | 99 | 99 | 99 | 99 | 99 | 99 |
| 99 | 99 | 99 | 99 | 99 | 99 | 99 | 99 |
| 99 | 99 | 99 | 99 | 99 | 99 | 99 | 99 |
| 99 | 99 | 99 | 99 | 99 | 99 | 99 | 99 |
| 99 | 99 | 99 | 99 | 99 | 99 | 99 | 99 |

Luminance                                   Chrominance

**Table 3.50:** Recommended Quantization Tables.

If the quantization is done right, very few nonzero numbers will be left in the DCT coefficients block, and they will typically be concentrated in the upper left part. These numbers are the output of JPEG, but they are further compressed before being written on the output file. In the JPEG literature this compression is called "entropy coding," and Section 3.7.5 shows in detail how it is done. Three techniques are used by entropy coding to compress the $8 \times 8$ matrix of integers:

1. The 64 numbers are collected by scanning the matrix in zigzags (Figure 3.5a). This produces a string of 64 numbers that starts with some nonzeros and typically ends with many consecutive zeros. Only the nonzero numbers are output (after further compressing them) and are followed by a special end-of-block (EOB) code. This way there is no need to output the trailing zeros (we can say that the EOB is the run-length encoding of all the trailing zeros).

**Example:** Table 3.51 lists 64 hypothetical DCT coefficients, only four of which are nonzero. The zigzag sequence of these coefficients is $1118, 2, 0, -2, \underbrace{0, \ldots, 0}_{13}, -1, \underbrace{0, \ldots, 0}_{46}$.

| 1118 | 2 | 0 | 0 | 0 | 0 | 0 |
|------|---|---|---|---|---|---|
| 0 | 0 | 0 | 0 | 0 | 0 | 0 |
| −2 | 0 | 0 | −1 | 0 | 0 | 0 | 0 |
| 0 | 0 | 0 | 0 | 0 | 0 | 0 |
| 0 | 0 | 0 | 0 | 0 | 0 | 0 |
| 0 | 0 | 0 | 0 | 0 | 0 | 0 |
| 0 | 0 | 0 | 0 | 0 | 0 | 0 |
| 0 | 0 | 0 | 0 | 0 | 0 | 0 |

**Table 3.51:** 64 Quantized Coefficients.

How can we write a software loop to traverse an $8 \times 8$ matrix in zigzag? A simple approach is to manually figure out the zigzag path and to record it in an array **zz** of structures, where each structure contains a pair of coordinates for the path as shown, e.g., in Figure 3.52.

(0,0) (0,1) (1,0) (2,0) (1,1) (0,2) (0,3) (1,2)
(2,1) (3,0) (4,0) (3,1) (2,2) (1,3) (0,4) (0,5)
(1,4) (2,3) (3,2) (4,1) (5,0) (6,0) (5,1) (4,2)
(3,3) (2,4) (1,5) (0,6) (0,7) (1,6) (2,5) (3,4)
(4,3) (5,2) (6,1) (7,0) (7,1) (6,2) (5,3) (4,4)
(3,5) (2,6) (1,7) (2,7) (3,6) (4,5) (5,4) (6,3)
(7,2) (7,3) (6,4) (5,5) (4,6) (3,7) (4,7) (5,6)
(6,5) (7,4) (7,5) (6,6) (5,7) (6,7) (7,6) (7,7)

**Figure 3.52:** Coordinates for the Zigzag Path.

If the two components of a structure are zz.r and zz.c, then the zigzag traversal can be done by a loop of the form

```
for (i=0; i<64; i++){
row:=zz[i].r; col:=zz[i].c
...data_unit[row][col]...}
```

2. The nonzero numbers are compressed using Huffman coding (Section 3.7.5).
3. The first of those numbers (the DC coefficient, page 109) is treated differently from the others (the AC coefficients).

### 3.7.5 Coding

We first discuss point 3 above. Each $8 \times 8$ matrix of quantized DCT coefficients contains one DC coefficient [at position $(0,0)$, the top left corner] and 63 AC coefficients. The DC coefficient is a measure of the average value of the 64 original pixels constituting the data unit. Experience shows that in a continuous-tone image, adjacent data units of pixels are normally correlated in the sense that the average values of the pixels in adjacent data units are close. We already know that the DC coefficient of a data unit is a multiple of the average of the 64 pixels constituting the unit. This implies that the DC coefficients of adjacent data units don't differ much. JPEG outputs the first one (encoded), followed by *differences* (also encoded) of the DC coefficients of consecutive data units.

**Example:** If the first three $8 \times 8$ data units of an image have quantized DC coefficients of 1118, 1114, and 1119, then the JPEG output for the first data unit is 1118 (Huffman encoded; see below) followed by the 63 (encoded) AC coefficients of that data unit. The output for the second data unit will be $1114 - 1118 = -4$ (also Huffman encoded), followed by the 63 (encoded) AC coefficients of that data unit, and the output for the third data unit will be $1119 - 1114 = 5$ (also Huffman encoded), again followed by the 63 (encoded) AC coefficients of that data unit. This way of handling the DC coefficients is worth the extra trouble, since the differences are small.

Coding the DC differences is done using Table 3.53. This table uses the so-called *unary code*, defined as follows: The unary code of the nonnegative integer $n$ consists of $n - 1$ ones followed by a single 0 or, alternatively, of $n - 1$ zeros followed by a single 1. The length of the unary code for the integer $n$ is therefore $n$ bits.

| 0: | 0 | | | | | | | | | 0 |
|---|---|---|---|---|---|---|---|---|---|---|
| 1: | -1 | 1 | | | | | | | | 10 |
| 2: | -3 | -2 | 2 | 3 | | | | | | 110 |
| 3: | -7 | -6 | -5 | -4 | 4 | 5 | 6 | 7 | | 1110 |
| 4: | -15 | -14 | . . . | -9 | -8 | 8 | 9 | 10 . . . | 15 | 11110 |
| 5: | -31 | -30 | -29 | . . . | -17 | -16 | 16 | 17 . . . | 31 | 111110 |
| 6: | -63 | -62 | -61 | . . . | -33 | -32 | 32 | 33 . . . | 63 | 1111110 |
| 7: | -127 | -126 | -125 | . . . | -65 | -64 | 64 | 65 . . . | 127 | 11111110 |
| ⋮ | | | ⋮ | | | | | | | |
| 14: | -16383 | -16382 | -16381 | . . . | -8193 | -8192 | 8192 | 8193 . . . | 16383 | 111111111111110 |
| 15: | -32767 | -32766 | -32765 | . . . | -16385 | -16384 | 16384 | 16385 . . . | 32767 | 1111111111111110 |
| 16: | 32768 | | | | | | | | | 1111111111111111 |

**Table 3.53:** Coding the Differences of DC Coefficients.

Each row of Table 3.53 has a row number (on the left), the unary code for the row (on the right), and several columns in between. Each row contains greater numbers (and also more numbers) than its predecessor but not the numbers contained in previous rows. Row $i$ contains the range of integers $[-(2^i-1), +(2^i-1)]$ but is missing the middle range $[-(2^{i-1}-1), +(2^{i-1}-1)]$. The rows thus get very long, which means that a simple two-dimensional array is not a good data structure for this table. In fact, there is no need to store these integers in a data structure, since the program can figure out where in the table any given integer $x$ is supposed to reside by analyzing the bits of $x$.

The first DC coefficient to be encoded in our example is 1118. It is found in row 11 column 930 of the table (column numbering starts at zero), so it is encoded as 111111111110|01110100010 (the unary code for row 11, followed by the 11-bit binary value of 930). The second DC difference is $-4$. It resides in row 3 column 3 of Table 3.53, so it is encoded as 1110|011 (the unary code for row 3, followed by the 3-bit binary value of 3). The third DC difference, 5, is located in row 3 column 5, so it is encoded as 1110|101.

Point 2 at the end of Section 3.7.4 has to do with the precise way the 63 AC coefficients of a data unit are compressed. This compression uses a combination of RLE and either Huffman or arithmetic coding. The idea is that the sequence of AC coefficients normally contains just a few nonzero numbers, with runs of zeros between them, and with a long run of trailing zeros. For each nonzero number $x$, (1) the encoder finds the number $Z$ of consecutive zeros preceding $x$; (2) it finds $x$ in Table 3.53 and prepares its row and column numbers (R and C); (3) the pair (R, Z) [that's (R, Z), not (R, C)] is used as row and column numbers for Table 3.54; and (4) the Huffman code found in that position in the table is concatenated to C (where C is written as an R-bit number) and the result is the code emitted by the JPEG encoder for the AC coefficient $x$ and all the consecutive zeros preceding it. (Quite a mouthful.)

The Huffman codes in Table 3.54 are arbitrary and are not the ones recommended by the JPEG standard. The standard recommends the use of Tables 3.55 and 3.56 and says that up to four Huffman code tables can be used by a JPEG codec, except that the baseline mode can use only two such tables. The reader should notice the EOB code at position $(0,0)$ and the ZRL code at position $(0,15)$. The former indicates end-of-block, and the latter is the code emitted for 15 consecutive zeros when the number of consec-

| R  Z: | 0 | 1 | ... | 15 |
|-------|---|---|-----|----|
| 0: | 1010 | | | 11111111001(ZRL) |
| 1: | 00 | 1100 | ... | 1111111111110101 |
| 2: | 01 | 11011 | ... | 1111111111110110 |
| 3: | 100 | 1111001 | ... | 1111111111110111 |
| 4: | 1011 | 111110110 | ... | 1111111111111000 |
| 5: | 11010 | 11111110110 | ... | 1111111111111001 |
| ⋮ | ⋮ | | | |

**Table 3.54:** Coding AC Coefficients.

utive zeros exceeds 15. These codes are the ones recommended for the luminance AC coefficients of Table 3.55. The EOB and ZRL codes recommended for the chrominance AC coefficients of Table 3.56 are 00 and 1111111010, respectively.

**Example:** Consider again the sequence $1118, 2, 0, -2, \underbrace{0, \ldots, 0}_{13}, -1, \underbrace{0, \ldots, 0}_{46}$. The first AC coefficient 2 has no zeros preceding it, so $Z = 0$. It is found in Table 3.53 in row 2 column 2, so $R = 2$ and $C = 2$. The Huffman code in position $(R, Z) = (2, 0)$ of Table 3.54 is 01, so the final code emitted for 2 is 01|10. The next nonzero coefficient, $-2$, has one zero preceding it, so $Z = 1$. It is found in Table 3.53 in row 2 column 1, so $R = 2$ and $C = 1$. The Huffman code in position $(R, Z) = (2, 1)$ of Table 3.54 is 11011, so the final code emitted for 2 is 11011|01. The last nonzero AC coefficient, $-1$, is preceded by thirteen consecutive zeros, so $Z = 13$. The coefficient itself is found in Table 3.53 in row 1 column 0, so $R = 1$ and $C = 0$. Assuming that the Huffman code in position $(R, Z) = (1, 13)$ of Table 3.54 is 1110101, the final code emitted for 1 is 1110101|0.

Finally, the sequence of trailing zeros is encoded as 1010 (EOB), so the output for the sequence of AC coefficients is 0110110111011101010101010. We saw earlier that the DC coefficient is encoded as 111111111110|1110100010, so the final output for the entire 64-pixel data unit is the 46-bit number

$$11111111111100111010001001101101110111010101010.$$

These 46 bits encode one color component of the 64 pixels of a data unit. Let's assume that the other two color components are also encoded into 46-bit numbers. If each pixel originally consists of 24 bits, then this corresponds to a compression factor of $64 \times 24/(46 \times 3) \approx 11.13$; very impressive!

(Notice that the DC coefficient of 1118 has contributed 23 of the 46 bits. Subsequent data units code differences of their DC coefficient, and these may typically consist of fewer than 10 bits instead of 23. They may feature much higher compression factors as a result.)

The same tables (Tables 3.53 and 3.54) used by the encoder should, of course, be used by the decoder. The tables may be predefined and used by a JPEG codec as defaults, or they may be specifically calculated for a given image in a special pass

| Z | R 1 / 6 | 2 / 7 | 3 / 8 | 4 / 9 | 5 / A |
|---|---|---|---|---|---|
| 0 | 00<br>1111000 | 01<br>11111000 | 100<br>1111110110 | 1011<br>1111111110000010 | 11010<br>1111111110000011 |
| 1 | 1100<br>1111111110000100 | 11011<br>1111111110000101 | 11110001<br>1111111110000110 | 111110110<br>1111111110000111 | 11111110110<br>1111111110001000 |
| 2 | 11100<br>111111110001010 | 11111001<br>111111110001011 | 1111110111<br>111111110001100 | 111111110100<br>111111110001101 | 111111110001001<br>111111110001110 |
| 3 | 111010<br>1111111110010001 | 111110111<br>1111111110010010 | 111111110101<br>1111111110010011 | 1111111110001111<br>1111111110010100 | 1111111110010000<br>1111111110010101 |
| 4 | 111011<br>1111111110011001 | 1111111000<br>1111111110011010 | 1111111110010110<br>1111111110011011 | 1111111110010111<br>1111111110011100 | 1111111110011000<br>1111111110011101 |
| 5 | 1111010<br>1111111110100001 | 11111110111<br>1111111110100010 | 1111111110011110<br>1111111110100011 | 1111111110011111<br>1111111110100100 | 1111111110100000<br>1111111110100101 |
| 6 | 1111011<br>1111111110101001 | 111111110110<br>1111111110101010 | 1111111110100110<br>1111111110101011 | 1111111110100111<br>1111111110101100 | 1111111110101000<br>1111111110101101 |
| 7 | 11111010<br>1111111110110001 | 111111110111<br>1111111110110010 | 1111111110101110<br>1111111110110011 | 1111111110101111<br>1111111110110100 | 1111111110110000<br>1111111110110101 |
| 8 | 111111000<br>1111111110111001 | 111111111000000<br>1111111110111010 | 1111111110110110<br>1111111110111011 | 1111111110110111<br>1111111110111100 | 1111111110111000<br>1111111110111101 |
| 9 | 111111001<br>1111111111000010 | 1111111110111110<br>1111111111000011 | 1111111110111111<br>1111111111000100 | 1111111111000000<br>1111111111000101 | 1111111111000001<br>1111111111000110 |
| A | 111111010<br>1111111111001011 | 1111111111000111<br>1111111111001100 | 1111111111001000<br>1111111111001101 | 1111111111001001<br>1111111111001110 | 1111111111001010<br>1111111111001111 |
| B | 1111111001<br>1111111111010100 | 1111111111010000<br>1111111111010101 | 1111111111010001<br>1111111111010110 | 1111111111010010<br>1111111111010111 | 1111111111010011<br>1111111111011000 |
| C | 1111111010<br>1111111111011101 | 1111111111011001<br>1111111111011110 | 1111111111011010<br>1111111111011111 | 1111111111011011<br>1111111111100000 | 1111111111011100<br>1111111111100001 |
| D | 11111111000<br>1111111111100110 | 1111111111100010<br>1111111111100111 | 1111111111100011<br>1111111111101000 | 1111111111100100<br>1111111111101001 | 1111111111100101<br>1111111111101010 |
| E | 1111111111101011<br>1111111111110000 | 1111111111101100<br>1111111111110001 | 1111111111101101<br>1111111111110010 | 1111111111101110<br>1111111111110011 | 1111111111101111<br>1111111111110100 |
| F | 11111111001<br>1111111111111001 | 1111111111110101<br>1111111111111010 | 1111111111110110<br>1111111111111011 | 1111111111110111<br>1111111111111101 | 1111111111111000<br>1111111111111110 |

**Table 3.55:** Recommended Huffman Codes for Luminance AC Coefficients.

| Z | R 1 6 | 2 7 | 3 8 | 4 9 | 5 A |
|---|---|---|---|---|---|
| 0 | 01<br>111000 | 100<br>1111000 | 1010<br>111110100 | 11000<br>1111110110 | 11001<br>111111110100 |
| 1 | 1011<br>111111110101 | 111001<br>111111110001000 | 11110110<br>111111110001001 | 111110101<br>111111110001010 | 11111110110<br>111111110001011 |
| 2 | 11010<br>1111111110001100 | 11110111<br>1111111110001101 | 1111110111<br>1111111110001110 | 111111110110<br>1111111110001111 | 111111111000010<br>1111111110010000 |
| 3 | 11011<br>1111111110010010 | 11111000<br>1111111110010011 | 1111111000<br>1111111110010100 | 111111110111<br>1111111110010101 | 111111111010001<br>1111111110010110 |
| 4 | 111010<br>1111111110011010 | 111110110<br>1111111110011011 | 1111111110010111<br>1111111110011100 | 1111111110011000<br>1111111110011101 | 1111111110011001<br>1111111110011110 |
| 5 | 111011<br>1111111110100010 | 1111111001<br>1111111110100011 | 1111111110011111<br>1111111110100100 | 1111111110100000<br>1111111110100101 | 1111111110100001<br>1111111110100110 |
| 6 | 1111001<br>1111111110101010 | 11111110111<br>1111111110101011 | 1111111110100111<br>1111111110101100 | 1111111110101000<br>1111111110101101 | 1111111110101001<br>1111111110101110 |
| 7 | 1111010<br>1111111110110010 | 111111111000<br>1111111110110011 | 1111111110101111<br>1111111110110100 | 1111111110110000<br>1111111110110101 | 1111111110110001<br>1111111110110110 |
| 8 | 11111001<br>1111111110111011 | 1111111110110111<br>1111111110111100 | 1111111110111000<br>1111111110111101 | 1111111110111001<br>1111111110111110 | 1111111110111010<br>1111111110111111 |
| 9 | 111110111<br>1111111111000100 | 1111111111000000<br>1111111111000101 | 1111111111000001<br>1111111111000110 | 1111111111000010<br>1111111111000111 | 1111111111000011<br>1111111111001000 |
| A | 111111000<br>1111111111001101 | 1111111111001001<br>1111111111001110 | 1111111111001010<br>1111111111001111 | 1111111111001011<br>1111111111010000 | 1111111111001100<br>1111111111010001 |
| B | 111111001<br>1111111111010110 | 1111111111010010<br>1111111111010111 | 1111111111010011<br>1111111111011000 | 1111111111010100<br>1111111111011001 | 1111111111010101<br>1111111111011010 |
| C | 111111010<br>1111111111011111 | 1111111111011011<br>1111111111100000 | 1111111111011100<br>1111111111100001 | 1111111111011101<br>1111111111100010 | 1111111111011110<br>1111111111100011 |
| D | 11111111001<br>1111111111101000 | 1111111111100100<br>1111111111101001 | 1111111111100101<br>1111111111101010 | 1111111111100110<br>1111111111101011 | 1111111111100111<br>1111111111101100 |
| E | 11111111100000<br>1111111111110001 | 1111111111101101<br>1111111111110010 | 1111111111101110<br>1111111111110011 | 1111111111101111<br>1111111111110100 | 1111111111110000<br>1111111111110101 |
| F | 111111111000011<br>1111111111111010 | 1111111111010110<br>1111111111111011 | 1111111111110111<br>1111111111111100 | 1111111111111000<br>1111111111111101 | 1111111111111001<br>1111111111111110 |

**Table 3.56:** Recommended Huffman Codes for Chrominance AC Coefficients.

preceding the actual compression. The JPEG standard does not specify any code tables, so any JPEG codec must use its own.

Some JPEG variants use a particular version of arithmetic coding, called the QM coder, that is specified in the JPEG standard. This version of arithmetic coding is adaptive, so it does not need Tables 3.53 and 3.54. It adapts its behavior to the image statistics as it goes along. Using arithmetic coding may produce 5–10% better compression than Huffman for a typical continuous-tone image. However, it is more complex to implement than Huffman coding, so in practice it is rarely implemented.

### 3.7.6 Lossless Mode

The lossless mode of JPEG uses differencing to reduce the values of pixels before they are compressed. This particular form of differencing is called *predicting*. The values of some near neighbors of a pixel are subtracted from the pixel to get a small number, which is then compressed further using Huffman or arithmetic coding. Figure 3.57a shows a pixel X and three neighbor pixels A, B, and C. Figure 3.57b shows eight possible ways (predictions) to combine the values of the three neighbors. In the lossless mode of JPEG, the user can select one of these predictions, and the encoder then uses it to combine the three neighbor pixels and subtract the combination from the value of X. The result is normally a small number, which is then entropy-coded in a way very similar to that described for the DC coefficient in Section 3.7.5.

Predictor 0 is used only in the hierarchical mode of JPEG. Predictors 1, 2, and 3 are called "one-dimensional." Predictors 4, 5, 6, and 7 are "two-dimensional."

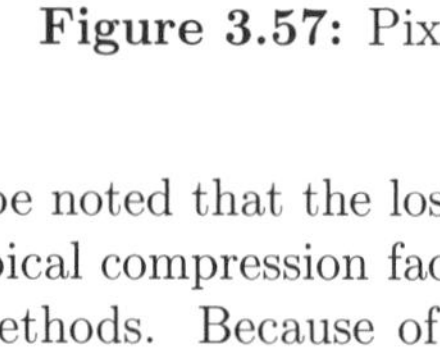

| Selection value | Prediction |
|:---:|:---:|
| 0 | no prediction |
| 1 | A |
| 2 | B |
| 3 | C |
| 4 | $A + B - C$ |
| 5 | $A + ((B - C)/2)$ |
| 6 | $B + ((A - C)/2)$ |
| 7 | $(A + B)/2$ |

|     |     |     |
|-----|-----|-----|
| C | B |  |
| A | X |  |
|   |   |  |

(a)   (b)

**Figure 3.57:** Pixel Prediction in the Lossless Mode.

It should be noted that the lossless mode of JPEG has never been very successful. It produces typical compression factors of 2 and is thus inferior to other lossless image compression methods. Because of this, popular JPEG implementations do not even implement this mode. Even the lossy (baseline) mode of JPEG does not perform well when asked to limit the amount of loss to a minimum. As a result, some JPEG implementations do not allow parameter settings that result in minimum loss. The strength of JPEG is in its ability to generate highly compressed images that when decompressed are indistinguishable from the original. Recognizing this, the ISO has decided to come up with another standard for lossless compression of continuous-tone images. This standard is now commonly known as JPEG-LS and is described in Section 3.8.

### 3.7.7 The Compressed File

A JPEG encoder outputs a compressed file that includes parameters, markers, and the compressed data units. The parameters are either 4 bits (these always come in pairs), one byte, or two bytes long. The markers serve to identify the various parts of the file. Each is two bytes long, where the first byte is X'FF' and the second one is not 0 or X'FF'. A marker may be preceded by a number of bytes with X'FF'. Table 3.59 lists all the JPEG markers (the first four groups are start-of-frame markers). The compressed data units are combined into MCUs (minimal coded unit), where an MCU is either a single data unit (in the noninterleaved mode) or three data units from the three image components (in the interleaved mode).

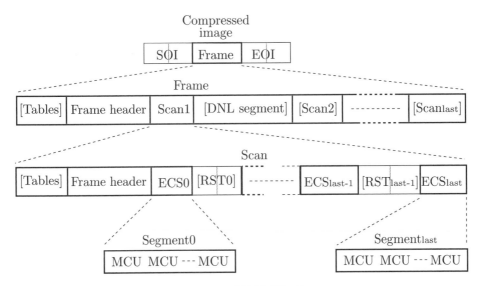

**Figure 3.58:** JPEG File Format.

Figure 3.58 shows the main parts of the JPEG compressed file (parts in square brackets are optional). The file starts with the SOI marker and ends with the EOI marker. Between these markers, the compressed image is organized in frames. In the hierarchical mode there are several frames, and in all other modes there is only one frame. In each frame, the image information is contained in one or more scans, but the frame also contains a header and optional tables (which, in turn, may include markers). The first scan may be followed by an optional DNL segment (define number of lines), which starts with the DNL marker and contains the number of lines in the image that's represented by the frame. A scan starts with optional tables, followed by the scan header, followed by several entropy-coded segments (ECS), which are separated by (optional) restart markers (RST). Each ECS contains one or more MCUs, where an MCU is, as explained earlier, either a single data unit or three such units.

| Value | Name | Description |
|-------|------|-------------|
| Nondifferential, Huffman coding | | |
| FFC0 | $SOF_0$ | Baseline DCT |
| FFC1 | $SOF_1$ | Extended sequential DCT |
| FFC2 | $SOF_2$ | Progressive DCT |
| FFC3 | $SOF_3$ | Lossless (sequential) |
| Differential, Huffman coding | | |
| FFC5 | $SOF_5$ | Differential sequential DCT |
| FFC6 | $SOF_6$ | Differential progressive DCT |
| FFC7 | $SOF_7$ | Differential lossless (sequential) |
| Nondifferential, arithmetic coding | | |
| FFC8 | JPG | Reserved for extensions |
| FFC9 | $SOF_9$ | Extended sequential DCT |
| FFCA | $SOF_{10}$ | Progressive DCT |
| FFCB | $SOF_{11}$ | Lossless (sequential) |
| Differential, arithmetic coding | | |
| FFCD | $SOF_{13}$ | Differential sequential DCT |
| FFCE | $SOF_{14}$ | Differential progressive DCT |
| FFCF | $SOF_{15}$ | Differential lossless (sequential) |
| Huffman table specification | | |
| FFC4 | DHT | Define Huffman table |
| Arithmetic coding conditioning specification | | |
| FFCC | DAC | Define arith coding conditioning(s) |
| Restart interval termination | | |
| FFD0–FFD7 | $RST_m$ | Restart with modulo 8 count $m$ |
| Other markers | | |
| FFD8 | SOI | Start of image |
| FFD9 | EOI | End of image |
| FFDA | SOS | Start of scan |
| FFDB | DQT | Define quantization table(s) |
| FFDC | DNL | Define number of lines |
| FFDD | DRI | Define restart interval |
| FFDE | DHP | Define hierarchical progression |
| FFDF | EXP | Expand reference component(s) |
| FFE0–FFEF | $APP_n$ | Reserved for application segments |
| FFF0–FFFD | $JPG_n$ | Reserved for JPEG extensions |
| FFFE | COM | Comment |
| Reserved markers | | |
| FF01 | TEM | For temporary private use |
| FF02–FFBF | RES | Reserved |

**Table 3.59:** JPEG Markers.

### 3.7.8 JFIF

It has been mentioned earlier that JPEG is a compression method, not a graphics file format, which is why it does not specify image features such as pixel aspect ratio, color space, or interleaving of bitmap rows. This is where JFIF comes in.

JFIF (JPEG file interchange format) is a graphics file format that makes it possible to exchange JPEG-compressed images between computers. The main features of JFIF are the use of the YCbCr triple-component color space for color images (only one component for grayscale images) and the use of a *marker* to specify features missing from JPEG, such as image resolution, aspect ratio, and features that are application-specific.

The JFIF marker (called the APP0 marker) starts with the zero-terminated string `JFIF`. Following this, there is pixel information and other specifications (see below). Following this, there may be additional segments specifying JFIF extensions. A JFIF extension contains more platform-specific information about the image.

Each extension starts with the zero-terminated string `JFXX`, followed by a 1-byte code identifying the extension. An extension may contain application-specific information, in which case it starts with a different string, not `JFIF` or `JFXX` but something that identifies the specific application or its maker.

The format of the first segment of an APP0 marker is as follows:

1. APP0 marker (4 bytes): `FFD8FFE0`.
2. Length (2 bytes): Total length of marker, including the 2 bytes of the "length" field but excluding the APP0 marker itself (field 1).
3. Identifier (5 bytes): $4A46494600_{16}$. This is the `JFIF` string that identifies the APP0 marker.
4. Version (2 bytes): Example: $0102_{16}$ specifies version 1.02.
5. Units (1 byte): Units for the X and Y densities. 0 means no units; the Xdensity and Ydensity fields specify the pixel aspect ratio. 1 means that Xdensity and Ydensity are dots per inch, 2, that they are dots per centimeter.
6. Xdensity (2 bytes), Ydensity (2 bytes): Horizontal and vertical pixel densities (both should be nonzero).
7. Xthumbnail (1 byte), Ythumbnail (1 byte): Thumbnail horizontal and vertical pixel counts.
8. (RGB)$n$ ($3n$ bytes): Packed (24-bit) RGB values for the thumbnail pixels. $n =$ Xthumbnail$\times$Ythumbnail.

The syntax of the JFIF extension APP0 marker segment is as follows:

1. APP0 marker.
2. Length (2 bytes): Total length of marker, including the 2 bytes of the "length" field but excluding the APP0 marker itself (field 1).
3. Identifier (5 bytes): $4A46585800_{16}$ This is the `JFXX` string identifying an extension.
4. Extension code (1 byte): $10_{16} =$ Thumbnail coded using JPEG. $11_{16} =$ Thumbnail coded using 1 byte/pixel (monochromatic). $13_{16} =$ Thumbnail coded using 3 bytes/pixel (eight colors).
5. Extension data (variable): This field depends on the particular extension.

## 3.8 JPEG-LS

This compression method uses the Golomb code, so we start with a short section describing this little-known code.

### 3.8.1 The Golomb Code

The *Golomb code* for nonnegative integers $n$ [Golomb 66] can be an effective Huffman code. The code depends on the choice of a parameter $b$. The first step is to compute the two quantities

$$q = \left\lfloor \frac{n-1}{b} \right\rfloor, \qquad r = n - qb - 1,$$

(where the notation $\lfloor x \rfloor$ implies truncation of $x$) following which the code is constructed of two parts; the first is the value of $q + 1$, coded in unary (page 150), and the second, the binary value of $r$ coded in either $\lfloor \log_2 b \rfloor$ bits (for the small remainders) or in $\lceil \log_2 b \rceil$ bits (for the large ones). Choosing $b = 3$, e.g., produces three possible remainders, 0, 1, and 2. They are coded 0, 10, and 11, respectively. Choosing $b = 5$ produces the five remainders 0 through 4, which are coded 00, 01, 100, 101, and 110. Table 3.60 shows some examples of the Golomb code for $b = 3$ and $b = 5$.

| $n$ | 1 | 2 | 3 | 4 | 5 | 6 | 7 | 8 | 9 | 10 |
|---|---|---|---|---|---|---|---|---|---|---|
| $b=3$ | 0\|0 | 0\|10 | 0\|11 | 10\|0 | 10\|10 | 10\|11 | 110\|0 | 110\|10 | 110\|11 | 1110\|0 |
| $b=5$ | 0\|00 | 0\|01 | 0\|100 | 0\|101 | 10\|110 | 10\|00 | 10\|01 | 10\|100 | 10\|101 | 110\|110 |

**Table 3.60:** Some Golomb Codes for $b = 3$ and $b = 5$.

Imagine an input data stream consisting of positive integers where the probability of integer $n$ appearing in the data is $P(n) = (1-p)^{n-1}p$, for some $0 \le p \le 1$. It can be shown that the Golomb code is an optimal code for this data if $b$ is chosen such that

$$(1-p)^b + (1-p)^{b+1} \le 1 < (1-p)^{b-1} + (1-p)^b.$$

Given the right data, it is easy to generate the best variable-size codes without going through the Huffman algorithm.

### 3.8.2 JPEG-LS Principles

As was mentioned in Section 3.7.6, the lossless mode of JPEG is inefficient and often is not even implemented. As a result, the ISO, in cooperation with the IEC, has decided to develop a new standard for the lossless (or near-lossless) compression of continuous-tone images. The result is recommendation ISO/IEC CD 14495, popularly known as JPEG-LS. The principles of this method are described here, but it should be noted that it is not simply an extension or a modification of JPEG. This is a new method, designed to be simple and fast. It does not use the DCT, does not use arithmetic coding, and uses quantization in a limited way and only in its near-lossless option. JPEG-LS is based on ideas developed in [Weinberger et al. 96] for their LOCO-I compression method. JPEG-LS (1) examines several of the previously seen neighbors of the current pixel, (2) uses them as the *context* of the pixel, (3) uses the context to predict the pixel and to select a probability distribution out of several such distributions, and (4) uses that distribution to encode the prediction error with a special Golomb code. There is also a run mode, where the length of a run of identical pixels is encoded.

The context used to predict the current pixel $x$ is shown in Figure 3.61. The encoder examines the context pixels and decides whether to encode the current pixel $x$ in the *run mode* or in the *regular mode*. If the context suggests that the pixels $y$, $z$,... following the current pixel are likely to be identical, the encoder selects the run mode. Otherwise, it selects the regular mode. In the near-lossless mode the decision is slightly different. If the context suggests that the pixels following the current pixel are likely to be almost identical (within the tolerance parameter NEAR), the encoder selects the run mode. Otherwise, it selects the regular mode. The rest of the encoding process depends on the mode selected.

|   |   |   |   |   |
|---|---|---|---|---|
|   | $c$ | $b$ | $d$ |   |
|   | $a$ | $x$ | $y$ | $z$ |
|   |   |   |   |   |

**Figure 3.61:** Context for Predicting $x$.

In the regular mode, the encoder uses the values of context pixels $a$, $b$, and $c$ to predict pixel $x$ and subtracts the prediction from $x$ to obtain the *prediction error*, denoted by *Errval*. This error is then *corrected* by a term that depends on the context (this correction is done to compensate for systematic biases in the prediction) and encoded with a Golomb code. The Golomb coding depends on all four pixels of the context and also on prediction errors that were previously encoded for the same context (this information is stored in arrays $A$ and $N$, mentioned in Section 3.8.3). If near-lossless compression is used, the error is quantized before it is encoded.

In the run mode, the encoder starts at the current pixel $x$ and finds the longest run of pixels that follow $x$ on the image row and are identical to context pixel $a$. The encoder does not extend this run beyond the end of the current image row. Since all the pixels in the run are identical to $a$ (and $a$ is already known to the decoder), only the length of the run needs be encoded, and this is done with a 32-entry array denoted by $J$ (Section 3.8.3). If near-lossless compression is used, the encoder selects a run of pixels that are close to $a$ within the tolerance parameter NEAR.

The decoder is not substantially different from the encoder, so JPEG-LS is a nearly symmetric compression method. The compressed file contains data segments (with the Golomb codes and the encoded run lengths), marker segments (with information needed by the decoder), and markers (some of the reserved markers of JPEG are used). A marker is a byte of all ones followed by a special code, signaling the start of a new segment. If a marker is followed by a byte whose most significant bit is 0, that byte is the start of a marker segment. Otherwise, that byte starts a data segment.

### 3.8.3 The Encoder

JPEG-LS is normally used as a lossless compression method. In this case, the reconstructed value of a pixel is identical to its original value. In the near lossless mode, the original and the reconstructed values may differ. In each case we denote the reconstructed value of a pixel $p$ by $Rp$.

When the top row of an image is encoded, context pixels $b$, $c$, and $d$ are not available and should therefore be considered zero. If the current pixel is located at the start or the end of an image row, either $a$ and $c$, or $d$ are not available. In such a case, the encoder uses for $a$ or $d$ the reconstructed value $Rb$ of $b$ (or zero if this is the top row), and for $c$ the reconstructed value that was assigned to $a$ when the first pixel of the previous line was encoded. This means that the encoder has to do part of the decoder's job and has to figure out the reconstructed values of certain pixels.

The first step in determining the context is to calculate the three *gradient* values

$$D1 = Rd - Rb, \quad D2 = Rb - Rc, \quad D3 = Rc - Ra.$$

If the three values are zero (or, for near-lossless, if their absolute values are less than or equal to the tolerance parameter NEAR), the encoder selects the run mode, where it looks for the longest run of pixels identical to $Ra$. Step 2 compares the three gradients $Di$ to certain parameters and calculates three region numbers $Qi$ according to certain rules (not discussed here). Each region number $Qi$ can take one of the nine integer values in the interval $[-4, +4]$, so there are $9 \times 9 \times 9 = 729$ different region numbers. The third step uses the absolute values of the three region numbers $Qi$ (there are 365 of them, since one of the 729 values is zero) to calculate an integer $Q$ in the range $[0, 364]$. The details of this calculation are not specified by the JPEG-LS standard, and the encoder can do it in any way it chooses. The integer $Q$ becomes the context for the current pixel $x$. It is used to index arrays $A$ and $N$ in Figure 3.65.

After determining the context $Q$, the encoder predicts pixel $x$ in two steps. The first step calculates the prediction $Px$ based on *edge rules*, as shown in Figure 3.62. The second step corrects the prediction, as shown in Figure 3.63, based on the quantity SIGN (determined from the signs of the three regions $Qi$), the correction values $C[Q]$ (derived from the bias and not discussed here), and parameter MAXVAL.

```
if(Rc>=max(Ra,Rb)) Px=min(Ra,Rb);
 else
  if(Rc<=min(Ra,Rb)) Px=max(Ra,Rb)
    else Px=Ra+Rb-Rc;
  endif;
endif;
```

**Figure 3.62:** Edge Detecting.

```
if(SIGN=+1) Px=Px+C[Q]
        else Px=Px-C[Q]
 endif;
if(Px>MAXVAL) Px=MAXVAL
   else if(Px<0) Px=0 endif;
 endif;
```

**Figure 3.63:** Prediction Correcting.

To understand the edge rules, let's consider the case where $b \leq a$. In this case the edge rules select $b$ as the prediction of $x$ in many cases where a vertical edge exists in the image just left of the current pixel $x$. Similarly, $a$ is selected as the prediction in many cases where a horizontal edge exists in the image just above $x$. If no edge is detected, the edge rules compute a prediction of $a+b-c$, and this has a simple geometric interpretation. If we interpret each pixel as a point in three-dimensional space, with the pixel's intensity as its height, then the value $a + b - c$ places the prediction $Px$ on the same plane as pixels $a$, $b$, and $c$ (see discussion of points and vectors in [Salomon 99], page 174).

Once the prediction $Px$ is known, the encoder computes the prediction error $Errval$ as the difference $x - Px$ but reverses its sign if the quantity SIGN is negative.

In the near-lossless mode the error is quantized, and the encoder uses it to compute the reconstructed value $Rx$ of pixel $x$ the way the decoder will do it in the future. The encoder needs this reconstructed value to encode future pixels. The basic quantization step is

$$Errval \leftarrow \frac{Errval + \text{NEAR}}{2 \times \text{NEAR} + 1}.$$

It uses parameter NEAR, but it involves more details that are not shown here. The basic reconstruction step is

$$Rx \leftarrow Px + \text{SIGN} \times Errval \times (2 \times \text{NEAR} + 1).$$

The prediction error (after possibly being quantized) now goes through a range reduction (whose details are omitted here) and is finally ready for the important step of encoding.

The Golomb code was introduced in Section 3.8.1, where its main parameter was denoted by $b$. JPEG-LS denotes this parameter by $m$. Once $m$ has been selected, the Golomb code of the nonnegative integer $n$ consists of two parts, the unary code of the integer part of $n/m$ and the binary representation of $n \bmod m$. These codes are ideal for integers $n$ that are distributed geometrically (i.e., when the probability of $n$ is $(1 - r)r^n$, where $0 < r < 1$). For any such geometric distribution there exists a value $m$ such that the Golomb code based on it yields the shortest possible average code length. The special case where $m$ is a power of 2 ($m = 2^k$) leads to simple encoding/decoding operations. The code for $n$ consists, in such a case, of the $k$ least-significant bits of $n$, preceded by the unary code of the remaining most significant bits of $n$. This particular Golomb code is denoted by $G(k)$.

As an example we compute the $G(2)$ code of $n = 19 = 10011_2$. Since $k = 2$, $m$ is 4. We start with the two least significant bits, 11, of $n$. They equal the integer 3, which is also $n \bmod m$ ($3 = 19 \bmod 4$). The remaining most significant bits, 100, are also the integer 4, which is the integer part of the quotient $n/m$ ($19/4 = 4.75$). The unary code of 4 is 00001, so the $G(2)$ code of $n = 19$ is 00001|11.

In practice, we always have a finite set of nonnegative integers, where the largest integer in the set is denoted by $I$. The maximum length of $G(0)$ is $I + 1$, and since $I$ can be large, it is desirable to limit the size of the Golomb code. This is done by the special Golomb code $LG(k, glimit)$, which depends on the two parameters $k$ and $glimit$. We first form a number $q$ from the most significant bits of $n$. If $q < glimit - \lceil \log I \rceil - 1$, the $LG(k, glimit)$ code is simply $G(k)$. Otherwise, the unary code of $glimit - \lceil \log I \rceil - 1$ is prepared (i.e., $glimit - \lceil \log I \rceil - 1$ zeros followed by a single 1). This acts as an escape code and is followed by the binary representation of $n - 1$ in $\lceil I \rceil$ bits.

Our prediction errors are not necessarily positive. They are differences, so they can also be zero or negative, but the various Golomb codes were designed for nonnegative integers. This is why the prediction errors must be mapped to nonnegative values before they can be coded. This is done by

$$MErrval = \begin{cases} 2Errval, & Errval \geq 0, \\ 2|Errval| - 1, & Errval < 0. \end{cases} \tag{3.18}$$

This mapping interleaves negative and positive values in the sequence

$$0, -1, +1, -2, +2, -3, \ldots.$$

Table 3.64 lists some prediction errors, their mapped values, and their $LG(2, 32)$ codes assuming an alphabet of size 256 (i.e., $I = 255$ and $\lceil \log I \rceil = 8$).

The next point to be discussed is how to determine the value of the Golomb code parameter $k$. This is done adaptively. Parameter $k$ depends on the context, and the value of $k$ for a context is updated each time a pixel with that context is found. The calculation of $k$ can be expressed by the single C-language statement

```
for (k=0; (N[Q]<<k)<A[Q]; k++);
```

where $A$ and $N$ are arrays indexed from 0 to 364. This statement uses the context $Q$ as an index to the two arrays. It initializes $k$ to 0 and goes into a loop. In each iteration it shifts array element $N[Q]$ by $k$ positions to the left and compares it to element $A[Q]$. If the shifted value of $N[Q]$ is greater than or equal to $A[Q]$, the current value of $k$ is chosen. Otherwise, $k$ is incremented by 1 and the test repeated.

After $k$ has been determined, the prediction error $Errval$ is mapped, by means of Equation (3.18), to $MErrval$, which is encoded using code $LG(k, LIMIT)$. The quantity LIMIT is a parameter. Arrays $A$ and $N$ (together with an auxiliary array $B$) are then updated as shown in Figure 3.65 (RESET is a user-controlled parameter).

Encoding in the run mode is done differently. The encoder selects this mode when it finds consecutive pixels $x$ whose values $Ix$ are identical and equal to the reconstructed value $Ra$ of context pixel $a$. For near-lossless compression, pixels in the run must have values $Ix$ that satisfy

$$|Ix - Ra| \leq \text{NEAR}.$$

A run is not allowed to continue beyond the end of the current image row. The length of the run is encoded (there is no need to encode the value of the run's pixels, since it equals $Ra$), and if the run ends before the end of the current row, its encoded length is followed by the encoding of the pixel immediately following it (the pixel *interrupting* the run). The two main tasks of the encoder in this mode are (1) run scanning and run-length encoding and (2) run-interruption coding. Run scanning is shown in Figure 3.66. Run-length encoding is shown in Figures 3.67 (for run segments of length $rm$) and 3.68 (for segments of length less than $rm$). Here are some of the details.

| Prediction error | Mapped value | Code |
|---|---|---|
| 0 | 0 | 1 00 |
| −1 | 1 | 1 01 |
| 1 | 2 | 1 10 |
| −2 | 3 | 1 11 |
| 2 | 4 | 01 00 |
| −3 | 5 | 01 01 |
| 3 | 6 | 01 10 |
| −4 | 7 | 01 11 |
| 4 | 8 | 001 00 |
| −5 | 9 | 001 01 |
| 5 | 10 | 001 10 |
| −6 | 11 | 001 11 |
| 6 | 12 | 0001 00 |
| −7 | 13 | 0001 01 |
| 7 | 14 | 0001 10 |
| −8 | 15 | 0001 11 |
| 8 | 16 | 00001 00 |
| −9 | 17 | 00001 01 |
| 9 | 18 | 00001 10 |
| −10 | 19 | 00001 11 |
| 10 | 20 | 000001 00 |
| −11 | 21 | 000001 01 |
| 11 | 22 | 000001 10 |
| −12 | 23 | 000001 11 |
| 12 | 24 | 0000001 00 |
| ... | | |
| 50 | 100 | 000000000000 |
| | | 000000000001 |
| | | 01100011 |

**Table 3.64:** Prediction Errors, Their Mappings, and $LG(2, 32)$ Codes.

```
B[Q]=B[Q]+Errval*(2*NEAR+1);
A[Q]=A[Q]+abs(Errval);
if(N[Q]=RESET) then
 A[Q]=A[Q]>>1; B[Q]=B[Q]>>1; N[Q]=N[Q]>>1
endif;
N[Q]=N[Q]+1;
```

**Figure 3.65:** Updating Arrays $A$, $B$, and $N$.

```
RUNval=Ra;
RUNcnt=0;
while(abs(Ix-RUNval)<=NEAR)
 RUNcnt=RUNcnt+1;
 Rx=RUNval;
 if(EOLine=1) break
   else GetNextSample()
 endif;
endwhile;
```

**Figure 3.66:** Run Scanning.

```
while(RUNcnt>=(1<<J[RUNindex]))
 AppendToBitfile(1,1);
 RUNcnt=RUNcnt-(1<<J[RUNindex]);
 if(RUNindex<31)
  RUNindex=RUNindex+1;
endwhile;
```

**Figure 3.67:** Run Encoding: I.

```
if(EOLine=0) then
 AppendToBitfile(0,1);
 AppendToBitfile
  (RUNcnt,J[RUNindex]);
 if(RUNindex>0)
  RUNindex=RUNindex-1;
 endif;
else if(RUNcnt>0)
 AppendToBitfile(1,1);
```

**Figure 3.68:** Run Encoding: II.

The encoder uses a 32-entry table $J$ containing values that are denoted by $rk$. $J$ is initialized to the 32 values

$$0, 0, 0, 0, 1, 1, 1, 1, 2, 2, 2, 2, 3, 3, 3, 3, 4, 4, 5, 5, 6, 6, 7, 7, 8, 9, 10, 11, 12, 13, 14, 15.$$

For each value $rk$, we use the notation $rm = 2^{rk}$. The 32 quantities $rm$ are called *code order*. The first 4 $rms$ have values $2^0 = 1$. The next four have values $2^1 = 2$, and the next four, $2^2 = 4$, up to the last $rm$, whose value is $2^{15} = 32768$. The encoder executes the procedure of Figure 3.66 to determine the run length, which it stores in variable RUNlen. This variable is then encoded by breaking it up into chunks whose sizes are the values of consecutive $rms$. For example, if RUNlen is 6, it can be expressed in terms of the $rms$ as $1 + 1 + 1 + 1 + 2$, so it is equivalent to the first five $rms$. It is encoded by writing five bits of 1 on the compressed file. Each of those bits is written by the statement AppendToBitfile(1,1) of Figure 3.67. Each time a 1 is written, the value of the corresponding $rm$ is subtracted from RUNlen. If RUNlen is originally 6, it goes down to 5, 4, 3, 2, and 0.

It may happen, of course, that the length RUNlen of a run is not equal to an integer number of $rms$. An example is a RUNlen of 7. This is encoded by writing five bits of 1, followed by a *prefix* bit, followed by the remainder of RUNlen (in our example, a 1), written on the compressed file as an $rk$-bit number (the current $rk$ in our example is 2). This last operation is performed by the procedure call AppendToBit-file(RUNcnt,J[RUNindex]) of Figure 3.68. The prefix bit is 0 if the run is interrupted by a different pixel. It is 1 if the run is terminated by the end of an image row.

The second main task of the encoder, encoding the interruption pixel, is similar to encoding the current pixel and is not discussed here.

There is nothing worse than a sharp image of a fuzzy concept

Ansel Adams, *Reader's Digest* May, 1997

# 4
# Wavelet Methods

As mentioned in the Introduction, wavelet methods are mathematically sophisticated and so present a challenge to both the author and the reader. The main aim of this chapter is to present—with the minimum of mathematics—the basics of the wavelet transform and how it is applied to data compression. The chapter starts by describing a sequence of simple averaging and differencing steps that transform a one-dimensional array of data items into a form that can easily be compressed. The sequence is then extended to the two-dimensional case, where it can be applied to digital images. This sequence is the simplest example of a *subband transform*, and we show that it is identical to the Haar transform of Section 3.5.7.

Section 4.2.1 shows how the Haar transform can be performed by matrix multiplication, which paves the way to introducing, in Section 4.4, the concept of filter banks. Section 4.3 is mathematical and can be skipped by nonmathematical readers. It discusses the concept of discrete convolution and how it is used in subband transforms. This material is followed, in Section 4.6, by a description of the discrete wavelet transform (DWT). The chapter ends with a description of SPIHT, an image compression method based on the wavelet transform.

Before any details are presented and explained, the following, frequently asked question should be answered: Why the term "wavelet"? This chapter does not fully answer the question, but Figures 4.14 and 4.35 provide a partial, intuitive answer.

## 4.1 Averaging and Differencing

We start with a one-dimensional array of $N$ values. In practice, these will be neighboring pixels or adjacent audio samples. For simplicity we assume that $N$ is a power of 2. (We use this assumption throughout this chapter, but there is no loss of generality. If $n$ has a different value, the data can be extended by appending zeros or by duplicating the last value as many times as needed. After decompression, the added items are removed.) An example is the array of eight values $(1, 2, 3, 4, 5, 6, 7, 8)$. We first compute the four averages $(1+2)/2 = 3/2$, $(3+4)/2 = 7/2$, $(5+6)/2 = 11/2$, and $(7+8)/2 = 15/2$. It is impossible to reconstruct the original eight values from these four averages, so we also compute the four differences $(1-2)/2 = -1/2$, $(3-4)/2 = -1/2$, $(5-6)/2 = -1/2$, and $(7-8)/2 = -1/2$. These differences are called *detail coefficients*, and in this section the terms "difference" and "detail" are used interchangeably. We can think of the averages as a coarse resolution representation of the original image and of the details as the data needed to reconstruct the original image from this coarse resolution. If the data items are correlated, the coarse representation will resemble the original items, while the details will be small.

The array $(3/2, 7/2, 11/2, 15/2, -1/2, -1/2, -1/2, -1/2)$ that consists of the four averages and four differences can be used to reconstruct the original eight values. This array has eight values, but its last four components, the differences, tend to be small numbers, which helps in compression. Encouraged by this, we repeat the process on the four averages, the large components of our array. They are transformed into two averages and two differences, yielding the array $(10/4, 26/4, -4/4, -4/4, -1/2, -1/2, -1/2, -1/2)$. The next and last iteration of this process transforms the first two components of the new array into one average (the average of all eight components of the original array) and one difference $(36/8, -16/8, -4/4, -4/4, -1/2, -1/2, -1/2, -1/2)$. The last array is the *Haar wavelet transform* of the original data items.

Because of the differences, the wavelet transform tends to have numbers smaller than the original pixel values, so it is easier to compress with quantization, run-length encoding, Huffman coding, and perhaps other methods such as move-to-front [Salomon 00]. Lossy compression can be obtained if some of the smaller differences are quantized or even completely deleted (changed to zero).

Before we continue, it is interesting (and also useful) to estimate the *complexity* of this transform, i.e., the number of arithmetic operations as a function of the size of the data. In our example we needed $8+4+2 = 14$ operations (additions and subtractions), a number that can also be expressed as $14 = 2(8-1)$. In the general case, assume that we start with $N = 2^n$ data items. In the first iteration we need $2^n$ operations, in the second one we need $2^{n-1}$ operations, and so on, until the last iteration, where $2^{n-(n-1)} = 2^1$ operations are needed. Thus, the total number of operations is

$$\sum_{i=1}^{n} 2^i = \left( \sum_{i=0}^{n} 2^i \right) - 1 = \frac{1 - 2^{n+1}}{1 - 2} - 1 = 2^{n+1} - 2 = 2(2^n - 1) = 2(N - 1).$$

The Haar wavelet transform of $N$ data items can therefore be performed with $2(N-1)$ operations, so its complexity is $\mathcal{O}(N)$, an excellent result.

It is useful to associate with each iteration a quantity called *resolution*, which is defined as the number of remaining averages at the end of the iteration. The resolutions after each of the three iterations above are $4(= 2^2)$, $2(= 2^1)$, and $1(= 2^0)$. Section 4.2.1 shows that each component of the wavelet transform should be normalized by dividing it by the square root of the resolution. (This is the *orthonormal Haar transform*, also discussed in Section 3.5.7.) Thus, our example wavelet transform becomes

$$\left(\frac{36/8}{\sqrt{2^0}}, \frac{-16/8}{\sqrt{2^0}}, \frac{-4/4}{\sqrt{2^1}}, \frac{-4/4}{\sqrt{2^1}}, \frac{-1/2}{\sqrt{2^2}}, \frac{-1/2}{\sqrt{2^2}}, \frac{-1/2}{\sqrt{2^2}}, \frac{-1/2}{\sqrt{2^2}}\right).$$

If the normalized wavelet transform is used, it can be shown that ignoring the smallest differences is the best choice for lossy image compression, since it causes the smallest loss of image information.

The two procedures of Figure 4.1 illustrate how the normalized wavelet transform of an array of $n$ components (where $n$ is a power of 2) can be computed. Reconstructing the original array from the normalized wavelet transform is illustrated by the pair of procedures of Figure 4.2.

These procedures seem at first to be different from the averages and differences discussed earlier. They don't compute averages, since they divide by $\sqrt{2}$ instead of by 2; the first one starts by dividing the entire array by $\sqrt{n}$, and the second one ends by doing the reverse. The final result, however, is the same as that shown above. Starting with array $(1, 2, 3, 4, 5, 6, 7, 8)$, the three iterations of procedure `NWTcalc` result in

$$\left(\frac{3}{\sqrt{2^4}}, \frac{7}{\sqrt{2^4}}, \frac{11}{\sqrt{2^4}}, \frac{15}{\sqrt{2^4}}, \frac{-1}{\sqrt{2^4}}, \frac{-1}{\sqrt{2^4}}, \frac{-1}{\sqrt{2^4}}, \frac{-1}{\sqrt{2^4}}\right),$$

$$\left(\frac{10}{\sqrt{2^5}}, \frac{26}{\sqrt{2^5}}, \frac{-4}{\sqrt{2^5}}, \frac{-4}{\sqrt{2^5}}, \frac{-1}{\sqrt{2^4}}, \frac{-1}{\sqrt{2^4}}, \frac{-1}{\sqrt{2^4}}, \frac{-1}{\sqrt{2^4}}\right),$$

$$\left(\frac{36}{\sqrt{2^6}}, \frac{-16}{\sqrt{2^6}}, \frac{-4}{\sqrt{2^5}}, \frac{-4}{\sqrt{2^5}}, \frac{-1}{\sqrt{2^4}}, \frac{-1}{\sqrt{2^4}}, \frac{-1}{\sqrt{2^4}}, \frac{-1}{\sqrt{2^4}}\right),$$

$$\left(\frac{36/8}{\sqrt{2^0}}, \frac{-16/8}{\sqrt{2^0}}, \frac{-4/4}{\sqrt{2^1}}, \frac{-4/4}{\sqrt{2^1}}, \frac{-1/2}{\sqrt{2^2}}, \frac{-1/2}{\sqrt{2^2}}, \frac{-1/2}{\sqrt{2^2}}, \frac{-1/2}{\sqrt{2^2}}\right).$$

### 4.1.1 Extending to Two Dimensions

The one-dimensional Haar wavelet transform performed by averaging and differencing is easy to generalize to two-dimensional data. This is an important step, since in practice this transform has to be applied to images which are two-dimensional. This generalization can be done in several ways, discussed in [Salomon 00]. Here we show two approaches, called the *standard decomposition* and the *pyramid decomposition*.

The former (Figure 4.3) starts by computing the wavelet transform of every row of the image. Each row goes through all the iterations, until the leftmost data item of the row is transformed into an average and all the other data items are transformed into differences. This results in a transformed image where the first column contains averages and all the other columns contain differences. The standard algorithm then computes the wavelet transform of every column. This results in one average value at the top-left corner, with the rest of the top row containing averages of differences, the rest of the leftmost column containing differences of averages, and with all other pixel values transformed into differences.

The latter method computes the wavelet transform of the image by alternating between rows and columns. The first step is to calculate averages and differences for all

```
procedure NWTcalc(a:array of real, n:int);
 comment n is the array size (a power of 2)
 a:=a/√n comment divide entire array
 j:=n;
 while j≥2 do
  NWTstep(a, j);
  j:=j/2;
 endwhile;
end;

procedure NWTstep(a:array of real, j:int);
 for i=1 to j/2 do
  b[i]:=(a[2i-1]+a[2i])/√2;
  b[j/2+i]:=(a[2i-1]-a[2i])/√2;
 endfor;
 a:=b; comment move entire array
end;
```

**Figure 4.1:** Computing the Normalized Wavelet Transform.

```
procedure NWTreconst(a:array of real, n:int);
 j:=2;
 while j≤n do
  NWTRstep(a, j);
  j:=2j;
 endwhile
 a:=a√n; comment multiply entire array
end;

procedure NWTRstep(a:array of real, j:int);
 for i=1 to j/2 do
  b[2i-1]:=(a[i]+a[j/2+i])/√2;
  b[2i]:=(a[i]-a[j/2+i])/√2;
 endfor;
 a:=b; comment move entire array
end;
```

**Figure 4.2:** Restoring from a Normalized Wavelet Transform.

```
procedure StdCalc(a:array of real, n:int);
 comment array size is nxn (n = power of 2)
 for r=1 to n do NWTcalc(row r of a, n);
 endfor;
 for c=n to 1 do comment loop backwards
  NWTcalc(col c of a, n);
 endfor;
end;
procedure StdReconst(a:array of real, n:int);
 for c=n to 1 do comment loop backwards
  NWTreconst(col c of a, n);
 endfor;
 for r=1 to n do
  NWTreconst(row r of a, n);
 endfor;
end;
```

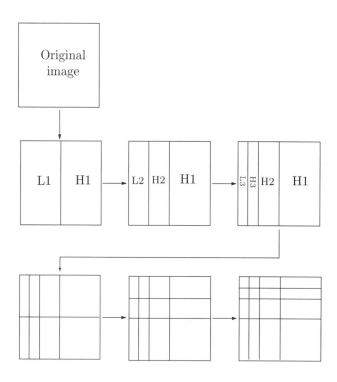

**Figure 4.3:** The Standard Image Wavelet Transform and Decomposition.

the rows (just one iteration, not the entire wavelet transform). This creates averages in the left half of the image and differences in the right half. The second step is to calculate averages and differences for all the columns, which results in averages in the top left quadrant of the image and differences elsewhere. Steps 3 and 4 operate on the rows and columns of that quadrant, resulting in averages concentrated in the top left subquadrant. Pairs of steps are repeatedly executed on smaller and smaller subsquares, until only one average is left, at the top left corner of the image, and all other pixel values have been reduced to differences. This process is summarized in Figure 4.5.

The transforms described in Section 3.5 are orthogonal. They transform the original pixels into a few large numbers and many small numbers. In contrast, wavelet transforms, such as the Haar transform, are *subband transforms*. They partition the image into regions such that one region contains large numbers (averages in the case of the Haar transform) and the other regions contain small numbers (differences). However, these regions, which are called *subbands*, are more than just sets of large and small numbers. They reflect different geometrical features of the image. To illustrate what this means, we examine a small, mostly uniform image with one vertical line and one horizontal line. Figure 4.4a shows an $8 \times 8$ image with pixel values of 12, except for a vertical line with pixel values of 14 and a horizontal line with pixel values of 16.

```
12 12 12 12 14 12 12 12      12 12 13 12│ 0  0  2  0        12 12 13 12│ 0  0  2  0
12 12 12 12 14 12 12 12      12 12 13 12│ 0  0  2  0        12 12 13 12│ 0  0  2  0
12 12 12 12 14 12 12 12      12 12 13 12│ 0  0  2  0        14 14 14 14│ 0  0  0  0
12 12 12 12 14 12 12 12      12 12 13 12│ 0  0  2  0        12 12 13 12│ 0  0  2  0
12 12 12 12 14 12 12 12      12 12 13 12│ 0  0  2  0        ─────────────────────────
16 16 16 16 14 16 16 16      16 16 15 16│ 0  0  2  0         0  0  0  0│ 0  0  0  0
12 12 12 12 14 12 12 12      12 12 13 12│ 0  0  2  0         0  0  0  0│ 0  0  0  0
12 12 12 12 14 12 12 12      12 12 13 12│ 0  0  2  0         4  4  2  4│ 0  0  4  0
                                                             0  0  0  0│ 0  0  0  0
            (a)                          (b)                             (c)
```

**Figure 4.4:** An $8 \times 8$ Image and Its Subband Decomposition.

Figure 4.4b shows the results of applying the Haar transform once to the rows of the image. The right half of this figure (the differences) is mostly zeros, reflecting the uniform nature of the image. However, traces of the vertical line can easily be seen (the notation 2 indicates a negative difference). Figure 4.4c shows the results of applying the Haar transform once to the columns of Figure 4.4b. The upper right subband now contains traces of the vertical line, whereas the lower left subband shows traces of the horizontal line. These subbands are denoted by HL and LH, respectively (see Figure 4.36, although there is inconsistency in the use of this notation by various authors). The lower right subband, denoted by HH, reflects diagonal image artifacts (which our example image lacks). Most interesting is the upper left subband, denoted by LL, that consists entirely of averages. This subband is a one-quarter version of the entire image, containing traces of both the vertical and the horizontal lines.

Figure 4.6 illustrates how subband HH reflects diagonal artifacts of the image. Part (a) of the figure shows a uniform $8 \times 8$ image with one diagonal line above the main

```
procedure NStdCalc(a:array of real, n:int);
 a:=a/√n comment divide entire array
 j:=n;
 while j≥ 2 do
  for r=1 to j do NWTstep(row r of a, j);
  endfor;
  for c=j to 1 do comment loop backwards
   NWTstep(col c of a, j);
  endfor;
  j:=j/2;
 endwhile;
end;
procedure NStdReconst(a:array of real, n:int);
 j:=2;
 while j≤n do
  for c=j to 1 do comment loop backwards
   NWTRstep(col c of a, j);
  endfor;
  for r=1 to j do
   NWTRstep(row r of a, j);
  endfor;
  j:=2j;
 endwhile
 a:=a√n; comment multiply entire array
end;
```

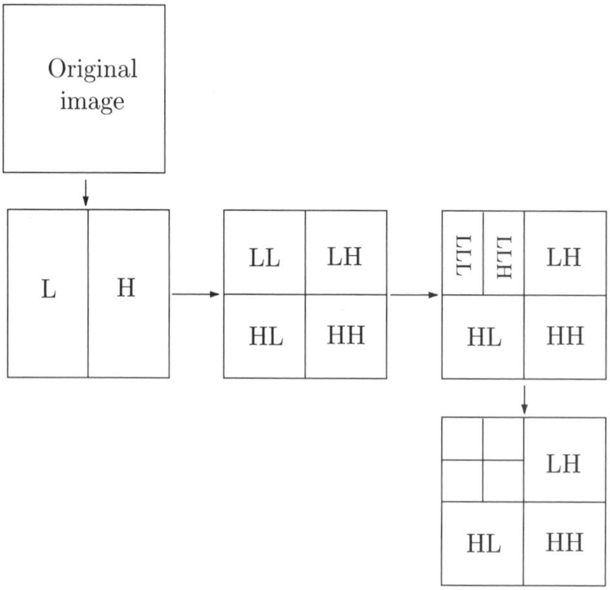

**Figure 4.5:** The Pyramid Image Wavelet Transform.

diagonal. Figure 4.6b,c shows the first two steps in its pyramid decomposition. It is obvious that the transform coefficients in the bottom right subband (HH) indicate a diagonal artifact located above the main diagonal. It is also easy to see that subband LL is a low-resolution version of the original image.

```
12 16 12 12 12 12 12 12      14 12 12 12 | 4 0 0 0      13 13 12 12 | 2 2 0 0
12 12 16 12 12 12 12 12      12 14 12 12 | 0 4 0 0      12 13 13 12 | 0 2 2 0
12 12 12 16 12 12 12 12      12 14 12 12 | 0 4 0 0      12 12 13 13 | 0 0 2 2
12 12 12 12 16 12 12 12      12 12 14 12 | 0 0 4 0      12 12 12 13 | 0 0 0 2
12 12 12 12 12 16 12 12      12 12 14 12 | 0 0 4 0      ─────────────────────
12 12 12 12 12 12 16 12      12 12 12 14 | 0 0 0 4       2 2 0 0 | 4 4 0 0
12 12 12 12 12 12 12 16      12 12 12 14 | 0 0 0 4       0 2 2 0 | 0 4 4 0
12 12 12 12 12 12 12 12      12 12 12 12 | 0 0 0 0       0 0 2 2 | 0 0 4 4
                                                         0 0 0 2 | 0 0 0 4
         (a)                        (b)                        (c)
```

**Figure 4.6:** The Subband Decomposition of a Diagonal Line.

Figure 4.36 shows four levels of subbands, where level 1 contains the detailed features of the image (also referred to as the high-frequency or fine-resolution wavelet coefficients) and the top level, level 4, contains the coarse image features (low-frequency or coarse-resolution coefficients). It is clear that the lower levels can be quantized coarsely without much loss of important image information, while the higher levels should be quantized finely or not at all. The subband structure is the basis of all the image compression methods that use the wavelet transform.

Figure 4.7 shows typical results of the pyramid wavelet transform. The original image is shown in Figure 4.7a, and Figure 4.7c is a general pyramid decomposition. In order to illustrate how the pyramid transform works, this image consists only of horizontal, vertical, and slanted lines. The four quadrants of Figure 4.7b show smaller versions of the image. The top left subband, containing the averages, is similar to the entire image, while each of the other three subbands shows image details. Because of the way the pyramid transform is constructed, the top right subband contains vertical details, the bottom left subband contains horizontal details, and the bottom right one contains the details of slanted lines. Figure 4.7c shows the results of repeatedly applying this transform. The image is transformed into subbands of horizontal, vertical, and diagonal details, while the top left subsquare, containing the averages, is shrunk to a single pixel.

Either method, standard or uniform, results in a transformed—although not yet compressed—image that has one average at the top left corner and smaller numbers, differences, or averages of differences everywhere else. This can now be compressed using a combination of methods, such as RLE, move-to-front [Salomon 00], and Huffman coding. If lossy compression is acceptable, some of the smallest differences can be quantized or even set to zero, which creates run lengths of zeros, making the use of RLE even more attractive.

**Color Images:** So far we have assumed that each pixel is a single number (i.e., we have a single-component image, in which all pixels are shades of the same color, normally

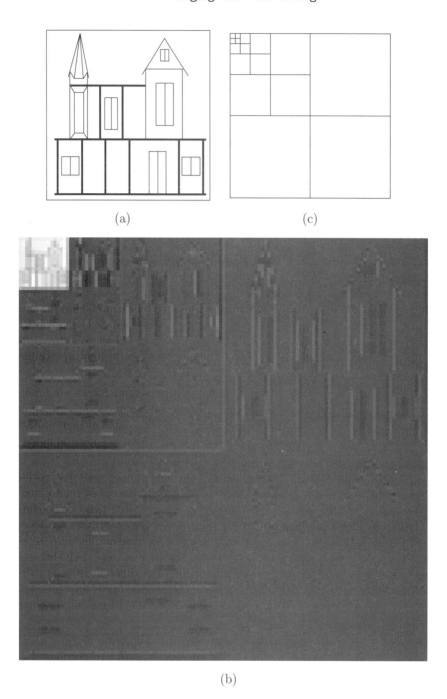

(a)                                        (c)

(b)

**Figure 4.7:** An Example of the Pyramid Image Wavelet Transform.

gray). Any compression method for single-component images can be extended to color (three-component) images by separating the three components, then transforming and compressing each individually. If the compression method is lossy, it makes sense to convert the three image components from their original color representation, which is normally RGB, to the YIQ color representation. The Y component of this representation is called *luminance,* and the I and Q (chrominance) components are responsible for the color information [Salomon 99]. The advantage of this color representation is that the human eye is most sensitive to Y and least sensitive to Q. A lossy method should therefore leave the Y component alone and delete some data from the I and more data from the Q components, resulting in good compression and in a loss for which the eye is not that sensitive. Section 3.7.1 offers more information on luminance and chrominance.

It is interesting to note that U.S. color television transmission also takes advantage of the YIQ representation. Signals are broadcast with bandwidths of 4 MHz for Y, 1.5 MHz for I, and only 0.6 MHz for Q.

### 4.1.2 Properties of the Haar Transform

The examples in this section illustrate several important properties of the Haar wavelet transform and of the discrete wavelet transform in general. Figure 4.8 shows a highly correlated $8 \times 8$ image and its Haar wavelet transform. Both the grayscale and numeric values of the pixels and of the *transform coefficients* are shown. Because the original image is so correlated, the wavelet coefficients are mostly small and there are many zeros.

**Note:** A glance at Figure 4.8 suggests that the last sentence is wrong. The wavelet transform coefficients listed in the figure are very large compared to the pixel values of the original image. In fact, we know that the top left Haar transform coefficient should be the average of all the image pixels. Since the pixels of our image have values that are (more or less) uniformly distributed in the interval $[0, 255]$, this average should be around 128 (in fact, it is 131.375), yet the top left transform coefficient is 1051 (which equals $131.375 \times 8$). The reason this coefficient is eight times the average is that the Matlab code that did the calculations uses $\sqrt{2}$ instead of 2 (see function `individ(n)` in Figure 4.12).

In a discrete wavelet transform, most of the wavelet coefficients are details (or differences). The details in the lower levels represent the fine details of the image. As we move higher in the subband level, we find details that correspond to coarser image features. Figure 4.9a illustrates this concept. It shows an image that is smooth on the left and has "activity" (i.e., adjacent pixels that tend to be different) on the right. Part (b) shows the wavelet transform of the image. Low levels (corresponding to fine details) have transform coefficients on the right, since this is where the image activity is located. High levels (coarse details) look similar but also have coefficients on the left side, since the image is not completely blank on the left.

The Haar transform is the simplest wavelet transform, but even this simple method illustrates the power of the wavelet transform. It turns out that the low levels of the discrete wavelet transform contain the unimportant image features, so quantizing or discarding these coefficients can lead to lossy compression that is both efficient and of high quality. Many times, the image can be reconstructed from very few transform co-

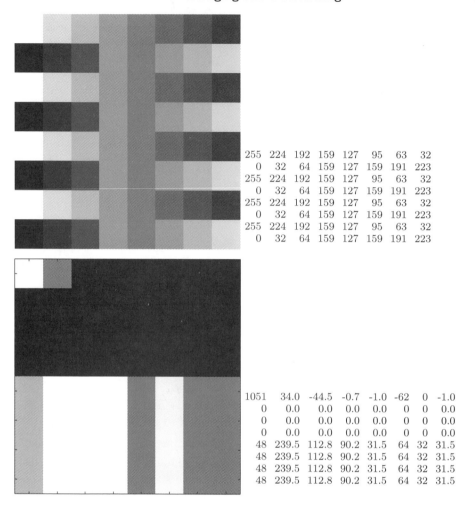

| 255 | 224 | 192 | 159 | 127 | 95  | 63  | 32  |
|-----|-----|-----|-----|-----|-----|-----|-----|
| 0   | 32  | 64  | 159 | 127 | 159 | 191 | 223 |
| 255 | 224 | 192 | 159 | 127 | 95  | 63  | 32  |
| 0   | 32  | 64  | 159 | 127 | 159 | 191 | 223 |
| 255 | 224 | 192 | 159 | 127 | 95  | 63  | 32  |
| 0   | 32  | 64  | 159 | 127 | 159 | 191 | 223 |
| 255 | 224 | 192 | 159 | 127 | 95  | 63  | 32  |
| 0   | 32  | 64  | 159 | 127 | 159 | 191 | 223 |

| 1051 | 34.0  | -44.5 | -0.7 | -1.0 | -62 | 0  | -1.0 |
|------|-------|-------|------|------|-----|----|------|
| 0    | 0.0   | 0.0   | 0.0  | 0.0  | 0   | 0  | 0.0  |
| 0    | 0.0   | 0.0   | 0.0  | 0.0  | 0   | 0  | 0.0  |
| 0    | 0.0   | 0.0   | 0.0  | 0.0  | 0   | 0  | 0.0  |
| 48   | 239.5 | 112.8 | 90.2 | 31.5 | 64  | 32 | 31.5 |
| 48   | 239.5 | 112.8 | 90.2 | 31.5 | 64  | 32 | 31.5 |
| 48   | 239.5 | 112.8 | 90.2 | 31.5 | 64  | 32 | 31.5 |
| 48   | 239.5 | 112.8 | 90.2 | 31.5 | 64  | 32 | 31.5 |

**Figure 4.8:** The $8 \times 8$ Image Reconstructed in Figure 4.11 and Its Haar Transform.

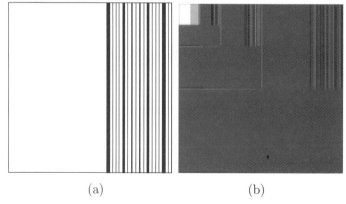

(a)                                  (b)

**Figure 4.9:** (a) A $128 \times 128$ Image with Activity on the Right. (b) Its Transform.

efficients without any noticeable loss of quality. Figure 4.11 shows three reconstructions of the simple $8 \times 8$ image of Figure 4.8. They were obtained from only 32, 13, and 5 wavelet coefficients, respectively.

Figure 4.10 is a similar example. Part (a) shows a bi-level image fully reconstructed from just 4% of its transform coefficients (653 coefficients shown in part (b) out of $128 \times 128$).

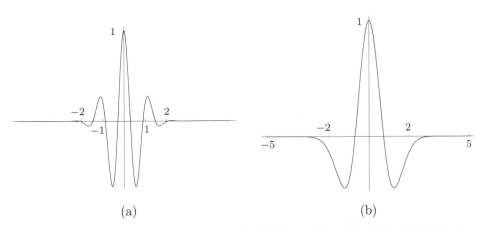

(a)                                    (b)

**Figure 4.10:** Reconstructing a $128 \times 128$ Simple Image from 4% of Its Coefficients.

My personal experience suggests that the best way to understand these concepts is to experiment extensively with images that have different correlations and activities. Proper mathematical software makes it easy to input images and to experiment with various features of the discrete wavelet transform. In order to help the interested reader, Figure 4.12 lists a Matlab program that inputs an image, computes its Haar wavelet transform, discards a given percentage of the smallest transform coefficients, then computes the inverse transform to reconstruct the image.

Lossy wavelet image compression involves the discarding of coefficients, so the concept of *sparseness ratio* is defined to measure the number of coefficients discarded. It is defined as the number of nonzero wavelet coefficients divided by the number of coefficients left after some are discarded. The higher the sparseness ratio, the fewer coefficients are left. Higher sparseness ratios lead to better compression but may result in poorly reconstructed images. The sparseness ratio is distantly related to the *compression factor*, a compression measure defined in the Preface.

The line "`filename='lena128'; dim=128;`" contains the image file name and the dimension of the image. The image files used by the author were in raw form and contained just the grayscale values, each as a single byte. There is no header, and not even the image resolution (number of rows and columns) is contained in the file. However, Matlab can read other types of files. The image is assumed to be square,

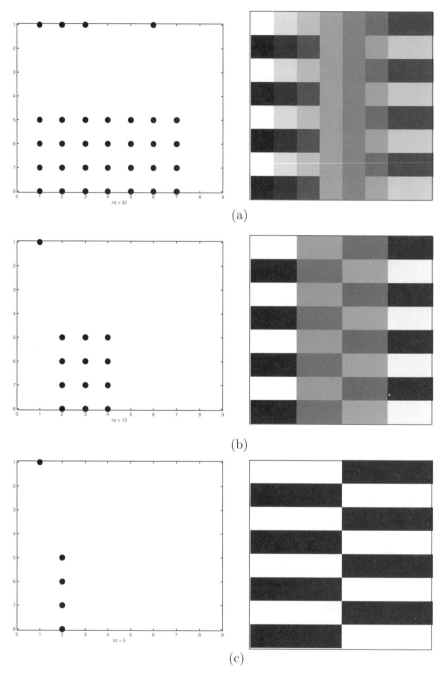

**Figure 4.11:** Three Lossy Reconstructions of an $8 \times 8$ Image.

```
clear; % main program
filename='lena128'; dim=128;
fid=fopen(filename,'r');
if fid==-1 disp('file not found')
else img=fread(fid,[dim,dim])'; fclose(fid);
end
thresh=0.0;        % percent of transform coefficients deleted
figure(1), imagesc(img), colormap(gray), axis off, axis square
w=harmatt(dim);  % compute the Haar dim x dim transform matrix
timg=w*img*w';    % forward Haar transform
tsort=sort(abs(timg(:)));
tthresh=tsort(floor(max(thresh*dim*dim,1)));
cim=timg.*(abs(timg) > tthresh);
[i,j,s]=find(cim);
dimg=sparse(i,j,s,dim,dim);
% figure(2) displays the remaining transform coefficients
%figure(2), spy(dimg), colormap(gray), axis square
figure(2), image(dimg), colormap(gray), axis square
cimg=full(w'*sparse(dimg)*w);        % inverse Haar transform
density = nnz(dimg);
disp([num2str(100*thresh) '% of smallest coefficients deleted.'])
disp([num2str(density) ' coefficients remain out of ' ...
 num2str(dim) 'x' num2str(dim) '.'])
figure(3), imagesc(cimg), colormap(gray), axis off, axis square

File harmatt.m with two functions

function x = harmatt(dim)
num=log2(dim);
p = sparse(eye(dim)); q = p;
i=1;
while i<=dim/2;
 q(1:2*i,1:2*i) = sparse(individ(2*i));
 p=p*q; i=2*i;
end
x=sparse(p);

function f=individ(n)
x=[1, 1]/sqrt(2);
y=[1,-1]/sqrt(2);
while min(size(x)) < n/2
 x=[x, zeros(min(size(x)),max(size(x)));...
   zeros(min(size(x)),max(size(x))), x];
end
while min(size(y)) < n/2
 y=[y, zeros(min(size(y)),max(size(y)));...
   zeros(min(size(y)),max(size(y))), y];
end
f=[x;y];
```

**Figure 4.12:** Matlab Code for the Haar Transform of an Image.

and parameter "dim" should be a power of 2. The assignment "thresh=" specifies the percentage of transform coefficients to be deleted. This provides an easy way to experiment with lossy wavelet image compression.

File "harmatt.m" contains two functions that compute the Haar wavelet coefficients in a matrix form (Section 4.2.1).

(A technical note: A Matlab m file may include either commands or a function but not both. It may, however, contain more than one function, provided that only the top function is invoked from outside the file. All the other functions must be called from within the file. In our case, function harmatt(dim) calls function individ(n).)

**Example:** The code of Figure 4.12 is used to compute the Haar transform of the well-known "Lena" image. The image is then reconstructed three times by discarding more and more detail coefficients. Figure 4.13 shows the results of reconstructing the original image from 3277, 1639, and 820 coefficients, respectively. Despite the heavy loss of wavelet coefficients, only a very small loss of image quality is noticeable. The number of wavelet coefficients is, of course, the same as the image resolution $128 \times 128 = 16,384$. Using 820 out of 16,384 coefficients corresponds to discarding 95% of the smallest of the transform coefficients (notice, however, that some of the coefficients were originally zero, so the actual loss may amount to less than 95%).

## 4.2 The Haar Transform

The Haar transform uses a scale function $\phi(t)$ and a wavelet $\psi(t)$, both shown in Figure 4.14a, to represent a large number of functions $f(t)$. The representation is the infinite sum

$$f(t) = \sum_{k=-\infty}^{\infty} c_k \phi(t-k) + \sum_{k=-\infty}^{\infty} \sum_{j=0}^{\infty} d_{j,k} \psi(2^j t - k),$$

where $c_k$ and $d_{j,k}$ are coefficients to be calculated.

The basic scale function $\phi(t)$ is the unit pulse

$$\phi(t) = \begin{cases} 1, & 0 \le t < 1, \\ 0, & \text{otherwise.} \end{cases}$$

The function $\phi(t-k)$ is a copy of $\phi(t)$, shifted $k$ units to the right. Similarly, $\phi(2t-k)$ is a copy of $\phi(t-k)$ scaled to half the width of $\phi(t-k)$. The shifted copies are used to approximate $f(t)$ at different times $t$. The scaled copies are used to approximate $f(t)$ at higher resolutions. Figure 4.14b shows the functions $\phi(2^j t - k)$ for $j = 0, 1, 2$, and 3 and for $k = 0, 1, \ldots, 7$.

The basic Haar wavelet is the step function

$$\psi(t) = \begin{cases} 1, & 0 \le t < 0.5, \\ -1, & 0.5 \le t < 1. \end{cases}$$

From this we can see that the general Haar wavelet $\psi(2^j t - k)$ is a copy of $\psi(t)$ shifted $k$ units to the right and scaled such that its total width is $1/2^j$. The four Haar wavelets $\psi(2^2 t - k)$ for $k = 0, 1, 2$, and 3 are shown in Figure 4.14c.

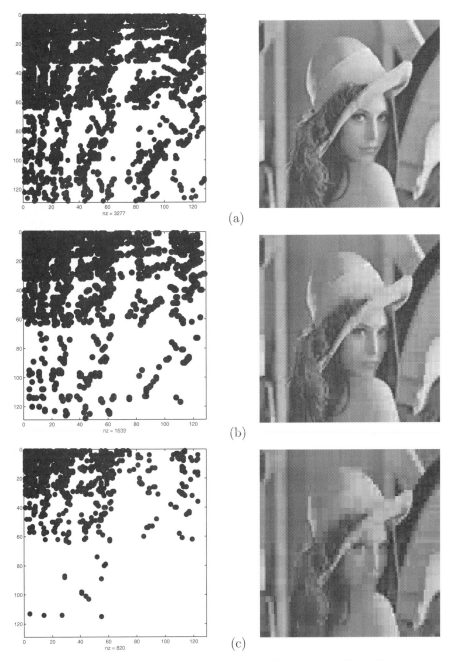

**Figure 4.13:** Three Lossy Reconstructions of the $128 \times 128$ Lena Image.

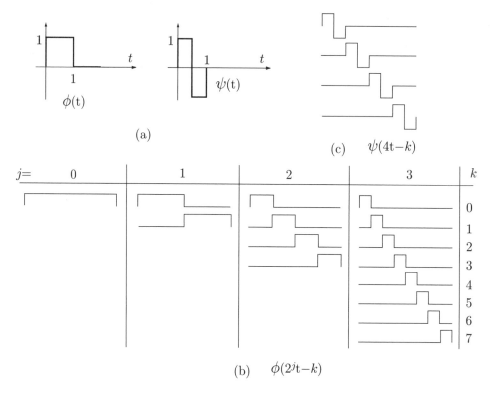

Figure 4.14: The Haar Basis Scale and Wavelet Functions.

Both $\phi(2^j t - k)$ and $\psi(2^j t - k)$ are nonzero in an interval of width $1/2^j$. This interval is their *support*. Since this interval tends to be short, we say that these functions have *compact support*.

We illustrate the basic transform on the simple step function

$$f(t) = \begin{cases} 5, & 0 \le t < 0.5, \\ 3, & 0.5 \le t < 1. \end{cases}$$

It is easy to see that $f(t) = 4\phi(t) + \psi(t)$. We say that the original steps $(5,3)$ have been transformed to the (low resolution) average 4 and the (high resolution) detail $-1$. Using matrix notation, this can be expressed as $(5,3)\mathbf{A}_2 = (4,-1)$, where $\mathbf{A}_2$ is the order-2 Haar transform matrix of Equation (3.16).

### 4.2.1 A Matrix Approach

The principle of the Haar transform is to calculate averages and differences. It turns out that this can be done by means of matrix multiplication ([Mulcahy 96] and [Mulcahy 97]). As an example, we select the top row of the simple $8 \times 8$ image of Figure 4.8. Anyone with a little experience with matrices can construct a matrix that when multiplied by this vector creates a vector with four averages and four differences. Matrix $A_1$

of Equation (4.1) does that and, when multiplied by the top row of pixels of Figure 4.8, generates $(239.5, 175.5, 111.0, 47.5, 15.5, 16.5, 16.0, 15.5)$. Similarly, matrices $A_2$ and $A_3$ perform the second and third steps of the transform, respectively. The results are shown in Equation (4.2):

$$A_1 = \begin{pmatrix} \frac{1}{2} & \frac{1}{2} & 0 & 0 & 0 & 0 & 0 & 0 \\ 0 & 0 & \frac{1}{2} & \frac{1}{2} & 0 & 0 & 0 & 0 \\ 0 & 0 & 0 & 0 & \frac{1}{2} & \frac{1}{2} & 0 & 0 \\ 0 & 0 & 0 & 0 & 0 & 0 & \frac{1}{2} & \frac{1}{2} \\ \frac{1}{2} & -\frac{1}{2} & 0 & 0 & 0 & 0 & 0 & 0 \\ 0 & 0 & \frac{1}{2} & -\frac{1}{2} & 0 & 0 & 0 & 0 \\ 0 & 0 & 0 & 0 & \frac{1}{2} & -\frac{1}{2} & 0 & 0 \\ 0 & 0 & 0 & 0 & 0 & 0 & \frac{1}{2} & -\frac{1}{2} \end{pmatrix}, \quad A_1 \begin{pmatrix} 255 \\ 224 \\ 192 \\ 159 \\ 127 \\ 95 \\ 63 \\ 32 \end{pmatrix} = \begin{pmatrix} 239.5 \\ 175.5 \\ 111.0 \\ 47.5 \\ 15.5 \\ 16.5 \\ 16.0 \\ 15.5 \end{pmatrix}, \quad (4.1)$$

$$A_2 = \begin{pmatrix} \frac{1}{2} & \frac{1}{2} & 0 & 0 & 0 & 0 & 0 & 0 \\ 0 & 0 & \frac{1}{2} & \frac{1}{2} & 0 & 0 & 0 & 0 \\ \frac{1}{2} & -\frac{1}{2} & 0 & 0 & 0 & 0 & 0 & 0 \\ 0 & 0 & \frac{1}{2} & -\frac{1}{2} & 0 & 0 & 0 & 0 \\ 0 & 0 & 0 & 0 & 1 & 0 & 0 & 0 \\ 0 & 0 & 0 & 0 & 0 & 1 & 0 & 0 \\ 0 & 0 & 0 & 0 & 0 & 0 & 1 & 0 \\ 0 & 0 & 0 & 0 & 0 & 0 & 0 & 1 \end{pmatrix}, \quad A_3 = \begin{pmatrix} \frac{1}{2} & \frac{1}{2} & 0 & 0 & 0 & 0 & 0 & 0 \\ \frac{1}{2} & -\frac{1}{2} & 0 & 0 & 0 & 0 & 0 & 0 \\ 0 & 0 & 1 & 0 & 0 & 0 & 0 & 0 \\ 0 & 0 & 0 & 1 & 0 & 0 & 0 & 0 \\ 0 & 0 & 0 & 0 & 1 & 0 & 0 & 0 \\ 0 & 0 & 0 & 0 & 0 & 1 & 0 & 0 \\ 0 & 0 & 0 & 0 & 0 & 0 & 1 & 0 \\ 0 & 0 & 0 & 0 & 0 & 0 & 0 & 1 \end{pmatrix},$$

$$A_2 \begin{pmatrix} 239.5 \\ 175.5 \\ 111.0 \\ 47.5 \\ 15.5 \\ 16.5 \\ 16.0 \\ 15.5 \end{pmatrix} = \begin{pmatrix} 207.5 \\ 79.25 \\ 32.0 \\ 31.75 \\ 15.5 \\ 16.5 \\ 16.0 \\ 15.5 \end{pmatrix}, \quad A_3 \begin{pmatrix} 207.5 \\ 79.25 \\ 32.0 \\ 31.75 \\ 15.5 \\ 16.5 \\ 16.0 \\ 15.5 \end{pmatrix} = \begin{pmatrix} 143.375 \\ 64.125 \\ 32. \\ 31.75 \\ 15.5 \\ 16.5 \\ 16. \\ 15.5 \end{pmatrix}. \quad (4.2)$$

Instead of calculating averages and differences of image rows, all we have to do is construct matrices $A_1$, $A_2$, and $A_3$, multiply them to get $W = A_1 A_2 A_3$, and apply $W$ to all the rows of image $I$ by multiplying $W \cdot I$:

$$W \begin{pmatrix} 255 \\ 224 \\ 192 \\ 159 \\ 127 \\ 95 \\ 63 \\ 32 \end{pmatrix} = \begin{pmatrix} \frac{1}{8} & \frac{1}{8} & \frac{1}{8} & \frac{1}{8} & \frac{1}{8} & \frac{1}{8} & \frac{1}{8} & \frac{1}{8} \\ \frac{1}{8} & \frac{1}{8} & \frac{1}{8} & \frac{1}{8} & \frac{-1}{8} & \frac{-1}{8} & \frac{-1}{8} & \frac{-1}{8} \\ \frac{1}{4} & \frac{1}{4} & \frac{-1}{4} & \frac{-1}{4} & 0 & 0 & 0 & 0 \\ 0 & 0 & 0 & 0 & \frac{1}{4} & \frac{1}{4} & \frac{-1}{4} & \frac{-1}{4} \\ \frac{1}{2} & \frac{-1}{2} & 0 & 0 & 0 & 0 & 0 & 0 \\ 0 & 0 & \frac{1}{2} & \frac{-1}{2} & 0 & 0 & 0 & 0 \\ 0 & 0 & 0 & 0 & \frac{1}{2} & \frac{-1}{2} & 0 & 0 \\ 0 & 0 & 0 & 0 & 0 & 0 & \frac{1}{2} & \frac{-1}{2} \end{pmatrix} \begin{pmatrix} 255 \\ 224 \\ 192 \\ 159 \\ 127 \\ 95 \\ 63 \\ 32 \end{pmatrix} = \begin{pmatrix} 143.375 \\ 64.125 \\ 32 \\ 31.75 \\ 15.5 \\ 16.5 \\ 16 \\ 15.5 \end{pmatrix}.$$

This, of course, is only half the task. In order to compute the complete transform, we still have to apply $W$ to the rows of the product $W \cdot I$, and we do this by applying it to the columns of the transpose $(W \cdot I)^T$, then transposing the result. Thus, the complete transform is (see line `timg=w*img*w`' in Figure 4.12)

$$I_{\mathrm{tr}} = \left(W(W \cdot I)^T\right)^T = W \cdot I \cdot W^T.$$

The inverse transform is done by

$$W^{-1}(W^{-1} \cdot I_{\mathrm{tr}}^T)^T = W^{-1}\left(I_{\mathrm{tr}} \cdot (W^{-1})^T\right),$$

and this is where the normalized Haar transform (mentioned on page 168) becomes important. Instead of calculating averages [quantities of the form $(d_i + d_{i+1})/2$] and differences [quantities of the form $(d_i - d_{i+1})/2$], it is better to use the quantities $(d_i + d_{i+1})/\sqrt{2}$ and $(d_i - d_{i+1})/\sqrt{2}$. This results is an *orthonormal* matrix $W$, and it is well known that the inverse of such a matrix is simply its transpose. Thus, we can write the inverse transform in the simple form $W^T I_{\mathrm{tr}} W$ [see line `cimg=full(w'*sparse(dimg)*w)` in Figure 4.12].

In between the forward and inverse transforms, some transform coefficients may be quantized or deleted. Alternatively, matrix $I_{\mathrm{tr}}$ may be compressed by means of run-length encoding and/or Huffman codes.

Function `individ(n)` of Figure 4.12 starts with a $2 \times 2$ Haar transform matrix (notice that it uses $\sqrt{2}$ instead of 2), then uses it to construct as many individual matrices $A_i$ as necessary. Function `harmatt(dim)` combines those individual matrices to form the final Haar matrix for an image of `dim` rows and `dim` columns.

**Example:** The Matlab code of Figure 4.15 calculates $W$ as the product of the three matrices $A_1$, $A_2$, and $A_3$, then transforms the $8 \times 8$ image of Figure 4.8 by computing the product $W \cdot I \cdot W^T$. The result is an $8 \times 8$ matrix of transform coefficients whose top left value, 131.375, is the average of all 64 image pixels.

## 4.3 Subband Transforms

The transforms discussed in Section 3.5 are *orthogonal* because each is based on an orthogonal matrix. An orthogonal transform can also be expressed as an *inner product* of the data (pixel values or audio samples) with a set of *basis functions*. The result of an orthogonal transform is a set of transform coefficients that can be compressed with RLE, Huffman coding, or other methods. Lossy compression is obtained when the transform coefficients are quantized before being compressed.

The discrete inner product of the two vectors $f_i$ and $g_i$ is defined by

$$\langle f, g \rangle = \sum_i f_i \, g_i,$$

and Section 3.5.1 starts with a transform of the form $c_i = \sum_j d_j w_{ij}$, where $d_j$ are the data items and $w_{ij}$ are certain weights.

```
a1=[1/2 1/2 0 0 0 0 0 0; 0 0 1/2 1/2 0 0 0 0;
 0 0 0 0 1/2 1/2 0 0; 0 0 0 0 0 0 1/2 1/2;
 1/2 -1/2 0 0 0 0 0 0; 0 0 1/2 -1/2 0 0 0 0;
 0 0 0 0 1/2 -1/2 0 0; 0 0 0 0 0 0 1/2 -1/2];
% a1*[255; 224; 192; 159; 127; 95; 63; 32];
a2=[1/2 1/2 0 0 0 0 0 0; 0 0 1/2 1/2 0 0 0 0;
 1/2 -1/2 0 0 0 0 0 0; 0 0 1/2 -1/2 0 0 0 0;
 0 0 0 0 1 0 0 0; 0 0 0 0 0 1 0 0;
 0 0 0 0 0 0 1 0; 0 0 0 0 0 0 0 1];
a3=[1/2 1/2 0 0 0 0 0 0; 1/2 -1/2 0 0 0 0 0 0;
 0 0 1 0 0 0 0 0; 0 0 0 1 0 0 0 0;
 0 0 0 0 1 0 0 0; 0 0 0 0 0 1 0 0;
 0 0 0 0 0 0 1 0; 0 0 0 0 0 0 0 1];
w=a3*a2*a1;
dim=8; fid=fopen('8x8','r');
img=fread(fid,[dim,dim])'; fclose(fid);
w*img*w' % Result of the transform
```

| | | | | | | | |
|---|---|---|---|---|---|---|---|
| 131.375 | 4.250 | −7.875 | −0.125 | −0.25 | −15.5 | 0 | −0.25 |
| 0 | 0 | 0 | 0 | 0 | 0 | 0 | 0 |
| 0 | 0 | 0 | 0 | 0 | 0 | 0 | 0 |
| 0 | 0 | 0 | 0 | 0 | 0 | 0 | 0 |
| 12.000 | 59.875 | 39.875 | 31.875 | 15.75 | 32.0 | 16 | 15.75 |
| 12.000 | 59.875 | 39.875 | 31.875 | 15.75 | 32.0 | 16 | 15.75 |
| 12.000 | 59.875 | 39.875 | 31.875 | 15.75 | 32.0 | 16 | 15.75 |
| 12.000 | 59.875 | 39.875 | 31.875 | 15.75 | 32.0 | 16 | 15.75 |

**Figure 4.15:** Code and Results for the Matrix Wavelet Transform $W \cdot I \cdot W^T$.

The wavelet transform, on the other hand, is a *subband transform*. It is done by computing a *convolution* of the data items (pixel values or audio samples) with a set of *bandpass filters*. Each resulting subband encodes a particular portion of the frequency content of the data.

The word "convolution" means coiling together. The discrete convolution of the two vectors $f_i$ and $g_i$ is denoted by $f \star g$. Each element $(f \star g)_i$ of the convolution is defined by

$$(f \star g)_i = \sum_j f_j\, g_{i-j}. \tag{4.3}$$

(Convolution is also defined for functions, but the field of data compression deals with discrete quantities, so only the discrete convolution is discussed here.) Notice that the limits of the sum above have not been stated explicitly. They depend on the sizes of vectors $f$ and $g$, and Equation (4.9) is an example.

The remainder of this section discusses linear systems and why convolution is defined in this peculiar way. This material can be skipped by nonmathematical readers.

We start with the simple, intuitive concept of a *system*. This is anything that receives input and generates output in response. The input and output can be one-dimensional (a function of the time) two-dimensional (a function of two spatial variables), or it can have any number of dimensions. We will be concerned with the relation of the output to the input, not with the internal operation of the system. We will also concentrate on *linear systems*, since they are both simple and important. A linear system is defined as follows: If input $x_1(t)$ produces output $y_1(t)$ [we denote this by $x_1(t) \rightarrow y_1(t)$] and if $x_2(t) \rightarrow y_2(t)$, then $x_1(t) + x_2(t) \rightarrow y_1(t) + y_2(t)$. Any system that does not satisfy this condition is considered nonlinear.

This definition implies that $2x_1(t) = x_1(t) + x_1(t) \rightarrow y_1(t) + y_1(t) = 2y_1(t)$ or, in general, that $a\,x_1(t) \rightarrow a\,y_1(t)$ for any real $a$.

Some linear systems are *shift invariant*. If such a linear system satisfies $x(t) \rightarrow y(t)$, then $x(t-T) \rightarrow y(t-T)$; i.e., shifting the input by an amount $T$ shifts the output by the same amount but does not otherwise affect the output. In the discussion of convolution, we assume that the systems in question are linear and shift invariant. This is true (or true to a very good approximation) for electrical networks and optical systems, the main pieces of hardware used in image processing and compression.

It is useful to have a general relation between the input and output of a linear, shift-invariant system. It turns out that the expression

$$y(t) = \int_{-\infty}^{+\infty} f(t,\tau)x(\tau)\,d\tau \qquad (4.4)$$

is general enough for this purpose. In other words, there is always a two-parameter function $f(t,\tau)$ that can be used to predict the output $y(t)$ if the input $x(\tau)$ is known. However, we want to express this relation with a one-parameter function, and we use the shift invariance of the system for this purpose. For a linear, shift-invariant system we can write

$$y(t-T) = \int_{-\infty}^{+\infty} f(t,\tau)x(\tau - T)\,d\tau.$$

If we change variables by adding $T$ to both $t$ and $\tau$, we get

$$y(t) = \int_{-\infty}^{+\infty} f(t+T,\tau + T)x(\tau)\,d\tau. \qquad (4.5)$$

Comparing Equations (4.4) and (4.5) shows that $f(t,\tau) = f(t+T,\tau+T)$. Thus, function $f$ has the property that if we add $T$ to both its parameters, it does not change. The function is constant as long as the difference between its parameters is constant. Function $f$ depends only on the difference of its parameters, so it is essentially a single parameter function. We can therefore write $g(t-\tau) = f(t,\tau)$, which changes Equation (4.4) to

$$y(t) = \int_{-\infty}^{+\infty} g(t-\tau)x(\tau)\,d\tau. \qquad (4.6)$$

This is the *convolution integral*, an important relation between $x(t)$ and $y(t)$ or between $x(t)$ and $g(t)$. This relation is denoted by $y = g \star x$ and it says that the output $y$ of a linear, shift-invariant system is given by the convolution of its input $x$ with a certain function $g(t)$ (or by *convolving* $x$ with $g$). Function $g$, which is characteristic of the system, is called the *impulse response* of the system. Figure 4.16 shows a graphical description of a convolution, where the final result (the integral) is the gray area under the curve.

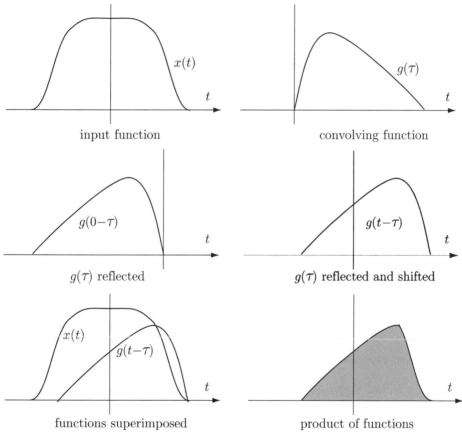

**Figure 4.16:** The Convolution of $x(t)$ and $g(t)$.

The convolution has a number of important properties. It is commutative, associative, and distributive over addition. These properties are listed in Equation (4.7)

$$
\begin{aligned}
f \star g &= g \star f, \\
f \star (g \star h) &= (f \star g) \star h, \\
f \star (g + h) &= f \star g + f \star h.
\end{aligned}
\tag{4.7}
$$

Practical problems normally involve discrete sequences of numbers, rather than continuous functions, so the *discrete convolution* is useful. The discrete convolution of the two sequences $f(i)$ and $g(i)$ is defined as

$$h(i) = f(i) \star g(i) = \sum_j f(j)\, g(i - j). \tag{4.8}$$

If the lengths of $f(i)$ and $g(i)$ are $m$ and $n$, respectively, then $h(i)$ has length $m + n - 1$.

**Example:** Given the two sequences $f = \big(f(0), f(1), \ldots, f(5)\big)$ (six elements) and $g = \big(g(0), g(1), \ldots, g(4)\big)$ (five elements), Equation (4.8) yields the ten elements of the convolution $h = f \star g$:

$$h(0) = \sum_{j=0}^{0} f(j)g(0 - j) = f(0)g(0)$$

$$h(1) = \sum_{j=0}^{1} f(j)g(1 - j) = f(0)g(1) + f(1)g(0)$$

$$h(2) = \sum_{j=0}^{2} f(j)g(2 - j) = f(0)g(2) + f(1)g(1) + f(2)g(0)$$

$$h(3) = \sum_{j=0}^{3} f(j)g(3 - j) = f(0)g(3) + f(1)g(2) + f(2)g(1) + f(3)g(0)$$

$$h(4) = \sum_{j=0}^{4} f(j)g(4 - j) = f(0)g(4) + f(1)g(3) + f(2)g(2) + f(3)g(1) + f(4)g(0)$$

$$h(5) = \sum_{j=1}^{5} f(j)g(5 - j) = f(1)g(4) + f(2)g(3) + f(3)g(2) + f(4)g(1) + f(5)g(0)$$

$$h(6) = \sum_{j=2}^{5} f(j)g(6 - j) = f(2)g(4) + f(3)g(3) + f(4)g(2) + f(5)g(1)$$

$$h(7) = \sum_{j=3}^{5} f(j)g(7 - j) = f(3)g(4) + f(4)g(3) + f(5)g(2)$$

$$h(8) = \sum_{j=4}^{5} f(j)g(8 - j) = f(4)g(4) + f(5)g(3)$$

$$h(9) = \sum_{j=5}^{5} f(j)g(9 - j) = f(5)g(4) \tag{4.9}$$

A simple example of the use of a convolution is smoothing (or denoising). This shows how convolution can be used as a filter. Given a noisy function $f(t)$ (Figure 4.17), we select a rectangular pulse as the convolving function $g(t)$. It is defined as

$$g(t) = \begin{cases} 1, & -a/2 < t < a/2, \\ \frac{1}{2}, & t = \pm a/2, \\ 0, & \text{elsewhere}, \end{cases}$$

where $a$ is a suitably small value (typically 1, but it could be anything). As the convolution proceeds, the pulse is moved from left to right and is multiplied by $f(t)$. The result of the product is a local average of $f(t)$ over an interval of width $a$. This has the effect of suppressing the high frequency fluctuations of $f(t)$.

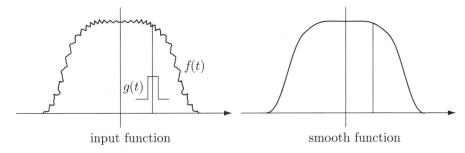

input function                    smooth function

**Figure 4.17:** Applying Convolution to Denoising a Function.

"Oh no," George said. "It was more than money."

   He leaned his forehead in his hand and tried to remember what else more than money. The darkness inside his head was full of convolutions. His eardrums were too tight. Only the higher registers of sound were getting through.

—Paul Scott, *The Bender*

## 4.4 Filter Banks

The matrix approach to the Haar transform is used in this section to introduce the idea of *filter banks* [Strang and Nguyen 96]. We show how the Haar transform can be interpreted as a bank of two filters, a lowpass and a highpass. We explain the terms "filter," "lowpass," and "highpass" and show how the idea of filter banks leads naturally to the concept of subband transform [Simoncelli et al. 90] The Haar transform, of course, is the simplest wavelet transform, so it is used here to illustrate the new concepts. However, using it as a filter bank may not be very efficient. Most practical applications of wavelet filters use more sophisticated sets of filter coefficients, but they are all based on the concept of filters and filter banks.

   A *filter* is a linear operator defined in terms of its *filter coefficients* $h(0)$, $h(1)$, $h(2),\ldots$. The filter coefficients can be applied to an input vector $x$ to produce an output vector $y$ according to

$$y(n) = \sum_k h(k)x(n-k) = h \star x.$$

Notice that the limits of the sum above have not been stated explicitly. They depend on the sizes of vectors $x$ and $h$. Since our independent variable is the time $t$, it is convenient to assume that the inputs (and, as a result, also the outputs) come at all times $t = \ldots, -2, -1, 0, 1, 2, \ldots$. Thus, we use the notation

$$x = (\ldots, a, b, c, d, e, \ldots),$$

where the central value $c$ is the input at time zero $[c = x(0)]$, values $d$ and $e$ are the inputs at times 1 and 2, respectively, and $b = x(-1)$ and $a = x(-2)$. In practice, the inputs are always finite, so the infinite vector $x$ will have only a finite number of nonzero elements.

Deeper insight into the behavior of a linear filter can be gained by considering the simple input $x = (\ldots, 0, 0, 1, 0, 0, \ldots)$. This input is zero at all times except at $t = 0$. It is called a *unit pulse* or a *unit impulse*. Even though the limits of the sum in the convolution have not been specified, it is easy to see that for any $n$ there is only one nonzero term in the sum, so $y(n) = h(n)x(0) = h(n)$. We say that the output $y(n) = h(n)$ at time $n$ is the *response* at time $n$ to the unit impulse $x(0) = 1$. Since the number of filter coefficients $h(i)$ is finite, the filter is a *finite impulse response*, or FIR.

Figure 4.18 shows the basic idea of a filter bank. It shows an *analysis bank* consisting of two filters, a lowpass filter $H_0$ and a highpass filter $H_1$. The lowpass filter employs convolution to remove the high frequencies from the input signal $x$ and let the low frequencies go through. The highpass filter does the opposite. Together, they separate the input into *frequency bands*.

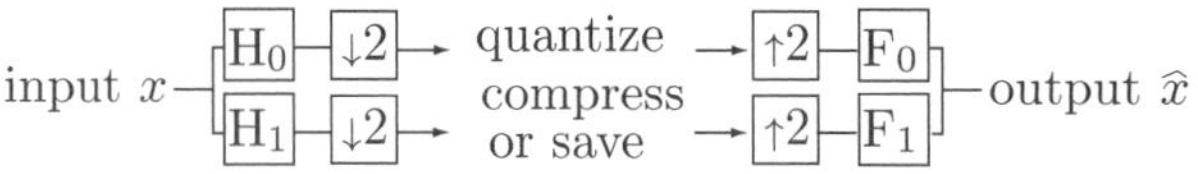

**Figure 4.18:** A Two-Channel Filter Bank.

The input $x$ can be a one-dimensional signal (a vector of real numbers, which is what we assume in this section) or a two-dimensional signal, an image. The elements $x(n)$ of $x$ are fed into the filters one by one, and each filter computes and outputs one number $y(n)$ in response to $x(n)$. The number of responses is therefore double the number of inputs (because there are two filters), an unfortunate result, since we are interested in compression. To correct this situation, each filter is followed by a *downsampling* process where the odd-numbered outputs are thrown away. This operation is also called *decimation* and is represented by the boxes marked "↓2". After decimation, the number of outputs from the two filters together equals the number of inputs.

**Example:** It is easy to construct a filter bank where the lowpass part produces averaging and the highpass part produces differences, essentially generating the Haar transform of the input. The filter coefficients for the lowpass filter are $h(0) = h(1) = 1/2$ and the ones for the highpass filter are $h(0) = -1/2$ and $h(1) = 1/2$. Applying these filters to the one-dimensional input sequence

$$\bigl(x(0), \ldots, x(7)\bigr) = (255, 224, 192, 159, 127, 95, 63, 32)$$

produces the sequence of averages $a(i)$

$$a(0) = \frac{1}{2}x(0) + x(-1) = \frac{1}{2}(255 + 0) = 127.5,$$

$$a(1) = \frac{1}{2}x(1) + x(0) = \frac{1}{2}(224 + 255) = 239.5,$$

$$a(2) = \frac{1}{2}x(2) + x(1) = \frac{1}{2}(192 + 224) = 208,$$

$$a(3) = \frac{1}{2}x(3) + x(2) = \frac{1}{2}(159 + 192) = 175.5,$$

$$a(4) = \frac{1}{2}x(4) + x(3) = \frac{1}{2}(127 + 159) = 143,$$

$$a(5) = \frac{1}{2}x(5) + x(4) = \frac{1}{2}(95 + 127) = 111,$$

$$a(6) = \frac{1}{2}x(6) + x(5) = \frac{1}{2}(63 + 95) = 79,$$

$$a(7) = \frac{1}{2}x(7) + x(6) = \frac{1}{2}(32 + 63) = 47.5,$$

$$a(8) = \frac{1}{2}x(8) + x(7) = \frac{1}{2}(0 + 32) = 16,$$

and the sequence of differences $d(i)$

$$d(0) = -\frac{1}{2}x(0) + x(-1) = \frac{1}{2}(-255 + 0) = -127.5,$$

$$d(1) = -\frac{1}{2}x(1) + x(0) = \frac{1}{2}(-224 + 255) = 15.5,$$

$$d(2) = -\frac{1}{2}x(2) + x(1) = \frac{1}{2}(-192 + 224) = 16,$$

$$d(3) = -\frac{1}{2}x(3) + x(2) = \frac{1}{2}(-159 + 192) = 16.5,$$

$$d(4) = -\frac{1}{2}x(4) + x(3) = \frac{1}{2}(-127 + 159) = 16,$$

$$d(5) = -\frac{1}{2}x(5) + x(4) = \frac{1}{2}(-95 + 127) = 16,$$

$$d(6) = -\frac{1}{2}x(6) + x(5) = \frac{1}{2}(-63 + 95) = 16,$$

$$d(7) = -\frac{1}{2}x(7) + x(6) = \frac{1}{2}(-32 + 63) = 15.5,$$

$$d(8) = -\frac{1}{2}x(8) + x(7) = \frac{1}{2}(-0 + 32) = 16.$$

After decimation, the first sequence is reduced to $(239.5, 175.5, 111, 47.5)$ and the second sequence is reduced to $(15.5, 16.5, 16, 15.5)$. These values can be concatenated to produce the combined sequence $(239.5, 175.5, 111, 47.5, 15.5, 16.5, 16, 15.5)$, which is identical to that produced by Equation (4.1).

Reconstructing the original sequence is done by upsampling (inserting zeros), followed by the synthesis filter bank, which is different from the analysis filter bank. The lowpass synthesis filter uses the two filter coefficients 1 and 1 to produce the four reconstructed values $y(0)$, $y(2)$, $y(4)$, and $y(6)$, while the highpass synthesis filter uses the two filter coefficients 1 and $-1$ to produce the four reconstructed values $y(1)$, $y(3)$, $y(5)$, and $y(7)$. These eight values are then interleaved to reconstruct the original sequence.

$$y(0) = a(1) + d(1) = (239.5 + 15.5) = 255,$$
$$y(2) = a(3) + d(3) = (175.5 + 16.5) = 192,$$
$$y(4) = a(5) + d(5) = (111 + 16) = 127,$$
$$y(6) = a(7) + d(7) = (47.5 + 15.5) = 63,$$
$$\overline{y(1) = a(1) - d(1) = (239.5 - 15.5) = 224,}$$
$$y(3) = a(3) - d(3) = (175.5 - 16.5) = 159,$$
$$y(5) = a(5) - d(5) = (111 - 16) = 95,$$
$$y(7) = a(7) - d(7) = (47.5 - 15.5) = 32.$$

Filter banks are a general way of looking at the Haar transform, but they are the key to designing other, more sophisticated discrete wavelet transforms. This technique is discussed in Section 4.5.

The reason for having a bank of filters as opposed to just one filter is that several filters working together, with downsampling, can exhibit behavior that is impossible to obtain with just a single filter. The most important feature of a filter bank is its ability to reconstruct the input from the outputs $H_0x$ and $H_1x$, even though each has been decimated.

Downsampling is not time invariant. After downsampling, the output is the even-numbered values $y(0)$, $y(2)$, $y(4)$,..., but if we delay the inputs by one time unit, the new outputs will be $y(-1)$, $y(1)$, $y(3)$,..., and these are different from and independent of the original outputs. These two sequences of signals are two phases of vector $y$.

The outputs of the analysis bank are called *subband coefficients*. They can be quantized (if lossy compression is acceptable), and they can be compressed by means of RLE, Huffman, arithmetic coding, or any other method. Eventually, they are fed into the *synthesis bank*, where they are first upsampled (by inserting zeros for each odd-numbered coefficient that was thrown away), then passed through the inverse filters $F_0$ and $F_1$, and finally combined to form a single output vector $\hat{x}$. The output of each analysis filter (after decimation) is

$$(\downarrow y) = (\ldots, y(-4), y(-2), y(0), y(2), y(4), \ldots).$$

Upsampling inserts zeros for the decimated values, so it converts the output vector above to

$$(\uparrow y) = (\ldots, y(-4), 0, y(-2), 0, y(0), 0, y(2), 0, y(4), 0, \ldots).$$

Downsampling causes loss of data. Upsampling alone cannot compensate for it, because it simply inserts zeros for the missing data. In order to achieve lossless reconstruction of the original signal $x$, the filters have to be designed such that they compensate for this loss of data. One feature that is commonly used in the design of good filters is *orthogonality*. The Haar analysis filter bank uses the two coefficients $(1/2, 1/2)$ in the lowpass filter and the two coefficients $(-1/2, 1/2)$ in the highpass filter. The dot product of these two 2-element vectors is $(1/2, 1/2) \cdot (-1/2, 1/2) = 0$. Similarly, the Haar synthesis filter bank uses the two sets $(1, 1)$ and $(1, -1)$ of orthogonal filter coefficients.

Figure 4.19 shows a set of orthogonal filters of size 4. The filters of the set are orthogonal because their dot product is zero:

$$(a, b, c, d) \cdot (d, -c, b, -a) = 0.$$

Notice how similar $H_0$ and $F_0$ are (and also $H_1$ and $F_1$). It still remains, of course, to choose actual values for the four filter coefficients $a$, $b$, $c$, and $d$. A full discussion of this topic is outside the scope of this book, but Section 4.5 illustrates some of the methods and rules used in practice to determine the values of various filter coefficients. An example is the Daubechies D4 filter, whose values are listed in Equation (4.12).

**Figure 4.19:** An Orthogonal Filter Bank with Four Filter Coefficients.

Simulating the operation of this filter manually shows that the reconstructed input is identical to the original input but lags three time units behind it.

A filter bank can also be *biorthogonal*, a less restricted type of filter. Figure 4.20 shows an example of such a set of filters that can reconstruct a signal exactly. Notice the similarity of $H_0$ and $F_1$ and also of $H_1$ and $F_0$.

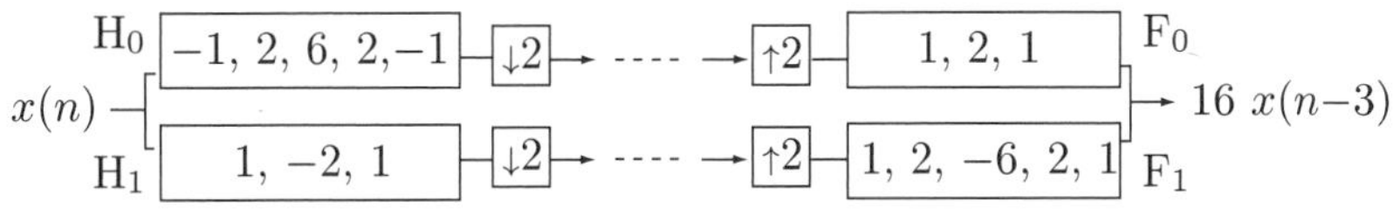

**Figure 4.20:** A Biorthogonal Filter Bank with Perfect Reconstruction.

We already know, from the discussion in Section 4.2, that the outputs of the lowpass filter $H_0$ are normally passed through the analysis filter several times, creating shorter and shorter outputs. This recursive process can be illustrated as a tree (Figure 4.21). Since each node of this tree produces half the number of outputs as its predecessor, the tree is called a *logarithmic tree*. Figure 4.21 shows how the scaling function $\phi(t)$ and the wavelet $\psi(t)$ are obtained at the limit of the logarithmic tree. This is the connection

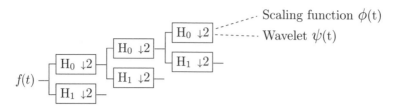

**Figure 4.21:** Scaling Function and Wavelet as Limits of a Logarithmic Tree.

between the discrete wavelet transform (using filter banks) and the continuous wavelet transform (CWT, [Salomon 00]).

As we "climb" up the logarithmic tree from level $i$ to the next finer level $i+1$, we compute the new averages from the new, higher-resolution scaling functions $\phi(2^i t - k)$ and the new details from the new wavelets $\psi(2^i t - k)$:

signal at level $i$ (averages) $\searrow$

$+$ signal at level $i+1$.

details at level $i$ (differences) $\nearrow$

Each level of the tree corresponds to twice the frequency (or twice the resolution) of the preceding level, which is why the logarithmic tree is also called a *multiresolution tree*. Successive filtering through the tree separates lower and lower frequencies.

Those who do quantitative work with sound and music know that two tones at frequencies $\omega$ and $2\omega$ sound like the same note and differ only in pitch. The frequency interval between $\omega$ and $2\omega$ is divided into 12 subintervals (the so-called *chromatic scale*), but Western music has a tradition of favoring just eight of the twelve tones that result from this division (a *diatonic scale*, made up of seven notes, with the eighth note as the "octave"). This is why the basic frequency interval used in music is traditionally called an *octave*. We therefore say that adjacent levels of the multiresolution tree differ in an octave of frequencies.

**Summary:** The discussion of filter banks in this section should be compared to the discussion of image transforms in Section 3.5. Even though both sections describe transforms, they differ in their approach, since they describe different classes of transforms. Each of the transforms described in Section 3.5 is based on a set of *orthogonal* basis functions (or orthogonal basis images) and is computed as an inner product of the input signal with the basis functions. The result is a set of transform coefficients that are subsequently compressed either losslessly (by RLE or some entropy encoder) or lossily (by quantization followed by entropy coding).

This section deals with *subband transforms*, a different type of transform that is computed by taking the *convolution* of the input signal with a set of bandpass filters and decimating the results. Each decimated set of transform coefficients is a subband signal that encodes a specific range of the frequencies of the input. Reconstruction is done by upsampling, followed by computing the inverse transforms, and adding the resulting sets of outputs from the inverse filters.

The main advantage of subband transforms is that they isolate the different frequencies of the input signal, thereby making it possible for the user to precisely control the loss of data in each frequency range. In practice, such a transform decomposes an image into several subbands, corresponding to different image frequencies, and each subband can be quantized differently.

The main disadvantage of this type of transform is the introduction of artifacts, such as aliasing and ringing, into the reconstructed image because of the downsampling. This is why the Haar transform is not satisfactory, and most of the research in this field has been aimed at finding better sets of filters.

Figure 4.22 shows a general subband filter bank with $N$ bandpass filters and three stages. Notice how the output of the highpass filter $H_0$ of each stage is sent to the next stage for further decomposition and how the combined output of the synthesis bank of a stage is sent to the top inverse filter of the synthesis bank of the preceding stage.

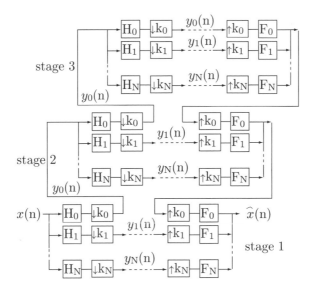

**Figure 4.22:** A General Filter Bank.

## 4.5 Deriving the Filter Coefficients

After presenting the basic operation of filter banks, the natural question is "How are the filter coefficients derived?" A full answer is outside the scope of this book (see, for example, [Akansu and Haddad 92]), but this section provides a glimpse at the rules and methods used to figure out the values of various filter banks.

Given a set of two forward and two inverse $N$-tap filters $H_0$ and $H_1$ and $F_0$ and $F_1$ (where $N$ is even), we denote their coefficients by

$$h_0 = \big(h_0(0), h_0(1), \ldots, h_0(N-1)\big), \quad h_1 = \big(h_1(0), h_1(1), \ldots, h_1(N-1)\big),$$
$$f_0 = \big(f_0(0), f_0(1), \ldots, f_0(N-1)\big), \quad f_1 = \big(f_1(0), f_1(1), \ldots, f_1(N-1)\big).$$

The four vectors $h_0$, $h_1$, $f_0$, and $f_1$ are the *impulse responses* of the four filters. Following is the simplest set of conditions that these quantities have to satisfy:

1. Normalization: Vector $h_0$ is normalized (i.e., its length is one unit).
2. Orthogonality: For any integer $i$ that satisfies $1 \le i < N/2$, the vector formed by the first $2i$ elements of $h_0$ should be orthogonal to the vector formed by the last $2i$ elements of the same $h_0$.
3. Vector $f_0$ is the reverse of $h_0$.
4. Vector $h_1$ is a copy of $f_0$ where the signs of the odd-numbered elements (the first, third, etc.) are reversed. We can express this by saying that $h_1$ is computed by coordinate multiplication of $h_1$ and $(-1, 1, -1, 1, \ldots, -1, 1)$.
5. Vector $f_1$ is a copy of $h_0$ where the signs of the even-numbered elements (the second, fourth, and so on) are reversed. We can express this by saying that $f_1$ is computed by coordinate multiplication of $h_0$ and $(1, -1, 1, -1, \ldots, 1, -1)$.

For two-tap filters, rule 1 implies

$$h_0^2(0) + h_0^2(1) = 1. \tag{4.10}$$

Rule 2 is not applicable because $N = 2$, so $i < N/2$ implies $i < 1$. Rules 3–5 yield

$$f_0 = \big(h_0(1), h_0(0)\big), \quad h_1 = \big(-h_0(1), h_0(0)\big), \quad f_1 = \big(h_0(0), -h_0(1)\big).$$

It all depends on the values of $h_0(0)$ and $h_0(1)$, but the single Equation (4.10) is not enough to determine them. However, it is not hard to see that the choice $h_0(0) = h_0(1) = 1/\sqrt{2}$ satisfies Equation (4.10).

For four-tap filters, rules 1 and 2 imply

$$h_0^2(0) + h_0^2(1) + h_0^2(2) + h_0^2(3) = 1, \quad h_0(0)h_0(2) + h_0(1)h_0(3) = 0, \tag{4.11}$$

and rules 3–5 yield

$$f_0 = \big(h_0(3), h_0(2), h_0(1), h_0(0)\big),$$
$$h_1 = \big(-h_0(3), h_0(2), -h_0(1), h_0(0)\big),$$
$$f_1 = \big(h_0(0), -h_0(1), h_0(2), -h_0(3)\big).$$

Again, Equation (4.11) is not enough to determine four unknowns, and other considerations (aided by mathematical intuition) are needed to derive the four values. These values are listed in Equation (4.12)—the Daubechies D4 filter.

For eight-tap filters, rules 1 and 2 imply

$$h_0^2(0) + h_0^2(1) + h_0^2(2) + h_0^2(3) + h_0^2(4) + h_0^2(5) + h_0^2(6) + h_0^2(7) = 1,$$
$$h_0(0)h_0(2) + h_0(1)h_0(3) + h_0(2)h_0(4) + h_0(3)h_0(5) + h_0(4)h_0(6) + h_0(5)h_0(7) = 0,$$
$$h_0(0)h_0(4) + h_0(1)h_0(5) + h_0(2)h_0(6) + h_0(3)h_0(7) = 0,$$
$$h_0(0)h_0(6) + h_0(1)h_0(7) = 0,$$

and rules 3–5 yield

$$f_0 = \big(h_0(7), h_0(6), h_0(5), h_0(4), h_0(3), h_0(2), h_0(1), h_0(0)\big),$$
$$h_1 = \big(-h_0(7), h_0(6), -h_0(5), h_0(4), -h_0(3), h_0(2), -h_0(1), h_0(0)\big),$$
$$f_1 = \big(h_0(0), -h_0(1), h_0(2), -h_0(3), h_0(4), -h_0(5), h_0(6), -h_0(7)\big).$$

The eight coefficients are listed in Table 4.23 (this is the Daubechies D8 filter).

| | | | |
|---|---|---|---|
| .230377813309 | .714846570553 | .630880767930 | $-.027983769417$ |
| $-.187034811719$ | .030841381836 | .032883011667 | $-.010597401785$ |

**Table 4.23:** Coefficients for the Daubechies 8-Tap Filter.

Determining the $N$ filter coefficients for each of the four filters $H_0$, $H_1$, $F_0$, and $F_1$ depends on $h_0(0)$ through $h_0(N-1)$, so it requires $N$ equations. However, in each of the cases, rules 1 and 2 supply only $N/2$ equations. Other conditions have to be imposed and satisfied before the $N$ quantities $h_0(0)$ through $h_0(N-1)$ can be determined. Here are some examples:

*Lowpass $H_0$ filter*: We want $H_0$ to be a lowpass filter, so it makes sense to require that the frequency response $H_0(\omega)$ be zero for the highest frequency $\omega = \pi$.

*Minimum phase filter*: This condition requires the zeros of the complex function $H_0(z)$ to lie on or inside the unit circle in the complex plane.

*Controlled collinearity*: The linearity of the phase response can be controlled by requiring that the sum

$$\sum_i \big(h_0(i) - h_0(N-1-i)\big)^2$$

be a minimum.

Other conditions are discussed in [Akansu and Haddad 92].

## 4.6 The DWT

Information that is produced and analyzed in real-life situations is discrete. It comes in the form of numbers, rather than as a continuous function. This is why the discrete wavelet transform (DWT) is used in practical calculations. There is also a continuous wavelet transform (CWT, [Lewalle 95] and [Rao and Bopardikar 98]) and studying the CWT may help in understanding the operation of the DWT.

The DWT involves a convolution, but experience shows that the quality of this type of transform depends heavily on two things, the choice of scale factors and time shifts and the choice of wavelet.

In practice, the DWT is computed with scale factors that are negative powers of 2 and with time shifts that are nonnegative powers of 2. Figure 4.24 shows the so-called *dyadic lattice* that illustrates this particular choice. The wavelets used are those that generate orthonormal (or biorthogonal) wavelet bases.

The main thrust in wavelet research has therefore been the search for wavelet families that form orthogonal bases. Of those wavelets, the preferred ones are those that

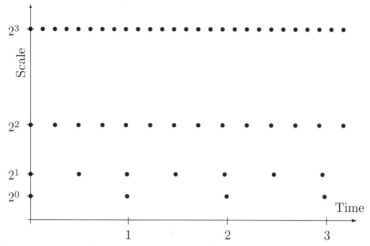

**Figure 4.24:** The Dyadic Lattice Showing the Relation between Scale Factors and Time.

have compact support, because they allow for DWT computations with *finite impulse response* (FIR) filters.

The simplest way to describe the discrete wavelet transform is by means of matrix multiplication, along the lines developed in Section 4.2.1. The Haar transform depends on two *filter coefficients* $c_0$ and $c_1$, both with a value of $1/\sqrt{2} \approx 0.7071$. The smallest transform matrix that can be constructed in this case is $\left(\begin{smallmatrix} 1 & 1 \\ 1 & -1 \end{smallmatrix}\right)/\sqrt{2}$. This is a $2 \times 2$ matrix, and it generates two transform coefficients, an average and a difference. (Notice that these are not exactly an average and a difference, because $\sqrt{2}$ is used instead of 2. Better names for them are *coarse detail* and *fine detail*, respectively.) In general, the DWT can use any set of wavelet filters, but it is computed in the same way regardless of the particular filter used.

We start with one of the most popular wavelets, the Daubechies D4. As its name implies, it is based on four filter coefficients $c_0$, $c_1$, $c_2$, and $c_3$, whose values are listed in Equation (4.12). The transform matrix $W$ is [compare with matrix $A_1$, Equation (4.1)]

$$
W = \begin{pmatrix}
c_0 & c_1 & c_2 & c_3 & 0 & 0 & \cdots & 0 \\
c_3 & -c_2 & c_1 & -c_0 & 0 & 0 & \cdots & 0 \\
0 & 0 & c_0 & c_1 & c_2 & c_3 & \cdots & 0 \\
0 & 0 & c_3 & -c_2 & c_1 & -c_0 & \cdots & 0 \\
\vdots & \vdots & & & & \ddots & & \\
0 & 0 & \cdots & 0 & c_0 & c_1 & c_2 & c_3 \\
0 & 0 & \cdots & 0 & c_3 & -c_2 & c_1 & -c_0 \\
c_2 & c_3 & 0 & \cdots & 0 & 0 & c_0 & c_1 \\
c_1 & -c_0 & 0 & \cdots & 0 & 0 & c_3 & -c_2
\end{pmatrix}.
$$

When this matrix is applied to a column vector of data items $(x_1, x_2, \ldots, x_n)$, its top row generates the weighted sum $s_1 = c_0x_1 + c_1x_2 + c_2x_3 + c_3x_4$, its third row generates the weighted sum $s_2 = c_0x_3 + c_1x_4 + c_2x_5 + c_3x_6$, and the other odd-numbered rows generate similar weighted sums $s_i$. Such sums are *convolutions* of the data vector $x_i$ with the four filter coefficients. In the language of wavelets, each of them is called a *smooth coefficient*, and together they are called an $H$ smoothing filter.

In a similar way, the second row of the matrix generates the quantity $d_1 = c_3x_1 - c_2x_2 + c_1x_3 - c_0x_4$, and the other even-numbered rows generate similar convolutions. Each $d_i$ is called a *detail coefficient*, and together they are called a $G$ filter. $G$ is not a smoothing filter. In fact, the filter coefficients are chosen such that the $G$ filter generates small values when the data items $x_i$ are correlated. Together, $H$ and $G$ are called *quadrature mirror filters* (QMF).

The discrete wavelet transform of an image can therefore be viewed as passing the original image through a QMF that consists of a pair of lowpass ($H$) and highpass ($G$) filters.

If $W$ is an $n \times n$ matrix, it generates $n/2$ smooth coefficients $s_i$ and $n/2$ detail coefficients $d_i$. The transposed matrix is

$$
W^T = \begin{pmatrix}
c_0 & c_3 & 0 & 0 & \cdots & & & & & c_2 & c_1 \\
c_1 & -c_2 & 0 & 0 & \cdots & & & & & c_3 & -c_0 \\
c_2 & c_1 & c_0 & c_3 & \cdots & & & & & 0 & 0 \\
c_3 & -c_0 & c_1 & -c_2 & \cdots & & & & & 0 & 0 \\
& & & & \ddots & & & & & & \\
& & & & & c_2 & c_1 & c_0 & c_3 & 0 & 0 \\
& & & & & c_3 & -c_0 & c_1 & -c_2 & 0 & 0 \\
& & & & & & & c_2 & c_1 & c_0 & c_3 \\
& & & & & & & c_3 & -c_0 & c_1 & -c_2
\end{pmatrix}.
$$

It can be shown that in order for $W$ to be orthonormal, the four coefficients have to satisfy the two relations $c_0^2 + c_1^2 + c_2^2 + c_3^2 = 1$ and $c_2c_0 + c_3c_1 = 0$. The other two equations used to calculate the four filter coefficients are $c_3 - c_2 + c_1 - c_0 = 0$ and $0c_3 - 1c_2 + 2c_1 - 3c_0 = 0$. They represent the vanishing of the first two moments of the sequence $(c_3, -c_2, c_1, -c_0)$. The solutions of these four equations are

$$
\begin{aligned}
c_0 &= (1 + \sqrt{3})/(4\sqrt{2}) \approx 0.48296, & c_1 &= (3 + \sqrt{3})/(4\sqrt{2}) \approx 0.8365, \\
c_2 &= (3 - \sqrt{3})/(4\sqrt{2}) \approx 0.2241, & c_3 &= (1 - \sqrt{3})/(4\sqrt{2}) \approx -0.1294.
\end{aligned}
\tag{4.12}
$$

Using a transform matrix $W$ is conceptually simple but not very practical, since $W$ should be of the same size as the image, which can be large. However, a look at $W$ shows that it is very regular, so there is really no need to construct the full matrix. It is enough to have just the top row of $W$. In fact, it is enough to have just an array with the filter coefficients. Figure 4.25 is Matlab code that performs this calculation. Function `fwt1(dat,coarse,filter)` takes a row vector `dat` of $2^n$ data items, and another array, `filter`, with filter coefficients. It then calculates the first `coarse` levels of the discrete wavelet transform.

```
function wc1=fwt1(dat,coarse,filter)
%  The 1D Forward Wavelet Transform
%  dat must be a 1D row vector of size 2^n,
%  coarse is the coarsest level of the transform
%  (note that coarse should be <<n)
%  filter is an orthonormal quadrature mirror filter
%  whose length should be <2^(coarse+1)
n=length(dat); j=log2(n); wc1=zeros(1,n);
beta=dat;
for i=j-1:-1:coarse
  alfa=HiPass(beta,filter);
  wc1((2^(i)+1):(2^(i+1)))=alfa;
  beta=LoPass(beta,filter) ;
end
wc1(1:(2^coarse))=beta;

function d=HiPass(dt,filter) % highpass downsampling
d=iconv(mirror(filter),lshift(dt));
% iconv is matlab convolution tool
n=length(d);
d=d(1:2:(n-1));

function d=LoPass(dt,filter) % lowpass downsampling
d=aconv(filter,dt);
% aconv is matlab convolution tool with time-
% reversal of filter
n=length(d);
d=d(1:2:(n-1));

function sgn=mirror(filt)
% return filter coefficients with alternating signs
sgn=-((-1).^(1:length(filt))).*filt;
```

A simple test of `fwt1` is

```
n=16; t=(1:n)./n;
dat=sin(2*pi*t)
filt=[0.4830 0.8365 0.2241 -0.1294];
wc=fwt1(dat,1,filt)
```

which outputs

```
dat=
0.3827  0.7071  0.9239 1.0000 0.9239 0.7071 0.3827 0
-0.3827 -0.7071 -0.9239 -1.0000 -0.9239 -0.7071 -0.3827 0
wc=
1.1365 -1.1365 -1.5685 1.5685 -0.2271 -0.4239 0.2271 0.4239
-0.0281 -0.0818 -0.0876 -0.0421 0.0281 0.0818 0.0876 0.0421
```

**Figure 4.25:** Code for the One-Dimensional Forward Discrete Wavelet Transform.

```
function dat=iwt1(wc,coarse,filter)
% Inverse Discrete Wavelet Transform
dat=wc(1:2^coarse);
n=length(wc); j=log2(n);
for i=coarse:j-1
 dat=ILoPass(dat,filter)+ ...
   IHiPass(wc((2^(i)+1):(2^(i+1))),filter);
end

function f=ILoPass(dt,filter)
f=iconv(filter,AltrntZro(dt));

function f=IHiPass(dt,filter)
f=aconv(mirror(filter),rshift(AltrntZro(dt)));

function sgn=mirror(filt)
% return filter coefficients with alternating signs
sgn=-((-1).^(1:length(filt))).*filt;

function f=AltrntZro(dt)
% returns a vector of length 2*n with zeros
% placed between consecutive values
n =length(dt)*2; f =zeros(1,n);
f(1:2:(n-1))=dt;
```

A simple test of iwt1 is

```
n=16; t=(1:n)./n;
dat=sin(2*pi*t)
filt=[0.4830 0.8365 0.2241 -0.1294];
wc=fwt1(dat,1,filt)
rec=iwt1(wc,1,filt)
```

**Figure 4.26:** Code and Test for the One-Dimensional Inverse Discrete Wavelet Transform.

Figure 4.26 lists the Matlab code of the inverse one-dimensional discrete wavelet transform function iwt1(wc,coarse,filter) and includes a test.

Readers who take the trouble to read and understand functions fwt1 and iwt1 (Figures 4.25 and 4.27) may be interested in their two-dimensional equivalents, functions fwt2 and iwt2, listed in Figures 4.28 and 4.29, respectively, with a simple test routine.

In addition to the Daubechies family of filters (by the way, the Haar wavelet can be considered the Daubechies filter of order 2) there are many other families of wavelets, each with its own properties. Some well-known filters are Beylkin, Coifman, Symmetric, and Vaidyanathan.

The Daubechies family of wavelets is a set of orthonormal, compactly supported functions where consecutive members are increasingly smoother. Section 4.8 discusses the Daubechies D4 wavelet and its building block. The term *compact support* means that these functions are zero (exactly zero, not just very small) outside a finite interval.

```
function dat=iwt1(wc,coarse,filter)
% Inverse Discrete Wavelet Transform
dat=wc(1:2^coarse);
n=length(wc); j=log2(n);
for i=coarse:j-1
 dat=ILoPass(dat,filter)+ ...
  IHiPass(wc((2^(i)+1):(2^(i+1))),filter);
end

function f=ILoPass(dt,filter)
f=iconv(filter,AltrntZro(dt));

function f=IHiPass(dt,filter)
f=aconv(mirror(filter),rshift(AltrntZro(dt)));

function sgn=mirror(filt)
% return filter coefficients with alternating signs
sgn=-((-1).^(1:length(filt))).*filt;

function f=AltrntZro(dt)
% returns a vector of length 2*n with zeros
% placed between consecutive values
n =length(dt)*2; f =zeros(1,n);
f(1:2:(n-1))=dt;
```

A simple test of iwt1 is

```
n=16; t=(1:n)./n;
dat=sin(2*pi*t)
filt=[0.4830 0.8365 0.2241 -0.1294];
wc=fwt1(dat,1,filt)
rec=iwt1(wc,1,filt)
```

**Figure 4.27:** Code for the One-Dimensional Inverse Discrete Wavelet Transform.

```
function wc=fwt2(dat,coarse,filter)
%  The 2D Forward Wavelet Transform
%  dat must be a 2D matrix of size (2^n:2^n),
%  "coarse" is the coarsest level of the transform
%  (note that coarse should be <<n)
%  filter is an orthonormal qmf of length<2^(coarse+1)
q=size(dat); n = q(1); j=log2(n);
if q(1)~=q(2), disp('Nonsquare image!'), end;
wc = dat; nc = n;
for i=j-1:-1:coarse,
 top = (nc/2+1):nc; bot = 1:(nc/2);
 for ic=1:nc,
  row = wc(ic,1:nc);
  wc(ic,bot)=LoPass(row,filter);
  wc(ic,top)=HiPass(row,filter);
 end
 for ir=1:nc,
  row = wc(1:nc,ir)';
  wc(top,ir)=HiPass(row,filter)';
  wc(bot,ir)=LoPass(row,filter)';
 end
nc = nc/2;
end

function d=HiPass(dt,filter) % highpass downsampling
d=iconv(mirror(filter),lshift(dt));
% iconv is matlab convolution tool
n=length(d);
d=d(1:2:(n-1));

function d=LoPass(dt,filter) % lowpass downsampling
d=aconv(filter,dt);
% aconv is matlab convolution tool with time-
% reversal of filter
n=length(d);
d=d(1:2:(n-1));

function sgn=mirror(filt)
% return filter coefficients with alternating signs
sgn=-((-1).^(1:length(filt))).*filt;
```

A simple test of `fwt2` and `iwt2` is

```
filename='house128'; dim=128;
fid=fopen(filename,'r');
if fid==-1 disp('file not found')
 else img=fread(fid,[dim,dim])'; fclose(fid);
end
filt=[0.4830 0.8365 0.2241 -0.1294];
fwim=fwt2(img,4,filt);
figure(1), imagesc(fwim), axis off, axis square
rec=iwt2(fwim,4,filt);
figure(2), imagesc(rec), axis off, axis square
```

**Figure 4.28:** Code for the Two-Dimensional Forward Discrete Wavelet Transform.

```
function dat=iwt2(wc,coarse,filter)
% Inverse Discrete 2D Wavelet Transform
n=length(wc); j=log2(n);
dat=wc;
nc=2^(coarse+1);
for i=coarse:j-1,
 top=(nc/2+1):nc; bot=1:(nc/2); all=1:nc;
 for ic=1:nc,
  dat(all,ic)=ILoPass(dat(bot,ic)',filter)'  ...
   +IHiPass(dat(top,ic)',filter)';
 end % ic
 for ir=1:nc,
  dat(ir,all)=ILoPass(dat(ir,bot),filter)   ...
   +IHiPass(dat(ir,top),filter);
 end % ir
nc=2*nc;
end % i

function f=ILoPass(dt,filter)
f=iconv(filter,AltrntZro(dt));

function f=IHiPass(dt,filter)
f=aconv(mirror(filter),rshift(AltrntZro(dt)));

function sgn=mirror(filt)
% return filter coefficients with alternating signs
sgn=-((-1).^(1:length(filt))).*filt;

function f=AltrntZro(dt)
% returns a vector of length 2*n with zeros
% placed between consecutive values
n =length(dt)*2; f =zeros(1,n);
f(1:2:(n-1))=dt;
```

A simple test of `fwt2` and `iwt2` is

```
filename='house128'; dim=128;
fid=fopen(filename,'r');
if fid==-1 disp('file not found')
 else img=fread(fid,[dim,dim])'; fclose(fid);
end
filt=[0.4830 0.8365 0.2241 -0.1294];
fwim=fwt2(img,4,filt);
figure(1), imagesc(fwim), axis off, axis square
rec=iwt2(fwim,4,filt);
figure(2), imagesc(rec), axis off, axis square
```

**Figure 4.29:** Code for the Two-Dimensional Inverse Discrete Wavelet Transform.

The Daubechies D4 wavelet is based on four coefficients, shown in Equation (4.12). The D6 wavelet is, similarly, based on six coefficients. They are calculated by solving six equations, three of which represent orthogonality requirements and the other three, the vanishing of the first three moments. The result is listed in Equation (4.13):

$$c_0 = (1 + \sqrt{10} + \sqrt{5 + 2\sqrt{10}})/(16\sqrt{2}) \approx .3326,$$

$$c_1 = (5 + \sqrt{10} + 3\sqrt{5 + 2\sqrt{10}})/(16\sqrt{2}) \approx .8068,$$

$$c_2 = (10 - 2\sqrt{10} + 2\sqrt{5 + 2\sqrt{10}})/(16\sqrt{2}) \approx .4598,$$

$$c_3 = (10 - 2\sqrt{10} - 2\sqrt{5 + 2\sqrt{10}})/(16\sqrt{2}) \approx -.1350,$$

$$c_4 = (5 + \sqrt{10} - 3\sqrt{5 + 2\sqrt{10}})/(16\sqrt{2}) \approx -.0854,$$

$$c_5 = (1 + \sqrt{10} - \sqrt{5 + 2\sqrt{10}})/(16\sqrt{2}) \approx .0352.$$

(4.13)

Each member of this family has two more coefficients than its predecessor and is smoother. The derivation of these functions is discussed in [Daubechies 88], [DeVore et al. 92], and [Vetterli and Kovacevic 95].

## 4.7 Examples

We already know that the discrete wavelet transform can reconstruct images from a small number of transform coefficients. The first example in this section illustrates an important property of the discrete wavelet transform, namely its ability to reconstruct images that degrade *gracefully*, without exhibiting any artifacts, when more and more transform coefficients are zeroed or are coarsely quantized. Other transforms, most notably the DCT, may introduce artifacts in the reconstructed image, but this property of the DWT makes it ideal for applications such as fingerprint compression [Salomon 00].

The example uses functions fwt2 and iwt2 of Figures 4.28 and 4.29 to blur an image. The idea is to compute the four-step subband transform of an image (thus ending up with 13 subbands), then set most of the transform coefficients to zero and heavily quantize some of the others. This, of course, results in a loss of image information and in a nonperfectly reconstructed image. The point is that the reconstructed image is *blurred* rather than being coarse or having artifacts.

Figure 4.30 shows the result of blurring the Lena image. Parts (a) and (b) show the logarithmic multiresolution tree and the subband structure, respectively. Part (c) shows the results of the quantization. The transform coefficients of subbands 5–7 have been divided by two, and all the coefficients of subbands 8–13 have been cleared. At first, most of the image in part (b) looks uniformly black (i.e., all zeros), but a careful examination shows many nonzero elements in subbands 5–10. We can say that the blurred image of part (d) has been reconstructed from the coefficients of subbands 1–4 (1/64th of the total number of transform coefficients) and half of the coefficients of subbands 5-7 (half of 3/64, or 3/128). On average, the image has been reconstructed from $5/128 \approx 0.039$ or 3.9% of the transform coefficients. Notice that the Daubechies

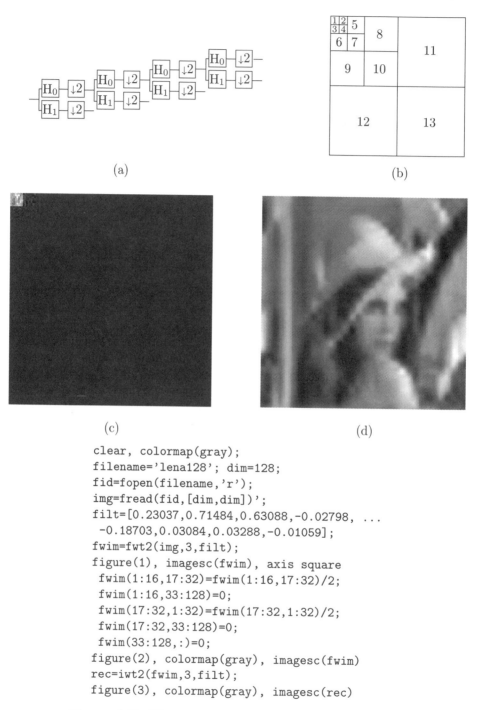

(a)

(b)

(c)

(d)

```
clear, colormap(gray);
filename='lena128'; dim=128;
fid=fopen(filename,'r');
img=fread(fid,[dim,dim])';
filt=[0.23037,0.71484,0.63088,-0.02798, ...
 -0.18703,0.03084,0.03288,-0.01059];
fwim=fwt2(img,3,filt);
figure(1), imagesc(fwim), axis square
 fwim(1:16,17:32)=fwim(1:16,17:32)/2;
 fwim(1:16,33:128)=0;
 fwim(17:32,1:32)=fwim(17:32,1:32)/2;
 fwim(17:32,33:128)=0;
 fwim(33:128,:)=0;
figure(2), colormap(gray), imagesc(fwim)
rec=iwt2(fwim,3,filt);
figure(3), colormap(gray), imagesc(rec)
```

**Figure 4.30:** Blurring as a Result of Coarse Quantization.

D8 filter was used in the calculations. Readers are encouraged to use this code and experiment with the performance of other filters.

The second example illustrates the performance of the Daubechies D4 filter and shows how it compacts the energy much better than the simple Haar filter, which is based on averaging and differencing.

Table 4.31a lists the values of the 128 pixels that constitute row 64 (the middle row) of the $128 \times 128$ grayscale Lena image. Tables 4.31b,c list the transform coefficients of the Daubechies D4 and the Haar wavelet transforms, respectively, of this data. The first transform coefficient is the same in both cases, but the remaining 127 coefficients are smaller, on average, in the Daubechies transform, which shows that this transform produces better energy compaction. The average of the absolute values of these 127 coefficients in the Daubechies D4 transform is 2.1790, whereas the corresponding average in the Haar transform is 9.8446, about 4.5 times greater.

*Mathematica* code for Table 4.31b and Matlab code for Table 4.31c are listed in Figure 4.32. Note that the former uses `WaveletTransform.m`, a *Mathematica* package by Alistair C. H. Rowe and Paul C. Abbott and available from [Alistair and Abbott 01].

## 4.8 The Daubechies Wavelets

Many useful mathematical functions are defined explicitly. A polynomial is perhaps the simplest such function. However, many other functions, not less useful, are defined recursively, in terms of themselves. Defining anything in terms of itself seems a contradiction, but the point is that a valid recursive definition must have several parts, and at least one part must be explicit. This part normally defines an initial value for whatever is defined. A simple example is the factorial function. It can be defined explicitly by

$$n! = n(n-1)(n-2)\cdots 3 \cdot 2 \cdot 1$$

but can also be defined recursively, by the 2-part definition

$$1! = 1, \quad n! = n \cdot (n-1)!.$$

Another interesting example is the exponential function $e$ (or "exp"), which is defined by the differential recursive relation

$$e^0 = 1, \quad \frac{d\,e^x}{dx} = e^x.$$

Ingrid Daubechies has introduced a wavelet $\psi$ and a scaling function (or building block) $\varphi$. One requirement was that the scaling function have finite support. It had to be zero outside a finite range. Daubechies selected the range $(0,3)$ to be the support of the function and has proved that this function cannot be expressed in terms of elementary functions such as polynomials, trigonometric, or exponential. She also showed that $\varphi$ can be defined recursively, in terms of several initial values and a recursion relation. The initial values selected by her are

$$\varphi(0) = 0, \quad \varphi(1) = \frac{1+\sqrt{3}}{2}, \quad \varphi(2) = \frac{1-\sqrt{3}}{2}, \quad \text{and} \quad \varphi(3) = 0,$$

| 148 | 141 | 137 | 124 | 101 | 104 | 105 | 103 | 98 | 89 | 100 | 136 |
|---|---|---|---|---|---|---|---|---|---|---|---|
| 156 | 173 | 175 | 176 | 179 | 171 | 152 | 116 | 80 | 82 | 92 | 99 |
| 103 | 102 | 101 | 100 | 100 | 102 | 106 | 104 | 112 | 139 | 155 | 149 |
| 139 | 107 | 90 | 126 | 90 | 65 | 65 | 93 | 62 | 87 | 61 | 84 |
| 48 | 64 | 42 | 75 | 72 | 35 | 42 | 53 | 73 | 45 | 58 | 130 |
| 156 | 176 | 185 | 196 | 167 | 185 | 178 | 121 | 113 | 126 | 113 | 122 |
| 133 | 109 | 106 | 92 | 91 | 133 | 162 | 165 | 174 | 189 | 193 | 190 |
| 190 | 167 | 120 | 97 | 92 | 106 | 103 | 81 | 55 | 43 | 60 | 150 |
| 126 | 55 | 61 | 65 | 61 | 50 | 52 | 53 | 52 | 79 | 135 | 132 |
| 147 | 163 | 161 | 158 | 157 | 157 | 156 | 156 | 156 | 158 | 159 | 156 |
| 155 | 154 | 155 | 155 | 157 | 157 | 154 | 150 | | | | |

(a)

| 117.95 | −10.38 | −5.99 | −0.19 | −11.64 | 12.6 | −5.95 | 4.15 |
|---|---|---|---|---|---|---|---|
| −2.57 | 6.61 | −17.08 | −0.50 | 7.88 | −15.53 | 4.10 | −10.80 |
| −5.29 | 2.94 | −0.63 | 5.42 | −2.39 | 0.53 | −5.96 | 2.67 |
| −6.4 | 9.71 | −5.43 | 0.56 | −0.13 | 0.83 | −0.02 | 1.17 |
| −1.38 | −2.68 | 1.92 | 3.14 | −3.71 | 0.62 | −0.02 | −0.04 |
| −1.41 | −2.37 | 0.08 | −1.62 | −1.03 | −3.50 | 2.52 | 2.81 |
| −1.68 | 1.41 | −1.79 | 1.11 | 3.55 | −0.24 | −7.44 | 0.28 |
| −0.49 | −2.56 | 1.98 | −0.00 | 0.10 | −0.17 | 0.42 | 0.65 |
| 0.35 | −1.00 | 0.15 | 0.21 | −1.30 | 0.31 | 0.21 | 0.45 |
| 0.85 | −1.62 | 0.04 | 0.25 | 0 | −0.10 | 0.23 | −0.93 |
| 1.06 | 0.98 | −2.43 | 0.35 | −1.48 | −1.72 | −1.51 | −1.54 |
| −1.91 | 1.86 | −0.67 | 1.95 | −2.99 | 0.78 | 0.04 | −1.55 |
| 2.42 | −1.46 | −0.64 | 1.47 | 0.23 | −1.98 | 1.26 | −0.32 |
| 0.42 | 0.95 | −0.75 | −1.02 | 1.01 | −0.55 | −3.45 | 3.31 |
| −0.80 | 0.39 | −0.11 | −1.17 | 2.19 | −0.25 | 0.25 | −0.07 |
| −0.03 | −0.09 | 0.18 | −0.02 | 0.02 | 0.06 | 0.08 | 0.19 |

(b)

| 117.95 | −9.68 | −16.44 | 1.31 | −20.81 | 3.31 | 14.38 | −29.44 |
|---|---|---|---|---|---|---|---|
| −6.63 | 8.38 | −20.56 | 39.38 | 10.44 | −31.50 | −14.25 | 1.13 |
| 7.75 | 22.13 | 4.25 | −13.88 | −24.38 | 21.50 | 24.00 | 9.25 |
| 0.13 | 11.38 | −22.75 | −28.88 | 0.38 | −0.38 | 1.25 | 0.13 |
| 7.25 | 13.25 | 15.00 | 1.00 | −1.75 | 11.00 | −6.50 | −25.75 |
| −9.00 | −5.00 | 6.50 | 35.00 | 4.75 | 3.50 | 21.50 | −28.00 |
| 7.25 | 13.75 | 3.75 | 1.50 | −6.50 | −34.00 | −10.75 | −2.25 |
| 1.25 | 0.50 | −0.50 | −0.25 | 1.50 | −0.25 | −1.00 | 2.50 |
| 14.50 | −9.00 | 3.50 | 28.50 | 4.00 | −6.50 | 6.50 | −4.50 |
| −5.50 | 12.00 | 1.50 | 7.00 | 0.50 | −21.00 | −14.50 | −1.50 |
| −4.50 | −7.50 | −2.00 | 1.50 | 0 | 11.50 | 23.50 | 11.50 |
| 2.50 | −7.00 | 1.50 | 11.00 | 13.00 | 6.00 | −8.50 | −45.00 |
| 12.00 | 35.50 | −3.00 | −2.00 | 2.00 | 5.50 | −1.00 | −0.50 |
| 0.50 | −13.50 | −28.00 | 1.50 | −7.50 | −8.00 | 1.00 | 1.50 |
| 0.50 | 0 | 0.50 | 0 | 0 | −1.00 | −0.50 | 1.50 |
| 0.50 | 0.50 | −0.50 | 0 | −1.00 | 0 | 1.50 | 2.00 |

(c)

**Table 4.31:** Daubechies and Haar Transforms of Middle Row in Lena Image.

```
<<WaveletTransform.m
(* Middle row of 128x128 Lena image *)
data={148,141,137,124,101,104,105,103, 98, 89,100,136
 ...
,155,154,155,155,157,157,154,150};
forward = Wavelet[data, Daubechies[4]]
NumberForm[forward,{6,2}]
inverse = InverseWavelet[forward,Daubechies[4]]
data == inverse
```

(a)

```
% Haar transform (averages & differences)
data=[148 141 137 124 101 104 105 103  98  89 100 136 ...
 ...
155 154 155 155 157 157 154 150];
n=128; ln=7; %log_2 n=7
for k=1:ln,
 for i=1:n/2,
  i1=2*i; j=n/2+i;
  newdat(i)=(data(i1-1)+data(i1))/2;
  newdat(j)=(data(j-1)-data(j))/2;
 end
 data=newdat; n=n/2;
end
round(100*data)/100
```

(b)

**Figure 4.32:** (a) *Mathematica* and (b) Matlab Codes for Table 4.31.

and the recursion relation is

$$
\begin{aligned}
\varphi(r) &= \frac{1+\sqrt{3}}{4}\varphi(2r) + \frac{3+\sqrt{3}}{4}\varphi(2r-1) + \frac{3-\sqrt{3}}{4}\varphi(2r-2) + \frac{1-\sqrt{3}}{4}\varphi(2r-3) \\
&= h_0\varphi(2r) + h_1\varphi(2r-1) + h_2\varphi(2r-2) + h_3\varphi(2r-3) \\
&= (h_0, h_1, h_2, h_3) \cdot \big(\varphi(2r), \varphi(2r-1), \varphi(2r-2), \varphi(2r-3)\big).
\end{aligned}
\tag{4.14}
$$

Notice that the initial values add up to 1:

$$
\varphi(0) + \varphi(1) + \varphi(2) + \varphi(3) = 0 + \frac{1+\sqrt{3}}{2} + \frac{1-\sqrt{3}}{2} + 0 = 1.
$$

Further computations of $\varphi$ must be performed in steps. In step 1, the finite support requirement, the four initial values of $\varphi$ and the recurrence relation [Equation (4.14)] are applied to compute the values of $\varphi(r)$ at the three points $r = 0.5,\ 1.5$, and $2.5$.

$$\varphi(1/2) = h_0\varphi(2/2) + h_1\varphi(2/2 - 1) + h_2\varphi(2/2 - 2) + h_3\varphi(2/2 - 3)$$
$$= \frac{1 + \sqrt{3}}{4} \cdot \frac{1 + \sqrt{3}}{2} + h_1 \cdot 0 + h_2 \cdot 0 + h_3 \cdot 0$$
$$= \frac{2 + \sqrt{3}}{4},$$

$$\varphi(3/2) = h_0\varphi(6/2) + h_1\varphi(6/2 - 1) + h_2\varphi(6/2 - 2) + h_3\varphi(6/2 - 3)$$
$$= h_0 \cdot 0 + \frac{1 + \sqrt{3}}{4} \cdot \frac{1 - \sqrt{3}}{2} + \frac{1 - \sqrt{3}}{4} \cdot \frac{1 + \sqrt{3}}{2} + h_3 \cdot 0$$
$$= 0,$$

$$\varphi(5/2) = h_0\varphi(10/2) + h_1\varphi(10/2 - 1) + h_2\varphi(10/2 - 2) + h_3\varphi(10/2 - 3)$$
$$= h_0 \cdot 0 + h_1 \cdot 0 + h_2 \cdot 0 + \frac{1 - \sqrt{3}}{2} \cdot \frac{1 - \sqrt{3}}{2}$$
$$= \frac{2 - \sqrt{3}}{4}.$$

The values of $\varphi$ are now known at the four initial points 0, 1, 2, and 3 and at the three additional points 0.5, 1.5, and 2.5 midway between them, a total of seven points. In step 2, six more values are computed at the six points 1/4, 3/4, 5/4, 7/4, 9/4, and 11/4. The computations are similar and the results are

$$\frac{5 + 3\sqrt{3}}{16},\quad \frac{9 + 5\sqrt{3}}{16},\quad \frac{1 + \sqrt{3}}{8},\quad \frac{1 - \sqrt{3}}{8},\quad \frac{9 - 5\sqrt{3}}{16},\quad \frac{5 - 3\sqrt{3}}{16}.$$

The values of $\varphi$ are now known at $4 + 3 + 6 = 13$ points (Figure 4.33).

Step 3 computes the 12 values midway between these 13 points, resulting in $12 + 13 = 25$ values. Further steps compute 24, 48, 96, and so on, values. After $n$ steps, the values of $\varphi$ are known at $4 + 3 + 6 + 12 + 24 + \cdots + 3 \cdot 2^n = 4 + 3(2^{n+1} - 1)$ points. After nine steps, $4 + 3(2^{10} - 1) = 3073$ values are known (Figure 4.34).

Function $\varphi$ serves as a building block for the construction of the Daubechies wavelet $\psi$, which is defined recursively by

$$\psi(r) = -\frac{1 + \sqrt{3}}{4}\varphi(2r - 1) + \frac{3 + \sqrt{3}}{4}\varphi(2r) - \frac{3 - \sqrt{3}}{4}\varphi(2r + 1) + \frac{1 - \sqrt{3}}{4}\varphi(2r + 2)$$
$$= -h_0\varphi(2r - 1) + h_1\varphi(2r) - h_2\varphi(2r + 1) + h_3\varphi(2r + 2).$$

Recall that $\varphi$ is nonzero only in the interval $(0, 3)$. The definition above implies that $\psi(r)$ is nonzero in the interval $(-1, 2)$. This definition is also the basis for the recursive calculation of $\psi$, similar to that of $\varphi$. Figure 4.35 shows the values of the wavelet at 3073 points. A glance at Figures 4.34 and 4.35 also explains (albeit very late in this chapter) the reason for the term "wavelet."

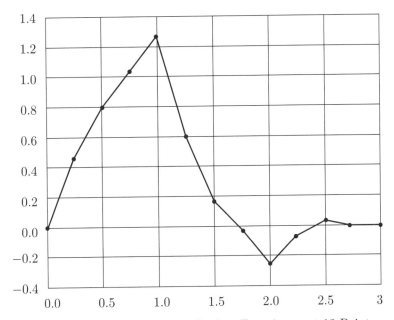

**Figure 4.33:** The Daubechies Scaling Function $\varphi$ at 13 Points.

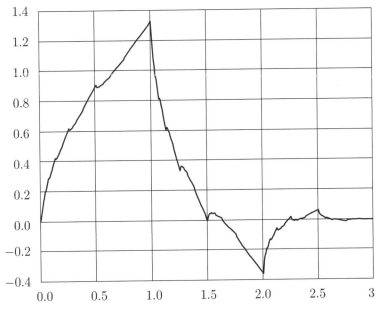

**Figure 4.34:** The Daubechies Scaling Function $\varphi$ at 3073 Points.

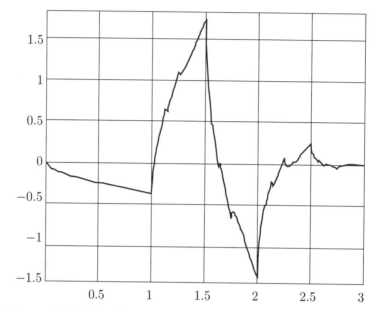

**Figure 4.35:** The Daubechies Wavelet $\psi$ at 3073 Points.

## 4.9 SPIHT

SPIHT is an image compression method, but it is included in this chapter because it uses the wavelet transform as one of its compression steps and because its main data structure, the spatial orientation tree, uses the fact (mentioned on page 172) that the various subbands reflect the geometrical artifacts of the image.

Section 4.2 shows how the Haar transform can be applied several times to an image, creating regions (or subbands) of averages and details. The Haar transform is simple, and better compression can be achieved by other wavelet filters that produce better energy compaction. It seems that different wavelet filters produce different results depending on the image type, but it is currently not clear what filter is the best for any given image type. Regardless of the particular filter used, the image is decomposed into subbands such that lower subbands correspond to higher image frequencies and higher subbands correspond to lower image frequencies, where most of the image energy is concentrated (Figure 4.36). This is why we can expect the detail coefficients to get smaller as we move from high to low levels. Also, there are spatial similarities among the subbands (Figure 4.7b). An image part, such as an edge, occupies the same spatial position in each subband. These features of the wavelet decomposition are exploited by the SPIHT (set partitioning in hierarchical trees) method [Said and Pearlman 96].

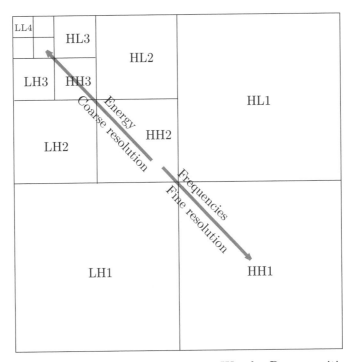

**Figure 4.36:** Subbands and Levels in Wavelet Decomposition.

SPIHT was designed for optimal progressive transmission, as well as for compression. One of the important features of SPIHT (perhaps a unique feature) is that at any point during the decoding of an image, the quality of the displayed image is the best that can be achieved for the number of bits input by the decoder up to that moment.

Another important SPIHT feature is its use of embedded coding. This feature is defined as follows: If an (embedded coding) encoder produces two files, a large one of size $M$ and a small one of size $m$, then the smaller file is identical to the first $m$ bits of the larger file.

The following example aptly illustrates the meaning of this definition. Suppose that three users wait for a certain compressed image to be sent them, but they need different image qualities. The first one needs the quality contained in a 10 KB file. The image qualities required by the second and third users are contained in files of sizes 20 KB and 50 KB, respectively. Most lossy image compression methods would have to compress the same image three times, at different qualities, to generate three files with the right sizes. SPIHT, on the other hand, produces one file and then three chunks—of lengths 10 KB, 20 KB, and 50 KB, all starting at the beginning of the file—that can be sent to the three users, thereby satisfying their needs.

We start with a general description of SPIHT. We denote the pixels of the original image $\mathbf{p}$ by $p_{i,j}$. Any set $\mathbf{T}$ of wavelet filters can be used to transform the pixels to wavelet coefficients (or transform coefficients) $c_{i,j}$. These coefficients constitute the transformed image **c**. The transformation is denoted by $\mathbf{c} = \mathbf{T}(\mathbf{p})$. In a progressive transmission method, the decoder starts by setting the reconstruction image $\hat{\mathbf{c}}$ to zero. It then inputs (encoded) transform coefficients, decodes them, and uses them to generate an improved reconstruction image $\hat{\mathbf{c}}$, which, in turn, is used to produce a better image $\hat{\mathbf{p}}$. We can summarize this operation by $\hat{\mathbf{p}} = \mathbf{T}^{-1}(\hat{\mathbf{c}})$.

The main aim in progressive transmission is to transmit the most important image information first. This is the information that results in the largest reduction of the distortion (the difference between the original and the reconstructed images). SPIHT uses the mean squared error (MSE) distortion measure [Equation (3.2)],

$$D_{\mathrm{mse}}(\mathbf{p} - \hat{\mathbf{p}}) = \frac{|\mathbf{p} - \hat{\mathbf{p}}|^2}{N} = \frac{1}{N}\sum_i\sum_j(p_{i,j} - \hat{p}_{i,j})^2,$$

where $N$ is the total number of pixels. An important consideration in the design of SPIHT is the fact that this measure is invariant to the wavelet transform, a feature that allows us to write

$$D_{\mathrm{mse}}(\mathbf{p} - \hat{\mathbf{p}}) = D_{\mathrm{mse}}(\mathbf{c} - \hat{\mathbf{c}}) = \frac{|\mathbf{p} - \hat{\mathbf{p}}|^2}{N} = \frac{1}{N}\sum_i\sum_j(c_{i,j} - \hat{c}_{i,j})^2. \tag{4.15}$$

Equation (4.15) shows that the MSE decreases by $|c_{i,j}|^2/N$ when the decoder receives the transform coefficient $c_{i,j}$ (we assume that the exact value of the coefficient is received by the decoder; i.e., there is no loss of precision due to the limited precision of computer arithmetic). It is now clear that the largest coefficients $c_{i,j}$ (largest in absolute value, regardless of their signs) contain the information that reduces the MSE distortion most, so a progressive encoder should send those coefficients first. This is one important principle of SPIHT.

Another principle is based on the observation that the most significant bits of a binary integer whose value is close to maximum tend to be ones. (For example, in a 16-bit computer, the small 16-bit number +5 is represented by 0|000...0101 but the large 16-bit number +65,382 is represented by 0|111111101100110.) This suggests that the most significant bits contain the most important image information and that they should be sent to the decoder first (or written first on the compressed stream).

The progressive transmission method used by SPIHT incorporates these two principles. SPIHT sorts the coefficients and transmits their most significant bits first. To simplify the description of this method, we first assume that the sorting information is explicitly transmitted to the decoder; the next section discusses an efficient method to code this information.

We now show how the SPIHT encoder uses these principles to progressively transmit the wavelet coefficients to the decoder (or to write them on the compressed file), starting with the most important information. We assume that a wavelet transform has already been applied to the image (SPIHT is a coding method, so it can work with any wavelet transform) and that the transformed coefficients $c_{i,j}$ are already stored in memory. The coefficients are sorted (ignoring their signs) and the sorting information is contained in an array $m$ such that array element $m(k)$ contains the $(i,j)$ coordinates of a coefficient

$c_{i,j}$ and such that $|c_{m(k)}| \geq |c_{m(k+1)}|$ for all values of $k$. Table 4.37 lists hypothetical values of 16 coefficients. Each is shown as a 16-bit number where the most significant bit (bit 15) is the sign and the remaining 15 bits (numbered 14 through 0, top to bottom) are the magnitude. The first coefficient $c_{m(1)} = c_{2,3}$ is $s1aci\ldots r$ (where $s$, $a$, and so on are bits). The second one $c_{m(2)} = c_{3,4}$ is $s1bdj\ldots s$ and so on.

| k |  | 1 | 2 | 3 | 4 | 5 | 6 | 7 | 8 | 9 | 10 | 11 | 12 | 13 | 14 | 15 | 16 |
|---|---|---|---|---|---|---|---|---|---|---|----|----|----|----|----|----|----|
|  | sign | $s$ | $s$ | $s$ | $s$ | $s$ | $s$ | $s$ | $s$ | $s$ | $s$ | $s$ | $s$ | $s$ | $s$ | $s$ | $s$ |
| msb | 14 | 1 | 1 | 0 | 0 | 0 | 0 | 0 | 0 | 0 | 0 | 0 | 0 | 0 | 0 | 0 | 0 |
|  | 13 | $a$ | $b$ | 1 | 1 | 1 | 1 | 0 | 0 | 0 | 0 | 0 | 0 | 0 | 0 | 0 | 0 |
|  | 12 | $c$ | $d$ | $e$ | $f$ | $g$ | $h$ | 1 | 1 | 1 | 0 | 0 | 0 | 0 | 0 | 0 | 0 |
|  | 11 | $i$ | $j$ | $k$ | $l$ | $m$ | $n$ | $o$ | $p$ | $q$ | 1 | 0 | 0 | 0 | 0 | 0 | 0 |
|  | $\vdots$ | $\vdots$ | $\vdots$ | $\vdots$ |  |  |  |  |  |  |  |  |  |  |  |  | $\vdots$ |
| lsb | 0 | $r$ | $s$ | $t$ | $u$ | $v$ | $w$ | $x$ | $y$ |  | $\ldots$ |  | $\ldots$ |  | $\ldots$ |  | $z$ |
| $m(k) = i,j$ |  | 2,3 | 3,4 | 3,2 | 4,4 | 1,2 | 3,1 | 3,3 | 4,2 | 4,1 | $\ldots$ |  | $\ldots$ |  | $\ldots$ |  | 4,3 |

**Table 4.37:** Transform Coefficients Ordered by Absolute Magnitudes.

The sorting information that the encoder has to transmit is the sequence $m(k)$, or

$$(2,3),\ (3,4),\ (3,2),\ (4,4),\ (1,2),\ (3,1),\ (3,3),\ (4,2),\ldots,(4,3).$$

In addition, it has to transmit the 16 signs and the 16 coefficients in order of significant bits. A direct transmission would send the 16 numbers

$$ssssssssssssssss, \quad 1100000000000000, \quad ab11110000000000,$$
$$cdefgh1110000000, \quad ijklmnopq1000000, \ldots, rstuvwxy\ldots z,$$

but this is clearly wasteful. Instead, the encoder goes into a loop, where in each iteration it performs a *sorting step* and a *refinement step*. In the first iteration it transmits the number $l = 2$ (the number of coefficients $c_{i,j}$ in our example that satisfy $2^{14} \leq |c_{i,j}| < 2^{15}$) followed by the two pairs of coordinates $(2,3)$ and $(3,4)$ and by the signs of the first two coefficients. This is done in the first sorting pass. This information enables the decoder to construct approximate versions of the 16 coefficients as follows: Coefficients $c_{2,3}$ and $c_{3,4}$ are constructed as the 16-bit numbers $s100\ldots0$. The remaining 14 coefficients are constructed as all zeros. This is how the most significant bits of the largest coefficients are transmitted to the decoder first.

The next step of the encoder is the refinement pass, but it is not performed in the first iteration.

In the second iteration the encoder performs both passes. In the sorting pass it transmits the number $l = 4$ (the number of coefficients $c_{i,j}$ in our example that satisfy $2^{13} \leq |c_{i,j}| < 2^{14}$), followed by the four pairs of coordinates $(3,2)$, $(4,4)$, $(1,2)$, and $(3,1)$

and by the signs of the four coefficients. In the refinement step it transmits the two bits $a$ and $b$. These are the 14th most significant bits of the two coefficients transmitted in the previous iteration.

The information received so far enables the decoder to improve the 16 approximate coefficients constructed in the previous iteration. The first six become

$$c_{2,3} = s1a0\ldots0, \; c_{3,4} = s1b0\ldots0, \; c_{3,2} = s0100\ldots0,$$
$$c_{4,4} = s0100\ldots0, \; c_{1,2} = s0100\ldots0, \; c_{3,1} = s0100\ldots0,$$

and the remaining 10 coefficients are not changed.

In the sorting pass of the third iteration the encoder transmits the number $l = 3$ (the number of coefficients $c_{i,j}$ in our example that satisfy $2^{12} \le |c_{i,j}| < 2^{13}$), followed by the three pairs of coordinates $(3,3)$, $(4,2)$, and $(4,1)$ and by the signs of the three coefficients. In the refinement step it transmits the six bits $cdefgh$. These are the 13th most significant bits of the coefficients transmitted in all the previous iterations.

The information received so far enables the decoder to further improve the 16 approximate coefficients. The first nine become

$$c_{2,3} = s1ac0\ldots0, \; c_{3,4} = s1bd0\ldots0, \; c_{3,2} = s01e00\ldots0,$$
$$c_{4,4} = s01f00\ldots0, \; c_{1,2} = s01g00\ldots0, \; c_{3,1} = s01h00\ldots0,$$
$$c_{3,3} = s0010\ldots0, \; c_{4,2} = s0010\ldots0, \; c_{4,1} = s0010\ldots0,$$

and the remaining seven are not changed.

The main steps of the SPIHT encoder should now be easy to understand. They are as follows:

*Step 1:* Given an image to be compressed, calculate its wavelet transform using any suitable wavelet filter, decompose it into transform coefficients $c_{i,j}$, and represent the resulting coefficients with a fixed number of bits. (In the discussion that follows we use the terms *pixel* and *coefficient* interchangeably.) We assume that the coefficients are represented as 16-bit signed-magnitude numbers. The leftmost bit is the sign, and the remaining 15 bits are the magnitude. (Notice that the sign-magnitude representation is different from the 2's complement method, which is used by computer hardware to represent signed numbers.) Such numbers can have values from $-(2^{15} - 1)$ to $2^{15} - 1$. Set $n$ to $\lfloor \log_2 \max_{i,j}(c_{i,j}) \rfloor$. In our case $n$ will be set to $\lfloor \log_2(2^{15} - 1) \rfloor = 14$.

*Step 2:* Sorting pass: Transmit the number $l$ of coefficients $c_{i,j}$ that satisfy $2^n \le |c_{i,j}| < 2^{n+1}$. Follow with the $l$ pairs of coordinates and the $l$ sign bits of those coefficients.

*Step 3:* Refinement pass: Transmit the $n$th most significant bit of all the coefficients satisfying $|c_{i,j}| \ge 2^{n+1}$. These are the coefficients that were selected in previous sorting passes (not including the immediately preceding sorting pass).

*Step 4:* Iterate: Decrement $n$ by 1. If more iterations are needed (or desired), go to Step 2.

The last iteration is normally performed for $n = 0$, but the encoder can stop earlier, in which case the least important image information (some of the least significant bits of all the wavelet coefficients) will not be transmitted. This is the natural lossy option of SPIHT. It is equivalent to scalar quantization, but it produces better results than what is usually achieved with scalar quantization, since the coefficients are transmitted in sorted order. An alternative is for the encoder to transmit the entire image (i.e., all the bits of all the wavelet coefficients), and the decoder can stop decoding when the reconstructed image reaches a certain quality. This quality can either be predetermined by the user or automatically determined by the decoder at run time.

### 4.9.1 Set Partitioning Sorting Algorithm

The method as described so far is simple, since we have assumed that the coefficients were sorted before the loop started. In practice, the image may have $1K \times 1K$ pixels or more; there may be more than a million coefficients, so sorting all of them is too slow. Instead of sorting the coefficients, SPIHT uses the fact that sorting is done by comparing two elements at a time, and each comparison results in a simple yes/no result. Therefore, if both encoder and decoder use the same sorting algorithm, the encoder can simply send the decoder the sequence of yes/no results, and the decoder can use those to duplicate the operations of the encoder. This is true not just for sorting but for any algorithm based on comparisons or on any type of branching.

The actual algorithm used by SPIHT is based on the realization that there is really no need to sort *all* the coefficients. The main task of the sorting pass in each iteration is to select those coefficients that satisfy $2^n \leq |c_{i,j}| < 2^{n+1}$. This task is divided into two parts. For a given value of $n$, if a coefficient $c_{i,j}$ satisfies $|c_{i,j}| \geq 2^n$, then we say that it is *significant*; otherwise, it is called *insignificant*. In the first iteration, relatively few coefficients will be significant, but their number increases from iteration to iteration, since $n$ keeps getting decremented. The sorting pass has to determine which of the significant coefficients satisfies $|c_{i,j}| < 2^{n+1}$ and transmit their coordinates to the decoder. This is an important part of the algorithm used by SPIHT.

The encoder partitions all the coefficients into a number of sets $T_k$ and performs the significance test

$$\max_{(i,j) \in T_k} |c_{i,j}| \geq 2^n \ ?$$

on each set $T_k$. The result may be either "no" (all the coefficients in $T_k$ are insignificant, so $T_k$ itself is considered insignificant) or "yes" (some coefficients in $T_k$ are significant, so $T_k$ itself is significant). This result is transmitted to the decoder. If the result is "yes," then $T_k$ is partitioned by both encoder and decoder, using the same rule, into subsets and the same significance test is performed on all the subsets. This partitioning is repeated until all the significant sets are reduced to size 1 (i.e., they contain one coefficient each, and that coefficient is significant). This is how the significant coefficients are identified by the sorting pass in each iteration.

The significant test performed on a set $T$ can be summarized by

$$S_n(T) = \begin{cases} 1, & \max_{(i,j) \in T} |c_{i,j}| \geq 2^n, \\ 0, & \text{otherwise.} \end{cases} \tag{4.16}$$

The result, $S_n(T)$, is a single bit that is transmitted to the decoder. Since the result of each significance test becomes a single bit written on the compressed file, the number of tests should be minimized. To achieve this goal, the sets should be created and partitioned such that sets expected to be significant will be large and sets expected to be insignificant will contain just one element.

### 4.9.2 Spatial Orientation Trees

The sets $T_k$ are created and partitioned using a special data structure called a *spatial orientation tree*. This structure is defined in a way that exploits the spatial relationships between the wavelet coefficients in the different levels of the subband pyramid. Experience has shown that the subbands in each level of the pyramid exhibit spatial similarity (Figure 4.7b). Any special features, such as a straight edge or a uniform region, are visible in all the levels at the same location.

The spatial orientation trees are illustrated in Figure 4.38 for a $16 \times 16$ image. The figure shows two levels, level 1 (the highpass) and level 2 (the lowpass). Each level is divided into four subbands. Subband LL2 (the lowpass subband) is divided into four groups of $2 \times 2$ coefficients each. Figure 4.38a shows the top left group, while Figure 4.38b shows the bottom right one. In each group, each of the four coefficients (except the top left one, shaded gray) becomes the root of a spatial orientation tree. The arrows show examples of how the various levels of these trees are related. The thick arrows indicate how each group of $4 \times 4$ coefficients in level 2 is the parent of four such groups in level 1. In general, a coefficient at location $(i, j)$ in the image is the parent of the four coefficients at locations $(2i, 2j)$, $(2i + 1, 2j)$, $(2i, 2j + 1)$, and $(2i + 1, 2j + 1)$.

The roots of the spatial orientation trees of our example are located in subband LL2 (in general, they are located in the top left LL subband, which can be of any size), but any wavelet coefficient, except the gray ones on level 1 (also except the leaves), can be considered the root of some spatial orientation subtree. The leaves of all those trees are located on level 1 of the subband pyramid.

In our example, subband LL2 is of size $4 \times 4$, so it is divided into four $2 \times 2$ groups, and three of the four coefficients of a group become roots of trees. Thus, the number of trees in our example is 12. In general, the number of trees is $3/4$ the size of the highest LL subband.

Each of the 12 roots in subband LL2 in our example is the parent of four children located on the same level. However, the children of these children are located on level 1. This is true in general. The roots of the trees are located on the highest level and their children are on the same level, but from then on, the four children of a coefficient on level $k$ are themselves located on level $k - 1$.

We use the terms *offspring* for the four children of a node and *descendants* for the children, grandchildren, and all their descendants. The set partitioning sorting algorithm uses the following four sets of coordinates:

1. $\mathcal{O}(i, j)$: The set of coordinates of the four offspring of node $(i, j)$. If node $(i, j)$ is a leaf of a spatial orientation tree, then $\mathcal{O}(i, j)$ is empty.
2. $\mathcal{D}(i, j)$: The set of coordinates of the descendants of node $(i, j)$.
3. $\mathcal{H}(i, j)$: The set of coordinates of the roots of all the spatial orientation trees ($3/4$ of the wavelet coefficients in the highest LL subband).
4. $\mathcal{L}(i, j)$: The difference set $\mathcal{D}(i, j) - \mathcal{O}(i, j)$. This set contains all the descendants of tree node $(i, j)$ except its four offspring.

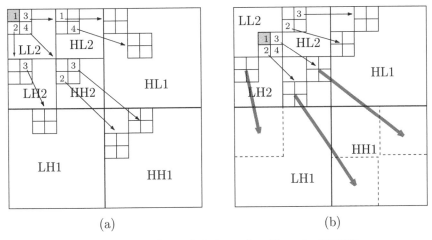

**Figure 4.38:** Spatial Orientation Trees in SPIHT.

The spatial orientation trees are used to create and partition the sets $T_k$. The set partitioning rules are as follows:

1. The initial sets are $\{(i,j)\}$ and $\mathcal{D}(i,j)$, for all $(i,j) \in \mathcal{H}$ (i.e., for all roots of the spatial orientation trees). In our example there are 12 roots, so there will initially be 24 sets: 12 sets each containing the coordinates of one root and 12 more sets each with the coordinates of all the descendants of one root.

2. If set $\mathcal{D}(i,j)$ is significant, then it is partitioned into $\mathcal{L}(i,j)$ plus the four single-element sets with the four offspring of $(i,j)$. In other words, if any of the descendants of node $(i,j)$ is significant, then its four offspring become four new sets and all its other descendants become another set (to be significance tested in rule 3).

3. If $\mathcal{L}(i,j)$ is significant, then it is partitioned into the four sets $\mathcal{D}(k,l)$, where $(k,l)$ are the offspring of $(i,j)$.

Once the spatial orientation trees and the set partitioning rules are understood, the coding algorithm can be described.

### 4.9.3 SPIHT Coding

It is important to have the encoder and decoder test sets for significance in the same way, so the coding algorithm uses three lists called *list of significant pixels* (LSP), *list of insignificant pixels* (LIP), and *list of insignificant sets* (LIS). These are lists of coordinates $(i,j)$ that in the LIP and LSP represent individual coefficients and in the LIS represent either the set $\mathcal{D}(i,j)$ (a type $A$ entry) or the set $\mathcal{L}(i,j)$ (a type $B$ entry).

The LIP contains coordinates of coefficients that were insignificant in the previous sorting pass. In the current pass they are tested, and those that test significant are moved to the LSP. In a similar way, sets in the LIS are tested in sequential order, and when a set is found to be significant, it is removed from the LIS and is partitioned. The new subsets with more than one coefficient are placed back in the LIS, to be tested later, and the subsets with one element are tested and appended to the LIP or the

LSP, depending on the results of the test. The refinement pass transmits the $n$th most significant bit of the entries in the LSP.

Figure 4.39 shows this algorithm in detail. Figure 4.40 is a simplified version for readers who are intimidated by too many details.

The decoder executes the detailed algorithm of Figure 4.39. It always works in *lockstep* with the encoder, but the following notes shed more light on its operation:

1. Step 2.2 of the algorithm evaluates all the entries in the LIS. However, step 2.2.1 appends certain entries to the LIS (as type $B$) and step 2.2.2 appends other entries to the LIS (as type $A$). It is important to realize that all these entries are also evaluated by step 2.2 in the same iteration.

2. The value of $n$ is decremented in each iteration, but there is no need to bring it all the way to zero. The loop can stop after any iteration, resulting in lossy compression. Normally, the user specifies the number of iterations, but it is also possible to have the user specify the acceptable amount of distortion (in units of MSE), and the encoder can use Equation (4.15) to decide when to stop the loop.

3. The encoder knows the values of the wavelet coefficients $c_{i,j}$ and uses them to calculate the bits $S_n$ (Equation (4.16)), which it transmits (i.e., writes on the compressed file). These bits are input by the decoder, which uses them to calculate the values of $c_{i,j}$. The algorithm executed by the decoder is that of Figure 4.39 but with the word "output" changed to "input."

4. The sorting information, previously denoted by $m(k)$, is recovered when the coordinates of the significant coefficients are appended to the LSP in steps 2.1.2 and 2.2.1. This implies that the coefficients indicated by the coordinates in the LSP are sorted according to

$$\lfloor \log_2 |c_{m(k)}| \rfloor \geq \lfloor \log_2 |c_{m(k+1)}| \rfloor$$

for all values of $k$. The decoder recovers the ordering because its three lists (LIS, LIP, and LSP) are updated in the same way as those of the encoder (remember that the decoder works in lockstep with the encoder). When the decoder inputs data, its three lists are identical to those of the encoder at the moment it (the encoder) output that data.

5. The encoder starts with the wavelet coefficients $c_{i,j}$; it never gets to "see" the actual image. The decoder, however, has to display the image and update the display in each iteration. In each iteration, when the coordinates $(i, j)$ of a coefficient $c_{i,j}$ are moved to the LSP as an entry, it is known (to both encoder and decoder) that $2^n \leq |c_{i,j}| < 2^{n+1}$. As a result, the best value that the decoder can give the coefficient $\hat{c}_{i,j}$ that is being reconstructed is midway between $2^n$ and $2^{n+1} = 2 \times 2^n$. Thus, the decoder sets $\hat{c}_{i,j} = \pm 1.5 \times 2^n$ (the sign of $\hat{c}_{i,j}$ is input by the decoder just after the insertion). During the refinement pass, when the decoder inputs the actual value of the $n$th bit of $c_{i,j}$, it improves the value $1.5 \times 2^n$ by adding $2^{n-1}$ to it if the input bit was a 1 or subtracting $2^{n-1}$ from it if the input bit was a 0. This way, the decoder can improve the appearance of the image (or, equivalently, reduce the distortion) during *both* the sorting and refinement passes.

It is possible to improve the performance of SPIHT by entropy coding the encoder's output, but experience shows that the added compression gained this way is minimal

1. Initialization: Set $n$ to $\lfloor \log_2 \max_{i,j}(c_{i,j}) \rfloor$ and transmit $n$. Set the LSP to empty. Set the LIP to the coordinates of all the roots $(i,j) \in \mathcal{H}$. Set the LIS to the coordinates of all the roots $(i,j) \in \mathcal{H}$ that have descendants.

2. Sorting pass:
   2.1 for each entry $(i,j)$ in the LIP do:
       2.1.1 output $S_n(i,j)$;
       2.1.2 if $S_n(i,j) = 1$, move $(i,j)$ to the LSP and output the sign of $c_{i,j}$;
   2.2 for each entry $(i,j)$ in the LIS do:
       2.2.1 if the entry is of type $A$, then
           • output $S_n(\mathcal{D}(i,j))$;
           • if $S_n(\mathcal{D}(i,j)) = 1$, then
               ∗ for each $(k,l) \in \mathcal{O}(i,j)$ do:
                   · output $S_n(k,l)$;
                   · if $S_n(k,l) = 1$, add $(k,l)$ to the LSP, output the sign of $c_{k,l}$;
                   · if $S_n(k,l) = 0$, append $(k,l)$ to the LIP;
               ∗ if $\mathcal{L}(i,j) \neq 0$, move $(i,j)$ to the end of the LIS, as a type-$B$ entry, and go to step 2.2.2; else, remove entry $(i,j)$ from the LIS;
       2.2.2 if the entry is of type $B$, then
           • output $S_n(\mathcal{L}(i,j))$;
           • if $S_n(\mathcal{L}(i,j)) = 1$, then
               ∗ append each $(k,l) \in \mathcal{O}(i,j)$ to the LIS as a type-$A$ entry:
               ∗ remove $(i,j)$ from the LIS:

3. Refinement pass: for each entry $(i,j)$ in the LSP, except those included in the last sorting pass (the one with the same $n$), output the $n$th most significant bit of $|c_{i,j}|$;

4. Loop: decrement $n$ by 1 and go to step 2 if needed.

**Figure 4.39:** The SPIHT Coding Algorithm.

1. Set the threshold. Set LIP to all root nodes coefficients. Set LIS to all trees (assign type D to them). Set LSP to an empty set.

2. Sorting pass: Check the significance of all coefficients in LIP:
   2.1 If significant, output 1, output a sign bit, and move the coefficient to the LSP.
   2.2 If not significant, output 0.

3. Check the significance of all trees in the LIS according to the type of tree:
   3.1 For a tree of type D:
       3.1.1 If it is significant, output 1, and code its children:
           3.1.1.1 If a child is significant, output 1, then a sign bit, and add it to the LSP.
           3.1.1.2 If a child is insignificant, output 0 and add the child to the end of LIP.
           3.1.1.3 If the children have descendants, move the tree to the end of LIS as type L; otherwise remove it from LIS.
       3.1.2 If it is insignificant, output 0.
   3.2 For a tree of type L:
       3.2.1 If it is significant, output 1, add each of the children to the end of LIS as an entry of type D, and remove the parent tree from the LIS.
       3.2.2 If it is insignificant, output 0.

4. Loop: Decrement the threshold and go to step 2 if needed.

**Figure 4.40:** A Simplified SPIHT Coding Algorithm.

and does not justify the additional expense of both encoding and decoding time. It turns out that the signs and the individual bits of coefficients output in each iteration are uniformly distributed, so entropy coding them does not produce any compression. The bits $S_n(i,j)$ and $S_n(\mathcal{D}(i,j))$, on the other hand, are distributed nonuniformly and may gain from such coding.

### 4.9.4 Example

We assume that a $4 \times 4$ image has already been transformed, and the 16 coefficients are stored in memory as 6-bit signed-magnitude numbers (one sign bit followed by five magnitude bits). They are shown in Figure 4.41, together with the single spatial orientation tree. The coding algorithm initializes LIP to the one-element set $\{(1,1)\}$, the LIS to the set $\{\mathcal{D}(1,1)\}$, and the LSP to the empty set. The largest coefficient is 18, so $n$ is set to $\lfloor \log_2 18 \rfloor = 4$. The first two iterations are shown.

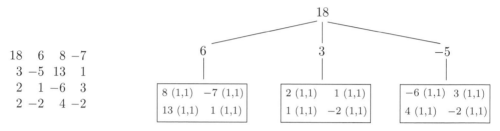

```
18   6   8  −7
 3  −5  13   1
 2   1  −6   3
 2  −2   4  −2
```

**Figure 4.41:** Sixteen Coefficients and One Spatial Orientation Tree.

Sorting Pass 1:
$2^n = 16$.
Is (1,1) significant? yes: output a 1.
LSP $= \{(1,1)\}$, output the sign bit: 0.
Is $\mathcal{D}(1,1)$ significant? no: output a 0.
LSP $= \{(1,1)\}$, LIP $= \{\}$, LIS $= \{\mathcal{D}(1,1)\}$.
Three bits output.
Refinement pass 1: no bits are output (this pass deals with coefficients from sorting pass $n-1$).
Decrement $n$ to 3.
Sorting Pass 2:
$2^n = 8$.
Is $\mathcal{D}(1,1)$ significant? yes: output a 1.
Is $(1,2)$ significant? no: output a 0.
Is $(2,1)$ significant? no: output a 0.
Is $(2,2)$ significant? no: output a 0.
LIP $= \{(1,2),(2,1),(2,2)\}$, LIS $= \{\mathcal{L}(1,1)\}$.
Is $\mathcal{L}(1,1)$ significant? yes: output a 1.
LIS $= \{\mathcal{D}(1,2),\mathcal{D}(2,1),\mathcal{D}(2,2)\}$.
Is $\mathcal{D}(1,2)$ significant? yes: output a 1.

Is $(1,3)$ significant? yes: output a 1.
LSP $= \{(1,1),(1,3)\}$, output sign bit: 1.
Is $(2,3)$ significant? yes: output a 1.
LSP $= \{(1,1),(1,3),(2,3)\}$, output sign bit: 1.
Is $(1,4)$ significant? no: output a 0.
Is $(2,4)$ significant? no: output a 0.
LIP $= \{(1,2),(2,1),(2,2),(1,4),(2,4)\}$,
LIS $= \{\mathcal{D}(2,1),\mathcal{D}(2,2)\}$.
Is $\mathcal{D}(2,1)$ significant? no: output a 0.
Is $\mathcal{D}(2,2)$ significant? no: output a 0.
LIP $= \{(1,2),(2,1),(2,2),(1,4),(2,4)\}$,
LIS $= \{\mathcal{D}(2,1),\mathcal{D}(2,2)\}$,
LSP $= \{(1,1),(1,3),(2,3)\}$.
Fourteen bits output.
Refinement pass 2: After iteration 1, the LSP included entry $(1,1)$, whose value is
$18 = 10010_2$.
One bit is output.
Sorting Pass 3:
$2^n = 4$.
Is $(1,2)$ significant? yes: output a 1.
LSP $= \{(1,1),(1,3),(2,3),(1,2)\}$, output a sign bit: 1.
Is $(2,1)$ significant? no: output a 0.
Is $(2,2)$ significant? yes: output a 1.
LSP $= \{(1,1),(1,3),(2,3),(1,2),(2,2)\}$, output a sign bit: 0.
Is $(1,4)$ significant? yes: output a 1.
LSP $= \{(1,1),(1,3),(2,3),(1,2),(2,2),(1,4)\}$, output a sign bit: 1.
Is $(2,4)$ significant? no: output a 0.
LIP $= \{(2,1),(2,4)\}$.
Is $D(2,1)$ significant? no: output a 0.
Is $D(2,2)$ significant? yes: output a 1.
Is $(3,3)$ significant? yes: output a 1.
LSP $= \{(1,1),(1,3),(2,3),(1,2),(2,2),(1,4),(3,3)\}$, output a sign bit: 0.
Is $(4,3)$ significant? yes: output a 1.
LSP $= \{(1,1),(1,3),(2,3),(1,2),(2,2),(1,4),(3,3),(4,3)\}$, output a sign bit: 1.
Is $(3,4)$ significant? no: output a 0.
LIP $= \{(2,1),(2,4),(3,4)\}$.
Is $(4,4)$ significant? no: output a 0.
LIP $= \{(2,1),(2,4),(3,4),(4,4)\}$.
LIP $= \{(2,1),(3,4),(3,4),(4,4)\}$, LIS $= \{\mathcal{D}(2,1)\}$,
LSP $= \{(1,1),(1,3),(2,3),(1,2),(2,2),(1,4),(3,3),(4,3)\}$.
Sixteen bits output.
Refinement Pass 3:
After iteration 2, the LSP included entries $(1,1)$, $(1,3)$, and $(2,3)$, whose values are
$18 = 10010_2$, $8 = 1000_2$, and $13 = 1101_2$. Three bits are output
After two iterations, a total of 37 bits has been output.

### 4.9.5 QTCQ

Closely related to SPIHT, the QTCQ (quadtree classification and trellis coding quantization) method [Banister and Fischer 99] uses fewer lists than SPIHT and explicitly forms classes of the wavelet coefficients for later quantization by means of the ACTCQ and TCQ (arithmetic and trellis coded quantization) algorithms of [Joshi, Crump, and Fischer 93].

The method uses the spatial orientation trees originally developed by SPIHT. This type of tree is a special case of a quadtree. The encoding algorithm is iterative. In the $n$th iteration, if any element of this quadtree is found to be significant, then the four highest elements in the tree are defined to be in class $n$. They also become roots for four new quadtrees. Each of the four new trees is tested for significance, moving down each tree until all the significant elements are found. All the wavelet coefficients declared to be in class $n$ are stored in a *list of pixels* (LP). The LP is initialized with all the wavelet coefficients in the lowest frequency subband (LFS). The test for significance is performed by the function $S_T(k)$, which is defined by

$$S_T(k) = \begin{cases} 1, & \max_{(i,j)\in k} |C_{i,j}| \geq T, \\ 0, & \text{otherwise,} \end{cases}$$

where $T$ is the current threshold for significance and $k$ is a tree of wavelet coefficients. The QTCQ encoding algorithm uses this test and is listed in Figure 4.42.

The QTCQ decoder is similar. All the outputs in Figure 4.42 should be replaced by inputs, and ACTCQ encoding should be replaced by ACTCQ decoding.

1. <u>Initialization:</u>
   Initialize LP with all $C_{i,j}$ in LFS,
   Initialize LIS with all parent nodes,
   Output $n = \lfloor \log_2(\max |C_{i,j}|/q) \rfloor$.
   Set the threshold $T = q2^n$, where $q$ is a quality factor.
2. <u>Sorting:</u>
   <u>for</u> each node $k$ in LIS <u>do</u>
     output $S_T(k)$
     <u>if</u> $S_T(k) = 1$ <u>then</u>
       <u>for</u> each child of $k$ <u>do</u>
       move coefficients to LP
       add to LIS as a new node
       <u>endfor</u>
       remove $k$ from LIS
     <u>endif</u>
   <u>endfor</u>
3. <u>Quantization:</u> For each element in LP,
     quantize and encode using ACTCQ.
     (use TCQ step size $\Delta = \alpha \cdot q$).
4. <u>Update:</u> Remove all elements in LP. Set $T = T/2$. Go to step 2.

**Figure 4.42:** QTCQ Encoding.

The QTCQ implementation, as described in [Banister and Fischer 99], does not transmit the image progressively, but the authors claim that this property can be added to it.

What are wavelets? Wavelets extend Fourier analysis.
How are wavelets computed? Fast transforms compute them.
—Yves Nievergelt, *Wavelets Made Easy*

# 5
# Video Compression

In the mid 1940s, with World War II over, several pioneers, among them Alan Turing, John Atanasoff, and John W. Mauchly and J. Presper Eckert, started developing the first electronic computers. They envisioned fast and reliable machines that perform numerical computations. It did not take long, however, for computer users to realize that the same computers could be used for nonnumerical applications. The first nonnumerical applications, developed in the 1950s, were concerned with text; then came still images (in the 1960s), computer animation (in the 1970s), and digital sound (in the 1980s). Today's computers are used mostly for communications and entertainment, so they run multimedia applications, where text, images, and video are created, displayed, edited, and transmitted.

All types of computer data benefit from efficient compression, but compression is especially important for video files. An image file tends to be large, but a video file may contain thousands of images together with the associated audio and can therefore be very large. Lossy compression is common with images and is even more important with video. Image compression is based on correlation among pixels, and video compression is based, as discussed in Section 5.1, both on correlations between pixels in a single frame and on correlations between consecutive video frames.

This short chapter presents the main principles and techniques used in video compression but does not describe any specific algorithms. Those interested in MPEG or other video compression methods should use [Salomon 00] as a starting point.

## 5.1 Basic Principles

Video compression is based on two principles. The first is the spatial redundancy that exists in each frame. The second is the fact that most of the time, a video frame is very similar to its immediate neighbors. This is called *temporal redundancy*. A typical technique for video compression should therefore start by encoding the first frame using a still image compression method. It should then encode each successive frame by identifying the differences between the frame and its predecessor, and encoding these differences. If the frame is very different from its predecessor (as happens with the first frame of a sequence), it should be coded independently of any other frames. In the video compression literature, a frame that is coded using its predecessor is called *inter frame* (or just *inter*), while a frame that is coded independently is called *intra frame* (or just *intra*).

Video compression is normally lossy. Encoding a frame $F_i$ in terms of its predecessor $F_{i-1}$ introduces some distortions. As a result, encoding frame $F_{i+1}$ in terms of $F_i$ increases the distortion. Even in lossless video compression, a frame may lose some bits. This may happen during transmission or after a long shelf stay. If a frame $F_i$ has lost some bits, then all the frames following it, up to the next intra frame, will be decoded improperly, perhaps even leading to accumulated errors. This is why intra frames should be used from time to time inside a sequence, not just at its beginning. An intra frame is labeled $I$, and an inter frame is labeled $P$ (for *predictive*).

Once this idea is grasped, it is possible to generalize the concept of an inter frame. Such a frame can be coded based on one of its predecessors and also on one of its *successors*. Obviously, an encoder should not use any information that's not available to the decoder, but video compression is special because of the large quantities of data involved. We usually don't mind if the encoder is slow, but the decoder has to be fast. A typical case is video recorded on a hard disk or on a DVD to be played back. The encoder can take minutes or hours to encode the data. The decoder, however, has to play it back at the correct frame rate (so many frames per second), so it has to be fast. This is why a typical video decoder works in parallel. It has several decoding circuits working simultaneously on several frames.

With this in mind we can imagine a situation where the encoder encodes frame 2 based on both frames 1 and 3 and writes the frames on the compressed stream in the order 1, 3, 2. The decoder reads them in this order, decodes frames 1 and 3 in parallel, outputs frame 1, then decodes frame 2 based on frames 1 and 3. The frames should, of course, be clearly tagged (or time stamped). A frame that is encoded based on both past and future frames is labeled $B$ (for *bidirectional*).

Predicting a frame based on its successor makes sense in cases where the movement of an object in the picture gradually uncovers a background area. Such an area may be only partly known in the current frame but may be better known in the next frame. Thus, the next frame is a natural candidate for predicting this area in the current frame.

The idea of a $B$ frame is so useful that most frames in a compressed video presentation may be of this type. We therefore end up with a sequence of compressed frames of the three types $I$, $P$, and $B$. An $I$ frame is decoded independently of any other frame. A $P$ frame is decoded using the preceding $I$ or $P$ frame. A $B$ frame is decoded using the preceding *and* following $I$ or $P$ frames. Figure 5.1a shows a sequence of such frames in the order in which they are generated by the encoder (and input by the decoder). Figure 5.1b shows the same sequence in the order in which the frames are output by the decoder and displayed. It is clear that the frame labeled 2 should be displayed after frame 5, which is why each frame should have two time stamps, its coding time and its display time.

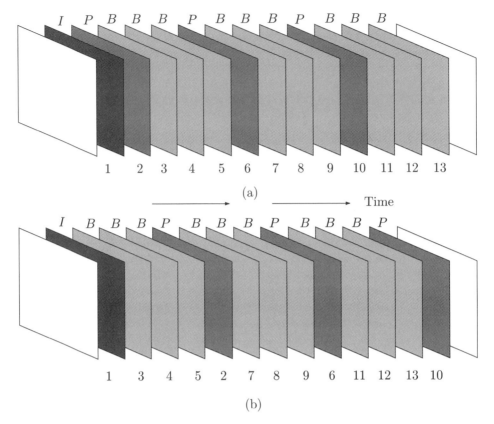

**Figure 5.1:** (a) Coding Order. (b) Display Order.

We start with a few intuitive video compression methods.

**Subsampling**: The encoder selects every other frame and writes it on the compressed stream. This yields a compression factor of 2. The decoder inputs a frame and duplicates it to create two frames.

**Differencing**: A frame is compared to its predecessor. If the difference between them is small (just a few pixels), the encoder encodes the pixels that are different by writing three numbers on the compressed stream for each pixel: its image coordinates and the difference between the values of the pixel in the two frames. If the difference between the frames is large, the current frame is written on the output in raw format.

A lossy version of differencing looks at the amount of change in a pixel. If the difference between the intensities of a pixel in the preceding frame and in the current frame is smaller than a certain threshold, the pixel is not considered different.

**Block Differencing**: This is a further improvement of differencing. The image is divided into blocks of pixels, and each block $B$ in the current frame is compared to the corresponding block $P$ in the preceding frame. If the blocks differ by more than a certain amount, then $B$ is compressed by writing its image coordinates, followed by the values of all its pixels (expressed as differences) on the compressed stream. The advantage is that the block coordinates are small numbers (smaller than a pixel's coordinates), and these coordinates have to be written just once for the entire block. On the downside, the values of all the pixels in the block, even those that haven't changed, have to be written on the output. However, since these values are expressed as differences, they are small numbers. Consequently, this method is sensitive to the block size.

**Motion Compensation**: Anyone who has watched movies knows that the difference between consecutive frames is small because it is the result of moving the scene, the camera, or both between frames. This feature can therefore be exploited to improve compression. If the encoder discovers that a part $P$ of the preceding frame has been rigidly moved to a different location in the current frame, then $P$ can be compressed by writing the following three items on the compressed stream: its previous location, its current location, and information identifying the boundaries of $P$. The following discussion of motion compensation is based on [Manning 98].

In principle, such a part can have any shape. In practice, we are limited to equal-size blocks (normally square but can also be rectangular). The encoder scans the current frame block by block. For each block $B$ it searches the preceding frame for an identical block $C$ (if compression is to be lossless) or for a similar one (if it can be lossy). On finding such a block, the encoder writes the difference between its past and present locations on the output. This difference is of the form

$$(C_x - B_x, C_y - B_y) = (\Delta x, \Delta y),$$

so it is called a *motion vector*. Figure 5.2 shows a simple example where the sun and trees are moved rigidly to the right (because of camera movement) while the child moves a different distance to the left (this is scene movement).

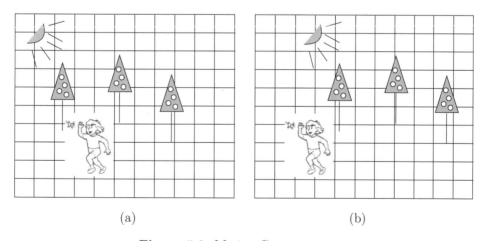

(a)                                                      (b)

**Figure 5.2:** Motion Compensation.

Motion compensation is effective if objects are just translated, not scaled or rotated. Drastic changes in illumination from frame to frame also reduce the effectiveness of this method. In general, motion compensation is lossy. The following paragraphs discuss the main aspects of motion compensation in detail.

**Frame Segmentation**: The current frame is divided into equal-size nonoverlapping blocks. The blocks may be square or rectangles. The latter choice assumes that motion in video is mostly horizontal, so horizontal blocks reduce the number of motion vectors without degrading the compression ratio. The block size is important, since large blocks reduce the chance of finding a match, and small blocks result in many motion vectors. In practice, block sizes that are integer powers of 2, such as 8 or 16, are used, since this simplifies the software.

**Search Threshold**: Each block $B$ in the current frame is first compared to its counterpart $C$ in the preceding frame. If they are identical, or if the difference between them is less than a preset threshold, the encoder assumes that the block hasn't been moved.

**Block Search**: This is a time-consuming process, so it has to be carefully designed. If $B$ is the current block in the current frame, then the previous frame has to be searched for a block identical to or very close to $B$. The search is normally restricted to a small area (called the *search area*) around $B$, defined by the *maximum displacement* parameters $dx$ and $dy$. These parameters specify the maximum horizontal and vertical distances, in pixels, between $B$ and any matching block in the previous frame. If $B$ is a square with side $b$, the search area will contain $(b+2dx)(b+2dy)$ pixels (Figure 5.3) and will consist of $(2dx+1)(2dy+1)$ distinct, overlapping $b \times b$ squares. The number of candidate blocks in this area is therefore proportional to $dx \cdot dy$.

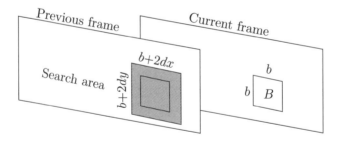

**Figure 5.3:** Search Area.

**Distortion Measure**: This is the most sensitive part of the encoder. The distortion measure selects the best match for block $B$. It has to be simple and fast, but also reliable. A few choices are discussed below.

The *mean absolute difference* (or *mean absolute error*) calculates the average of the absolute differences between a pixel $B_{ij}$ in $B$ and its counterpart $C_{ij}$ in a candidate block $C$:

$$\frac{1}{b^2} \sum_{i=1}^{b} \sum_{j=1}^{b} |B_{ij} - C_{ij}|.$$

This involves $b^2$ subtractions and absolute value operations, $b^2$ additions, and one division. This measure is calculated for each of the $(2dx+1)(2dy+1)$ distinct, overlapping

$b \times b$ candidate blocks, and the smallest distortion (say, for block $C_k$) is examined. If it is smaller than the search threshold, than $C_k$ is selected as the match for $B$. Otherwise, there is no match for $B$, and $B$ has to be encoded without motion compensation.

An obvious question at this point is "How can such a thing happen? How can a block in the current frame match nothing in the preceding frame?" The answer is to imagine a camera panning from left to right. New objects will enter the field of view from the right all the time. A block on the right side of the frame may thus contain objects that did not exist in the previous frame.

The *mean square difference* is a similar measure, where the square, rather than the absolute value, of a pixel difference is calculated:

$$\frac{1}{b^2} \sum_{i=1}^{b} \sum_{j=1}^{b} (B_{ij} - C_{ij})^2.$$

The *pel difference classification* (PDC) measure counts how many differences $|B_{ij} - C_{ij}|$ are smaller than the PDC parameter $p$.

The *integral projection* measure computes the sum of a row of $B$ and subtracts it from the sum of the corresponding row of $C$. The absolute value of the difference is added to the absolute value of the difference of the columns sum:

$$\sum_{i=1}^{b} \left| \sum_{j=1}^{b} B_{ij} - \sum_{j=1}^{b} C_{ij} \right| + \sum_{j=1}^{b} \left| \sum_{i=1}^{b} B_{ij} - \sum_{i=1}^{b} C_{ij} \right|.$$

**Suboptimal Search Methods**: These methods search some instead of all the candidate blocks in the $(b+2dx)(b+2dy)$ area. They speed up the search for a matching block at the expense of compression efficiency. Several such methods are discussed in detail in Section 5.2.

**Motion Vector Correction**: Once a block $C$ has been selected as the best match for $B$, a motion vector is calculated as the difference between the upper left corner of $C$ and that of $B$. Regardless of how the matching was determined, the motion vector may be wrong because of noise, local minima in the frame, or because the matching algorithm is not ideal. It is possible to apply smoothing techniques to the motion vectors after they have been calculated, in an attempt to improve the matching. Spatial correlations in the image suggest that the motion vectors should also be correlated. If certain vectors are found to violate this, they can be corrected.

This step is costly and may even backfire. A video presentation may involve slow, smooth motion of most objects, but also swift, jerky motion of some small objects. Correcting motion vectors may interfere with the motion vectors of such objects and cause distortions in the compressed frames.

**Coding Motion Vectors**: A large part of the current frame (perhaps close to half of it) may be converted to motion vectors, so the way these vectors are encoded is crucial; it must also be lossless. Two properties of motion vectors help in encoding them: (1) They are correlated and (2) their distribution is nonuniform. As we scan the frame block by block, adjacent blocks normally have motion vectors that don't differ by much; they are correlated. The vectors also don't point in all directions. There are usually one or two preferred directions in which all or most motion vectors point; the vectors are thus nonuniformly distributed.

No single method has proved ideal for encoding the motion vectors. Arithmetic coding, adaptive Huffman coding, and various prefix codes have been tried, and all seem to perform well. Here are two different methods that may perform better:

1. Predict a motion vector based on its predecessors in the same row and its predecessors in the same column of the current frame. Calculate the difference between the prediction and the actual vector, and Huffman encode it. This method is important. It is used in MPEG-1 and other compression methods.

2. Group the motion vectors in blocks. If all the vectors in a block are identical, the block is encoded by encoding this vector. Other blocks are encoded as in 1 above. Each encoded block starts with a code identifying its type.

**Coding the Prediction Error**: Motion compensation is lossy, since a block $B$ is normally matched to a somewhat different block $C$. Compression can be improved by coding the difference between the current uncompressed and compressed frames on a block by block basis and only for blocks that differ much. This is usually done by transform coding. The difference is written on the output, following each frame, and is used by the decoder to improve the frame after it has been decoded.

## 5.2 Suboptimal Search Methods

Video compression includes many steps and computations, so researchers look for optimizations and faster algorithms, especially for steps that involve many calculations. One such step is the search for a block $C$ in the previous frame to match a given block $B$ in the current frame. An exhaustive search is time-consuming, so it pays to look for suboptimal search methods that search just some of the many overlapping candidate blocks. These methods do not always find the best match, but they can generally speed up the entire compression process while incurring only a small loss of compression efficiency.

**Signature-Based Methods**: Such a method performs a number of steps, restricting the number of candidate blocks in each step. In the first step, all the candidate blocks are searched using a simple, fast distortion measure such as pel difference classification. Only the best-matched blocks are included in the next step, where they are evaluated by a more restrictive distortion measure or by the same measure but with a smaller parameter. A signature method may involve several steps, each involving a different distortion measure.

**Distance-Diluted Search**: We know from experience that fast-moving objects look blurred in an animation even if they are sharp in all the frames. This suggests a way to lose data. We may require a good block match for slow-moving objects, but we could allow for a worse match for fast-moving ones. The result is a block-matching algorithm that searches all the blocks close to $B$ but fewer and fewer blocks as the search moves farther away from $B$. Figure 5.4a shows how such a method may work for maximum displacement parameters $dx = dy = 6$. The total number of blocks $C$ being searched drops from $(2dx + 1) \cdot (2dy + 1) = 13 \times 13 = 169$ to just 65, fewer than 39%!

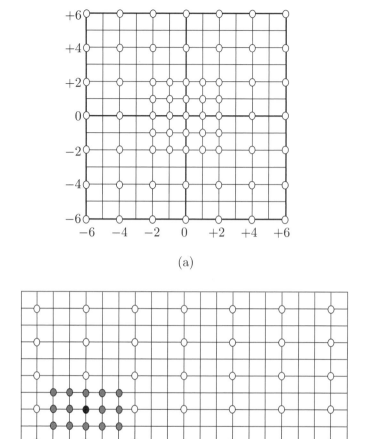

(a)

○ − first wave.   ● − best match of first wave.   ● − second wave.

(b)

**Figure 5.4:** (a) Distance-Diluted Search for $dx = dy = 6$. (b) A Locality Search.

**Locality-Based Search**: This method is based on the assumption that once a good match has been found, even better matches are likely to be located near it (remember that the blocks $C$ searched for matches highly overlap). An obvious algorithm is to start searching for a match in a sparse set of blocks, then use the best-matched block $C$ as the center of a second wave of searches, this time in a denser set of blocks. Figure 5.4b shows two waves of search: The first considers widely spaced blocks, selecting one as the best match; the second wave searches every block in the vicinity of the best match.

**Quadrant Monotonic Search**: This is a variant of locality-based search. It starts with a sparse set of blocks $C$ that are searched for a match. The distortion measure is computed for each of those blocks, and the result is a set of distortion values. The idea is that the distortion values increase as we move away from the best match. By examining the set of distortion values obtained in the first step, the second step may predict where the best match is likely to be found. Figure 5.5 shows how a search of a region of $4 \times 3$ blocks suggests a well-defined direction in which to continue searching.

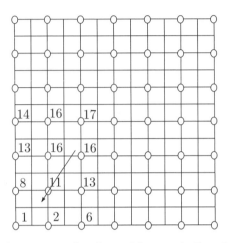

**Figure 5.5:** Quadrant Monotonic Search.

This method is less reliable than the previous ones since the direction proposed by the set of distortion values may lead to a local best block, whereas *the* best block may be located elsewhere.

**Dependent Algorithms**: As has been mentioned before, motion in a frame is the result of either camera movement or object movement. If we assume that objects in the frame are bigger than a block, we conclude that it is reasonable to expect the motion vectors of adjacent blocks to be correlated. The search algorithm can therefore start by estimating the motion vector of a block $B$ from the motion vectors that have already been found for its neighbors, then improve this estimate by comparing $B$ to some candidate blocks $C$. This is the basis of several *dependent algorithms*, which can be spatial or temporal.

*Spatial dependency*: In a spatial dependent algorithm, the neighbors of a block $B$ in the current frame are used to estimate the motion vector of $B$. These, of course, must be neighbors whose motion vectors have already been computed. Most blocks have eight neighbors each, but using all eight may not be the best strategy (also, when a block $B$ is considered, only some of its neighbors may have their motion vectors already computed). If blocks are matched in raster order, then it makes sense to use one, two, or three previously matched neighbors, as shown in Figure 5.6a,b,c. Because of symmetry, however, it is better to use four symmetric neighbors, as in Figure 5.6d,e. This can be done by a three-pass method that scans blocks as in Figure 5.6f. The first pass scans all the blocks shown in black (one-quarter of the blocks in the frame). Motion vectors for those blocks are calculated by some other method. Pass two scans the blocks shown in gray (25% of the blocks) and estimates a motion vector for each using the motion vectors of its four corner neighbors. The white blocks (the remaining 50%) are scanned in the third pass, and the motion vector of each is estimated using the motion vectors of its neighbors on all four sides. If the motion vectors of the neighbors are very different, they should not be used, and a motion vector for block $B$ is calculated using a different method.

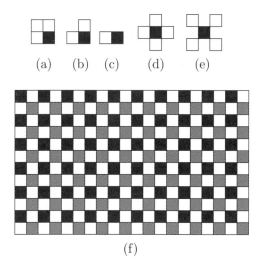

(a)     (b)   (c)     (d)       (e)

(f)

**Figure 5.6:** Strategies for Spatial Dependent Search Algorithms.

*Temporal dependency:* The motion vector of block $B$ in the current frame can be estimated as the motion vector of the same block in the previous frame. This makes sense if we can assume uniform motion. After the motion vector of $B$ is estimated this way, it should be improved and corrected using other methods.

**More Quadrant Monotonic Search Methods**: The following suboptimal block-matching methods use the main assumption of the quadrant monotonic search method.

**Two-Dimensional Logarithmic Search**: This multistep method reduces the search area in each step until it shrinks to one block. We assume that the current block $B$ is located at position $(a, b)$ in the current frame. This position becomes the initial center of the search. The algorithm uses a distance parameter $d$ that defines the search area. This parameter is user-controlled with a default value. The search area consists of the $(2d + 1) \times (2d + 1)$ blocks centered on the current block $B$.

*Step 1*: A step size $s$ is calculated by

$$s = 2^{\lfloor \log_2 d \rfloor - 1},$$

and the algorithm compares $B$ to the five blocks at positions $(a, b)$, $(a, b+s)$, $(a, b-s)$, $(a + s, b)$, and $(a - s, b)$ in the previous frame. These five blocks form the pattern of a plus sign $+$.

*Step 2*: The best match among the five blocks is selected. We denote the position of this block by $(x, y)$. If $(x, y) = (a, b)$, then $s$ is halved (this is the reason for the name *logarithmic*). Otherwise, $s$ stays the same, and the center $(a, b)$ of the search is moved to $(x, y)$.

*Step 3*: If $s = 1$, then the nine blocks around the center $(a, b)$ of the search are searched, and the best match among them becomes the result of the algorithm. Otherwise the algorithm goes to Step 2.

Any blocks that need be searched but are outside the search area are ignored and are not used in the search. Figure 5.7 illustrates the case where $d = 8$. For simplicity we assume that the current block $B$ has frame coordinates $(0, 0)$. The search is limited to the $17 \times 17$-block area centered on block $B$. Step 1 calculates

$$s = 2^{\lfloor \log_2 8 \rfloor - 1} = 2^{3-1} = 4$$

and searches the five blocks (labeled 1) at locations $(0, 0)$, $(4, 0)$, $(-4, 0)$, $(0, 4)$, and $(0, -4)$. We assume that the best match of these five is at $(0, 4)$, so this becomes the new center of the search, and the three blocks (labeled 2) at locations $(4, -4)$, $(4, 4)$, and $(8, 0)$ are searched in the second step.

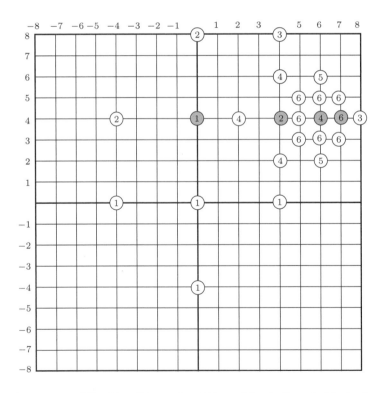

**Figure 5.7:** The Two-Dimensional Logarithmic Search Method.

Assuming that the best match among these three is at location $(4,4)$, the next step searches the two blocks labeled 3 at locations $(8,4)$ and $(4,8)$, the block (labeled 2) at $(4,4)$ and the "1" blocks at $(0,4)$ and $(4,0)$.

In the next step, we assume that $(4,4)$ is again the best match. Since $(4,4)$ is at the center of the $+$, the value of $s$ is halved to 2. The step searches the four blocks labeled 4, centered on $(4,4)$. Assuming that the best match is at $(6,4)$, the two blocks labeled 5 are searched. Assuming that $(6,4)$ is the best match, $s$ is halved to 1, and the eight blocks labeled 6 are searched. The diagram shows that the best match is finally found at location $(7,4)$.

**Three-Step Search**: This is somewhat similar to the two-dimensional logarithmic search. In each step it tests eight blocks, instead of four, around the center of search, then halves the step size. If $s = 3$ initially, the algorithm terminates after three steps, hence its name.

**Orthogonal Search**: This is a variation of both the two-dimensional logarithmic search and the three-step search. Each step of the orthogonal search involves a horizontal and a vertical search. The step size $s$ is initialized to $\lfloor(d+1)/2\rfloor$, and the block at the center of the search and two candidate blocks located on either side of it at a distance of $s$ are searched. The location of smallest distortion becomes the center of the vertical search, where two candidate blocks above and below the center, at distances of $s$, are searched. The best of these locations becomes the center of the next search. If the step size $s$ is 1, the algorithm terminates and returns the best block found in the current step. Otherwise, $s$ is halved, and another set of horizontal and vertical searches is performed.

**One-at-a-Time Search**: In this type of search there are again two steps, a horizontal and a vertical. The horizontal step searches all the blocks in the search area whose $y$ coordinates equal that of block $B$ (i.e., that are located on the same horizontal axis as $B$). Assuming that block $H$ has the minimum distortion among them, the vertical step searches all the blocks on the same vertical axis as $H$ and returns the best of them. A variation repeats this on smaller and smaller search areas.

**Cross Search**: All the steps of this algorithm, except the last one, search the five blocks at the edges of a multiplication sign $\times$. The step size is halved in each step until it gets down to 1. At the last step, the plus sign $+$ is used to search the areas located around the top left and bottom right corners of the preceding step.

This has been a survey of quadrant monotonic search methods. We follow with an outline of two advanced search methods.

**Hierarchical Search Methods**: Hierarchical methods take advantage of the fact that block matching is sensitive to block size. A hierarchical search method starts with large blocks and uses their motion vectors as starting points for more searches with smaller blocks. Large blocks are less likely to stumble on a local maximum, while a small block generally produces a better motion vector. A hierarchical search method is thus computationally intensive, and the main point is to speed it up by reducing the number of operations. This can be done in several ways as follows:

1. In the initial steps, when the blocks are still large, search just a sample of blocks. The resulting motion vectors are not the best, but they are going to be used only as starting points for better ones.

2. When searching large blocks, skip some of the pixels of a block. The algorithm may,

for example, use just one quarter of the pixels of the large blocks, one half of the pixels of smaller blocks, and so on.

3. Select the block sizes such that the block used in step $i$ is divided into several (typically four or nine) blocks used in the following step. This way a single motion vector calculated in step $i$ can be used as an estimate for several better motion vectors in step $i + 1$.

**Multidimensional Search Space Methods**: These methods are more complex. When searching for a match for block $B$, such a method looks for matches that are rotations or zooms of $B$, not just translations.

A multidimensional search space method may also find a block $C$ that matches $B$ but has different lighting conditions. This is useful when an object moves among areas that are illuminated differently. All the methods discussed so far compare two blocks by comparing the luminance values of corresponding pixels. Two blocks $B$ and $C$ that contain the same objects but differ in luminance would be declared different by such methods.

When a multidimensional search space method finds a block $C$ that matches $B$ but has different luminance, it may declare $C$ the match of $B$ and append a luminance value to the compressed frame $B$. This value (which may be negative) is added by the decoder to the pixels of the decompressed frame, to bring them back to their original values.

A multidimensional search space method may also compare a block $B$ to rotated versions of the candidate blocks $C$. This is useful if objects in the video presentation may be rotated in addition to being moved. The algorithm may also try to match a block $B$ to a block $C$ containing a scaled version of the objects in $B$. If, for example, $B$ is of size $8 \times 8$ pixels, the algorithm may consider blocks $C$ of size $12 \times 12$, shrink each to $8 \times 8$, and compare it to $B$.

This kind of block search involves many extra operations and comparisons. We say that it increases the size of the *search space* significantly, hence the name *multidimensional search space*. It seems that at present there is no multidimensional search space method that can account for scaling, rotation, and changes in illumination and also be fast enough for practical use.

Video meliora proboque deteriora sequor
(I see what is better and I approve it but follow the worse).

Ovid, *Metamorphoses,* 7:20

# 6
# Audio Compression

Text does not occupy much space in the computer. An average book, consisting of a million characters, can be stored uncompressed in about 1 MB, since each character of text occupies one byte (the Colophon at the end of the book illustrates this with precise data from the book itself).

It is a handy rule of thumb that an average book occupies about a million bytes. This is based on a "typical" 400-page book with 60 characters per line and 45 lines per page, which works out to $60 \times 45 \times 400 = 1,080,000$ characters, requiring one byte of storage each.

In contrast, images require much more space, lending another meaning to the phrase "a picture is worth a thousand words." Depending on the number of colors used in an image, a single pixel requires anywhere from one bit to three bytes. Thus, a $512 \times 512$-pixel image requires between 32 KB and 768 KB.

With the advent of powerful, inexpensive personal computers came multimedia applications, where text, images, movies, and *sound* are stored in the computer and can be displayed, edited, and played back. The storage requirements of sound are smaller than those of images or movies but bigger than those of text. This is why audio compression has become important and was the subject of much research and experimentation throughout the 1990s.

This chapter starts with a short introduction to sound and digitized sound. It then discusses those properties of the human auditory system (ear and brain) that make it possible to lose much audio information without losing sound quality. This is followed by two simple audio compression methods, namely, *silence compression* and *companding*. The chapter concludes with a description of the popular MP3 audio compression method that's part of the MPEG-1 standard.

## 6.1 Sound

To most of us, sound is a very familiar phenomenon, since we hear it all the time. Nevertheless, when we try to define sound, we find that we can approach this concept from two different points of view, and we end up with two definitions, as follows:

An intuitive definition: Sound is the sensation detected by our ears and interpreted by our brain in a certain way.

A scientific definition: Sound is a physical disturbance in a medium. It propagates in the medium as a pressure wave by the movement of atoms or molecules.

We normally hear sound as it propagates through the air and hits the diaphragm in our ears. However, sound can propagate in many different media. Marine animals produce sounds underwater and respond to similar sounds. Hitting the end of a metal bar with a hammer produces sound waves that propagate through the bar and can be detected at the other end. Good sound insulators are rare, and the best insulator is vacuum, where there are no particles to vibrate and propagate the disturbance.

Sound can also be considered a wave, even though its frequency may change all the time. It is a longitudinal wave, one where the disturbance is in the direction of the wave itself. In contrast, electromagnetic waves and ocean waves are transverse waves. Their undulations are perpendicular to the direction of the wave.

As any other wave, sound has three important attributes, its speed, amplitude, and period. The frequency of a wave is not an independent attribute; it is the number of periods that occur in one time unit (one second). The unit of frequency is the hertz (Hz). The speed of sound depends mostly on the medium it passes through, and on the temperature. In air, at sea level (one atmospheric pressure), and at 20° Celsius (68° Fahrenheit), the speed of sound is 343.8 meters per second (about 1128 feet per second).

The human ear is sensitive to a wide range of sound frequencies, normally from about 20 Hz to about 22,000 Hz, depending on the person's age and health. This is the range of *audible frequencies*. Some animals, most notably dogs and bats, can hear higher frequencies (ultrasound). A quick calculation reveals the periods associated with audible frequencies. At 22,000 Hz, each period is about 1.56 cm long, whereas at 20 Hz, a period is about 17.19 meters long.

The amplitude of sound is also an important property. We perceive it as loudness. We sense sound when air molecules strike the diaphragm of the ear and apply pressure on it. The molecules move back and forth tiny distances that are related to the *amplitude*, not to the period of the sound. The period of a sound wave may be several meters, yet an individual molecule in the air may move just a millionth of a centimeter in its oscillations. With very loud noise, an individual molecule may move about one thousandth of a centimeter. A device to measure noise levels should therefore have a sensitive diaphragm where the pressure of the sound wave is sensed and is converted to electrical voltage, which in turn is displayed as a numeric value.

The problem with measuring noise intensity is that the ear is sensitive to a very wide range of sound levels (amplitudes). The ratio between the sound level of a cannon at the muzzle and the lowest level we can hear (the threshold of hearing) is about 11 or 12 orders of magnitude. If we denote the lowest audible sound level by 1, then the cannon noise would have a magnitude of $10^{11}$! It is inconvenient to deal with measurements over such a wide range, which is why the units of sound loudness use a *logarithmic scale*. The logarithm of 1 is zero, and the (base-10) logarithm of $10^{11}$ is 11. Using logarithms, we have to deal only with numbers in the range 0 through 11. Actually, this range turns out to be too small, and we typically multiply it by 10 or by 20 to get numbers between zero and 110 or 220. This is the well-known (and sometimes confusing) *decibel* system of measurement.

The decibel (dB) unit is defined as the base-10 logarithm of the ratio of two physical quantities whose units are power (energy per time). The logarithm is then multiplied by the convenient scale factor 10. (If the scale factor is not used, the result is measured in units called "Bel." The Bel, however, was dropped long ago in favor of the decibel.) Thus, we have

$$\text{Level} = 10 \log_{10} \frac{P_1}{P_2} \text{ dB},$$

where $P_1$ and $P_2$ are measured in units of power such as watt, joule/sec, gram·cm/sec, or horsepower. This can be mechanical power, electrical power, or anything else. In measuring the loudness of sound, we have to use units of acoustical power. Since even loud sound can be produced with very little energy, we use the microwatt ($10^{-6}$ watt) as a convenient unit.

The decibel is the logarithm of a ratio. The numerator, $P_1$, is the power (in microwatts) of the sound whose intensity level is being measured. It is convenient to select as the denominator the number of microwatts that produce the faintest audible sound (the threshold of hearing). This number is shown by experiment to be $10^{-6}$ microwatt $= 10^{-12}$ watt. Thus, a stereo unit that produces 1 watt of acoustical power has an intensity level of

$$10 \log \frac{10^6}{10^{-6}} = 10 \log \left(10^{12}\right) = 10 \times 12 = 120 \text{ dB}$$

(this happens to be about the threshold of feeling; see Figure 6.1), whereas an earphone producing $3 \times 10^{-4}$ microwatt has a level of

$$10 \log \frac{3 \times 10^{-4}}{10^{-6}} = 10 \log \left(3 \times 10^2\right) = 10 \times (\log 3 + \log 100) = 10 \times (0.477 + 2) \approx 24.77 \text{ dB}.$$

In the field of electricity, there is a simple relation between (electrical) power $P$ and pressure (voltage) $V$. Electrical power is the product of the current and voltage $P = I \cdot V$. The current, however, is proportional to the voltage by means of Ohm's law $I = V/R$ (where $R$ is the resistance). We can therefore write $P = V^2/R$ and use pressure (voltage) in our electric decibel measurements.

In practical acoustics work, we don't always have access to the source of the sound, so we cannot measure its electrical power output. In practice, we may find ourselves in a busy location, holding a sound decibel meter in our hands, trying to measure the noise level around us. The decibel meter measures the pressure $Pr$ applied by the sound waves on its diaphragm. Fortunately, the acoustical power per area (denoted by $P$) is proportional to the square of the sound pressure $Pr$. This is because sound power $P$ is the product of the pressure $Pr$ and the speed $v$ of the sound and because the speed can be expressed as the pressure divided by the specific impedance of the medium through which the sound propagates. This is why sound loudness is commonly measured in units of dB SPL (sound pressure level) instead of sound power. The definition is

$$\text{Level} = 10\log_{10}\frac{P_1}{P2} = 10\log_{10}\frac{Pr_1^2}{Pr_2^2} = 20\log_{10}\frac{Pr_1}{Pr_2}\text{ dB SPL}.$$

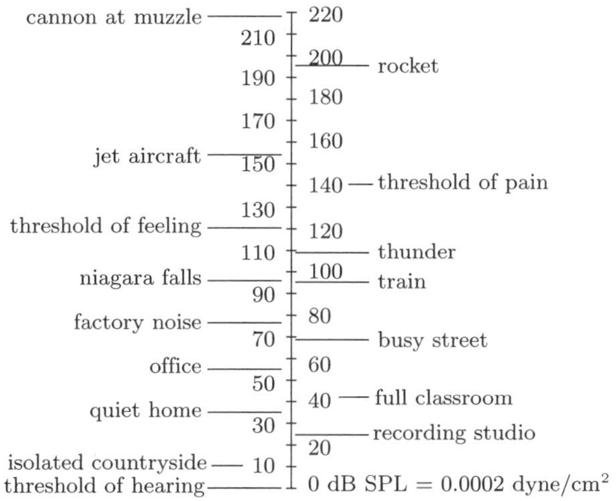

**Figure 6.1:** Common Sound Levels in dB PSL Units.

The zero reference level for dB SPL becomes 0.0002 dyne/cm$^2$, where the dyne, a small unit of force, is about 0.0010197 grams. Since a dyne equals $10^{-5}$ newtons and since 1 centimeter is 0.01 meter, that zero reference level (the threshold of hearing) equals 0.00002 newton/meter$^2$. Table 6.2 shows typical dB values in both units of power and SPL.

| watts | dB | pressure n/m$^2$ | dB SPL | source |
|---|---|---|---|---|
| 30000.0 | 165 | 2000.0 | 160 | jet |
| 300.0 | 145 | 200.0 | 140 | threshold of pain |
| 3.0 | 125 | 20.0 | 120 | factory noise |
| 0.03 | 105 | 2.0 | 100 | highway traffic |
| 0.0003 | 85 | 0.2 | 80 | appliance |
| 0.000003 | 65 | 0.02 | 60 | conversation |
| 0.00000003 | 45 | 0.002 | 40 | quiet room |
| 0.0000000003 | 25 | 0.0002 | 20 | whisper |
| 0.000000000001 | 0 | 0.00002 | 0 | threshold of hearing |

**Table 6.2:** Sound Levels in Power and Pressure Units.

The sensitivity of the human ear to sound level depends on the frequency. Experiments indicate that people are more sensitive to (and therefore more annoyed by) high-frequency sounds (which is why sirens have a high pitch). It is possible to modify the dB SPL system to make it more sensitive to high frequencies and less sensitive to low frequencies. This is called the dBA standard (ANSI standard S1.4-1983). There are also dBB and dBC standards of noise measurement. (Electrical engineers use also decibel standards called dBm, dBm0, and dBrn; see, for example, [Shenoi 95].)

Because of the use of logarithms, dB measures don't simply add up. If the first trumpeter starts playing his trumpet just before the concert, generating, say, a 70 dB noise level, and the second trombonist follows on his trombone, generating the same sound level, then the (poor) listeners hear twice the noise intensity, but this corresponds to just 73 dB, not 140 dB. To see this we notice that if

$$10 \log \left( \frac{P_1}{P_2} \right) = 70,$$

then

$$10 \log \left( \frac{2P_1}{P_2} \right) = 10 \left[ \log_{10} 2 + \log \left( \frac{P_1}{P_2} \right) \right] = 10(0.3 + 70/10) = 73.$$

Doubling the noise level increases the dB level by 3 (if SPL units are used, the 3 should be doubled to 6).

More information on sound, its properties, and its measurement can be found in [Shenoi 95].

## 6.2 Digital Audio

Much as an image can be digitized and broken up into pixels, where each pixel is a number, sound can also be digitized and broken up into numbers. When sound is played into a microphone, it is converted into a voltage that varies continuously with time. Figure 6.3 shows a typical example of sound that starts at zero and oscillates several times. Such voltage is the *analog* representation of the sound. Digitizing sound is done by measuring the voltage at many points in time, translating each measurement into a number, and writing the numbers on a file. This process is called *sampling*. The sound wave is sampled, and the samples become the digitized sound. The device used for sampling is called an analog-to-digital converter (ADC).

The difference between a sound wave and its samples can be compared to the difference between an analog clock, where the hands seem to move continuously, and a digital clock, where the display changes abruptly every second.

Since the sound samples are numbers, they are easy to edit. However, the main use of a sound file is to play it back. This is done by converting the numeric samples back into voltages that are continuously fed into a speaker. The device that does it is called a digital-to-analog converter (DAC). Intuitively, it is clear that a high sampling rate would result in better sound reproduction but also in many more samples and therefore bigger files. Thus, the main problem in sound sampling is how often to sample a given sound.

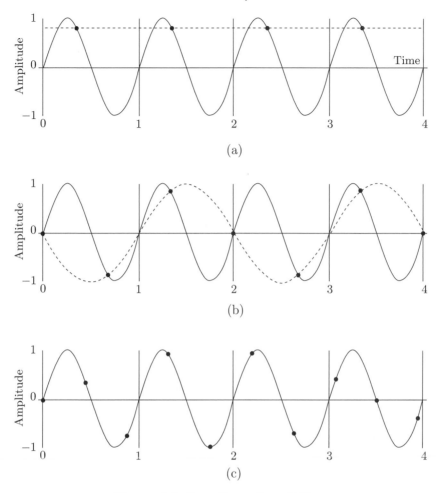

**Figure 6.3:** Sampling a Sound Wave.

Figure 6.3a shows what may happen if the sampling rate is too low. The sound wave in the figure is sampled four times, and all four samples happen to be identical. When these samples are used to play back the sound, the result is a uniform sound, resembling a buzz. Figure 6.3b shows seven samples, and they seem to "follow" the original wave fairly closely. Unfortunately, when they are used to reproduce the sound, they produce the dashed curve. There simply are not enough samples to reconstruct the original sound wave.

The solution to the sampling problem is to sample sound at a little over the *Nyquist rate*, which is twice the maximum frequency contained in the sound. Such a sampling rate guarantees true reproduction of the sound. This is illustrated in Figure 6.3c, which shows 10 equally-spaced samples taken over four periods. Notice that the samples do not have to be taken from the maxima or minima of the wave; they can come from any point.

The range of human hearing is typically from 16–20 Hz to 20,000–22,000 Hz, depending on the person and on age. When sound is digitized at high fidelity, it should therefore be sampled at a little over the Nyquist rate of $2 \times 22000 = 44000$ Hz. This is why high-quality digital sound is based on a 44,100 Hz sampling rate. Anything lower than this rate results in distortions, while higher sampling rates do not produce any improvement in the reconstruction (playback) of the sound. We can consider the sampling rate of 44,100 Hz a lowpass filter since it effectively removes all the frequencies above 22,000 Hz.

Many low-fidelity applications sample sound at 11,000 Hz, and the telephone system, originally designed for conversations, not for digital communications, samples sound at only 8 KHz. Thus, any frequency higher than 4000 Hz is distorted when sent over the phone, which is why it is hard to distinguish, on the phone, between the sounds of "f" and "s." This is also why, when someone gives you an address over the phone you should ask, "Is it H street, as in EFGH?" Often, the answer is, "No, it is Eighth street, as in sixth, seventh, eighth."

The second problem in sound sampling is the sample size. Each sample becomes a number, but how large should that number be? In practice, samples are normally either 8 or 16 bits, although some high-quality sound cards may optionally use 32-bit samples. Assuming that the highest voltage in a sound wave is 1 volt, an 8-bit sample can distinguish voltages as low as $1/256 \approx 0.004$ volt, or 4 millivolts (mv). A quiet sound, generating a wave lower than 2 mv, would be sampled as zero and played back as silence. In contrast, a 16-bit sample can distinguish sounds as low as $1/65,536 \approx 15$ microvolt ($\mu$v). We can think of the sample size as a quantization of the original audio data. Eight-bit samples are more coarsely quantized than 16-bit ones. As a result, they produce better compression but poorer reconstruction (the reconstructed sound has only 256 levels).

Audio sampling is also called *pulse code modulation* (PCM). We have all heard of AM and FM radio. These terms stand for *amplitude modulation* and *frequency modulation*, respectively. They indicate methods to modulate (i.e., to include binary information in) continuous waves. The term *pulse modulation* refers to techniques for converting a continuous wave to a file of binary numbers. There are several pulse modulation methods including pulse amplitude modulation (PAM), pulse position modulation (PPM), pulse width modulation (PWM), and pulse number modulation (PNM). [Pohlmann 85] is a good source of information on these methods. In practice, however, PCM has proved the most effective form of converting sound waves to numbers. When stereo sound is digitized, the PCM encoder multiplexes the left and right sound samples. Thus, stereo sound sampled at 22,000 Hz with 16-bit samples generates 44,000 16-bit samples per second for a total of 704,000 bits/s, or 88,000 bytes/s.

## 6.3 The Human Auditory System

The human ear is sensitive to frequencies from about 20 Hz to about 20,000 Hz, but its sensitivity is not uniform. It depends on the frequency of the sound, and experiments indicate that in a quiet environment the ear's sensitivity is maximal for frequencies in the range 2 KHz to 4 KHz. Figure 6.4a shows the *hearing threshold* for a quiet environment.

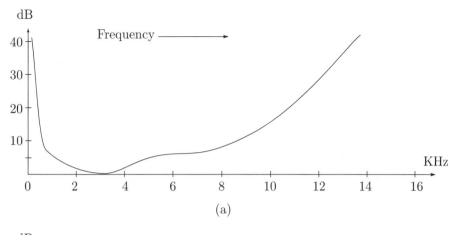

(a)

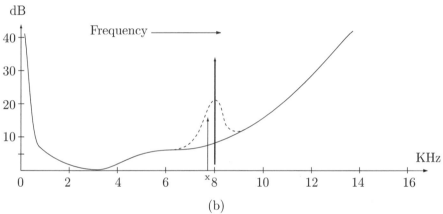

(b)

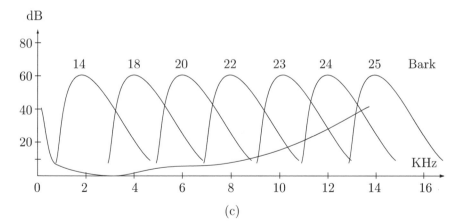

(c)

**Figure 6.4:** Threshold and Masking of Sound.

It should also be noted that the range of the human voice is much more limited. It is only from about 500 Hz to about 2 KHz.

The existence of the hearing threshold suggests an approach to lossy audio compression. Just delete any audio samples that are below the threshold. Since the threshold depends on the frequency, the encoder needs to know the frequency spectrum of the sound being compressed at any time. The encoder therefore has to save several of the previously input audio samples at any time ($n-1$ samples, where $n$ is either a constant or a user-controlled parameter). When the current sample is input, the first step is to transform the $n$ samples to the frequency domain. The result is a number $m$ of values (called *signals*) that indicate the strength of the sound at $m$ different frequencies. If a signal for frequency $f$ is smaller than the hearing threshold at $f$, it (the signal) should be deleted.

In addition to this, two more properties of the human hearing system are used in audio compression. They are *frequency masking* and *temporal masking*.

Frequency masking (also known as *auditory masking*) occurs when a sound that we can normally hear (because it is loud enough) is masked by another sound with a nearby frequency. The thick arrow in Figure 6.4b represents a strong sound source at 800 KHz. This source raises the normal threshold in its vicinity (the dashed curve), with the result that the nearby sound represented by the arrow at "x," a sound that would normally be audible because it is above the threshold, is now masked and is inaudible. A good lossy audio compression method should identify this case and delete the signals corresponding to sound "x," since it cannot be heard anyway. This is one way to lossily compress sound.

The frequency masking (the width of the dashed curve of Figure 6.4b) depends on the frequency. It varies from about 100 Hz for the lowest audible frequencies to more than 4 KHz for the highest. The range of audible frequencies can therefore be partitioned into a number of *critical bands* that indicate the declining sensitivity of the ear (rather, its declining resolving power) for higher frequencies. We can think of the critical bands as a measure similar to frequency. However, in contrast to frequency, which is absolute and has nothing to do with human hearing, the critical bands are determined according to the sound perception of the ear. Thus, they constitute a perceptually uniform measure of frequency. Table 6.5 lists 27 approximate critical bands.

| band | range | band | range | band | range |
|------|-------|------|-------|------|-------|
| 0 | 0–50 | 9 | 800–940 | 18 | 3280–3840 |
| 1 | 50–95 | 10 | 940–1125 | 19 | 3840–4690 |
| 2 | 95–140 | 11 | 1125–1265 | 20 | 4690–5440 |
| 3 | 140–235 | 12 | 1265–1500 | 21 | 5440–6375 |
| 4 | 235–330 | 13 | 1500–1735 | 22 | 6375–7690 |
| 5 | 330–420 | 14 | 1735–1970 | 23 | 7690–9375 |
| 6 | 420–560 | 15 | 1970–2340 | 24 | 9375–11625 |
| 7 | 560–660 | 16 | 2340–2720 | 25 | 11625–15375 |
| 8 | 660–800 | 17 | 2720–3280 | 26 | 15375–20250 |

**Table 6.5:** Twenty-Seven Approximate Critical Bands.

Another way to describe critical bands is to say that because of the ear's limited perception of frequencies, the threshold at a frequency $f$ is raised by a nearby sound only if the sound is within the critical band of $f$. This also points the way to designing a practical lossy compression algorithm. The audio signal should first be transformed into its frequency domain, and the resulting values (the frequency spectrum) should be divided into subbands that resemble the critical bands as much as possible. Once this is done, the signals in each subband should be quantized such that the quantization noise (the difference between the original sound sample and its quantized value) should be inaudible.

Yet another way to look at the concept of critical band is to consider the human auditory system a filter that lets through only frequencies in the range (bandpass) of 20 Hz to 20000 Hz. We visualize the ear–brain system as a collection of filters, each with a different bandpass. The bandpasses are called critical bands. They overlap and they have different widths. They are narrow (about 100 Hz) at low frequencies and become wider (to about 4–5 KHz) at high frequencies.

The width of a critical band is called its size. The widths of the critical bands introduce a new unit, the *Bark* (after H. G. Barkhausen) such that one Bark is the width (in Hz) of one critical band. The Bark is defined as

$$1 \text{ Bark} = \begin{cases} \frac{f}{100} & \text{for frequencies } f < 500 \text{ Hz,} \\ 9 + 4\log\left(\frac{f}{1000}\right) & \text{for frequencies } f \geq 500 \text{ Hz.} \end{cases}$$

Figure 6.4c shows some critical bands, with Barks between 14 and 25, positioned above the threshold.

Temporal masking may occur when a strong sound $A$ of frequency $f$ is preceded or followed in time by a weaker sound $B$ at a nearby (or the same) frequency. If the time interval between the sounds is short, sound $B$ may not be audible. Figure 6.6 illustrates an example of temporal masking. The threshold of temporal masking due to a loud sound at time 0 goes down, first sharply, then slowly. A weaker sound of 30 dB will not be audible if it occurs 10 ms before or after the loud sound but will be audible if the time interval between the sounds is 20 ms.

## 6.4 Conventional Methods

Conventional compression methods, such as RLE, statistical, and dictionary-based methods, can be used to losslessly compress sound files, but the results depend heavily on the specific sound. Some sounds may compress well with RLE but not with a statistical method. Other sounds may lend themselves to statistical compression but may expand when processed by a dictionary method. Here is how sounds respond to each of the three classes of compression methods.

RLE may work well when the sound contains long runs of identical samples. With 8-bit samples this may be common. Recall that the difference between the two 8-bit samples $n$ and $n + 1$ is about 4 mv. A few seconds of uniform music, where the wave does not oscillate more than 4 mv, may produce a run of thousands of identical samples. With 16-bit samples, long runs may be rare and RLE, consequently, ineffective.

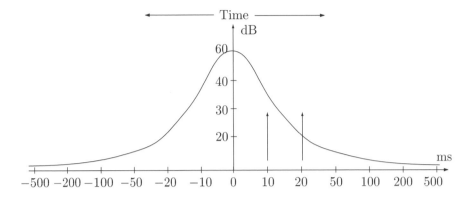

**Figure 6.6:** Threshold and Masking of Sound.

Statistical methods assign variable-size codes to the samples according to their frequency of occurrence. With 8-bit samples, there are only 256 different samples, so in a large sound file, the samples may sometimes have a flat distribution. Such a file will therefore not respond well to Huffman coding. With 16-bit samples there are more than 65,000 possible samples, so they may sometimes feature skewed probabilities (i.e., some samples may occur very often, while others may be rare). Such a file may therefore compress better with arithmetic coding, which works well even for skewed probabilities.

Dictionary-based methods expect to find the same phrases again and again in the data. This happens with text, where certain strings may repeat often. Sound, however, is an analog signal and the particular samples generated depend on the precise way the ADC works. With 8-bit samples, for example, a wave of 8 mv becomes a sample of size 2, but waves very close to that, say, 7.6 mv or 8.5 mv, may become samples of different sizes. This is why parts of speech that sound the same to us and should therefore have become identical phrases may end up being digitized slightly differently and go into the dictionary as different phrases, thereby reducing compression performance. Dictionary-based methods are thus not very well suited for sound compression.

It is possible to get better sound compression by developing lossy methods that take advantage of our perception of sound and discard data to which the human ear is not sensitive. This is similar to lossy image compression, where data to which the human eye is not sensitive is discarded. In both cases we use the fact that the original information (image or sound) is analog and has already lost some quality when digitized. Losing some more data, if done carefully, may not significantly affect the played-back sound and may therefore be indistinguishable from the original. We briefly describe two approaches, *silence compression* and *companding*.

The principle of silence compression is to treat small samples as if they were silence (i.e., as samples of zero). This generates run lengths of zero, so silence compression is actually a variant of RLE, suitable for sound compression. This method uses the fact that some people have less sensitive hearing than others and will tolerate the loss of sound that is so quiet they may not hear it anyway. Audio files containing long periods of low-volume sound will respond to silence compression better than other files with high-volume sound. This method requires a user-controlled parameter that specifies the largest sample that should be suppressed. Two other parameters are also necessary, although they may not have to be user-controlled. One specifies the shortest run length of small samples, typically 2 or 3. The other specifies the minimum number of consecutive large samples that should terminate a run of silence. For example, a run of 15 small samples followed by 2 large samples followed by 13 small samples may be considered one silence run of 30 samples, whereas the similar sequence 15, 3, 13 may become two distinct silence runs of 15 and 13 samples, with nonsilence in between.

Companding (short for "compressing/expanding") uses the fact that the ear requires more precise samples at low amplitudes (soft sounds) but is more forgiving at higher amplitudes. A typical ADC used in sound cards for personal computers converts voltages to numbers linearly. If an amplitude $a$ is converted to the number $n$, then amplitude $2a$ will be converted to the number $2n$. A compression method using companding examines every sample in the sound file and uses a nonlinear formula to reduce the number of bits devoted to it. For 16-bit samples, for example, a companding encoder may use a formula as simple as

$$\text{Mapped} = 32767 \left( 2^{\frac{\text{sample}}{65536}} - 1 \right) \qquad (6.1)$$

to reduce each sample. This formula maps the 16-bit samples nonlinearly to 15-bit numbers (i.e., numbers in the range [0, 32767]) such that small samples are less affected than large ones. Table 6.7 illustrates the nonlinearity of this mapping. It shows eight pairs of samples, where the two samples in each pair differ by 100. The two samples of the first pair are mapped to numbers that differ by 34, whereas the two samples of the last pair are mapped to numbers that differ by 65. The mapped 15-bit numbers can be decoded back into the original 16-bit samples by the inverse formula

$$\text{Sample} = 65536 \log_2 \left( 1 + \frac{\text{mapped}}{32767} \right). \qquad (6.2)$$

| sample | mapped | diff | sample | mapped | diff |
|---|---|---|---|---|---|
| 100 → | 35 | | 30000 → | 12236 | |
| 200 → | 69 | 34 | 30100 → | 12283 | 47 |
| 1000 → | 348 | | 40000 → | 17256 | |
| 1100 → | 383 | 35 | 40100 → | 17309 | 53 |
| 10000 → | 3656 | | 50000 → | 22837 | |
| 10100 → | 3694 | 38 | 50100 → | 22896 | 59 |
| 20000 → | 7719 | | 60000 → | 29040 | |
| 20100 → | 7762 | 43 | 60100 → | 29105 | 65 |

Table 6.7: 16-Bit Samples Mapped to 15-Bit Numbers.

Reducing 16-bit numbers to 15 bits doesn't produce much compression. Better compression can be achieved by substituting a smaller number for 32,767 in equations (6.1) and (6.2). A value of 127, for example, would map each 16-bit sample into an 8-bit one, producing a compression ratio of 0.5. However, decoding would be less accurate. A 16-bit sample of 60,100, for example, would be mapped into the 8-bit number 113, but this number would produce 60,172 when decoded by Equation (6.2). Even worse, the small 16-bit sample 1000 would be mapped into 1.35, which has to be rounded to 1. When Equation (6.2) is used to decode a 1, it produces 742, significantly different from the original sample. The amount of compression should thus be a user-controlled parameter, and this is an interesting example of a compression method where the compression ratio is known in advance.

In practice, there is no need to go through Equations (6.1) and (6.2), since the mapping of all the samples can be prepared in advance in a table. Both encoding and decoding are therefore fast.

Companding is not limited to Equations (6.1) and (6.2). More sophisticated methods, such as $\mu$-law and A-law, are commonly used and have been made into international standards.

## 6.5 MPEG-1 Audio Layers

The MPEG-1 movie compression standard consists of two main parts, video and audio compression. This section discusses the audio compression principles of MPEG-1, specifically, its third layer, popularly known as MP3. Readers are advised to read the first part of this chapter before trying to tackle this material.

The formal name of MPEG-1 is *the international standard for moving picture video compression, IS 11172*. It consists of five parts, of which part 3 [ISO/IEC 93] is the definition of the audio compression algorithm. Like other standards developed by ITU and ISO, the document describing MPEG-1 has *normative* and *informative* sections. A normative section is part of the standard specification. It is intended for implementers, it is written in a precise language, and it should be strictly followed in implementing the standard on actual computer platforms. An informative section, on the other hand, illustrates concepts discussed elsewhere, explains the reasons that led to certain choices and decisions, and contains background material.

An example of a normative section is the tables of the various parameters and of the Huffman codes used by the MPEG audio standard. An example of an informative section is the algorithm used by MPEG audio to implement a psychoacoustic model. MPEG does not require the use of any particular algorithm, and an MPEG encoder is free to use any method to implement the model. The section itself simply describes various alternatives.

The MPEG-1 audio standard specifies three compression methods called *layers* and designated I, II, and III. All three layers are part of the MPEG-1 standard but only layer III is discussed here. A movie compressed by MPEG-1 uses only one layer, and the layer number is specified in the compressed file. Any of the layers can be used to compress an audio file without any video. The functional modules of the lower layers are also used by the higher layers, but the higher layers have additional features that result in better compression. An interesting aspect of the design of the standard is that the layers form a hierarchy in the sense that a layer-III decoder can also decode audio files compressed by layers I or II.

The result of having three layers was an increasing popularity of layer III. The encoder is extremely complex, but it produces excellent compression, and this, combined with the fact that the decoder is much simpler, produced in the late 1990s an explosion of what is popularly known as MP3 sound files. It is easy to obtain a layer-III decoder and much music that's already encoded in layer III. So far, this has been a tremendous success of the audio part of the MPEG project.

The MPEG audio standard [ISO/IEC 93] starts with the normative description of the format of the compressed file for each of the three layers. It follows with a normative description of the decoder. The description of the encoder (it is different for the three layers) and of two psychoacoustic models follows and is informative; any encoder that generates a correct compressed file is a valid MPEG encoder. There are appendices (annexes) discussing related topics such as error protection.

In contrast with MPEG video, where many information sources are available, there is relatively little in the technical literature about MPEG audio. In addition to the references in the next paragraph, the reader is referred to the MPEG consortium [MPEG 00]. This site contains lists of other resources and is updated from time to time. Another resource is the Association of Audio Engineers (AES). Most of the ideas and techniques used in the MPEG audio standard (and also in other audio compression methods) were originally published in the many conference proceedings of this organization. Notice, however, that these are not freely available and have to be obtained from the AES.

For more information and details on the three layers see [Brandenburg and Stoll 94], [ISO/IEC 93], [Pan 95], [Rao and Hwang 96], and [Shlien 94].

When a movie is digitized, the audio part may many times consist of two sound tracks (stereo sound), each sampled at 44.1 KHz with 16-bit samples. The audio data rate is therefore $2 \times 44,100 \times 16 = 1,411,200$ bits/s, close to 1.5 Mbits/s. In addition to the 44.1 KHz sampling rate, the MPEG standard allows sampling rates of 32 KHz and 48 KHz. An important feature of MPEG audio is its compression ratio, which the standard specifies in advance! The standard calls for a compressed file with one of several bitrates ranging from 32 to 224 Kbits/s per audio channel (there normally are two channels, for stereo sound). Depending on the original sampling rate, these bitrates translate to compression factors of from 2.7 (low) to 24 (impressive)! The reason for specifying the bitrates of the compressed file is that the file also includes compressed data for the video and system parts.

The principle of MPEG audio compression is quantization. The values being quantized, however, are not the audio samples but numbers (called signals) taken from the frequency domain of the sound (this is discussed in the next paragraph). The fact that the compression ratio (or equivalently, the bitrate) is known to the encoder means that the encoder knows at any time how many bits it can allocate to the quantized signals. Thus, the (adaptive) *bit allocation algorithm* is an important part of the encoder. This algorithm uses the known bitrate and the frequency spectrum of the most recent audio samples to determine the size of the quantized signals such that the quantization noise (the difference between an original signal and a quantized one) will be inaudible (i.e., will be below the *masked threshold*, a concept discussed in Section 6.3).

The psychoacoustic models use the frequency of the sound that is being compressed, but the input file contains audio samples, not sound frequencies. The frequencies have to be computed from the samples. This is why the first step in MPEG audio encoding is a discrete Fourier transform, where a set of 512 consecutive audio samples is transformed to the frequency domain. Since the number of frequencies can be huge, they are grouped into 32 equal-width frequency subbands. For each subband, a number is obtained that indicates the intensity of the sound at that subband's frequency range. These numbers (called *signals*) are then quantized. The coarseness of the quantization in each subband is determined by the masking threshold in the subband and by the number of bits still available to the encoder. The masking threshold is computed for each subband using a psychoacoustic model.

MPEG uses two psychoacoustic models to implement frequency masking and temporal masking. Each model describes how loud sound masks other sounds that happen to be close to it in frequency or in time. The model partitions the frequency range into 24 critical bands and specifies how masking effects apply within each band. The masking effects depend, of course, on the frequencies and amplitudes of the tones. When the sound is decompressed and played, the user (listener) may select any playback amplitude, which is why the psychoacoustic model has to be designed for the worst case. The masking effects also depend on the nature of the source of the sound being compressed. The source may be tone-like or noise-like. The two psychoacoustic models used by MPEG are based on experimental work done by researchers over many years.

The decoder must be fast, since it may have to decode the entire movie (video and audio) in real time, so it must be simple. As a result it does not use any psychoacoustic model or bit allocation algorithm. The compressed file must therefore contain all the information the decoder needs for dequantizing the signals. This information (the size of the quantized signals) must be written by the encoder on the compressed file, and it constitutes overhead that should be subtracted from the number of remaining available bits.

Figure 6.8 is a block diagram of the main components of the MPEG audio encoder and decoder. The ancillary data is user-definable and would normally consist of information related to specific applications. This data is optional.

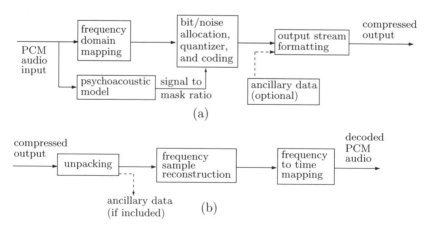

**Figure 6.8:** MPEG Audio Encoder (a) and Decoder (b).

### 6.5.1 Frequency Domain Coding

The first step in encoding the audio samples is to transform them from the time domain to the frequency domain. This is done by a bank of *polyphase filters* that transform the samples into 32 equal-width frequency subbands. The filters were designed to provide fast operation combined with good time and frequency resolutions. As a result, their design involved three compromises.

The first compromise is the equal widths of the 32 frequency bands. This simplifies the filters but is in contrast to the behavior of the human auditory system, whose sensitivity is frequency-dependent. Ideally, the filters should divide the input into the critical bands discussed in Section 6.3. These bands are formed such that the perceived loudness of a given sound and its audibility in the presence of another, masking, sound are consistent within a critical band, but different across these bands. Unfortunately, each of the low-frequency subbands overlaps several critical bands, with the result that the bit allocation algorithm cannot optimize the number of bits allocated to the quantized signal in those subbands. When several critical bands are covered by a subband X, the bit allocation algorithm selects the critical band with the least noise masking and uses that critical band to compute the number of bits allocated to the quantized signals in subband X.

The second compromise involves the inverse filter bank, the one used by the decoder. The original time-to-frequency transformation involves loss of information (even before any quantization). The inverse filter bank therefore receives data that is slightly bad and uses it to perform the inverse frequency-to-time transformation, resulting in more distortions. Therefore, the design of the two filter banks (for direct and inverse transformations) had to use compromises to minimize this loss of information.

The third compromise has to do with the individual filters. Adjacent filters should ideally pass different frequency ranges. In practice, they have considerable frequency overlap. Sound of a single, pure frequency can therefore penetrate through two filters and produce signals (that are later quantized) in two of the 32 subbands instead of in just one subband.

The polyphase filter bank uses (in addition to other intermediate data structures) a buffer $X$ with room for 512 input samples. The buffer is a FIFO queue and always contains the most recent 512 samples input. Figure 6.9 shows the five main steps of the polyphase filtering algorithm.

The next 32 audio samples read from the input are shifted into the buffer. Thus, the buffer always holds the 512 most recent audio samples. The signals $S_t[i]$ for the 32 subbands are computed by

$$S_t[i] = \sum_{k=0}^{63} \sum_{j=0}^{7} M_{i,k}\big(C[k+64j] \times X[k+64j]\big), \ i = 0, \ldots, 31. \qquad (6.3)$$

The notation $S_t[i]$ stands for the signal of subband $i$ at time $t$. Vector $C$ contains 512 coefficients of the analysis window and is fully specified by the standard. $M$ is the

1. Shift in 32 new input samples into FIFO buffer $X$

2. Window samples: $Z_i = C_i \times X_i$, for $i = 0, 1, \ldots, 511$

3. Partial computation: $Y_i = \sum_{j=0}^{7} Z_{i+64j}$, for $i = 0, 1, \ldots, 63$

4. Compute 32 signals: $S_i = \sum_{k=0}^{63} M_{i,k} \times Y_k$, for $i = 0, 1, \ldots, 31$

5. Output the 32 subband signals $S_i$

**Figure 6.9:** Polyphase Filter Bank.

analysis matrix defined by

$$M_{i,k} = \cos\left(\frac{(2i+1)(k-16)\pi}{64}\right), \; i = 0, \ldots, 31, \; k = 0, \ldots, 63. \tag{6.4}$$

Notice that the expression in parentheses in Equation (6.3) does not depend on $i$, while $M_{i,k}$ in Equation (6.4) does not depend on $j$. (This matrix is a modified version of the well-known DCT, so it is called the MDCT matrix.) This feature is a compromise that results in fewer arithmetic operations. In fact, the 32 signals $S_t[i]$ are computed by only $512 + 32 \times 64 = 2560$ multiplications and $64 \times 7 + 32 \times 63 = 2464$ additions, which come to about 80 multiplications and 80 additions per signal. Another point worth mentioning is the decimation of samples (Section 4.4). The entire filter bank produces 32 output signals for 32 input samples. Since each of the 32 filters produces 32 signals, its output has to be decimated, retaining only one signal per filter.

Figure 6.10 illustrates graphically the operations performed by the encoder and decoder during the polyphase filtering step. Part (a) of the figure shows how the $X$ buffer holds 64 segments of 32 audio samples each. The buffer is shifted one segment to the right before the next segment of 32 new samples is read from the input file and is entered on the left. After multiplying the $X$ buffer by the coefficients of the $C$ window, the products are moved to the $Z$ vector. The contents of this vector are partitioned into segments of 64 numbers each, and the segments are added. The result is vector $Y$, which is multiplied by the MDCT matrix, to produce the final vector of 32 subband signals.

Part (b) of the figure illustrates the operations performed by the decoder. A group of 32 subband signals is multiplied by the IMDCT matrix $N_{i,k}$ to produce the $V$ vector, consisting of two segments of 32 values each. The two segments are shifted into the $V$ FIFO buffer from the left. The $V$ buffer has room for the last 16 V vectors (i.e., $16 \times 64$, or 1024, values). A new 512-entry $U$ vector is created from 32 alternate segments in the $V$ buffer, as shown. The $U$ vector is multiplied by the 512 coefficients $D_i$ of the synthesis window (similar to the $C_i$ coefficients of the analysis window used by the encoder), to

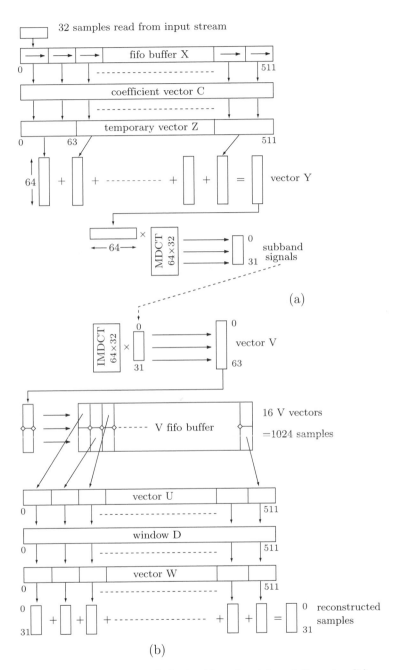

**Figure 6.10:** MPEG Audio Encoder (a) and Decoder (b).

create the $W$ vector. This vector is divided into 16 segments of 32 values each and the segments added. The result is 32 reconstructed audio samples. Figure 6.11 is a flowchart illustrating this process. The IMDCT synthesis matrix $N_{i,k}$ is given by

$$N_{i,k} = \cos\left(\frac{(2k+1)(i+16)\pi}{64}\right), \ i = 0, \ldots, 63, \ k = 0, \ldots, 31.$$

> 1. Input 32 new signals $S_i$, for $i = 0, \ldots, 31$

> 2. Shift* the FIFO buffer $V_i = V_{i-64}$, $i = 1023, \ldots, 64$

> 3. Multiply $V_i = \sum_{k=0}^{31} N_{ik}S_k$, $i = 0, \ldots, 63$

> 4. Construct 512 values in vector $U$
> for $i = 0$ to 7 do
> for $j = 0$ to 31 do
> $U_{j+64i} = V_{j+128i}$
> $U_{32+j+64i} = V_{96+j+128i}$

> 5. Construct $W$. For $i = 0$ to 511 do, $W_i = U_i \times D_i$

> 6. Compute 32 samples. For $j = 0$ to 31 do, $S_j = \sum_{i=0}^{15} W_{j+32i}$

> 7. Output the 32 audio samples $S_j$

> * $V$ is initialized to all zeros at startup.

**Figure 6.11:** Reconstructing Audio Samples.

The subband signals computed by the filtering stage of the encoder are collected and packaged into *frames* containing 1152 signals each. The signals in a frame are then scaled and quantized according to the psychoacoustic model used by the encoder and the bit allocation algorithm. The quantized values, together with the scale factors and quantization information (the number of quantization levels in each subband) are written on the compressed file (Huffman codes are also used to encode the quantized values even further).

### 6.5.2 Format of Compressed Data

Each frame consists of 36 signals per subband, for a total of 1152 signals. The signals in the frame are quantized (this is how compression is achieved) and written on the compressed file together with other information.

Each frame written on the output starts with a 32-bit header whose format is identical for the three layers. The header contains a synchronization code (12 1-bits) and 20 bits of coding parameters listed below. If error protection is used, the header is immediately followed by a 16-bit CRC check word. Next comes a frame of the quantized signals, followed by an (optional) ancillary data block. The formats of the last two items depend on the layer.

The synchronization code is used by the decoder to verify that what it is reading is, in fact, the header. This code is a string of 12 bits of 1, so the entire format of the compressed file had to be designed to avoid an accidental occurrence of a string of 12 ones elsewhere.

The remaining 20 bits of the header are divided into 12 fields as follows:

Field 1. An ID bit whose value is 1 (this indicates that MPEG is used). A value of zero is reserved and is currently unused.

Field 2. Two bits to indicate the layer number. Valid values are 11—layer I, 10—layer II, and 01—layer III. The value 00 is reserved.

Field 3. An error protection indicator bit. A value of zero indicates that redundancy has been added to the compressed file to help in error detection.

Field 4. Four bits to indicate the bitrate. A zero index indicates a "fixed" bitrate, where a frame may contain an extra slot, depending on the padding bit (field 6).

Field 5. Two bits to indicate one of three sampling frequencies. The three values are 00—44.1 KHz, 01—48 KHz, and 10—32 KHz. The value 11 is reserved.

Field 6. One bit to indicate whether padding is used. Padding may add a slot (slots are not discussed here) to the compressed file after a certain number of frames, to make sure that the total size of the frames either equals or is slightly less than the sum

$$\sum_{\text{first frame}}^{\text{current frame}} \frac{\text{frame-size} \times \text{bitrate}}{\text{sampling frequency}},$$

where frame-size is 384 signals for layer I and 1152 signals for layers II and III. The following algorithm may be used by the encoder to determine whether or not padding is necessary.

```
for first audio frame:
  rest:=0;
  padding:=no;
for each subsequent audio frame:
  if layer=I
     then dif:=(12 × bitrate) modulo (sampling-frequency)
     else dif:=(144 × bitrate) modulo (sampling-frequency);
  rest:=rest−dif;
  if rest<0 then
     padding:=yes;
     rest:=rest+(sampling-frequency)
  else padding:=no;
```

This algorithm has a simple interpretation. A frame is divided into $N$ or $N + 1$ slots, where $N$ depends on the layer. For layer I, $N$ is given by

$$N = 12 \times \frac{\text{bitrate}}{\text{sampling frequency}}.$$

For layers II and II, it is given by

$$N = 144 \times \frac{\text{bitrate}}{\text{sampling frequency}}.$$

If this does not produce an integer, the result is truncated and padding is used.

Field 7. One bit for private use of the encoder. This bit will not be used by ISO/IEC in the future.

Field 8. A two-bit stereo mode field. Values are 00—stereo, 01—joint-stereo (intensity-stereo and/or ms-stereo), 10—dual-channel, and 11—single-channel.

Stereo information is encoded in one of four modes: stereo, dual channel, joint stereo, and ms-stereo. In the first two modes, samples from the two stereo channels are compressed and written on the output. The encoder does not check for any correlations between the two. The stereo mode is used to compress the left and right stereo channels, while the dual channel mode is used to compress different sets of audio samples, such as a bilingual broadcast. The joint stereo mode exploits redundancies between the left and right channels, since many times they are identical, similar, or differ by a small time lag. The ms-stereo mode ("ms" stands for "middle side") is a special case of joint stereo, where two signals, a middle value $M_i$ and a side value $S_i$, are encoded instead of the left and right audio channels $L_i$ and $R_i$. The middle-side values are computed by the following sum and difference:

$$L_i = \frac{M_i + S_i}{\sqrt{2}}, \text{ and } R_i = \frac{M_i - S_i}{\sqrt{2}}.$$

Field 9. A two-bit mode extension field. This is used in the joint-stereo mode. In layers I and II the bits indicate which subbands are in intensity-stereo. All other subbands are coded in "stereo" mode. The four values are:

00—subbands 4–31 in intensity stereo, bound = 4.
01—subbands 8–31 in intensity stereo, bound = 8.
10—subbands 12–31 in intensity stereo, bound = 12.
11—subbands 16–31 in intensity stereo, bound = 16.

In layer III these bits indicate which type of joint stereo coding method is applied. The values are

00—intensity stereo off, ms stereo off.
01—intensity stereo on, ms stereo off.
10—intensity stereo off, ms stereo on.
11—intensity stereo on, ms stereo on.

Field 10. Copyright bit. If the compressed file is copyright protected, this bit should be 1.

Field 11. One bit indicating original/copy. A value of 1 indicates an original compressed file.

Field 12. A two-bit emphasis field. This indicates the type of deemphasis that is used. The values are 00—none, 01—50/15 microseconds, 10—reserved, and 11 indicates CCITT J.17 deemphasis.

### 6.5.3 Psychoacoustic Models

The task of a psychoacoustic model is to make it possible for the encoder to easily decide how much quantization noise to allow in each subband. This information is then used by the bit allocation algorithm, together with the number of available bits, to determine the number of quantization levels for each subband. The MPEG audio standard specifies two psychoacoustic models. Either model can be used with any layer, but only model II generates the specific information needed by layer III. In practice, model I is the only one used in layers I and II. Layer III can use either model, but it achieves better results when using model II.

The MPEG standard allows considerable freedom in the way the models are implemented. The sophistication of the model that is actually implemented in a given MPEG audio encoder depends on the desired compression factor. For consumer applications, where large compression factors are not critical, the psychoacoustic model can be completely eliminated. In such a case, the bit allocation algorithm does not use an SMR (signal to mask ratio). It simply assigns bits to the subband with the minimum SNR (signal to noise ratio).

A complete description of the models is outside the scope of this book and can be found in the text of the MPEG audio standard [ISO/IEC 93], pp. 109–139. The main steps of the two models are as follows:

1. A Fourier transform is used to convert the original audio samples to their frequency domain. This transform is separate and different from the polyphase filters because the models need finer frequency resolution in order to accurately determine the masking threshold.

2. The resulting frequencies are grouped into critical bands, not into the same 32 subbands used by the main part of the encoder.

3. The spectral values of the critical bands are separated into tonal (sinusoid-like) and nontonal (noise-like) components.

4. Before the noise masking thresholds for the different critical bands can be determined, the model applies a masking function to the signals in the different critical bands. This function has been determined empirically, by experimentation.

5. The model computes a masking threshold for each subband.

6. The SMR (signal to mask ratio) is calculated for each subband. It is the signal energy in the subband divided by the minimum masking threshold for the subband. The set of 32 SMRs, one per subband, constitutes the output of the model.

### 6.5.4 Encoding: Layer III

Layer III uses a much more refined and complex algorithm than the first two layers. This is reflected in the compression factors, which are much higher. The difference between layer III and layers I and II starts at the very first step, filtering. The same polyphase filter bank is used, but is followed by a modified version of the discrete cosine transform. The MDCT corrects some of the errors introduced by the polyphase filters and also subdivides the subbands to bring them closer to the critical bands. The layer III decoder has to use the inverse MDCT, so it has to work harder. The MDCT can be performed on either a short block of 12 samples (resulting in six transform coefficients) or a long block of 36 samples (resulting in 18 transform coefficients). Regardless of the block size chosen, consecutive blocks transformed by the MDCT have considerable overlap, as shown in Figure 6.12. In this figure, the blocks are shown above the thick line, and the resulting groups of 18 or 6 coefficients are below the line. The long blocks produce better frequency spectrum for stationary sound (sound where adjacent samples don't differ much), while the short blocks are preferable when the sound varies often.

The MDCT uses $n$ input samples $x_k$ (where $n$ is either 36 or 12) to obtain $n/2$ (i.e., 18 or 6) transform coefficients $S_i$. The transform and its inverse are given by

$$S_i = \sum_{k=0}^{n-1} x_k \cos\left(\frac{\pi}{2n}\left[2k+1+\frac{n}{2}\right](2i+1)\right), \; i = 0, 1, \ldots, \frac{n}{2}-1,$$

$$x_k = \sum_{i=0}^{n/2-1} S_i \cos\left(\frac{\pi}{2n}\left[2k+1+\frac{n}{2}\right](2i+1)\right), \; k = 0, 1, \ldots, n-1.$$

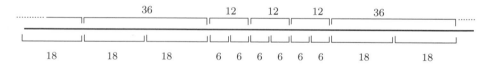

**Figure 6.12:** Overlapping MDCT Windows.

The size of a short block is one-third that of a long block, so they can be mixed. When a frame is constructed, the MDCT can use all long blocks, all short blocks (three times as many), or long blocks for the two lowest-frequency subbands and short blocks for the remaining 30 subbands. This is a compromise where the long blocks provide finer frequency resolution for the lower frequencies, where it is most useful, and the short blocks maintain better time resolution for the high frequencies.

Since the MDCT provides better frequency resolution, it has to result in poorer time resolution because of the uncertainty principle [Salomon 00]. What happens in practice is that the quantization of the MDCT coefficients causes errors that are spread over time and cause audible distortions that manifest themselves as preechoes (read: "pre-echoes").

The psychoacoustic model used by layer III has extra features that detect conditions for preechoes. In such cases, layer III uses a complex bit allocation algorithm that borrows bits from the pool of available bits in order to temporarily increase the number of quantization levels and thus reduce preechoes. Layer III can also switch to short MDCT blocks, thereby reducing the size of the time window, if it "suspects" that conditions are favorable for preechoes.

(The layer-III psychoacoustic model calculates a quantity called "psychoacoustic entropy" (PE) and the layer-III encoder "suspects" that conditions are favorable for preechoes if PE > 1800.)

The MDCT coefficients go through some processing to remove artifacts caused by the frequency overlap of the 32 subbands. This is called *aliasing reduction*. Only the long blocks are sent to the aliasing reduction procedure. The MDCT uses 36 input samples to compute 18 coefficients, and the aliasing reduction procedure uses a butterfly operation between two sets of 18 coefficients. This operation is illustrated graphically in Figure 6.13a with a C-language code shown in Figure 6.13b. Index $i$ in the figure is the distance from the last line of the previous block to the first line of the current block. Eight butterflies are computed, with different values of the weights $cs_i$ and $ca_i$ that are given by

$$cs_i = \frac{1}{\sqrt{1 + c_i^2}}, \quad ca_i = \frac{c_i}{\sqrt{1 + c_i^2}}, \quad i = 0, 1, \ldots, 7.$$

The eight $c_i$ values specified by the standard are $-0.6$, $-0.535$, $-0.33$, $-0.185$, $-0.095$, $-0.041$, $-0.0142$, and $-0.0037$. Figures 6.13c,d show the details of a single butterfly for the encoder and decoder, respectively.

Quantization in layer III is nonuniform. The quantizer raises the values to be quantized to $3/4$ power before quantization. This provides a more consistent SNR. The decoder reverses this operation by dequantizing a value and raising it to $4/3$ power. The quantization is done by

$$is(i) = \text{nint}\left[\left(\frac{xr(i)}{\text{quant}}\right)^{3/4} - 0.0946\right],$$

where $xr(i)$ is the absolute value of the signal of subband $i$, "quant" is the quantization step size, "nint" is the nearest-integer function, and $is(i)$ is the quantized value. As in layers I and II, the quantization is midtread; i.e., values around zero are quantized to zero and the quantizer is symmetric about zero.

In layers I and II, each subband can have its own scale factor. Layer III uses *bands* of scale factors. These bands cover several MDCT coefficients each, and their widths are close to the widths of the critical bands. There is a noise allocation algorithm that selects values for the scale factors.

Layer III uses Huffman codes to compress the quantized values even further. The encoder produces 18 MDCT coefficients per subband. It sorts the resulting 576 coefficients ($= 18 \times 32$) by increasing order of frequency (for short blocks, there are three sets of coefficients within each frequency). Notice that the 576 MDCT coefficients correspond to 1152 transformed audio samples. The set of sorted coefficients is divided into three regions, and each region is encoded with a different set of Huffman codes. This is because the values in each region have a different statistical distribution. The values for the higher frequencies tend to be small and to have runs of zeros, whereas the values for the lower frequencies tend to be large. The code tables are provided by the standard (32 tables on pp. 54–61 of [ISO/IEC 93]). Dividing the quantized values into three regions also helps to control error propagation.

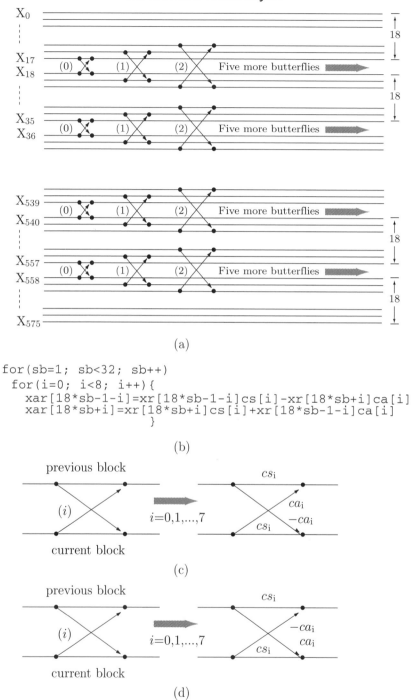

```
for(sb=1; sb<32; sb++)
  for(i=0; i<8; i++){
    xar[18*sb-1-i]=xr[18*sb-1-i]cs[i]-xr[18*sb+i]ca[i]
    xar[18*sb+i]=xr[18*sb+i]cs[i]+xr[18*sb-1-i]ca[i]
    }
```

(b)

**Figure 6.13:** Layer III Aliasing Reduction Butterfly.

Starting at the values for the highest frequencies, where there are many zeros, the encoder selects the first region as the continuous run of zeros from the highest frequency. It is rare but possible not to have any run of zeros. The run is limited to an even number of zeros. This run does not have to be encoded, since its value can be deduced from the sizes of the other two regions. Its size, however, should be even, since the other two regions code their values in even-numbered groupings.

The second region consists of a continuous run of the three values $-1$, 0, and 1. This is called the "count1" region. Each Huffman code for this region encodes four consecutive values, so the number of codes must be $3^4 = 81$. The length of this region must, of course, be a multiple of 4.

The third region, known as the "big values" region, consists of the remaining values. It is (optionally) further divided into three subregions, each with its own Huffman code table. Each Huffman code encodes two values.

The largest Huffman code table specified by the standard has $16 \times 16$ codes. Larger values are encoded using an escape mechanism.

A frame $F$ in layer III is organized as follows: It starts with the usual 32-bit header, which is followed by the optional 16-bit CRC. This is followed by 59 bits of side information. The last part of the frame is the main data. The side information is followed by a segment of main data (the side information contains, among other data, the length of the segment) but the data in this segment does not have to be that of frame $F$! The segment may contain main data from several frames because of the encoder's use of a *bit reservoir*.

The concept of the bit reservoir is especially useful. The encoder can borrow bits from this reservoir when it decides to increase the number of quantization levels because it suspects preechoes. The encoder can also donate bits to the reservoir when it needs fewer than the average number of bits to encode a frame. Borrowing, however, can be done only from past donations; the reservoir cannot have a negative number of bits.

The side information of a frame includes a 9-bit pointer that points to the start of the main data for the frame, and the entire concept of main data, fixed-size segments, pointers, and bit reservoirs is illustrated in Figure 6.14. In this diagram, frame 1 needed only about half of its bit allocation, so it left the other half in the reservoir, where it was eventually used by frame 2. Frame 2 needed a little additional space in its "own" segment, leaving the rest of the segment in the reservoir. This was eventually used by frames 3 and 4. Frame 3 did not need any of its own segment, so the entire segment was left in the reservoir and was eventually used by frame 4. That frame also needed some of its own segment, and the rest was used by frame 5.

Bit allocation in layer III is similar to that in the other layers but includes the added complexity of noise allocation. The encoder (Figure 6.15) computes the bit allocation, performs the actual quantization of the subband signals, encodes them with the Huffman codes, and counts the total number of bits generated in this process. This is the bit allocation inner loop. The noise allocation algorithm (also called analysis-by-synthesis procedure) becomes an outer loop where the encoder calculates the quantization noise (i.e., it dequantizes and reconstructs the subband signals and computes the differences between each signal and its reconstructed counterpart). If it finds that certain scale-factor bands have more noise than the psychoacoustic model allows, the

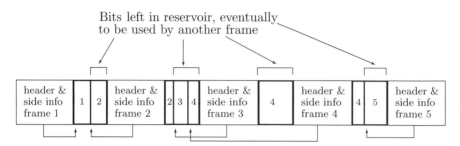

**Figure 6.14:** Layer III Compressed File.

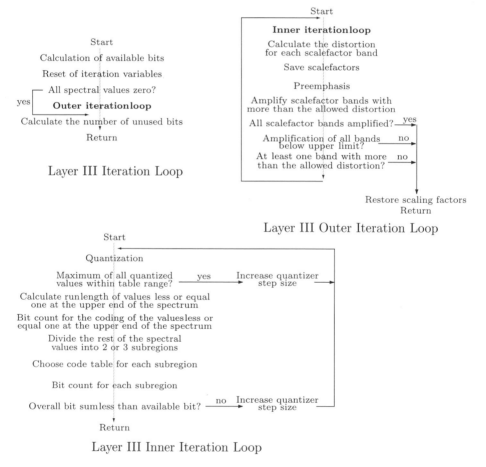

**Figure 6.15:** Layer III Iteration Loop.

encoder increases the number of quantization levels for these bands and repeats the process. This process terminates when any of the following three conditions becomes true:

1. All the scale-factor bands have the allowed noise or less.
2. The next iteration would require a requantization of ALL the scale-factor bands.
3. The next iteration would need more bits than are available in the bit reservoir.

The layer III (MP3) encoder is extremely complex and hard to implement. The decoder, on the other hand, is simple since it does not use a psychoacoustic model, nor does it have to anticipate preechoes and maintain the bit reservoir. This is why there are so many free and low-cost programs available to play MP3 audio files on all computer platforms.

> There were times when Bowman, well aware how unnecessary this was—for the alarm would sound instantly if anything was wrong—would switch over to audio output. He would listen, half hypnotized, to the infinitely slow heartbeats of his sleeping colleagues, keeping his eyes fixed on the sluggish waves that marched in synchronism across the screen.
>
> Arthur C. Clarke, *2001: A Space Odyssey*

# Bibliography

Ahmed, N., T. Natarajan, and R. K. Rao (1974) "Discrete Cosine Transform," *IEEE Transactions on Computers* C-23:90–93.

Akansu, Ali, and R. Haddad (1992) *Multiresolution Signal Decomposition*, San Diego, CA, Academic Press.

Alistair and Abbott (2001) is `ftp://ftp.pd.uwa.edu.au/pub/Wavelets/`.

Anderson, K. L., et al., (1987) "Binary-Image-Manipulation Algorithm in the Image View Facility," *IBM Journal of Research and Development* **31**(1):16–31, January.

Banister, Brian, and Thomas R. Fischer (1999) "Quadtree Classification and TCQ Image Coding," in Storer, James A., and Martin Cohn (eds.) (1999) *DCC '99: Data Compression Conference*, Los Alamitos, CA, IEEE Computer Society Press, pp. 149–157.

Blinn, J. F. (1993) "What's the Deal with the DCT," *IEEE Computer Graphics and Applications* pp. 78–83, July.

Brandenburg, KarlHeinz, and Gerhard Stoll (1994) "ISO-MPEG-1 Audio: A Generic Standard for Coding of High-Quality Digital Audio," *Journal of the Audio Engineering Society*, **42**(10):780–792, October.

ccitt (2001) is URL `src.doc.ic.ac.uk/computing/ccitt/ccitt-standards/1988/`.

Cleary, J. G., and I. H. Witten (1984) "Data Compression Using Adaptive Coding and Partial String Matching," *IEEE Transactions on Communications* COM-32(4):396–402, April.

Daubechies, Ingrid (1988) "Orthonormal Bases of Compactly Supported Wavelets," *Communications on Pure and Applied Mathematics*, **41**:909–996.

DeVore R., et al. (1992) "Image Compression Through Wavelet Transform Coding," *IEEE Transactions on Information Theory* **38**(2):719–746, March.

Ekstrand, Nicklas (1996) "Lossless Compression of Gray Images via Context Tree Weighting," in Storer, James A. (ed.), *DCC '96: Data Compression Conference*, Los Alamitos, CA, IEEE Computer Society Press, pp. 132–139, April.

Feig, Ephraim N., and Elliot Linzer (1990) "Discrete Cosine Transform Algorithms for Image Data Compression," in *Proceedings Electronic Imaging '90 East*, pages 84–87, Boston, MA.

Funet (2001) is URL `ftp://nic.funet.fi/pub/graphics/misc/test-images/`.

Gardner, Martin (1972) "Mathematical Games," *Scientific American*, **227**(2):106, August.

Golomb, S. W. (1966) "Run-Length Encodings," *IEEE Transactions on Information Theory* IT-12(3):399–401.

Gonzalez, Rafael C., and Richard E. Woods (1992) *Digital Image Processing*, Reading, MA, Addison-Wesley.

Grafica (1996) is URL `http://www.sgi.com/grafica/huffman/`.

Gray, Frank (1953) "Pulse Code Communication," United States Patent 2,632,058, March 17.

Heath, F. G. (1972) "Origins of the Binary Code," *Scientific American*, **227**(2):76, August.

Huffman, David (1952) "A Method for the Construction of Minimum Redundancy Codes," *Proceedings of the IRE* **40**(9):1098–1101.

Hunter, R., and A. H. Robinson (1980) "International Digital Facsimile Coding Standards," *Proceedings of the IEEE* **68**(7):854–867, July.

ISO/IEC (1993) International Standard IS 11172-3 "Information Technology—Coding of Moving Pictures and Associated Audio for Digital Storage Media at up to about 1.5 Mbits/s—Part 3: Audio."

Joshi, R. L., V. J. Crump, and T. R. Fischer (1993) "Image Subband Coding Using Arithmetic and Trellis Coded Quantization," *IEEE Transactions on Circuits and Systems Video Technology*, **5**(6):515–523, December.

Knuth, D. E. (1985) "Dynamic Huffman Coding," *Journal of Algorithms* **6**:163–180.

Lelewer, D. A., and D. S. Hirschberg (1987) "Data compression," *Computing Surveys* **19**,3, 261–297. Reprinted in Japanese BIT Special issue in Computer Science (1989), 16–195. Available at `http://www.ics.uci.edu/~dan/pubs/DataCompression.html`.

Lewalle, Jacques (1995) "Tutorial on Continuous Wavelet Analysis of Experimental Data," available anonymously from `ftp.mame.syr.edu/pub/jlewalle/tutor.ps.Z`.

Linde, Y., A. Buzo, and R. M. Gray (1980) "An Algorithm for Vector Quantization Design," *IEEE Transactions on Communications*, COM-28:84–95, January.

Loeffler, C., A. Ligtenberg, and G. Moschytz (1989) "Practical Fast 1-D DCT Algorithms with 11 Multiplications," *Proceedings of the International Conference on Acoustics, Speech, and Signal Processing (ICASSP '89)*, pp. 988–991.

Manning (1998), is URL `http://www.newmediarepublic.com/dvideo/compression/` file `adv08.html`.

Marking, Michael P. (1990) "Decoding Group 3 Images," *The C Users Journal*, pp. 45–54, June.

McConnell, Kenneth R. (1992) *FAX: Digital Facsimile Technology and Applications*, Norwood, MA, Artech House.

Moffat, Alistair (1990) "Implementing the PPM Data Compression Scheme," *IEEE Transactions on Communications* COM-38(11):1917–1921, November.

Moffat, Alistair, Radford Neal, and Ian H. Witten (1998) "Arithmetic Coding Revisited," *ACM Transactions on Information Systems*, **16**(3):256–294, July.

MPEG (2000), see URL `http://www.mpeg.org/`.

Mulcahy, Colm (1996) "Plotting and Scheming with Wavelets," *Mathematics Magazine*, **69**(5):323–343, December. Also available as `http://www.spelman.edu/~colm/csam.ps`.

Mulcahy, Colm (1997) "Image Compression Using the Haar Wavelet Transform," *Spelman College Science and Mathematics Journal*, **1**(1):22–31, April. Also available as `http://www.spelman.edu/~colm/wav.ps`. (It has been claimed that any smart 15-year-old could follow this introduction to wavelets.)

Ohio-state (2001) is URL `http://www.cis.ohio-state.edu/htbin/rfc/rfc804.html`.

Pan, Davis Yen (1995) "A Tutorial on MPEG/Audio Compression," *IEEE Multimedia*, **2**:60–74, Summer.

Pennebaker, William B., and Joan L. Mitchell (1992) *JPEG Still Image Data Compression Standard*, New York, Van Nostrand Reinhold.

Phillips, Dwayne (1992) "LZW Data Compression," *The Computer Application Journal*, Circuit Cellar Inc., **27**:36–48, June/July.

Pohlmann, Ken (1985) *Principles of Digital Audio*, Indianapolis, IN, Howard Sams & Co.

Rao, K. R., and P. Yip (1990) *Discrete Cosine Transform—Algorithms, Advantages, Applications*, London, Academic Press.

Rao, K. R., and J. J. Hwang (1996) *Techniques and Standards for Image, Video, and Audio Coding*, Upper Saddle River, NJ, Prentice Hall.

Rao, Raghuveer M., and Ajit S. Bopardikar (1998) *Wavelet Transforms: Introduction to Theory and Applications*, Reading, MA, Addison-Wesley.

Said, A., and W. A. Pearlman (1996) "A New Fast and Efficient Image Codec Based on Set Partitioning in Hierarchical Trees," *IEEE Transactions on Circuits and Systems for Video Technology*, **6**(6):243–250, June.

Salomon, David (1999) *Computer Graphics and Geometric Modeling*, New York, NY, Springer-Verlag.

Salomon, David (2000) *Data Compression: The Complete Reference*, New York, NY, Springer-Verlag.

Shenoi, Kishan (1995) *Digital Signal Processing in Telecommunications*, Upper Saddle River, NJ, Prentice Hall.

Shlien, Seymour (1994) "Guide to MPEG-1 Audio Standard," *IEEE Transactions on Broadcasting* **40**(4):206–218, December.

Simoncelli, Eero P., and Edward. H. Adelson (1990) "Subband Transforms," in Woods, John, editor, *Subband Coding*, Boston, Kluwer Academic Press, 143–192.

Stollnitz, E. J., T. D. DeRose, and D. H. Salesin (1996) *Wavelets for Computer Graphics*, San Francisco, Morgan Kaufmann.

Storer, J. A., and T. G. Szymanski (1982) "Data Compression via Textual Substitution," *Journal of the ACM* **29**:928–951.

Strang, Gilbert, and Truong Nguyen (1996) *Wavelets and Filter Banks*, Wellesley, MA, Wellesley-Cambridge Press.

Vetterli, M., and J. Kovacevic (1995) *Wavelets and Subband Coding*, Englewood Cliffs, NJ, Prentice Hall.

Vitter, Jeffrey S. (1987) "Design and Analysis of Dynamic Huffman Codes," *Journal of the ACM* **34**(4):825–845, October.

Wallace, Gregory K. (1991) "The JPEG Still Image Compression Standard," *Communications of the ACM* **34**(4):30–44, April.

Watson, Andrew (1994) "Image Compression Using the Discrete Cosine Transform," *Mathematica Journal*, **4**(1):81–88.

Weinberger, M. J., G. Seroussi, and G. Sapiro (1996) "LOCO-I: A Low Complexity, Context-Based, Lossless Image Compression Algorithm," in *Proceedings of Data Compression Conference*, Storer J., editor, Los Alamitos, CA, IEEE Computer Society Press, pp. 140–149.

Welch, T. A. (1984) "A Technique for High-Performance Data Compression," *IEEE Computer* **17**(6):8–19, June.

Witten, Ian H., Radford M. Neal, and John G. Cleary (1987) "Arithmetic Coding for Data Compression," *Communications of the ACM*, **30**(6):520–540.

Ziv, J., and A. Lempel (1977) "A Universal Algorithm for Sequential Data Compression," *IEEE Transactions on Information Theory*, IT-23(3):337–343.

Ziv, J., and A. Lempel (1978) "Compression of Individual Sequences via Variable-Rate Coding," *IEEE Transactions on Information Theory* IT-24(5):530–536.

"You've always been sloppy with bibliography, haven't you?" demanded the beard. "Phonetes would have been utterly embarrassed to have said that."

Robert Harris, *Stories From the Old Attic*

# Glossary

**Adaptive Compression**

A compression method that modifies its operations and/or its parameters according to new data read from the input stream. Examples are the adaptive Huffman method of Section 1.5 and the dictionary-based methods of Chapter 2.

**Alphabet**

The set of all possible symbols in the input stream. In text compression the alphabet is normally the set of 128 ASCII codes. In image compression it is the set of values a pixel can take (2, 16, 256, or anything else). (See also Symbol.)

**Arithmetic Coding**

A statistical compression method (Section 1.7) that assigns one (normally long) code to the entire input stream, instead of assigning codes to the individual symbols. The method reads the input stream symbol by symbol and appends more bits to the code each time a symbol is input and processed. Arithmetic coding is slow, but it compresses at or close to the entropy, even when the symbol probabilities are skewed. (See also Model of Compression, Statistical Methods.)

**Bark**

Unit of critical band rate. Named after Heinrich Georg Barkhausen and used in audio applications. The Bark scale is a nonlinear mapping of the frequency scale over the audio range, a mapping that matches the frequency selectivity of the human ear.

**Bi-level Image**

An image whose pixels have two different colors. The colors are normally referred to as black and white, "foreground" and "background," or 1 and 0. (See also Bitplane.)

## Bitplane

Each pixel in a digital image is represented by several bits. The set of all the $k$th bits of all the pixels in the image is the $k$th bitplane of the image. A bi-level image, for example, consists of two bitplanes. (See also Bi-level Image.)

## Bitrate

In general, the term "bitrate" refers to both bpb and bpc. In MPEG audio, however, this term is used to indicate the rate at which the compressed stream is read by the decoder. This rate depends on where the stream comes from (such as disk, communications channel, memory). If the bitrate of an MPEG audio file is, e.g., 128Kbps, then the encoder will convert each second of audio into 128K bits of compressed data, and the decoder will convert each group of 128K bits of compressed data into one second of sound. Lower bitrates mean smaller file sizes. However, as the bitrate decreases, the encoder must compress more audio data into fewer bits, eventually resulting in a noticeable loss of audio quality. For CD-quality audio, experience indicates that the best bitrates are in the range of 112Kbps to 160Kbps. (See also Bits/Char.)

## Bits/Char

Bits per character (bpc). A measure of the performance in text compression. Also a measure of entropy. (See also Bitrate.)

## Bits/Symbol

Bits per symbol. A general measure of compression performance.

## Codec

A term that refers to both encoder and decoder.

## Codes

A code is a symbol that stands for another symbol. In computer and telecommunications applications, codes are virtually always binary numbers. The ASCII code is the de facto standard, although the new Unicode is used on several new computers and the older EBCDIC is still used on some old IBM computers.

## Compression Factor

The inverse of compression ratio. It is defined as

$$\text{compression factor} = \frac{\text{size of the input stream}}{\text{size of the output stream}}.$$

Values greater than 1 mean compression and values less than 1 imply expansion. (See also Compression Ratio.)

## Compression Gain

This measure is defined as

$$100 \log_e \frac{\text{reference size}}{\text{compressed size}},$$

where the reference size is either the size of the input stream or the size of the compressed stream produced by some standard lossless compression method.

## Compression Ratio

One of several measures that are commonly used to express the efficiency of a compression method. It is the ratio

$$\text{compression ratio} = \frac{\text{size of the output stream}}{\text{size of the input stream}}.$$

A value of 0.6 means that the data occupies 60% of its original size after compression. Values greater than 1 mean an output stream bigger than the input stream (negative compression).

Sometimes the quantity $100 \times (1 - \text{compression ratio})$ is used to express the quality of compression. A value of 60 means that the output stream occupies 40% of its original size (or that the compression has resulted in a savings of 60%). (See also Compression Factor.)

## Continuous-Tone Image

A digital image with a large number of colors, such that adjacent image areas with colors that differ by just one unit appear to the eye as having continuously varying colors. An example is an image with 256 grayscale values. When adjacent pixels in such an image have consecutive gray levels, they appear to the eye as a continuous variation of the gray level. (See also Bi-level image, Discrete-Tone Image, Grayscale Image.)

## Correlation

A statistical measure of the linear relation between two paired variables. The values of $R$ range from $-1$ (perfect negative relation) to 0 (no relation) to $+1$ (perfect positive relation).

## Data Compression Conference

A meeting of researchers and developers in the area of data compression. The DCC takes place every year in Snowbird, Utah, USA. It lasts three days and the next few meetings are scheduled for late March.

## Decibel

A logarithmic measure that can be used to measure any quantity that takes values over a very wide range. A common example is sound intensity. The intensity (amplitude) of sound can vary over a range of 11–12 orders of magnitude. Instead of using a linear measure, where numbers as small as 1 and as large as $10^{11}$ would be needed, a logarithmic scale is used, where the range of values is $[0, 11]$.

## Decoder

A decompression program (or algorithm).

## Dictionary-Based Compression

Compression methods (Chapter 2) that save pieces of the data in a "dictionary" data structure (normally a tree). If a string of new data is identical to a piece already saved in the dictionary, a pointer to that piece is output to the compressed stream. (See also LZ Methods.)

## Digram

A pair of consecutive symbols.

## Discrete Cosine Transform

A variant of the discrete Fourier transform (DFT) that produces just real numbers. The DCT (Sections 3.5.3 and 3.7.2) transforms a set of numbers by combining $n$ numbers to become an $n$-dimensional point and rotating it in $n$ dimensions such that the first coordinate becomes dominant. The DCT and its inverse, the IDCT, are used in JPEG (Section 3.7) to compress an image with acceptable loss by isolating the high-frequency components of an image so that they can later be quantized.

## Discrete-Tone Image

A discrete-tone image may be bi-level, grayscale, or color. Such images are (with few exceptions) artificial, having been obtained by scanning a document or grabbing a computer screen. The pixel colors of such an image do not vary continuously or smoothly, but have a small set of values such that adjacent pixels may differ much in intensity or color. (See also Continuous-Tone Image.)

## Discrete Wavelet Transform

The discrete version of the continuous wavelet transform. A wavelet is represented by means of several filter coefficients, and the transform is carried out by matrix multiplication (or a simpler version thereof) instead of by calculating an integral.

## Encoder

A compression program (or algorithm).

## Entropy Encoding

A lossless compression method where data can be compressed such that the average number of bits/symbol approaches the entropy of the input symbols.

## Facsimile Compression

Transferring a typical page between two fax machines can take up to 10 or 11 minutes without compression. This is why the ITU has developed several standards for compression of facsimile data. The current standards (Section 1.6) are T4 and T6, also called Group 3 and Group 4, respectively.

## Gray Codes

These are binary codes for the integers, where the codes of consecutive integers differ by one bit only. Gray codes are used when a grayscale image is separated into bitplanes, each a bi-level image. (See also Grayscale Image.)

## Grayscale Image

A continuous-tone image with shades of a single color. (See also Continuous-Tone Image.)

## Huffman Coding

A popular method for data compression (Section 1.4). It assigns a set of "best" variable-size codes to a set of symbols based on their probabilities. It serves as the basis for several popular programs used on personal computers. Some of them use just the Huffman method, while others use it as one step in a multistep compression process. The Huffman method is somewhat similar to the Shannon-Fano method. It generally produces better codes, and like the Shannon-Fano method, it produces best code when the probabilities of the symbols are negative powers of 2. The main difference between the two methods is that Shannon-Fano constructs its codes top to bottom (from the leftmost to the rightmost bits), while Huffman constructs a code tree from the bottom up (builds the codes from right to left).

## Information Theory

A mathematical theory that quantifies information. It shows how to measure information so that one can answer the question, How much information is included in this piece of data? with a precise number! Information theory is the creation, in 1948, of Claude Shannon, of Bell Labs.

## JFIF

The full name of this method (Section 3.7.8) is JPEG File Interchange Format. It is a graphics file format that makes it possible to exchange JPEG-compressed images between different computers. The main features of JFIF are the use of the YCbCr triple-component color space for color images (only one component for grayscale images) and the use of a *marker* to specify features missing from JPEG, such as image resolution, aspect ratio, and features that are application-specific.

## JPEG

A sophisticated lossy compression method (Section 3.7) for color or grayscale still images (not movies). It also works best on continuous-tone images, where adjacent pixels have similar colors. One advantage of JPEG is the use of many parameters, allowing the user to adjust the amount of data loss (and thus also the compression ratio) over a very wide range. There are two main modes: lossy (also called baseline) and lossless (which typically gives a 2:1 compression ratio). Most implementations support just the lossy mode. This mode includes progressive and hierarchical coding.

The main idea behind JPEG is that an image exists for people to look at, so when the image is compressed, it is acceptable to lose image features to which the human eye is not sensitive.

The name JPEG is an acronym that stands for Joint Photographic Experts Group. This was a joint effort by the CCITT and the ISO that started in June 1987. The JPEG standard has proved successful and has become widely used for image presentation, especially in Web pages. (See also JPEG-LS, MPEG.)

## JPEG-LS

The lossless mode of JPEG is inefficient and often is not even implemented. As a result, the ISO decided to develop a new standard for the lossless (or near-lossless) compression of continuous-tone images. The result became popularly known as JPEG-LS. This method is not simply an extension or a modification of JPEG. It is a new method, designed to be simple and fast. It does not use the DCT, does not use arithmetic coding, and uses quantization in a limited way and only in its near-lossless option. JPEG-LS examines several of the previously seen neighbors of the current pixel, uses them as the *context* of the pixel, uses the context to predict the pixel and to select a probability distribution out of several such distributions, and uses that distribution to encode the prediction error with a special Golomb code. There is also a run mode, where the length of a run of identical pixels is encoded. (See also JPEG.)

## Lossless Compression

A compression method where the output of the decoder is identical to the original data compressed by the encoder. (See also Lossy Compression.)

## Lossy Compression

A compression method where the output of the decoder is different from the original data compressed by the encoder, but is nevertheless acceptable to a user. Such methods are common in image and audio compression, but not in text compression, where the loss of even one character may result in ambiguous or incomprehensible text. (See also Lossless Compression.)

## LZ Methods

All dictionary-based compression methods are based on the work of J. Ziv and A. Lempel, published in 1977 and 1978. Today, these are called LZ77 and LZ78 methods, respectively. Their ideas have been a source of inspiration to many researchers, who generalized, improved, and combined them with RLE and statistical methods to form many commonly used adaptive compression methods for text, images, and audio. (See also Dictionary-Based Compression, Sliding-Window Compression.)

## LZSS

This version of LZ77 (Section 2.2) was developed by Storer and Szymanski in 1982 [Storer 82]. It improves on the basic LZ77 in three ways: (1) It holds the look-ahead buffer in a circular queue, (2) it holds the search buffer (the dictionary) in a binary search tree, and (3) it creates tokens with two fields instead of three. (See also LZ Methods.)

## LZW

This is a popular variant (Section 2.4) of LZ78, developed by Terry Welch in 1984. Its main feature is eliminating the second field of a token. An LZW token consists of just a pointer to the dictionary. As a result, such a token always encodes a string of more than one symbol.

## Model of Compression

A model is a method to "predict" (to assign probabilities to) the data to be compressed. This concept is important in statistical data compression. When a statistical method is used, a model for the data has to be constructed before compression can begin. A simple model can be built by reading the entire input stream, counting the number of times each symbol appears (its frequency of occurrence), and computing the probability of occurrence of each symbol. The data stream is then input again, symbol by symbol, and is compressed using the information in the probability model. (See also Statistical Methods, Statistical Model.)

One feature of arithmetic coding is that it is easy to separate the statistical model (the table with frequencies and probabilities) from the encoding and decoding operations. It is easy to encode, for example, the first half of a data stream using one model and the second half using another model.

## Pel

The smallest unit of a facsimile image; a dot. (See also Pixel.)

## Pixel

The smallest unit of a digital image; a dot. (See also Pel.)

## Prediction

Assigning probabilities to symbols.

## Prefix Property

One of the principles of variable-size codes. Once a certain bit pattern has been assigned as the code of a symbol, no other codes should start with that pattern (the pattern cannot be the *prefix* of any other code). Once the string 1, for example, is assigned as the code of $a_1$, no other codes should start with 1 (i.e., they all have to start with 0). Once 01, for example, is assigned as the code of $a_2$, no other codes can start with 01 (they all should start with 00). (See also Variable-Size Codes, Statistical Methods.)

## Progressive Image Compression

An image compression method where the compressed stream consists of "layers," where each layer contains more detail of the image. The decoder can very quickly display the entire image in a low-quality format, then improve the display quality as more and more layers are being read and decompressed. A user watching the decompressed image develop on the screen can normally recognize most of the image features after only 5–10% of it has been decompressed. Improving image quality over time can be done by (1) sharpening it, (2) adding colors, or (3) adding resolution.

## Psychoacoustic Model

A mathematical model of the sound-masking properties of the human auditory (ear–brain) system.

## RLE

A general name for methods that compress data by replacing a run length of identical symbols with one code, or token, containing the symbol and the length of the run. RLE sometimes serves as one step in a multistep statistical or dictionary-based method.

## Scalar Quantization

The dictionary definition of the term "quantization" is "to restrict a variable quantity to discrete values rather than to a continuous set of values." If the data to be compressed is in the form of large numbers, quantization is used to convert them to small numbers. This results in (lossy) compression. If the data to be compressed is analog (e.g., a voltage that changes with time), quantization is used to digitize it into small numbers. This aspect of quantization is used by several audio compression methods. (See also Vector Quantization.)

## Sliding Window Compression

The LZ77 method (Section 2.1) uses part of the previously seen input stream as the dictionary. The encoder maintains a window to the input stream, and shifts the input in that window from right to left as strings of symbols are being encoded. The method is thus based on a *sliding window*. (See also LZ Methods.)

## SPIHT

A progressive image encoding method that efficiently encodes the image after it has been transformed by any wavelet filter. SPIHT is embedded, progressive, and has a natural lossy option. It is also simple to implement, fast, and produces excellent results for all types of images. (See also EZW, Progressive Image Compression, Embedded Coding, Discrete Wavelet Transform.)

## Statistical Methods

These methods (Chapter 1) work by assigning variable-size codes to symbols in the data, with the shorter codes assigned to symbols or groups of symbols that appear more often in the data (have a higher probability of occurrence). (See also Variable-Size Codes, Prefix Property, Huffman Coding, and Arithmetic Coding.)

## Statistical Model

See Model of Compression.

## Symbol

The smallest unit of the data to be compressed. A symbol is normally a byte but may also be a bit, a trit $\{0, 1, 2\}$, or anything else.

## Taps

Wavelet filter coefficients. (See also Discrete Wavelet Transform.)

## Transform

An image can be compressed by transforming its pixels (which are correlated) to a representation where they are *decorrelated*. Compression is achieved if the new values are smaller, on average, than the original ones. Lossy compression can be achieved by quantizing the transformed values. The decoder inputs the transformed values from the compressed stream and reconstructs the (precise or approximate) original data by applying the opposite transform. (See also Discrete Cosine Transform, Discrete Wavelet Transform.)

## Variable-Size Codes

These are used by statistical methods. Such codes should satisfy the prefix property (Section 1.2) and should be assigned to symbols based on their probabilities. (See also Prefix Property, Statistical Methods.)

## Vector Quantization

This is a generalization of the scalar quantization method. It is used for both image and sound compression. In practice, vector quantization is commonly used to compress data that has been digitized from an analog source, such as sampled sound and scanned images (drawings or photographs). Such data is called *digitally sampled analog data* (DSAD). (See also Scalar Quantization.)

## Video Compression

Video compression is based on two principles. The first is the spatial redundancy that exists in each video frame. The second is the fact that very often, a video frame is very similar to its immediate neighbors. This is called *temporal redundancy*. A typical technique for video compression should thus start by encoding the first frame using an image compression method. It should then encode each successive frame by identifying the differences between the frame and its predecessor, and encoding these differences.

> Necessity is the mother of compression.
>
> —Aesop (paraphrased)

# Joining the Data Compression Community

Those interested in a personal touch can join the "DC community" and communicate with researchers and developers in this area in person by attending the Data Compression Conference (DCC). It has taken place every year since 1991, in Snowbird, Utah, USA. The conference lasts three days and the next few meetings are scheduled for late March. Detailed information on the conference can be found at `http://www.cs.brandeis.edu/~dcc/index.html`. This Web page includes information about the conference itself, the organizers, and the geographical location.

In addition to invited presentations and technical sessions, there are "Midday Talks" on issues of current interest and the poster session; the central event of the DCC. Each presenter places a description of recent work (including text, diagrams, photographs, and charts) on a 4-foot-wide by 3-foot-high poster. They then discuss the work with anyone interested in a relaxed atmosphere, with refreshments served.

The Capocelli prize is awarded annually for the best student-written DCC paper, in memory of Renato M. Capocelli [1940–1992].

The program committee reads like a who's who of data compression, but the two central figures are James Andrew Storer and Martin Cohn, both of Brandeis University, who chair the conference and the conference program, respectively.

The conference proceedings have traditionally been edited by Storer and Cohn. They are published by the IEEE Computer Society (`http://www.computer.org/`) and are distributed prior to the conference, an attractive feature.

A complete bibliography (in bibTEX format) of papers published in past DCCs can be found at `http://www.cs.mu.oz.au/~alistair/dccrefs.bib`.

> I have the honor of joining with my brethren the
> Committee of Correspondence for the town.
> —Samuel Adams

# Appendix of Algorithms

# Index

Happening one day to mention Mr. Flexman, a Dissenting Minister, with some compliment to his exact memory in chronological matters; the Doctor replied, "Let me hear no more of him, Sir. That is the fellow who made the Index to my Ramblers, and set down the name of Milton thus: Milton, MR. John."

—James Boswell, *Life of Johnson* (1750)

# Colophon

Most of this book was culled from the second edition of *Data Compression: The Complete Reference* during winter 2001. As its predecessors, this book was designed by the author and was typeset by him with the TₑX typesetting system developed by D. Knuth. The text and tables were done with Textures, a commercial TₑX implementation for the Macintosh. The diagrams were done with Adobe Illustrator, also on the Macintosh. Diagrams that require calculations were done either with *Mathematica* or Matlab, but even those were "polished" in Adobe Illustrator. The following points illustrate the amount of work that went into the book:

- The book contains about 128,100 words, consisting of about 744,500 characters. As is now so common with any technical text, much reference material, including some *Mathematica* and Matlab codes, were obtained from the World Wide Web.

- The text is typeset mainly in font cmr10, but about 30 other fonts were used.

- The raw index file contained about 1350 items.

- There are about 310 cross references in the book.

That which shrinks must first expand.
—Lao-Tzu, verse 36 of *Tao Te Ching*